THE SOCIOLO(

# The Sociology of Financial Markets

*Edited by*

Karin Knorr Cetina and Alex Preda

OXFORD
UNIVERSITY PRESS

# OXFORD
UNIVERSITY PRESS

Great Clarendon Street, Oxford OX2 6DP

Oxford University Press is a department of the University of Oxford.
It furthers the University's objective of excellence in research, scholarship,
and education by publishing worldwide in

Oxford New York

Auckland Cape Town Dar es Salaam Hong Kong Karachi Kuala Lumpur
Madrid Melbourne Mexico City Nairobi New Delhi Shanghai Taipei Toronto

With offices in

Argentina Austria Brazil Chile Czech Republic France Greece
Guatemala Hungary Italy Japan South Korea Poland Portugal
Singapore Switzerland Thailand Turkey Ukraine Vietnam

Oxford is a registered trade mark of Oxford University Press
in the UK and in certain other countries

Published in the United States
by Oxford University Press Inc., New York

© Oxford University Press 2005

British Library Cataloguing in Publication Data

Data available

Library of Congress Cataloging in Publication Data

Data available

Typeset by Newgen Imaging Systems (P) Ltd., Chennai, India

Printed in Great Britain
on acid-free paper by
Biddles Ltd., King's Lynn, Norfolk

ISBN 0-19-927559-9   978-0-19-927559-5
ISBN 0-19-929692-8 (pbk.)   978-0-19-929692-7 (pbk.)

# ACKNOWLEDGMENTS

The project for this book was born during a conference organized by the editors at Lake Konstanz in Germany in May 2003 (*Inside Financial Markets: Financial Knowledge and Interaction Patterns in Global Financial Markets*). We want to present to the reader the complex and multifaceted research topics which can be uncovered in the field of financial markets; a selection of themes and problems was nevertheless unavoidable. But we also believe that financial markets—a crucial domain of modern societies—deserve a heightened sociological attention, and hope to make a contribution in this respect too.

The Fritz-Thyssen Foundation and the University of Konstanz have provided generous financial support for the conference. In addition to this, the Fritz-Thyssen Foundation has provided financial support for editorial help at the University of Konstanz. Richard Swedberg and Barbara Czarniawska encouraged us to edit a book based on (but not limited to) a set of conference papers. David Musson has manifested a keen interest in this project and offered his constant support. The anonymous reviewers gave us very valuable advice. Barbara Grimpe, Pat Skorge, Peimaneh Riahi, and Aaron Pitluck have provided great editorial help. Last but not least, we want to thank our families for their support and understanding.

# CONTENTS

# LIST OF FIGURES

# LIST OF TABLES

# LIST OF CONTRIBUTORS

**Mitchel Y. Abolafia** is Associate Professor in the Department of Public Administration and Policy, Rockefeller College, SUNY/Albany.

**Daniel Beunza** is Assistant Professor in the Economics and Business Department of the Universitat Pompeu Fabra.

**Gordon L. Clark** is Head of School and Halford Mackinder Professor of Geography, and a Fellow of St Peter's College, University of Oxford.

**Barbara Czarniawska** holds the Swedish Research Council/Malmsten Foundation Chair in Management Studies at the Göteborg Research Institute, School of Economics and Commercial Law, Göteborg University.

**Gerald Davis** is the Sparks/Whirlpool Corporation Professor and Chair of Management and Organizations at the University of Michigan Business School.

**Werner De Bondt** is Richard H. Driehaus Professor of Finance, and Director of the Driehaus Center for Behavioral Finance at De Paul University.

**Julian Dierkes** is Assistant Professor and the Keidanren Chair in Japanese Research at the Institute of Asian Research of the University of British Columbia.

**Frank Dobbin** is Professor of Sociology at Harvard University.

**Jean-Pierre Hassoun** is Research Fellow in Sociology at the French National Scientific Research Center. He teaches at the École Normale Supérieure and the École des Hautes Études en Sciences Sociales, Paris.

**Karin Knorr Cetina** is Professor of Sociology at the University of Konstanz and Visiting Professor of Sociology at the University of Chicago.

**Man-shan Kwok** is a Ph.D. candidate in the Department of Sociology at Princeton University. He teaches at the Chinese University of Hong Kong.

**Donald MacKenzie** holds a Personal Chair in Sociology at the University of Edinburgh.

**Michael Power** is P. D. Leake Professor of Accounting and Co-Director of the ESRC Center for the Analysis of Risk and Regulation, London School of Economics.

**Alex Preda** is Lecturer in Social Theory at the University of Edinburgh.

**Gregory Robbins** is an Assistant Professor of Strategic Management in the College of Management of the Georgia Institute of Technology.

**Saskia Sassen** is Ralph Lewis Professor of Sociology at the University of Chicago and Centennial Visiting Professor of Sociology at the London School of Economics.

**David Stark** is Arthur Lehman Professor of Sociology and International Affairs, at Columbia University and External Faculty Member of the Santa Fe Institute.

**Richard Swedberg** is Professor of Sociology at Cornell University.

**Nigel Thrift** is Head of the Division of Life and Environmental Sciences, and a Student of Christ Church College at Oxford University.

**Dirk Zorn** is a Ph.D. candidate at Princeton University and visiting fellow at Harvard University.

# Introduction

KARIN KNORR CETINA AND ALEX PREDA

This book is about the social and cultural study of finance, of the markets and institutions used for financial transactions, and the trading of assets and risks. The financial system controls and manages credit; in contemporary societies, the ultimate users of real capital rely heavily on others (investors) to provide the funds with which to acquire the resources they need. Investors make the transfers of money to those seeking credit in the hope of reaping profits at later points in time; the debts the receivers of the funds incur are claims investors can make on future income and on economic output and development. Characteristically, these claims (which take the form of company shares, governments bonds, etc.) and their derivatives are marketed and traded on *financial markets*—with the help of financial intermediaries (e.g. banks, brokerage houses, insurance companies) who package the deals, assume some of the risks, and facilitate the trading of claims and risks among market participants. The existence of such markets allows participants to sell claims and risks they no longer want, and to pursue additional profits through clever trading. Financial markets, then, are a major, if not the most important component of the credit mechanism in risk-based economies. Economists regard them as constituting an efficient mechanism that fulfills vital functions of, and for, the financial system: for instance, they pool and transfer wealth for capital use, decrease the costs of finance (through the elimination of banks as direct lenders), and spread and control risks—risk being more widely distributed when credit is obtained in financial markets through the splitting of shares and through derivative products that can be used for hedging risky investments (e.g. Merton and Bodie 1995: 4f., 13–15).

In contemporary Western societies, financial activities are a defining characteristic not only of the corporate economy, but also of politics, the welfare and social security system, and general culture. For example, the corporate economy has long depended on credit to finance production and investments. A Robinson Crusoe with nothing to invest could not hope to produce much. He would first have to invest his own time and labor in order to build the rudiments of a productive capital structure (Shapiro 1985: 77). As Susan Strange argues (1994: 30), if we had had to wait for profits to be accumulated there would have been none of the economic growth of the past decades in industry and agriculture. The state has long needed credit and borrowed vast amounts of money. From the seventeenth century onward, states systematically financed costly military interventions by issuing debt (government bonds) and borrowing money from banks and financial intermediaries, habits in which the financial sector might well have its earliest roots (Neal 1990). State borrowing continues to be strong today, though now it is more oriented toward deficit management and investment spending. In general terms, Western governments operate in interaction with the developments on financial markets. State officials and central bankers observe the price movements of currencies and financial indicators whose value may have an impact in a given geographic area, and they respond to them by talk and policy changes in an attempt to manage market participants' expectations and behavior (see Abolafia, Chapter 10, this volume). The state is interlinked with the financial system through government fiscal and regulatory policies which impact on the financial markets (e.g. Fligstein 2001: 201–2), and through the incentives states provide to attract financial investments and systems. A central component of modern welfare societies, pension systems, also depend on and interact with financial markets. Reserves that pay benefits to retirees are assets managed through investment vehicles. Finance is, moreover, now an ever more present part of the larger culture, as exemplified by the expansion of media attention given to finance. The first all-news financial television network appeared in the United States in 1983. It was soon followed by and absorbed into other networks (e.g. CNBC, CNNfn, Bloomberg Television and Radio). Newspapers also expanded their business section into enhanced 'Money' sections; together, these media provide an uninterrupted stream of financial and business news consulted by both a lay and a professional audience (Shiller 2000: 28–9). Barbara Czarniawska (Chapter 6, this volume) shows that the world of finance is present in popular culture—in consultancy books that dispense useful tips about personal investing mingled at times with autobiographical accounts (e.g. Schwager 1989, 1992), and in films and novels (e.g. Lewis 1989; Ridpath 1996; Partnoy 1997) that capture the dominant view of finance in our times.

Ours is not, of course, the first period in history to demonstrate a heightened curiosity in investment and some breathtaking movements of financial markets (see below and Preda, Chapter 7, this volume). But finance has perhaps risen in importance in the last quarter century more rapidly than any other sector of the economy. Since it bottomed out in 1982, the US stock market has experienced the most dramatic price increases in its history, if long-term data (1871–2000) are considered, and large stock price increases also occurred in Europe, Asia, and Australia (Shiller 2000: 5 ff.). In the period between 1981 and 1986 alone the volume of US public bond issues rose at an annual rate of 37%, equity issues almost tripled, the dollar volume of mergers and acquisitions activity tripled, and the volume of international bonds multiplied fivefold (Eccles and Crane 1988: 1). Since then there have been various dramatic falls in prices (examples are the 'Black Monday' of October 19, 1987 when the Dow Jones Industrial Average dropped 508 points, and the market declines of 2001 and 2002). Nonetheless, the level and diversity of financial activities appears to have increased significantly since the 1980s. More importantly, perhaps, awareness of the financial system and of the risks and benefits it offers to individuals and organizations has also risen. As Sassen points out (Chapter 1, this volume), since 1980 the stock of financial assets has increased three times faster than the aggregate gross domestic product (GDP) of the twenty-three highly developed Organization for Economic Cooperation and Development (OECD) countries, and the volume of trading in currencies, stocks, and bonds has increased five times faster. Most of this activity is financial market activity. For example, the global foreign direct investment stock was US$6 trillion in 2000, while the worldwide value of internationally traded derivatives was over US$80 trillion, and rose to US$192 trillion in 2002. In 1983, on the largest financial market in terms of volume of transactions, the foreign exchange market, transactions were ten times as large as world trade (the economic exchange of goods and services), but in 1999 they were seventy times larger, even though world trade also grew significantly during this period (Sassen, Chapter 1, this volume).

Financial markets in particular, then, have risen in importance since the early 1980s, and their power to determine outcomes in production, consumption, and social welfare is enormous. Yet to date they have not been paid much attention by sociologists. This is somewhat surprising in the light of the sharp upturn economic sociology has taken in the last twenty years, and the pioneering work that has been done in this field (e.g. White 1981; Granovetter 1985; Burt 1992; Fligstein 2001; Podolny 2001). Why the relative lack of interest in financial markets then? One answer surely is that the new economic sociology has focused on aspects of the *economy*, an area which has to be distinguished from that of finance. Economists have defined economic activities as that set of pursuits which involves the use of scarce resources to satisfy various human needs or wants—and they have broadly classified these activities into the categories of production, consumption, and exchange (Dholakia and Oza 1996: 7). Economic sociology also defines economic behavior in these terms—in terms of the institutions and relations of production, consumption, and social distribution (e.g. DiMaggio 1994: 28; Smelser and Swedberg 1994: 3; Portes 1995: 3). In their research, economic sociologists have focused on the production side of the economy, taking the firm as their point of departure—in line with the distinctive role production has played in the discipline's understanding of capitalism and with the focus early economic sociologists placed on the internal working of organizations (Swedberg 1991; Baron and Hannan 1994; Carruthers and Uzzi 2000: 486). Though a number of early studies were concerned with financial markets (Smith 1981; Adler and Adler 1984; Baker 1984), most recent research has not been in this area but has involved a shift from what goes on within firms to what goes on between them. The dominant line of research specializes in the analysis of interorganizational ties, in effect joining organizational analysis and market analysis through the use of network approaches that analyze the nature of the relationships and networks and how these affect labor, product, and credit-seeking (e.g. White 1981; Burt 1983; Baker 1990; Baker, Faulkner, and Fisher 1998; DiMaggio and Louch 1998; Uzzi 1999). When markets are analyzed they tend to be producer markets, for example, markets for industrial products and nonfinancial services. Characteristically, the research glosses over distinctions between producer markets and financial markets in an effort to address the question of how economic activities are embedded in social structure (Granovetter 1985). While this research does not reject differences between markets, it is also not designed to capture the types and patterns of social structural and cultural variation that a 'multiple market' model (Zelizer 1988) suggests. Yet differences between producer markets and financial markets are consequential for almost every level of analysis of markets.

Financial markets are not primarily concerned with the production of goods or with their distribution to clients but with the trading of financial instruments not designed for consumption. No 'production' effort on the trader's part is involved in 'spot' transactions, the direct sale or buying of a financial instrument. When more complex instruments are traded (options, futures, etc.), their value tends to be calculated on the spot by traders themselves without recourse to production facilities. Financial markets belong to a second-order economy where the 'goods' are contracts (equities, bonds, currencies, derivatives) that *circulate* rather than being channeled to end consumers. There are two aspects to the sense in which these markets are steps removed from the ordinary economy of production and consumption. The first pertains to the instruments traded, which are not the funds investors provide but the shares and obligations they obtain in return for their investment and the contracts they enter into so as to protect these investments. Thus financial market participants do not withdraw credit directly from a company when they sell company shares; what may happen is that the sale influences the value of these shares. The shares and other instruments are abstract entities which may not even be pieces of paper but merely an entry in the books of the respective parties; the value of these entities is determined by financial market activities and is only tenuously related to the underlying referent (e.g. a company). The shift from concrete funds to abstract entities epitomizes the decoupling of financial markets from the ordinary economy of production, consumption, and exchange. The second aspect of this decoupling has to do with the form of action prevalent in financial markets, which is 'speculation.' Consider the example of the foreign exchange market, where 'actuals' (currencies) rather than contracts are traded in spot transactions (though these currencies nonetheless take the form of abstract entities). Historically, currency (foreign exchange) dealers provided services for importers, exporters, and others who needed foreign exchange to pay bills and pay for goods. They were intermediaries in conventional trading oriented to the transfer of goods from producers to consumers. But only a tiny percentage of the current daily trading volume in foreign exchange (about US$1.2 trillion in 2001; Bank for International Settlements 2002) reflects any 'real' requirements of companies; the daily volume of dollar transactions in this market is approximately 200 times larger than the added volume of US merchandise imports and exports, plus other sales that require foreign exchange (e.g. Caves, Frankel, and Jones 1999: 420). Thus, most foreign exchange dealing today is speculation not motivated by a need for the product obtained but by the motive of gaining from expected price changes of the currency when it is resold. Speculation and the seemingly endless circulation of the entities traded also differentiate other financial markets not only from producer markets, but also from merchandise and service trading, which is oriented toward the transportation of goods from one location to another and toward consumption at the end of the trading chain.

There is another sense too in which financial markets and the associated institutions differ from national economies: financial markets tend to be global markets, and the financial system can arguably be considered a global system. It is, if you wish, a structure of the world as one place rather than one of national societies. Economies, on the other hand, have typically been localized; they are the economies of nation states. They depend on national regulatory frameworks and institutions, tax and social security systems, national policies and interventions. They use national currencies and presuppose the existence of a national central bank. Their localized character is reflected in national economic indicators and in the attention given to them. Larger economic systems such as the European Union pose problems for analysts precisely because they do not correspond to this pattern; European statistics are often problematic since they average out the internal dynamics of localized economic activities and their causal dependencies on national frameworks of policymaking. To make predictions about the European Union's economic development, analysts tend to resort to the indicators of leading national economies and to disregard aggregate statistics that reflect the European level. The global architecture of financial markets is reflected in their concentration in global centers and cities (Leyshon and Thrift 1997; Sassen 2001), in the bridgehead construction of their infrastructure and the global 'scopic systems' they employ (Knorr Cetina, Chapter 2, this volume). All this will become clearer in the first section of this book. Not all financial markets, one should add, are equally global. While currency markets are inherently transnational markets, bond and equity markets are not, though they have become increasingly global in the most recent wave of globalization. As Sassen shows (Chapter 1, this volume), the value of cross-border transactions in bonds and equities as a percentage of GDP in the leading economies was 4% in 1975 in the United States, 35% in 1985 when the financial era was in full swing, and had risen to 230% in 1998. This share grew from 5% to 334% in Germany and from 5% to 415% in France.

## A Brief Look at the History of Financial Markets

The world economy was born with the dawn of international trade, and foreign exchange trading has played a role in this economy from this time onward. Some financial transactions are ancient; of others we have had evidence only more recently. We need to distinguish here between the existence of public debt or of company shares (with occasional trades) and the emergence of financial markets and of stock exchanges. Financial securities were well known and privately owned in the eighteenth century in North America, but they were not traded (Wright 2001: 21–2). Financial markets can only be assumed to exist when there are routinized, systematic forms of trading, relatively stable settings, a minimal degree of standardization of financial securities, and established cognitive procedures for their evaluation. When stock exchanges emerged they involved, in addition, agreements about formal rules, an established organizational structure, and a regulatory framework for exchange activities. Economic historians agree that informally organized financial markets preceded stock exchanges and shaped the ways they were set up (Michie 1999: 15). For that reason, the social and cultural history of financial markets does not begin with the analysis of the institutional structure and dynamics of exchanges. One must also investigate forms of interaction, social relationships, and cognitive and technological patterns that indicate the existence of more or less informal financial markets.

Sociologists and economic historians have distinguished at least two patterns of market emergence. The first pattern, proposed by Max Weber, is that of functional differentiation. Weber ties the rise of financial markets to the emergence of modern, large-scale commerce (Weber 2000 [1894]: 306). In the seventeenth century, wholesale merchants began to exchange certificates of the ownership of goods and brought only samples to the market. This saved transportation costs and expanded the circulation of goods. In time, certificates began to be traded independently of the goods. When early modern states turned to financing their wars through public debt instead of costly private debt, this innovation gave financial markets an additional and decisive impetus (Neal 1990; Carruthers 1996: 71). Previous trading in paper certificates facilitated the move to trading government bonds, which states unloaded on the market. The growth of maritime trade—a costly enterprise—led to the emergence of joint-stock companies in the late seventeenth century; their shares added to the supply of trading instruments.

The second pattern of market emergence has been proposed by Winifred Barr Rothenberg, who ties the emergence of financial markets to the separation between property rights and exchange rights. Rothenberg (2000: 5) shows how in eighteenth century rural Massachusetts, in a cash-poor economy, in the absence of a banking network and of other financial institutions, members of rural communities issued mortgage deeds as financial securities without renouncing their property rights. The deeds were issued for the sole purpose of exchange; they were designed to facilitate trades in agricultural products. Over time, mortgage deeds were traded and accumulated without any reference to the underlying agricultural products, and a network of informal exchange relationships was thus established.

In Western Europe, financial markets emerged in the late seventeenth and early eighteenth centuries in Amsterdam, London, and Paris. The Paris Bourse was created already in 1724 by royal decree. In contrast, the London Stock Exchange was not completely institutionalized until 1801 (Michie 1999: 35). The New York Stock Exchange emerged from the 'Buttonwood Agreement' of May 17, 1792, by which the participating stockbrokers agreed to ask the same commission rate on transactions. The first formal stock exchange in North America was founded in Philadelphia in 1790 (Markham 2002: 115). Before that, there had been an incipient financial market in Philadelphia in the 1750s, but on a comparatively modest scale. Initially, financial transactions were conducted in the street and in the pubs and coffee houses where merchants came together. After the institutionalization of stock exchanges, the formal market moved indoors while the informal market continued to trade in the street. This situation continued until well into the twentieth century. In the nineteenth century, several formal exchanges existed in parallel in New York city; they specialized in various classes of securities (oil, mines, cotton, listed or unlisted, etc.). For most of the nineteenth century, trading in derivatives was not regulated by law, and was therefore practiced mostly in informal markets.

In the second half of the nineteenth century, markets underwent a process of technological remaking. While financial markets had benefited from communication technologies such as the telegraph and the telephone since the 1840s and the 1870s, respectively, what developed in the 1870s were custom-tailored technologies for the recording of security prices and for their simultaneous display in several places. This process was not free of tension; there were conflicts over the access to market technologies, to financial news, and to price information. Since then, financial markets have been reshaped repeatedly by revolutionary new technologies, a process that is ongoing. Several European stock exchanges have recently become entirely automated; the now empty trading floors of the Paris Bourse are occasionally used for staging fashion shows. The technological remake of financial markets in the nineteenth century had a number of consequences. The introduction of price recording technologies promoted the standardization of price information. Official price quotations appeared in London and New York in the late 1860s; with this innovation, producing business analyses and company statistics became more feasible and popular. As a further consequence of price standardization, one of the first market indexes was created by Dow Jones in 1884. Shortly afterward, security ratings and systematic financial analyses of industrial stocks were introduced. Technological innovation, along with processes of economic expansion, urbanization, and international migration have contributed further to the speed of transactions and the expansion of markets throughout the nineteenth and twentieth centuries. This expansion has been accompanied by the cross-border integration of these markets, manifest in the increased speed of capital flows, the growing interdependence of markets, and their previously mentioned concentration in global centers.

## Outline of the Book

Economic sociology, we said, has focused very much on the production side of the economy. Yet an incipient sociology of financial markets has also emerged since the 1980s, exemplified by Smith's work on trading strategies and auctions (e.g. 1981, 1989), Baker's studies of trading networks (e.g. 1984), Abolafia's ethnography of bond traders (1996), and Sassen's continued work on the location of financial markets in global cities (e.g. 2001), amongst others (e.g. Lie 1997). The studies collected in this volume extend this tradition and that of recent or ongoing work not represented in this volume (e.g. Hertz 1998; Miyazaki 2003; Zaloom 2003). The studies cover a whole spectrum of approaches focused on the internal working and governance of financial markets, on the rise of the investor and investors' concerns, and on the influence financial markets exert on other areas, for example, on popular culture and the internal structure of firms.

Section I, *Inside Financial Markets*, looks at the transaction practices in various financial markets, at market globality, and at mechanisms of market coordination and integration—followed by a reflexive study of how women fare in this world as reflected in popular culture. In Chapter 1, *The Embeddedness of Electronic Markets: The Case of Global Capital Markets*, Saskia Sassen addresses the technological transformations behind the emergence of global markets and the growth of capital flows since the early 1980s—as indicated by a number of highly telling statistics. These developments ensure, Sassen argues, the consolidation of an upper stratum of select financial centers, forming the top layer of the 30–40 global cities through which the global financial industry operates, and a weakening of national attachments for the elites and firms which make up the stratum. Yet the global market also remains embedded in national policies and state agencies in terms of the guarantees and protections it receives, and by producing norms and cognitions that become integrated into 'sound' national economic policies and standards. Chapter 2 (Karin Knorr Cetina) poses the question *How are Global Markets Global? The Architecture of a Flow World* with regard to a specific case, that of the foreign exchange markets, which by all accounts are the most genuinely global and the largest market worldwide in terms of daily volume of trading. The chapter draws a distinction between network markets and flow markets, arguing that foreign exchange markets have become decoupled from networks and exhibit a scopic architecture based on reflexive mechanisms of observation and projection that project market reality and enable it to flow. The argument challenges the notion that networks are the fundamental stuff of which today's markets (or other forms of new organization) are made, and the idea that electronic interconnectedness can be equated with a network form of organization. The chapter also spells out the characteristics of a flow market. In Chapter 3, *How a Super-Portfolio Emerges: Long-Term Capital Management and the Sociology of Arbitrage*, Donald MacKenzie turns to the actual trading practices of global arbitrage trading. MacKenzie's study focuses on Long-Term Capital Management (LTCM), a hedge fund that had been hugely successful for several years but was driven to the brink of bankruptcy in 1998. The chapter describes in detail LTCM's trading strategies, explaining its failure in terms of a sociological hypothesis: LTCM's success led to widespread imitation in the arbitrage community of people who personally knew each other and who ended up holding overlapping arbitrage positions. Sales by some holders then led to a cascade of self-reinforcing adverse price movements that exhausted LTCM's means to hold out against the losses it incurred. Daniel Beunza and David Stark (Chapter 4), *How to Recognize Opportunities: Heterarchical Search in a Trading Room*, also look at arbitrage trading, but from the perspective of how a Wall Street trading room of a major international investment bank is organized for the process of price discovery. Beunza and Stark conceptualize the trading room as a kind of laboratory characterized by heterarchy, that is, a flattened hierarchy where the evaluative principles and information of one trading desk can be exploited by other desks in a process by which intelligence is distributed across desks. The authors show how trading involves heterogeneous principles of valuation and collaborative efforts which have received hardly any attention hitherto in the literature on trading (but see Heath et al. 1994). Chapter 5 (Jean-Pierre Hassoun), *Emotions on the Trading Floor: Social and Symbolic Expressions*, also focuses on the financial trading floor—from yet another perspective, that of the role and management of emotions in trading. Drawing extensively on the metaphors traders use, Hassoun provides a typology of market emotions, which he associates with the contexts in which emotions emerge—those of performance, violence, and gaming and gambling. He also discusses the social effects of these emotions and specifies three 'registers' of market activity that range from the macro- to the micro-level. The final chapter in this section (Chapter 6), Barbara Czarniawska on *Women in Financial Services: Fiction and More Fiction*, provides a reflexive commentary on the way financial markets are exclusionary and represented in this way in popular culture. Czarniawska compares the portrayal of 'exceptional' women such as the Swedish analyst Elin Friman in novels and journalistic accounts with that of certain semi-fictitious male characters in films and autobiographies (examples are the movies *Rogue Trader*, which is based on the autobiography of Nicholas Leeson, who brought down the Baring Bank, and *Boiler Room*, a movie based on the story of Michael Milken, 'the king of junk bonds', who was later imprisoned). She finds that risk-taking women who try their hand at masculine pursuits come to sticky ends in the plots of such fiction, confirming conventional stereotypes expressed by male traders when they assert that women have no place in financial markets.

Section II, *The Age of the Investor*, turns from trading and the architecture of markets to the historical and contemporary construction and self-understanding of investors. While governments, firms, and markets all refer to the investor and conduct their business in the name of the investor, there are few sociological investigations of investor attitudes and investment behavior. Chapter 7, by Alex Preda, on *The Investor as a Cultural Figure of Global Capitalism* takes a step toward remedying this situation. Drawing on primary historical sources, Preda describes the emergence and understanding of the investor in the eighteenth and nineteenth centuries as one of capitalism's cultural figures, comparable to those of the entrepreneur and the capitalist. Preda argues that investment, originally denounced as a kind of gambling, became legitimate during the first wave of globalization (1850–1914); it began to be seen as intrinsic to human nature and a human right regardless of social status. The process involved a reconfiguration of the investor as a person in possession of these rights and of certain cognitive and technical skills (a kind of scientist) that allowed him or her to pursue his or her financial goals in universally valid and rational ways. These rights continue to play an important role today—in various governments' attempt to institute standards of business that work to the advantage of investors, in legal investigations, and in the various national and international negotiations over how to make financial information more transparent. In Chapter 8, *The Values and Beliefs of European Investors*, Werner De Bondt extends the historical analysis to contemporary investor culture. Using a survey of more than 3,100 affluent and semi-affluent investors in six Western European countries as a basis, De Bondt shows how investment strategies and the perceived attractiveness of asset classes are influenced by the values and beliefs of investors— and by their self-confidence, financial sophistication, and trust in expert advisors. De Bondt finds that investors' values and beliefs correlate with national character, gender, age, and religion and are predictors of portfolio choice and investment strategy. The final chapter (Chapter 9) in this section is by Richard Swedberg, who writes on the *Conflicts of Interest in the US Brokerage Industry*. This returns to the topic of investor rights, which Swedberg examines in the context of a case analysis of recent corporate scandals. Swedberg starts from the sociological assumption that interests are always socially defined or constructed and that interests can only be realized through social relations. He shows that interests manifest in these scandals were the outcome of definitional struggles centered on the notion of 'general investor interest', and that social relations and institutions played a key role in substituting particular definitions of interests for the general investor interest in determining the outcomes of these struggles. This analysis differs from the greed-centered psychological analysis of corporate scandals predominant in public discourse. Swedberg calls on economic sociology to pay more attention to the dynamic of interests in economic behavior, arguing, with reference to Weber, that interests are a dynamizing factor in economic and general behavior.

Section III, *Finance and Governance*, presents two kinds of sociocultural processes: those which mediate and control market transactions (Chapters 10–12) and those through which financial markets affect the structure and organizing principles of corporations (Chapters 13 and 14). In Chapter 10, *Interpretive Politics at the Federal Reserve*, Mitchel Y. Abolafia takes the reader into the normally closed meeting room of the Open Market Committee of the Federal Reserve System. Analyzing meeting transcripts, Abolafia details the interpretive politics of the Fed during a period of a major policy change. The chapter identifies the temporal structure of Fed meetings and the framing moves that participants use to contest existing policy frames and project new ones. By looking at interpretive politics as an interactional process that relies on a repertoire of moves, the chapter exemplifies the social process of meaning construction in finance and provides a template for the mediating role of interpretive reasoning processes in other areas. In Chapter 11, *The Return of Bureaucracy: Managing Dispersed Knowledge in Global Finance*, Gordon Clark and Nigel Thrift shift the analysis away from such mediating interpretive processes to the question of how banks exercise control over trading rooms and financial market transactions. The authors describe a bureaucratic process of control through risk management that is dependent upon assessing dispersed knowledge about market conditions and response within the firm and across the globe. In financial markets more than in most other kinds of firms and industries, this kind of bureaucratic control is seen to be essential to corporate financial integrity and performance; indeed, the authors argue that it may also be essential to global financial stability. Chapter 12, *Enterprise Risk Management and the Organization of Uncertainty in Financial Institutions*, continues to explore risk analysis, but with a broader focus. Michael Power shows how new instruments of risk analysis, based in sophisticated financial metrics, have gained global prominence and are being adopted as regulatory tools for financial markets by national and international bodies. Power's argument is that the rapid rise to success of these tools is not necessarily due to their technical accuracy, but rather to the fact that they embody a new conception of the relationship between firms and financial markets (the shareholder concept of the firm). Power also argues, in line with Clark and Thrift, that risk analysis tools are adopted to increase the internal control of corporations. The shareholder concept of the firm is also central to Chapter 13, *Managing Investors: How Financial Markets Reshaped the*

*American Firm*, Dirk Zorn, Frank Dobbin, Julian Dierkes, and Man-shan Kwok start from the question of what causes large numbers of firms to change strategy and structure in tandem. They find that the new model, the shareholder concept of the firm, which emerged between the 1960s and the 1990s, could not be traced to internal functional demands but came from institutional investors, financial analysts, and hostile takeover firms which began to articulate a new ideal that suited the interests of these three groups. The chapter thus illustrates how professional groups in financial markets can act as agents of change in an area with which they have little direct contact by expressing their preferences for firm structure and strategy through their roles in the market—for example, by lowering the price of firms that did not abide by the new ideal, recommending against buying stock in them, or taking firms over and restructuring them themselves. Chapter 14 demonstrates another aspect of the effect such agents can have on the internal structure of firms. In *Nothing but Net? Networks and Status in Corporate Governance*, Gerald Davis and Gregory Robbins show that corporate boards seek to appoint well-connected directors above all when they have a strong need for a display of status—which is the case when they are owned by institutional investors rather than individuals, and when they have been the subject of shareholder proposals suggesting a change in firm governance. By examining a panel of the several hundred largest US firms observed at four-year intervals over a twelve-year period, the authors explore these findings in connection with firms' network centrality. Central boards are better able to attract central directors and CEOs of major corporations, but there is no evidence that boards composed of these individuals enhance subsequent performance (Khurana 2002).

The intention here is not to present the reader with a single point of view or argument, but rather to highlight the diversity of theoretical perspectives and approaches, as well as the complexity of the field. Some topics of research are just emerging; others are being approached under a new angle. Still others did not find their way in this book for reasons of space and structure. Nonetheless, the present book aims to deepen the sociological study of financial markets as a fundamental domain of modern societies. It hopes to convey to the reader the intellectual excitement triggered by studying them.

# References

Abolafia, M. Y. 1996. *Making Markets: Opportunism and Restraint on Wall Street.* Cambridge, MA: Harvard University Press.

Adler, P. and Adler, P. (eds.). 1984. *The Social Dynamics of Financial Markets.* Greenwich, CT: JAI Press.

Baker, W. E. 1984. 'The Social Structure of a National Securities Market', *American Journal of Sociology* 89(4): 775–811.

—— 1990. 'Market Networks and Corporate Behavior', *American Journal of Sociology* 96(3): 589–625.

Baker, W. E., Faulkner, R. R., and Fisher, G. A. 1998. 'Hazards of the Market: the Continuity and Dissolution of Interorganizational Market Relationships', *American Sociological Review* 63(2): 147–77.

Bank for International Settlements. 2002. 'Triennial Central Bank Survey of Foreign Exchange and Derivatives Market Activity in March 2001: Final results'. Preliminary Global Data. Basel: Bank for International Settlements.

Baron, J. N. and Hannan, M. T. 1994. 'The Impact of Economics on Contemporary Sociology', *Journal of Economic Literature* 32: 1111–46.

Burt, R. 1983. *Corporate Profits and Cooptation: Networks of Market Constraints and Directorate Ties in the American Economy*. New York, NY: Academic Press.

—— 1992. *Structural Holes: The Social Structure of Competition*. Cambridge, MA: Harvard University Press.

Carruthers, B. 1996. *City of Capital. Politics and Markets in the English Financial Revolution*. Princeton, NJ: Princeton University Press.

Carruthers, B. and Uzzi, B. 2000. 'Economic Sociology in the New Millenium', *Contemporary Sociology* 29(3): 486–94.

Caves, R. E., Frankel, J. A., and Jones, R. W. 1999. *World Trade and Payments*. Redwood City, CA: Addison-Wesley.

Dholakia, R. H. and Oza, A. N. 1996. *Microeconomics for Management Students*. Delhi: Oxford University Press.

DiMaggio, P. 1994. 'Culture and the Economy', in *The Handbook of Economic Sociology*, Smelser, N. J. and Swedberg, R. (eds.). Princeton, NJ: Princeton University Press, 27–57.

DiMaggio, P. and Louch, H. 1998. 'Socially Embedded Consumer Transactions. For What Sort of Purchases Do People Use Networks Most?', *American Sociological Review* 63(5): 619–737.

Eccles, R. and Crane, D. B. 1988. *Doing Deals*. Boston, MA: Harvard Business School.

Fligstein, N. 2001. *The Architecture of Markets. An Economic Sociology of Twenty-First Century Capitalist Societies*. Princeton, NJ: Princeton University Press.

Granovetter, M. 1985. 'Economic Action and Social Structure: The Problem of Embeddedness', *American Journal of Sociology* 89: 481–510.

Heath, C., Jirotka, M., Luff, P., and Hindmarsh, J. 1994. 'Unpacking Collaboration: The Interactional Organisation of Trading in a City Dealing Room', *Computer Supported Cooperative Work* 3: 147–65.

Hertz, E. 1998. *The Trading Crowd. An Ethnography of the Shanghai Stock Market*. Cambridge: Cambridge University Press.

Khurana, R. 2002. *Searching for a Corporate Savior: the Irrational Quest for Charismatic CEOs*. Princeton, NJ: Princeton University Press.

Lewis, M. 1989. *Liar's Poker*. London: Hodder and Stoughton Ltd.

Leyshon, A. and Thrift, N. J. 1997. *Money–Space. Geographies of Monetary Transformation*. London: Routledge.

Lie, J. 1997. 'Sociology of Markets', *Annual Review of Sociology* 23: 341–60.

Markham, J. W. 2002. *A Financial History of the United States*, Vol. I. Armonk, NY: M.E. Sharpe.

Merton, R. C. and Bodie, Z. 1995. 'A Conceptual Framework for Analyzing the Financial Environment', in *The Global Financial System: A Functional Perspective*, Crane, D. B. et al. (eds.). Boston, MA: Harvard Business School Press, 3–33.

Michie, R. 1999. *The London Stock Exchange. A History*. Oxford: Oxford University Press.

Miyazaki, H. 2003. 'The Temporalities of the Market', *American Anthropologist* 105(2): 255–65.

Neal, L. 1990. *The Rise of Financial Capitalism. International Capital Markets in the Age of Reason*. Cambridge: Cambridge University Press.

Partnoy, F. 1997. *F.I.A.S.C.O. Blood in the Water on Wall Street*. New York and London: W.W. Norton & Company.

Podolny, J. 2001. 'Networks as the Pipes and Prisms of the Market', *American Journal of Sociology* 107(1): 33–60.

Portes, A. 1995. *The Economic Sociology of Immigration*. New York, NY: Russell Sage Foundation.

Ridpath, M. 1996. *Free to Trade*. London: Mandarin.

Rothenberg, W. 2000. 'Mortgage Credit at the Origins of a Capital Market, Middlesex County, MA 1642–1773', PAES Working Paper.

Sassen, S. 2001. *The Global City: New York, London, Tokyo, 2nd ed*. Princeton, NJ: Princeton University Press.

Schwager, J. 1989. *Market Wizards. Interviews with Top Traders*. New York, NY: New York Institute of Finance.

—— 1992. *The New Market Wizards. Conversations with America's Top Traders*. New York, NY: Harper Business.

Shapiro, M. M. 1985. *Foundations of the Market-Price System*. Lanham, MD: University Press of America.

Shiller, R. J. 2000. *Irrational Exuberance*. Princeton, NJ: Princeton University Press.

Smelser, N. J. and Swedberg, R. 1994. *The Handbook of Economic Sociology*. Princeton, NJ: Princeton University Press.

Smith, C. W. 1981. *The Mind of the Market. A Study of Stock Market Philosophies, their Uses, and Implications*. Totowa, NJ: Rowman & Littlefield.

—— 1989. *Auctions: The Social construction of Value*. New York, NY: Free Press.

Strange, S. 1994. *States and Markets*. London: Pinter.

Swedberg, R. 1991. 'Major Traditions of Economic Sociology', *Annual Review of Sociology* 17: 251–76.

Uzzi, B. 1999. 'Embeddedness in the Making of Financial Capital: How Social Relations and Networks Benefit Firms Seeking Financing', *American Sociological Review* 64: 481–505.

Weber, M. 2000 [1894]. 'Die Börse', *Theory & Society* 29: 305–38.

White, H. 1981. 'Productions Markets as Induced Role Structures', *Sociological Methodology*, 12: 1–57.

Wright, R. E. 2001. *Origins of Commercial Banking in America, 1750–1800*. Lanham, MD: Rowman & Littlefield.

Zaloom, C. 2003. 'Ambiguous Numbers: Trading Technologies and Interpretation in Financial Markets', *American Ethnologist* 30(2): 258–72.

Zelizer, V. 1988. 'Beyond the Polemics on the Markets: Establishing a Theoretical and Empirical Agenda', *Sociological Forum* 3: 614–34.

# Section I
## Inside Financial Markets

# 1

# The Embeddedness of Electronic Markets: The Case of Global Capital Markets

SASKIA SASSEN

## Introduction

We might expect today's global financial market to be generally unlike other current and past markets and to approximate, and even enact, key principles of neoclassical market theory. The effort of this chapter is to understand the limits of this electronic, transjurisdictional, globally interconnected market, and to lay bare its modes of embeddedness and its conditionalities. The argument is that while today's global capital market is indeed a complex formation markedly different from earlier global financial markets, this does not necessarily mean that it is totally disembedded. The new technologies have had a deeply transformative effect that I specify below. One research strategy to capture the specificity of the technical transformation along with the possible embeddedness of this market is to explore the existence of imbrications with non-digital environments and conditions that shape and give content to technical features and to the effects of technology. Such imbrications would then signal the limits of the technological transformation.

To examine the validity of this point it is actually important to show that the current market for capital is different from earlier phases in this market, in good part due to the specific capacities associated with the new computer centered interactive technologies. The first section, 'The Global Capital Market Today' then examines in what ways this market is different. In the second section, 'Continuing Utility of Social Agglomeration,' I argue that even as it is different, it remains deeply embedded and conditioned by non-market and non-digital dynamics, agendas, contents, powers.

## The Global Capital Market Today

The global market for capital would seem to be as close an approximation to the neoclassical model of the market as has been possible yet. Because it is

The author thanks Cambridge University Press for allowing the reprinting of this paper. The paper was originally prepared for presentation at the Conference *Inside Financial Markets* (Konstanz, May 2003).

increasingly an electronic market, with pervasive use of cutting edge computer applications, it is open to millions of simultaneous investors and conceivably able to maximize the chances that market participants have basically instantaneous access to the same information no matter where they are. This should then ensure that supply and demand forces are in full operation, guided by information universally available to participants. Since it is a market centered in an industry that produces dematerialized outputs, these can respond 'freely' to demand–supply forces, in that they experience little if any distance friction or other obstacles to circulation which can distort the operation of these forces. Crucial to this possibility is the fact that growing numbers of governments have been persuaded or led to deregulate the industry and its markets, thereby enhancing the operation of supply and demand forces, rather than being encumbrances to their operation. Further, as a global, deregulated, and electronic market, it has particular capabilities for overriding existing jurisdictions.

In brief, one might posit that this is as close an approximation to the model of supply and demand as one might hope for: a market that is not encumbered by geography, weight, unequal access to information, government regulation, or particularistic agendas given its highly technical character and the participation of millions of investors. Has the ultimate market arrived?

Insofar as an economic analysis of markets excludes firms, states, and courts from its explanatory variables, the global market for capital would seem to be a good case through which to explore these assumptions and propositions. In saying this, one of my assumptions is that today's global market for capital is actually distinct and needs to be differentiated from earlier cases of worldwide financial markets. There is by no means agreement on this. In what follows I briefly explain the main reasons for my asserting that it is different. Some of these differences with past financial markets and with other types of markets today are in turn the features that conceivably would seem to make this market one of the closest approximations to the economists' model of the market.

There has long been a market for capital and it has long consisted of multiple, variously specialized financial markets (Eichengreen and Fishlow 1996). It has also long had global components (Arrighi 1994). Indeed, a strong line of interpretation in the literature is that today's market for capital is nothing new and represents a return to an earlier global era at the turn of the twentieth century and, then again, in the interwar period (Hirst and Thompson 1996).

And yet, I will argue that all of this holds at a high level of generality, but that when we factor in the specifics of today's capital market some significant differences emerge with those past phases. There are, in my reading, two major sets of differences. One has to do with the level of formalization and institutionalization of the global market for capital today, which is partly an outcome of the interaction with national regulatory systems that themselves gradually became far more elaborate over the last hundred years (see generally

Hall and Biersteker 2002). I will not focus on this aspect here (but see Sassen 1996: ch. 2, 2001: ch. 4). The second set of differences concerns the transformative impact of the new information and communication technologies, particularly computer based technologies (henceforth referred to for short as digitization). In combination with the various dynamics and policies we usually refer to as globalization they have constituted the capital market as a distinct institutional order, one different from other major markets and circulation systems such as global trade.

One of the key and most significant outcomes of digitization on finance has been the jump in orders of magnitude and the extent of worldwide interconnectedness. Elsewhere I have posited that there are basically three ways in which digitization has contributed to this outcome (Sassen 2001: 110–26, 2005). One is the use of sophisticated software, a key feature of the global financial markets today and a condition that in turn has made possible an enormous amount of innovation. It has raised the level of liquidity as well as increased the possibilities of liquefying forms of wealth hitherto considered non-liquid. This can require complex instruments; the possibility of using computers facilitated not only the development of these instruments, but also enabled the widespread use of these instruments insofar as much of the complexity could be contained in the software. It allows users who might not fully grasp either the mathematics or the software design issues to be effective in their deployment of the instruments.

Second, the distinctive features of digital networks can maximize the implications of global market integration by producing the possibility of simultaneous interconnected flows and transactions, and decentralized access for investors. Since the late 1980s, a growing number of financial centers have become globally integrated as countries deregulated their economies. This non-digital condition raised the impact of the digitization of markets and instruments.

Third, because finance is particularly about transactions rather than simply flows of money, the technical properties of digital networks assume added meaning. Interconnectivity, simultaneity, decentralized access, all contribute to multiply the number of transactions, the length of transaction chains (i.e. distance between instrument and underlying asset), and thereby the number of participants. The overall outcome is a complex architecture of transactions.

The combination of these conditions has contributed to the distinctive position of the global capital market in relation to other components of economic globalization. We can specify two major features, one concerning orders of magnitude and the second the spatial organization of finance. In terms of the first, indicators are the actual monetary values involved and, though more difficult to measure, the growing weight of financial criteria in economic transactions, sometimes referred to as the financialization of the economy. Since 1980, the total stock of financial assets has increased three times faster than the aggregate gross domestic product (GDP) of the twenty-three highly developed countries that formed the Organization for Economic Cooperation and Development (OECD) for much of this period; and the volume of trading in currencies, bonds, and equities has increased about five times faster and now surpasses it by far. This aggregate GDP stood at US$30 trillion in 2000 while the worldwide value of internationally traded derivatives reached over US$65 trillion in the late 1990s, a figure that rose to over US$80 trillion by 2000, US$168 trillion by late 2001, and US$192 trillion in 2002. To put this in perspective we can make a comparison with the value of other major high-growth components of the global economy, such as the value of cross-border trade (ca. US$8 trillion in 2000), and global foreign direct investment stock (US$6 trillion in 2000) (Bank for International Settlements 2002). Foreign exchange transactions were ten times as large as world trade in 1983, but seventy times larger in 1999, even though world trade also grew sharply over this period.[1]

As for the second major feature, the spatial organization of finance, it has been deeply shaped by regulation. In theory, regulation has operated as one of the key locational constraints keeping the industry, its firms and markets, from spreading to every corner of the world.[2] The wave of deregulations that began in the mid-1980s has lifted this set of major constraints to geographic spread. Further, since today it is a highly digitized industry, its dematerialized outputs can circulate instantaneously worldwide, financial transactions can be executed digitally, and both, circulation and transactions, can cut across conventional borders. This raises a host of locational issues that are quite specific and different from those of most other economic sectors (Budd 1995; Parr and Budd 2000). The large scale deregulation of the industry in a growing number of countries since the mid-1980s has brought with it a sharp increase in access to what were still largely national financial centers and it enabled innovations which, in turn, facilitated its expansion both geographically and institutionally. This possibility of locational and institutional spread also brings with it a heightened level of risk, clearly a marking feature of the current phase of the market for capital.

Though there is little agreement on the subject, in my reading these current conditions make for important differences between today's global capital market and the period of the gold standard before the First World War. In many ways the international financial market from the late 1800s to the interwar period was as massive as today's. This appears to be the case if we measure its volume as a share of national economies and in terms of the relative size of international flows. The international capital market in that earlier period was large and dynamic, highly internationalized, and backed by a healthy dose of Pax Britannica to keep order. The extent of its internationalization can be seen in the fact that in 1920, for example, Moody's rated bonds issued by about fifty governments to raise money in the American capital markets (Sinclair 1994). The depression brought on a radical decline in the extent of this internationalization, and it was not till very recently that Moody's was once again rating the bonds of fifty governments. Indeed, as late as 1985, only fifteen foreign governments were borrowing in the US capital markets. Not until after 1985 did the international financial markets re-emerge as a major factor.[3]

One type of difference concerns the growing concentration of market power in institutions such as pension funds and insurance companies. Institutional investors are not new. What is different beginning in the 1980s is the diversity of types of funds and the rapid escalation of the value of their assets. There are two phases in this short history, one going into the early 1990s and the second one taking off in the later 1990s. Just focusing briefly on the first phase, and considering pension funds, for instance, their assets more than doubled in the United States from $1.5 trillion in 1985 to $3.3 trillion in 1992. Pension funds grew threefold in the United Kingdom and fourfold in Japan over that same period, and they more than doubled in Germany and in Switzerland. In the United States, institutional investors as a group came to manage two-fifths of US households' financial assets by the early 1990s, up from one-fifth in 1980. Further, the global capital market is increasingly a necessary component of a growing range of types of transactions, such as the diversity of government debts that now get financed through the global market: increasingly, kinds of debt that were thought to be basically local, such as municipal debt, are now entering this market. The overall growth in the value of financial instruments and assets also was evident with institutional investors whose assets rose as a share of GDP (Table 1.1).

Besides the growth of older types of institutional investors, the late 1990s also saw a proliferation of institutional investors with extremely speculative investment strategies. Hedge funds are among the most speculative of these institutions; they sidestep certain disclosure and leverage regulations by having a small private clientele and, frequently, by operating offshore. While they are not new, the growth in their size and their capacity to affect the functioning of markets certainly grew enormously in the 1990s and they emerged as

TABLE 1.1. Financial Assets of Institutional Investors, 1990–7, Selected Years and Countries (bn USD)

| Country | 1990 | 1993 | 1996 | 1997 |
|---|---|---|---|---|
| Canada | 332.6 | 420.4 | 560.5 | 619.8 |
| France | 655.7 | 906.4 | 1278.1 | 1263.2 |
| Germany | 599.0 | 729.7 | 1167.9 | 1201.9 |
| Japan | 2427.9 | 3475.5 | 3563.6 | 3154.7 |
| Netherlands | 378.3 | 465.0 | 671.2 | 667.8 |
| United Kingdom | 1116.8 | 1547.3 | 2226.9 | n/a |
| United States | 6875.7 | 9612.8 | 13382.1 | 15867.5 |
| Total OECD | 13768.2 | 19013.9 | 26001.2 | n/a |

*Source*: Based on OECD, International Direct Investment. Statistical Yearbook 1999, table 8.1.

a major force by the late 1990s. According to some estimates they numbered 1,200 with assets of over $150 billion by mid-1998 (Bank for International Settlements 2000), which was more than the $122 billion in assets of the total of almost 1,500 equity funds as of October 1997 (United Nations Conference 1998). Both of these types of funds need to be distinguished from asset management funds, of which the top ten are estimated to have $10 trillion under management.[4]

A second set of differences has to do with the properties that the new information technologies bring to the financial markets, already briefly addressed earlier. Two sets of properties need to be emphasized here: one, instantaneous transmission, interconnectivity, and speed; and the other, increased digitization of transactions and the associated increase in capacities to liquefy assets. Gross volumes have increased enormously. And the speed of transactions has brought its own consequences. Trading in currencies and securities is instant thanks to vast computer networks. Further, the high degree of interconnectivity in combination with instantaneous transmission signals the potential for exponential growth.

A third major difference is the explosion in financial innovations, also partly discussed above. Innovations have raised the supply of financial instruments that are tradable—sold on the open market. There are significant differences by country. Securitization is well advanced in the United States, but just beginning in most of Europe. The proliferation of derivatives has furthered the linking of national markets by making it easier to exploit price differences between different financial instruments, that is, to arbitrage.[5] By 1994 the total stock of derivatives sold over the counter or traded in exchanges had risen to over US$30 trillion, a historical high; this had doubled to US$65 trillion only a few years later, in 1999.

One indicator of this growing importance of cross-border transactions is the value of cross-border transactions in bonds and equities as a percentage of GDP in the leading developed economies. Table 1.2 presents this information for a handful of these countries and shows the recency of this accelerated increase. For instance, the value of such transactions represented 4% of GDP in 1975 in the United States, 35% in 1985 when the new financial era is in full swing, but had quadrupled by 1995 and risen to 230% in 1998. Other countries show even sharper increases. In Germany, this share grew from 5% in 1975 to 334% in 1998; in France it went from 5% in 1980 to 415% in 1998. In part, this entails escalating levels of risk and innovation driving the industry. It is only over the last decade and a half that we see this acceleration.

The drive to produce innovations is one of the marking features of the financial era that begins in the 1980s. The history of finance is in many ways a long history of innovations. But what is perhaps different today is the intensity of the current phase and the multiplication of instruments that lengthen the distance between the financial instrument and actual underlying asset. This is reflected, for instance, in the fact that stock market capitalization and

TABLE 1.2. Cross-border Transactions in Bonds and Equities, (*) 1975 to 1998, Selected Years and Countries as a percentage of GDP

| Country | 1975 | 1980 | 1985 | 1990 | 1995 | 1998 |
|---|---|---|---|---|---|---|
| United States | 4 | 9 | 35 | 89 | 135 | 230 |
| Japan | 2 | 8 | 62 | 119 | 65 | 91 |
| Germany | 5 | 7 | 33 | 57 | 172 | 334 |
| France | n/a | 5 | 21 | 54 | 187 | 415 |
| Italy | 1 | 1 | 4 | 27 | 253 | 640 |
| Canada | 3 | 9 | 27 | 65 | 187 | 331 |

*Note*: (*) Denotes gross purchases and sales of securities between residents and non-residents.
*Source*: Bank for International Settlements (BIS), Annual Report 1999, April 1998–June 1999: 10.

securitized debt, before the financial crisis of 1997–8, in North America, the European Union, and Japan amounted to $46.6 trillion in 1997, while their aggregate GDP was $21.4 and global GDP was $29 trillion. Further, the value of outstanding derivatives in these same sets of countries stood at $68 trillion, which was about 146% of the size of the underlying capital markets (International Monetary Fund 1999).

## In the Digital Era: More Concentration than Dispersal?

Today, after considerable deregulation in the industry, the incorporation of a growing number of national financial centers into a global market, and the sharp use of electronic trading, the actual spatial organization of the industry can be seen as a closer indicator of its market-driven locational dynamics than was the case in the earlier regulatory phase. This would hold especially for the international level given the earlier prevalence of highly regulated and closed national markets; but also in some cases for domestic markets, given barriers to interstate banking, for example, in the United States.

There has, indeed, been geographic decentralization of certain types of financial activities, aimed at securing business in the growing number of countries becoming integrated into the global economy. Many of the leading investment banks have operations in more countries than they had twenty years ago. The same can be said for the leading accounting, legal, and other specialized corporate services whose networks of overseas affiliates have seen explosive growth (Johnston, Taylor, and Watts 2002; Taylor et al. 2002). And it can be said for some markets: for example, in the 1980s all basic wholesale foreign exchange operations were in London. Today these are distributed among London and several other centers (even though their number is far smaller than the number of countries whose currency is being traded).

But empirically what stands out in the evidence about the global financial markets after a decade and a half of deregulation, worldwide integration, and major advances in electronic trading is the extent of locational concentration and the premium firms are willing to pay to be in major centers. Large shares of many financial markets are disproportionately concentrated in a few financial centers. This trend toward consolidation in a few centers also is evident within countries. Further, this pattern toward the consolidation of one leading financial center per country is a function of rapid growth in the sector, not of decay in the losing cities.

The sharp concentration in leading financial markets can be illustrated with a few facts.[6] London, New York, Tokyo (notwithstanding a national economic recession), Paris, Frankfurt, and a few other cities regularly appear at the top and represent a large share of global transactions. This holds even after the September 11 attacks that destroyed the World Trade Center (albeit that this was not largely a financial complex) in NY and were seen by many as a wake-up call about the vulnerabilities of strong concentration in a limited number of sites. Table 1.3 shows the extent to which the pre-September 11 levels of concentration in stock market capitalization in a limited number of global financial centers held after the attacks. Table 1.4 shows the foreign listings in the major markets, further indicating that location in a set of financial markets is one of the features of the global capital market, rather than a reduced need for being present in multiple markets. London, Tokyo, New York, Paris (now consolidated with Amsterdam and Brussels as Euronext), Hong Kong, and Frankfurt account for a major share of worldwide stock market capitalization. London, Frankfurt, and New York account for an

TABLE 1.3. The Ten Biggest Stock Markets in the World by Market Capitalization (bn USD)

| Stock Market | Market capitalization 2001 | 2001 Percentage of members capitalization (%) | Market capitalization 2000 | 2000 Percentage of members capitalization (%) |
|---|---|---|---|---|
| NYSE | 11,026.6 | 41.4 | 11,534.6 | 37.1 |
| NASDAQ | 2,739.7 | 10.3 | 3,597.1 | 8.8 |
| Tokyo | 2,264.5 | 8.5 | 3,157.2 | 7.3 |
| London | 2,164.7 | 8.1 | 2,612.2 | 7.0 |
| Euronext | 1,843.5 | 6.9 | 2,271.7 | 5.9 |
| Deutsche Börse | 1,071.7 | 4.0 | 1,270.2 | 3.4 |
| Toronto | 611.5 | 2.3 | 766.2 | 2.0 |
| Italy | 527.5 | 2.0 | 768.3 | 1.7 |
| Swiss Exchange | 527.3 | 2.0 | 792.3 | 1.7 |
| Hong Kong | 506.1 | 1.9 | 506.1 | 1.6 |
| Total for Federation Members | 26,610.0 | 87.5 | 31,125.0 | 76.4 |

*Note*: Euronext includes Brussels, Amsterdam, and Paris; 2001 figures are year end figures.

*Source*: Compiled from the BIS 2001 Annual Report: 92, with calculations of percentages added.

TABLE 1.4 Foreign Listings in Major Stock Exchanges

| Exchange | 2000 Number of foreign listings | 2000 Percentage of foreign listings (%) | 2001 Number of foreign listings | 2001 Percentage of foreign listings (%) |
|---|---|---|---|---|
| NASDAQ | 445 | 11.0 | 488 | 10.3 |
| NYSE | 461 | 19.2 | 433 | 17.5 |
| London | 409 | 17.5 | 448 | 18.9 |
| Deutsche Börse | 235 | 23.9 | 241 | 24.5 |
| Euronext | — | — | — | — |
| Swiss Exchange | 149 | 36.2 | 164 | 39.4 |
| Tokyo | 38 | 1.8 | 41 | 2.0 |

*Note*: Euronext includes Brussels, Amsterdam, and Paris; 2001 figures are year end figures.

*Source*: Compiled from the BIS 2001 Annual Report: 86, with calculations of percentages added.

enormous world share in the export of financial services. London, New York, and Tokyo account for over one-third of global institutional equity holdings, this as of the end of 1997 after a 32% decline in Tokyo's value over 1996. London, New York, and Tokyo account for 58% of the foreign exchange market, one of the few truly global markets; together with Singapore, Hong Kong, Zurich, Geneva, Frankfurt, and Paris, they account for 85% in this, the most global of markets.

This trend toward consolidation in a few centers, even as the network of integrated financial centers expands globally, also is evident within countries. In the United States for instance, New York concentrates the leading investment banks with only one other major international financial center in this enormous country, Chicago. Sydney and Toronto have equally gained power in continentally sized countries and have taken over functions and market share from what were once the major commercial centers, respectively Melbourne and Montreal. So have Sao Paulo and Mumbai, which have gained share and functions from respectively Rio de Janeiro in Brazil and New Delhi and Calcutta in India. These are all enormous countries and one might have thought that they could sustain multiple major financial centers. This pattern is evident in many countries.[7] Consolidation of one leading financial center in each country is an integral part of the growth dynamics in the sector rather than the result of losses in the losing cities.

There is both consolidation in fewer major centers across and within countries and a sharp growth in the numbers of centers that become part of the global network as countries deregulate their economies. Mumbai, for instance, became incorporated in the global financial network in the early 1990s after India (partly) deregulated its financial system. This mode of incorporation into the global network is often at the cost of losing functions which these cities may have had when they were largely national centers. Today the leading, typically foreign, financial, accounting, and legal services firms enter their markets to handle many of the new cross-border operations. Incorporation in the global market typically happens without a gain in their global share of the particular segments of the market they are in even as capitalization may increase, often sharply, and even though they add to the total volume in the global market.

Why is it that at a time of rapid growth in the network of financial centers, in overall volumes, and in electronic networks, we have such high concentration of market shares in the leading global and national centers? Both globalization and electronic trading are about expansion and dispersal beyond what had been the confined realm of national economies and floor trading. Indeed, one might well ask why financial centers matter at all.

## The Continuing Utility of Spatial Agglomeration

The continuing weight of major centers is, in a way, countersensical, as is, for that matter, the existence of an expanding network of financial centers. The rapid development of electronic exchanges, the growing digitization of much financial activity, the fact that finance has become one of the leading sectors in a growing number of countries, and that it is a sector that produces a dematerialized, hypermobile product, all suggest that location should not matter. In fact geographic dispersal would seem to be a good option given the high cost of operating in major financial centers. Further, the last ten years have seen an increased geographic mobility of financial experts and financial services firms.

There are, in my view, at least three reasons that explain the trend toward consolidation in a few centers rather than massive dispersal.

### The Importance of Social Connectivity and Central Functions

First, while the new communication technologies do indeed facilitate geographic dispersal of economic activities without losing system integration, they have also had the effect of strengthening the importance of central coordination and control functions for firms and, even, for markets.[8] Indeed for firms in any sector, operating a widely dispersed network of branches and affiliates and operating in multiple markets has made central functions far more complicated. Their execution requires access to top talent, not only inside headquarters but also, more generally, to innovative milieus—in technology, accounting, legal services, economic forecasting, and all sorts of other, many new, specialized corporate services. Major centers have massive concentrations of state of the art resources that allow maximization of the benefits of the new communication technologies and to govern the new conditions for operating globally. Even electronic markets such as NASDAQ and E-Trade rely on traders and banks which are located somewhere, with at least some in a major financial center. The question of risk and how it is handled and perceived is yet another factor which has an impact on how the industry organizes itself, where it locates operations, what markets become integrated into the global capital market, and so on.

One fact that has become increasingly evident is that to maximize the benefits of the new information technologies firms need not only the infrastructure but a complex mix of other resources. In my analysis organizational complexity is a key variable allowing firms to maximize the utility/benefits they can derive from using digital technology (Sassen 2001: 110–26). In the case of financial exchanges we could make a parallel argument. Most of the value added that these technologies produce for advanced service firms and exchanges lies in so-called externalities. And this means the material and human resources—state of the art office buildings, top talent, and the social networking infrastructure that maximizes connectivity. Any town can have fiber optic cables, but this is not sufficient for global social connectivity (Garcia 2002).

A second fact that is emerging with greater clarity concerns the meaning of 'information'. There are two types of information. One is the datum, which may be complex yet is standard knowledge: the level at which a stock market closes, a privatization of a public utility, the bankruptcy of a bank. But there is a far more difficult type of 'information', akin to an interpretation/evaluation/judgment. It entails negotiating a series of datums and a series of interpretations of a mix of datums in the hope of producing a higher order datum. Access to the first kind of information is now global and immediate from just about any place in the highly developed world thanks to the digital revolution. But it is the second type of information that requires a complicated mixture of elements—the social infrastructure for global connectivity—which gives major financial centers a leading edge.

It is possible, in principle, to reproduce the technical infrastructure anywhere. Singapore, for example, has technical connectivity matching Hong Kong's. But does it have Hong Kong's social connectivity? At a higher level of global social connectivity we could probably say the same for Frankfurt and London. When the more complex forms of information needed to execute major international deals cannot be gotten from existing data bases, no matter what one can pay, then one needs the social information loop and the associated de facto interpretations and inferences that come with bouncing off information among talented, informed people. It is the weight of this input that has given a whole new importance to credit rating agencies, for instance. Part of the rating has to do with interpreting and inferring. When this interpreting becomes 'authoritative' it becomes 'information' available to all. The process of making inferences/interpretations into 'information' takes quite a mix of talents and resources.

In brief, financial centers provide the social connectivity that allows a firm or market to maximize the benefits of its technical connectivity.

**Cross-border Mergers and Alliances**

Global firms and markets in the financial industry need enormous resources, a trend which is leading to rapid mergers and acquisitions of firms and strategic alliances among markets in different countries. These are happening on a scale and in combinations few would have foreseen as recently as the early 1990s. There are growing numbers of mergers among respectively financial services firms, accounting firms, law firms, insurance brokers, in brief, firms that need to provide a global service. A similar evolution is also possible for the global telecommunications industry which will have to consolidate in order to offer a state of the art, globe-spanning service to its global clients, among which are the financial firms.

I would argue that yet another kind of 'merger' is the consolidation of electronic networks that connect a very select number of markets. There are a number of networks connecting markets that have been set up in the last few years. In 1999 NASDAQ, the second largest US stock market after the New York Stock Exchange (NYSE), set up NASDAQ Japan and in 2000 NASDAQ Canada. This gives investors in Japan and Canada direct access to the market in the United States. Europe's more than thirty stock exchanges have been seeking to shape various alliances. Euronext (NEXT) is Europe's largest stock exchange merger, an alliance among the Paris, Amsterdam, and Brussels Bourses. The Toronto Stock Exchange has joined an alliance with the NYSE to create a separate global trading platform. The NYSE is a founding member of a global trading alliance, Global Equity Market (GEM) which includes ten exchanges, among them Tokyo and NEXT. Also small exchanges are merging: in March 2001 the Tallinn Stock Exchange in Estonia and its Helsinki counterpart created an alliance. A novel pattern is hostile takeovers, not of firms, but of markets, such as the (failed) attempt by the owners of the Stockholm Stock Exchange to buy the London Stock Exchange (for a price of US$3.7 billion).

These developments may well ensure the consolidation of a stratum of select financial centers at the top of the worldwide network of thirty or forty cities through which the global financial industry operates.[9] Taking an indicator such as equities under management shows a similar pattern of spread and simultaneous concentration at the top of the hierarchy. The worldwide distribution of equities under institutional management is spread among a large number of cities which have become integrated in the global equity market along with deregulation of their economies and the whole notion of 'emerging markets' as an attractive investment destination. In 1999 (the latest year for which data are available), institutional money managers around the world controlled approximately US$14 trillion. Thomson Financials (1999), for instance, has estimated that at the end of 1999, twenty-five cities accounted for about 80% of the world's valuation. These twenty-five cities also accounted for roughly 48% of the total market capitalization of the world which stood at US$24 trillion at the end of 1999. On the other hand, this global market is characterized by a disproportionate concentration in the top six or seven cities. London, New York, and Tokyo together accounted for a third of the world's total equities under institutional management in 1999.

These developments make clear a second important trend that in many ways specifies the current global era. These various centers do not just compete with each other: there is collaboration and division of labor. In the international system of the postwar decades, each country's financial center, in principle, covered the universe of necessary functions to service its national companies and markets. The world of finance was, of course, much simpler than it is today. In the initial stages of deregulation in the 1980s there was a strong tendency to see the relation among the major centers as one of straight competition when it came to international transactions. New York, London, and Tokyo, then the major centers in the system, were seen as competing. But in my research in the late 1980s on these three top centers I found clear evidence of a division of labor already there. They remain the major centers in the system today with the addition of Frankfurt and Paris in the 1990s. What we are seeing now is an additional pattern whereby the cooperation or division of functions is somewhat institutionalized: strategic alliances not only between firms across borders but also between markets. There is competition, strategic collaboration, and hierarchy.

In brief, the need for enormous resources to handle increasingly global operations in combination with the growth of central functions described earlier, produces strong tendencies toward concentration and hence hierarchy even as the network of financial centers has expanded

## Denationalized Elites and Agendas

National attachments and identities are becoming weaker for global firms and their customers. This is particularly strong in the West, but may develop in Asia as well. Deregulation and privatization have weakened the need for *national* financial centers. The nationality question simply plays differently in these sectors than it did even a decade ago. Global financial products are accessible in national markets and national investors can operate in global markets. For instance, some of the major Brazilian firms now list on the NYSE, and bypass the Sao Paulo exchange, a new practice which has caused somewhat of an uproar in specialized circles in Brazil (Schiffer 2002). While it is as yet inconceivable in the Asian case, this may well change given the growing number of foreign acquisitions of major firms in several countries after the 1997–8 crisis. Another indicator of this trend is the fact that the major US and European investment banks have set up specialized offices in London to handle various aspects of their global business. Even French banks have set up some of their global specialized operations in London, inconceivable a decade ago and still not avowed in national rhetoric.

One way of describing this process is as what I call an incipient and highly specialized denationalization of particular institutional arenas (Sassen 2004). It can be argued that such denationalization is a necessary condition for economic globalization as we know it today. The sophistication of this system lies in the fact that it only needs to involve strategic institutional areas—most national systems can be left basically unaltered. China is a good example. It adopted international accounting rules in 1993, necessary to engage in international transactions. To do so it did not have to change much of its domestic economy. Japanese firms operating overseas adopted such standards long before Japan's government considered requiring them. In this regard the 'wholesale' side of globalization is quite different from the global consumer markets, in which success necessitates altering national tastes at a mass level. This process of denationalization has been strengthened by state policy enabling privatization and foreign acquisition. In some ways one might say that the Asian financial crisis has functioned as a mechanism to denationalize, at least partly, control over key sectors of economies which, while allowing the massive entry of foreign investment, never relinquished that control.[10]

Major international business centers produce what we could think of as a new subculture, a move from the 'national' version of international activities to the 'global' version. The long-standing resistance in Europe to M&As, especially hostile takeovers, or to foreign ownership and control in East Asia, signal national business cultures that are somewhat incompatible with the new global economic culture. I would posit that major cities, and the variety of so-called global business meetings (such as those of the World Economic Forum in Davos and other similar occasions), contribute to denationalize corporate elites. Whether this is good or bad is a separate issue; but it is, I would argue, one of the conditions for setting in place the systems and sub-cultures necessary for a global economic system.

## The Global Capital Market and the State

The explosive growth in financial markets in combination with the tight organizational structure of the industry described in the preceding section, suggest that the global capital market today contributes to a distinct political economy. The increase in volumes per se may be secondary in many regards. But when these volumes can be deployed, for instance, to overwhelm national central banks, as happened in the 1994 Mexico and the 1997 Thai crises, then the fact itself of the volume becomes a significant variable.[11]

Further, when globally integrated electronic markets can enable investors rapidly to withdraw well over US$100 billion from a few countries in South East Asia in the 1997–8 crisis, and the foreign currency markets had the orders of magnitude to alter exchange rates radically for some of these currencies, then the fact of digitization emerges as a significant variable that goes beyond its technical features.[12]

These conditions raise a number of questions concerning the impact of this concentration of capital in markets that allow for high degrees of circulation in and out of countries. Does the global capital market now have the power to 'discipline' national governments, that is to say, to subject at least some monetary and fiscal policies to financial criteria where before this was not quite the case? How does this affect national economies and government policies more generally? Does it alter the functioning of democratic governments? Does this kind of concentration of capital reshape the accountability relation that has operated through electoral politics between governments and their people? Does it affect national sovereignty? And, finally, do these changes reposition states and the interstate system in the broader world of cross-border relations? These are some of the questions raised by the particular ways in which digitization interacts with other variables to produce the distinctive features of the global capital market today. The responses in the scholarly literature vary, ranging from those who find that in the end the national state still exercises the ultimate authority in these matters (Gilbert and Helleiner 1999; Andrew, Henning, and Pauly 2002) to those who see an emergent power gaining at least partial ascendance over national states (Panitch 1996).

For me these questions signal the existence of a second type of embeddedness: the largely digitized global market for capital is embedded in a thick world of national policy and state agencies. It is so in a double sense. First, as has been widely recognized, in order to function these markets require specific types of guarantees of contract and protections, and specific types of deregulation of existing frameworks (Graham and Richardson 1997; Garrett 1998; Picciotto and Mayne 1999). An enormous amount of government work has gone into the development of standards and regimes to handle the new conditions entailed by economic globalization. Much work has been done on competition policy and on the development of financial regulations, and there has been considerable willingness to innovate and to accept whole new policy concepts by governments around the world. The content and specifications of much of this work is clearly shaped by the frameworks and traditions evident in the North Atlantic region. This is not to deny the significant differences between the United States and the European Union for instance, or among various individual countries. But rather to emphasize that there is a clear western style that is dominant in the handling of these issues and second, that we cannot simply speak of 'Americanization' since in some cases Western European standards emerge as the ruling ones.

Second, in my reading, today the global financial markets are not only capable of deploying the raw power of their orders of magnitude but also of producing 'standards' that become integrated into national public policy and shape the criteria for what has come to be considered 'proper' economic policy.[13] The operational logic of the capital market contains criteria for what leading financial interests today consider not only sound financial, but also economic policy. These criteria have been constructed as norms for important aspects of national economic policymaking going far beyond the financial sector as such.[14]

These dynamics have become evident in a growing number of countries as these became integrated into the global financial markets. For many of these countries, these norms have been imposed from the outside. As has often been said, some states are more sovereign than others in these matters. Some of the more familiar elements that have become norms of 'sound economic policy' are the new importance attached to the autonomy of central banks, anti-inflation policies, exchange rate parity and the variety of items usually referred to as 'IMF conditionality'.[15] The IMF has been an important vehicle for instituting standards that work to the advantage of global firms and markets generally, very often to the detriment of other types of economic actors (e.g. Ferleger and Mandle 2000).[16]

Digitization of financial markets and instruments played a crucial role in raising the orders of magnitude, the extent of cross-border integration, and hence the raw power of the global capital market. Yet this process was shaped by interests and logics that typically had little to do with digitization per se, even though the latter was crucial. This makes clear the extent to which these digitized markets are embedded in complex institutional settings. Second, while the raw power achieved by the capital markets through digitization also facilitated the institutionalizing of certain finance-dominated economic criteria in national policy, digitization per se could not have achieved this policy outcome.


## Conclusion

The vast new economic topography implemented through the emergence and growth of electronic markets is but one element in an even vaster economic chain that is in good part embedded in non-electronic spaces. There is today no fully virtualized market, firm or economic sector. Even finance, the most digitized, dematerialized, and globalized of all sectors has a topography that weaves back and forth between actual and digital space. This essay sought to show that these features produce a double type of embeddedness in the case of today's global and largely digitized market for capital.

One of these is that the globalization itself of the market has raised the level of complexity of this market and its dependence on multiple types of non-digital resources and conditions. Information technologies have not eliminated the importance of massive concentrations of material resources but have, rather, reconfigured the interaction of capital fixity and hypermobility. The complex management of this interaction is dependent in part on the mix of resources and talents concentrated in a network of financial centers. This has given a particular set of places, global cities, a new competitive advantage in the functioning of the global capital market at a time when the properties of the new information and communication technologies could have been expected to eliminate the advantages of agglomeration, particularly for leading and globalized economic sectors, and at a time when national governments have lost some authority over these markets.

In theory, the intensification of deregulation and the instituting of policies in various countries aimed at creating a supportive cross-border environment for financial market transactions, could have dramatically changed the locational logic of the industry. This is especially the case because it is a digitized and globalized industry that produces dematerialized outputs. It could be argued that the one feature that could keep this industry from having a very broad range of locational options would be regulation. With deregulation that constraint should be disappearing. Other factors such as the premium paid for location in major cities should be a deterrent to locate there and with the new developments of telecommunications there should be no need for such central locations.

The second type of embeddedness is that at the same time, these new technologies have raised the orders of magnitude and capabilities of finance to thresholds that make it a sector distinct from other major sectors in the economy. The effect has been a financializing of economies and the growing weight of the operational logic of financial markets in shaping economic norms for policymaking. This is significant in two ways. No matter how globalized and electronic, finance requires specific regulatory conditions and hence depends partly on the participation of national states to produce these conditions. The other is that this participation has taken the form of introducing into public policy a set of criteria that reflect the current operational logic of the global market for capital. The formation of a global capital market has come to represent a concentration of power that is capable of influencing national government economic policy, and by extension other policies.

The organizing effort in this essay was to map the locational and institutional embeddedness of the global capital market. In so doing, the paper also sought to signal that there might be more potential for governmental participation in the governance of the global economy than much current commentary on globalization allows for given its emphasis on hypermobility, telecommunications, and electronic markets. But the manner of this participation may well be quite different from long-established forms. Indeed, we may be seeing instances where the gap between these older established conceptions and actual global dynamics—particularly in the financial markets—is making possible the emergence of a distinct zone for transactions and governance mechanisms, which although electronic and cross-border in some of its key features, is nonetheless structured and partly located in a specific geography. By emphasizing the embeddedness of the most digitized and

*Saskia Sassen*

global of all markets, the market for capital, the analysis presented here points to a broader conceptual landscape within which to understand global electronic markets today, both in theoretical and in policy terms.


# Notes

1. The foreign exchange market was the first one to globalize, in the mid-1970s. Today it is the biggest and in many ways the only truly global market. It has gone from a daily turnover rate of about US$15 billion in the 1970s, to US$60 billion in the early 1980s, and an estimated US$1.3 trillion today. In contrast, the total foreign currency reserves of the rich industrial countries amounted to about 1 trillion in 2000.
2. Wholesale finance has historically had strong tendencies toward cross-border circulation, whatever the nature of the borders might have been. Venice based Jewish bankers had multiple connections with those in Frankfurt, and those in Paris with those in London; the Hawala system in the Arab world was akin to the Lombard system in western Europe. For a detailed discussion see Arrighi (1994).
3. Switzerland's international banking was, of course, the exception. But this was a very specific type of banking and does not represent a global capital market, particularly given the fact that it was a basically closed national financial system at the time.
4. The level of concentration is enormous among these funds, partly as a consequence of mergers and acquisitions driven by the need for firms to reach what are de facto the competitive thresholds in the global market today.
5. While currency and interest-rates derivatives did not exist until the early 1980s and represent two of the major innovations of the current period, derivatives on commodities, so-called futures, have existed in some version in earlier periods. Famously, Amsterdam's stock exchange in the seventeenth century—when it was the financial capital of the world—was based almost entirely on trading in commodity futures.
6. Among the main sources of data for the figures cited in this section are BIS (the Bank for International Settlements in Basel); IMF national accounts data; specialized trade publications such as *Wall Street Journal's WorldScope, MorganStanley Capital International, The Banker*, data listings in the *Financial Times* and in *The Economist* and, especially for a focus on cities, the data produced by Technimetrics, Inc., now part of Thomson Financial.
7. In France, Paris today concentrates larger shares of most financial sectors than it did ten years ago and once important stock markets like Lyon have become 'provincial', even though Lyon is today the hub of a thriving economic region. Milano privatized its exchange in September 1997 and electronically merged Italy's ten regional markets. Frankfurt now concentrates a larger share of the financial market in Germany than it did in the early 1980s, and so does Zurich, which once had Basel and Geneva as significant competitors.
8. This is one of the seven organizing hypotheses through which I specified my global city model. (For a full explanation see Sassen 2001, preface to new edition.)
9. We now also know that a major financial center needs to have a significant share of global operations to be such. If Tokyo does not succeed in getting more of such

operations, it is going to lose position in the global hierarchy notwithstanding its importance as a capital exporter. It is this same capacity for global operations that will keep New York at the top levels of the hierarchy even though it is largely fed by the resources and the demand of domestic (though state-of-the-art) investors.

10. For instance, Lehman Brothers bought Thai residential mortgages worth half a billion dollars for a 53% discount. This was the first auction conducted by the Thai government's Financial Restructuring Authority which conducted the sale of $21 billion of financial companies' assets. It also acquired the Thai operations of Peregrine, the failed Hong Kong investment bank. The fall in prices and in the value of the yen has made Japanese firms and real estate attractive targets for foreign investors. Merril Lynch's has bought thirty branches of Yamaichi Securities, Société Generale Group 80% of Yamaichi International Capital Management, Travelers Group is now the biggest shareholder of Nikko, the third largest brokerage, and Toho Mutual Insurance Co. announced a joint venture with GE Capital. These are but some of the best known examples. Much valuable property in the Ginza—Tokyo's high priced shopping and business district—is now being considered for acquisition by foreign investors in a twist on Mitsubishi's acquisition of Rockefeller Center in New York City a decade earlier.

11. The new financial landscape maximizes these impacts: the declining role of commercial banks and the ascendance of securities industry (with limited regulation and significant leverage), the greater technical capabilities built into the industry, and aggressive hedging activities by asset management funds. Rather than counteracting the excesses of the securities industries, banks added to this landscape by accepting the forecast of long-term growth in these economies (thus also adding to the capital inflow and to the fairly generalized disregard for risk and quality of investments), and then joining the outflow. Furthermore, at the center of these financial crises were institutions whose liabilities were perceived as having an implicit government guarantee, even though as institutions they were essentially unregulated, and thus subject to so-called 'moral hazard' problems, that is, the absence of market discipline. Anticipated protection from losses based on the IMF's willingness to assist in bailing out international banks and failed domestic banks in Mexico encouraged excessive risk-taking. It is not the first time that financial intermediaries with substantial access to government liability guarantees posed a serious problem of moral hazard, in the United States savings and loan crisis being an earlier instance (Brewer, Evanoff, and Jacky 2001).

12. Global capital market integration, much praised in the 1990s for enhancing economic growth, became the problem in the East Asian financial crisis. Although the institutional structure for regulating the economy is weak in many of these countries, as has been widely documented, the fact of global capital market integration played the crucial role in the East Asian crisis as it contributed to enormous over-leveraging and to a boom–bust attitude by investors, who rushed in at the beginning of the decade and rushed out when the crisis began even though the soundness of some of the economies involved did not warrant that fast a retreat. The magnitude of debt accumulation, only made possible by the availability of foreign capital, was a crucial factor: in 1996 the total bank debt of East Asia was $2.8 trillion, or 130% of GDP, nearly double that from a decade earlier. By 1996 leveraged debt for the median firm had reached 620% in South Korea, 340% in Thailand and averaged 150–200% across other East Asian countries. This was

     financed with foreign capital inflows that became massive outflows in 1997 (Bank for International Settlements 2000).

13. I (1996: ch. 2) try to capture this normative transformation in the notion of privatizing certain capacities for making norms that in the recent history of states under the rule of law were in the public domain. Now what are actually elements of a private logic emerge as public norms even though they represent particular rather than public interests. This is not a new occurrence in itself for national states under the rule of law; what is perhaps different is the extent to which the interests involved are global.

14. This is not to deny that other economic sectors, particularly when characterized by the presence of a limited number of very large firms, have exercised specific types of influence over government policymaking (Dunning 1997).

15. Since the Southeast Asian financial crisis there has been a revision of some of the specifics of these standards. For instance, exchange rate parity is now posited in less strict terms. The crisis in Argentina that broke in December 2001 has further raised questions about aspects of IMF conditionality. But neither crisis has eliminated the latter.

16. One instance here is the IMFs policy that makes it cheaper for investors to provide short-term loans protected by the IMF at the expense of other types of investments. The notion behind this capital standard is that short-term loans are generally thought to have less credit risk, and as a result the Basel capital rules weigh cross-border claims on banks outside the OECD system at 20% for short-term loans—under one year, and at 100% if over a year. This encouraged short-term lending by banks in developing countries. Borrowers, given lower rates, took short-term loans. The result was the accumulation of a large volume of repayment coming due in any given year. Thus Basle risk weights and market risk do not interact properly as a signal. According to the Basle weight risks, it was safer to lend to a Korean bank than to a Korean conglomerate as the latter would incur a 100% weight capital charge, compared to 20% for a bank. The official position was thus to extend more loans to the banks than to the conglomerates.

# References

Andrew, D., Henning, M. C., and Pauly, L. W. 2002. *Governing the World's Money.* Ithaca, NY: Cornell University Press.

Arrighi, G. 1994. *The Long Twentieth Century: Money, Power and the Origins of our Times.* London: Verso.

Bank for International Settlements. 2000. *BIS Quarterly Review: International Banking and Financial Market Developments.* Basel: BIS Monetary and Economic Development.

Brewer, E., Evanoff, D., and Jacky, S. 2001. *Pricing IPOs of Mutual Thrift Conversions: The Joint Effect of Regulation and Market Discipline.* Chicago, IL: Federal Reserve Bank of Chicago.

Budd, L. 1995. 'Globalisation, Territory, and Strategic Alliances in Different Financial Centres', *Urban Studies* 32: 345–60.

Dunning, J. 1997. *Alliance Capitalism and Global Business.* London: Routledge.

Eichengreen, B. and Fishlow, A. 1996. *Contending with Capital Flows*. New York, NY: Council on Foreign Relations.

Garcia, L. 2002. 'Architecture of Global Networking Technologies', in *Global Networks, Linked Cities*, Sassen, S. (ed.). London: Routledge, 39–70.

Garrett, G. 1998. 'Global Markets and National Politics: Collision Course or Virtuous Circle', *International Organization* 52(4): 787–824.

Gilbert, E. and Helleiner, E. 1999. *Nation-States and Money: The Past, Present and Future of National Currencies*. London: Routledge.

Graham, E. O. and Richardson, J. D. 1997. *Global Competition Policy*. Washington, DC: Institute for International Economics.

Hall, B. and Biersteker, T. 2002. *The Emergence of Private Authority and Global Governance*. Cambridge: Cambridge University Press.

Hirst, P. and Thompson, G. 1996. *Globalization in Question: The International Economy and the Possibilities of Governance*. Cambridge: Polity Press.

International Monetary Fund. 1999. *International Capital Markets: Developments, Prospects, and Key Policy Issues* 47. Washington, DC: IMF.

Johnston, R. J., Taylor P. J., and Watts, M. J. 2002. *Geographies of Global Change: Remapping the World*. Malden, MA: Rowman and Littlefield.

Panitch, L. 1996. 'Rethinking the Role of the State in an Era of Globalization', in *Globalization: Critical Reflections. International Political Yearbook* 9, Mittelman, J. (ed.). Boulder, CO: Lynne Rienner, 83–113.

Parr, J. B. and Budd, L. 2000. 'Financial Services and the Urban System: An Exploration', *Urban Studies* 37: 593–610.

Picciotto, S. and Mayne, R. 1999. *Regulating International Business: Beyond Liberalization*. London: Basingstoke Macmillan.

Sassen, S. 1996. *Losing Control? Sovereignty in an Age of Globalization*. New York, NY: Columbia University Press.

—— 2001. *The Global City: New York, London, Tokyo, 2nd edn*. Princeton, NJ: Princeton University Press.

—— (ed.). 2005. 'Electronic Markets and Activist Networks: The Weight of Social Logics in Digital Formations', *Digital Formations. New Architectures of Global Order*, Latham, K.S. and Sassen, S. (eds.), Princeton, NJ: Princeton University Press.

—— 2004. *Denationalization: Territory, Authority and Rights in a Global Digital Age*. Princeton, NJ: Princeton University Press, forthcoming.

Schiffer, R. S. 2002. 'Sao Paulo: Articulating a Cross-border Regional Economy', *Global Networks/Linked Cities*, Sassen, S. (ed.) New York and London: Routledge, 209–36.

Sinclair, T. 1994. 'Passing Judgment: Credit Rating Processes as Regulatory Mechanisms of Governance in the Emerging World Order', *Review Of International Political Economy* 1(1): 133–59.

Taylor, P. J., Walker, D. R. F., and Beaverstock, J. V. 2002. 'Firms and their Global Service Networks', in *Global Networks/Linked Cities*, Sassen, S. (ed.) New York and London: Routledge, 93–116.

Thomson Financial 1999. *International Target Cities Report*. New York: Thomson Financial Investor Relations.

United Nation Conference. 1998. United Nations Conference on Trade and Development (UNCTAD). World Investment Report: Trends and Determinants. New York, NY: UNCTAD.

# 2

# How are Global Markets Global?
# The Architecture of a Flow World

KARIN KNORR CETINA

## Introduction

A few years into the twenty-first century, globalization has captured the public
and scholarly imagination. For many, globalization epitomizes the sense of
rupture with the past that pervades the public perception, as well as whatever
future lies ahead. Globalization, some think, will take us beyond modernity
with its projects of rationality, nation state dominance, and industrialization.
Others object that globalization is little more than 'globaloney', an inflated
catchword for abstract, imprecise, and erroneous accounts that cite everything that can be linked to some transnational process as evidence for a
global age. In what follows I shall develop an analysis of a global sphere that
attempts to avoid abstractness and imprecision. I do not wish to address
globalization as a general process that crystallizes into a world society, molds
the whole world into a single place, or knits together world-spanning economic interests and groups. I maintain that the notion of 'world' as a natural
container of globalizing processes of many sorts is itself problematic; what a
global world involves as a presupposed and factual context will differ in
various areas of global practice, and needs to be investigated rather than
assumed. The phenomenon I want to examine is that of global currency (or
foreign exchange) markets, which by all accounts—participants, economists,
and, very rarely, social scientists—are genuinely global markets. As collective
disembodied systems generated entirely in a symbolic space, these markets
can in fact be seen as an icon of contemporary global high-technology culture. Yet we know very little about these cultures. They raise important questions for economists, who consider exchange rates to be a significant catalyst
of global markets with far-reaching effects on the income, wealth, and welfare

This chapter draws in part on Karin Knorr Cetina, 2003. 'From Pipes to Scopes: The Flow
Architecture of Financial Markets', *Distinktion* 7: 7–23. The parts are reprinted with the permission of the journal. I am heavily indebted to the managers, traders, salespersons, and analysts
whose activities I studied together with Urs Bruegger, my coauthor on other papers, and who so
generously shared with us the information we collected. Research for this chapter is supported
by a grant from the Deutsche Forschungsgemeinschaft. An earlier version was presented at the
conference 'Economies at Large', New York November 14–15, 2003.

of communities.[1] These cultures also raise important questions for sociologists, not the least of which is how we are to understand the global social systems embedded in the respective economic transactions. And it is important to realize that we are indeed confronted with global social systems here. Traders are the major operators in international currency markets, and they are interconnected by high-technology communication in real time, passing on their 'books', when accounts are not closed in the evening, from time zone to time zone, following the sun. This situation has to be distinguished from that of dispersed brokerage communities in major exchanges, in which members do not exhibit high-frequency dynamic interaction with one another across countries and exchanges. Traders in interbank currency dealing do not broker deals but trade for their banks' accounts via direct dealer-to-dealer contact or via electronic brokerage systems (EBS) disengaged from local settings.

## Theory

What, then, does globalization involve in a concrete case, that of global currency markets? What is the architecture of this smooth-running system that has the highest average daily turnover in all financial markets (US$1.2 trillion in 2001, Bank for International Settlements 2002) and spans all time zones? What are the nuts and bolts of its construction, and what sort of 'world' is implied? The answer I shall develop entails something of a 'discontinuist' interpretation of global developments. By this I mean that genuinely global forms are in some respects unique—global currency markets, for example, are distinct in design and mechanism from previous incidences of financial markets. To capture the nature of the discontinuities involved I draw a distinction between two types of markets: those based on a network architecture, where social relationships carry much of the burden of specifying market behavior and of explaining some market outcomes, and markets that have become disembedded and decoupled from networks and exhibit what I call a flow architecture.[2] Economic sociologists have recently tended to view markets as embedded in social relations and social networks, the structures they see as defining markets and framing economic action (e.g. Baker 1981; White 1981, 2002; Granovetter 1985; Burt 1992; Swedberg 1997; Uzzi 1997; Baker, Faulkner, and Fisher 1998; DiMaggio and Louch 1998; Podolny 2001). Global currency markets, I maintain, and other financial markets like them, are flow markets rather than network markets; they differ substantially from a market that is mainly relationally structured. Though flow architectures may include networks, these networks are not the salient structuring principle of today's global markets. I use the notion of a flow in this context to specify a second discontinuity, that between the spatial or physical world we usually conceive of, and that of a timeworld. Most of our world notions imply that the world is a place (however extended) or perhaps a totality of objects (e.g. the physical universe) 'wherein' we live, and 'in' which factual (e.g. globalization) and symbolic processes can be said to take place. The defining characteristic of this sort of world is that it is given or presupposed. In its presupposed nature, it cannot be made intelligible by the things that happen 'in' the world; the world has a distinctive structure of its own that differs from the things that happen in it. In a timeworld or flowworld of the sort I will specify the content itself is processual—a 'melt' of material that is continually in flux, and that exists only as it is being projected forward and calls forth participants' reactions and contribution to the flux. Only 'frames', it would seem, for example, the frames that computer screens represent in a global financial market, are presupposed in this flowworld. The content, the entire constellation of things that pass as the referential context wherein some action takes place, is not separate from the totality of ongoing activities.

All this will become clearer below. What still needs to be addressed here is what happens at the points of transition between a network architecture and a flow architecture of markets. My answer is that global scopic systems emerge, projecting market reality while at the same time carrying it forward and allowing it to flow. The crucial element, then, in the flow architecture of global currency markets is the scopic system that sustains them. The term '-scope', derived from the Greek 'scopein', to see, when combined with a qualifying notion, means an instrument etc. for seeing or observing, as in 'periscope'. Social scientists tend to think in terms of mechanisms of coordination, which is what the network notion stands for; a network is an arrangement of nodes tied together by relationships which serve as conduits of communication, resources, and other coordinating instances that hold the arrangement together by passing between the nodes. Cooperations, strategic alliances, exchange, emotional bonds, kinship ties, 'personal relations', and forms of grouping and entrenchment can all be seen to work through ties and to instantiate sociality in networks of relationships. But we should also think in terms of reflexive mechanisms of observation and projection, which the relational vocabulary does not capture. Like an array of crystals acting as lenses that collect light, focusing it on one point, such mechanisms collect and focus activities, interests, and events on one surface, from whence the result may then be projected again in different directions. When such a mechanism is in place, coordination and activities respond to the projected reality to which participants become oriented. The system acts as a centering and mediating device through which things pass and from which they flow forward. An ordinary observer who monitors events is an instrument for seeing. When such an ordinary observer constructs a textual or visual rendering of the observed and televises it to an audience, the audience may start to react to the features of the reflected, represented reality rather than to the embodied, pre-reflexive occurrences.

In the financial markets studied the reflexive mechanism and 'projection plane' is the computer screen; along with the screen come software and hardware systems that provide a vast range of observation, presentation, and interaction capabilities sustained by information and service provider firms. Given these affordances, the pre-reflexive reality is cut off and replaced; some of the mechanisms that we take for granted in a lifeworld, for example, its performative possibilities, have been integrated into the systems, while others have been replaced by specialized processes that feed the screen. The technical systems gather up a lifeworld while simultaneously projecting it. They also 'appresent' (bring near, see Schutz and Luckmann 1973) and project layers of context and horizons that are out of reach in ordinary lifeworlds—they deliver not only transnational situations, but a global world spanning all major time zones. As I shall argue in the section on 'The Mirrored Market: "GRS" Illustrated', they do this from trading floors located in global cities (Sassen 2001), which serve as the bridgehead centers of the flow architecture of financial markets. Raised to a level of analytic abstraction, the configuration of screens, capabilities, and contents that traders in financial markets confront corresponds to a global reflex system, or GRS, where R stands for the reflexively transmitted and reflex-like (instantaneously) projected action–and other capabilities of the system and G stands for the global, scopic view and reach of the reflex system. For the present purpose, which is that of distinguishing between forms of coordination relevant to understanding markets, the term is intended to denote a reflexive form of coordination that is flat (nonhierarchical) in character while at the same time being based on a comprehensive, aggregate view of things—the reflected and projected global context and transaction system. This form of coordination contrasts with network forms of coordination which, according to the present terminology, are pre-reflexive in character—networks are embedded in territorial space, and they do not suggest the existence of reflexive mechanisms of projection that aggregate, contextualize, and augment the relational activities within new frameworks that are analytically relevant to understanding the continuation of activities. With the notion of a GRS system, I am offering a simplifying term for the constellation of technical, visual, and behavioral components packaged together on financial screens that deliver to participants a global world in which they can participate on a common platform, that of their shared computer screens. On a technological level, the GRS mechanism postulated requires that we understand as analytically relevant for a conception of financial markets not only electronic connections, but computer terminals and screens—the sorts of teletechnologies (Clough 2000: 3) that are conspicuously present on trading floors and the focus of participants' attention—as well as the trading floors themselves, where these screens cluster and through which markets pass.

Providing the teletechnologies, and to a significant extent the activities of 'gathering up' and televising a global world, are the tasks of provider firms which own and distribute the equipment and feed the screens. What from the viewpoint of the phenomenology of the everyday world are historical and evolutionary processes that constitute 'the' world as always prior to our current ways of living in it, are here corporate processes of technological and semantic as-it-happens world construction. The 'world' of these financial markets is in the care of corporate specialists to whom it has been outsourced. This was not the case historically; as detailed below, the firms that now provide the GRS and its content originally took over and delivered only small tasks like that of collecting and displaying price quotes that had been an integral part of trading long before any computerization. As more functions and contents were added, and traders learned to take what became ready-to-hand on ever more screens as their essential points of reference, 'worldliness' emerged in the sense of an on screen referential context wherein everything takes place. Reuters, Bloomberg, and Telerate, the three most important provider firms today, do not of course deliver this global financial world as a kind of finished product. The world still must be seen as an emergent reality that opens itself and takes participants into its presence from the materials and capabilities that the firms provide. Participants co-constitute the screen world as they operate in the constellation of equipment, practices, and concerns which they share. They also quite literally contribute to it. Not only do Reuters, Bloomberg, and Telerate feed the screen, but traders do as well; they input deals and reference observations, and they act as informants for the provider industry that builds its world pictures partly in consultation with market participants. The whole universe is doubly reflexive, first in the sense of the GRS mechanism that continually projects financial reality as it emerges, and second in the sense of immediate market participants' contribution to the projection.

The whole universe is also informational. What discloses itself to participants in the mass of materials on their financial screens is not the presence of objects but the presence of information. What we are really dealing in, traders say, is information. This does not just mean that in doing deals, traders buy and sell information, which they also do. Rather it means that they act in a universe that continually 'frees' information as traders recognize and respond to the things that come up. As Dreyfus (1991: 338) has argued, for modern man, starting with Descartes, reality is such that we encounter objects to be controlled and organized to satisfy our desires. We may even experience ourselves as objects to be augmented and improved in the assumption that this will enhance our life. Traders do not encounter finished, pre-existing objects that can be made intelligible scientifically and that serve as resources for technological projects of transformation. What shows up on their screens are not 'beings' at all but rather moments of opportunity to act that pass quickly and that, as others to whom these moments also disclose themselves respond, occasion the next set of opportunities. Thus traders find themselves in a succession of shared informational situations or 'clearings'. The mundane economic meaning of an informational reality that opens itself is that it discloses opportunities for investment and speculation. The mundane meaning of information 'freeing' and emergence is that disclosure may require (interpretative and other) work, the sort of thing that is illustrated by the native vocabulary of information 'extraction'.

Using the notion 'world' necessarily raises the question of what its materiality consists of. I answered the question by claiming that this materiality is constituted of information. This answer is consistent I think with a world that is temporal not only in the sense that it moves, as a time context, across physical space, but also in the sense of the transient, decaying character of its material content. The key to the notion of information is not truth in the sense of a correspondence with an independent reality but *news*: the material on screen can disclose itself as information only in as far as it is new compared to earlier material. The new is 'presenced' as-things-happen and vanishes from the screens as newer things come to pass. This sort of reality is inherently temporal, which is what I shall also indicate by 'flow'.

To make things more concrete now, I begin in what follows with an analysis of global currency markets as focused upon computer screens, the centerpieces of a GRS form of coordination. I will also briefly sketch the historical innovation and emergence of the relevant systems in the 1970s and 1980s and point out how they led to a replacement of network markets. In the section that follows, I address the temporal features of the global markets studied. A flow architecture, I shall argue, results from the combination of these temporal features with the GRS form of coordination.

## The Mirrored Market: 'GRS' Illustrated

Unlike other financial markets, the foreign exchange market is not organized mainly in centralized exchanges but derives from inter-dealer transactions in a global banking network of institutions; it is what is called an 'over the counter' market (for excellent descriptions of bond- stock- and other financial markets see Abolafia 1996; Hertz 1998). Over the counter transactions are made on the trading floors of major investment firms and other banks. On the major trading floors of the global banks where we conducted our research[3] in Zurich and New York, between 200 (Zurich) and 800 (New York) traders were engaged in stock, bond, and currency trading involving various trading techniques and instruments. Smaller floors in Sydney, Zurich, and New York featured between 40 and 80 traders. Up to 20% of these traders will deal in foreign exchange at desks grouped together on the floors. The traders on these desks in inter-bank currency markets take their own 'positions' in the market in trying to gain from price differences while also offering trades to other market participants, thereby bringing liquidity to the market and sustaining it—if necessary, by trading against their own position. Foreign exchange deals via these channels start in the order of several hundred thousand dollars per transaction, going up to a hundred million dollars and more. The deals are made by investors, speculators, financial managers, central bankers, and others who want to profit from expected currency moves, or who need currencies to help them enter or exit transnational investments (e.g. in mergers and acquisitions). In doing deals, all traders on the floors have a range of technology at their disposal; most conspicuously, the up to five computer screens, which display the market and serve to conduct trading. When traders arrive in the morning they strap themselves to their seats, figuratively speaking, they bring up their screens, and from then on their eyes will be glued to these screens, their visual regard captured by it even when they talk or shout to each other, their bodies and the screen world melting together in what appears to be a total immersion in the action in which they are taking part. The market composes itself in these produced-and-analyzed displays to which traders are attached.

What do the screens show? The central feature of the screens and the centerpiece of the market for traders are the dealing prices displayed on the 'electronic broker', a special screen and automated dealing service that sorts orders according to best bids and offers. It displays prices for currency pairs (mainly dollars against other currencies such as the Swiss franc or the euro), deals being possible at these prices. Traders frequently deal through the electronic broker which has largely replaced the 'voice broker' (real life broker). The price action on EBS (electronic brokerage system) is central to the prices they make as 'market makers' on another special screen (and computer network) through which they trade, called the 'Reuters conversational dealing'. On the Reuters dealing, deals are concluded in and through bilateral 'conversations' conducted on screen. These resemble email message exchanges for which the Reuters dealing is also used in and between dealing conversations. On a further screen, traders watch prices contributed by different banks worldwide; these prices are merely indicative, they express interest rather than dealing with prices as such. Traders may also watch their own current position in the market (e.g. their being long or short on particular currencies), the history of deals made over recent periods, and their overall account balances (profits and losses over relevant periods) on this or another workstation at their disposal. Finally, the screens provide headline news, economic commentary, and interpretations which traders watch. An important source of information which also appears on these screens, but is closer to traders' actual dealing in terms of the specificity, speed, and currentness of the information, are internal bulletin boards on which participants input information.

Consider now the electronic infrastructures of these trading floors. All financial markets today are heavily dependent on electronic information and communication technologies. Some markets, for example, the foreign exchange market that is the focus of this work, are entirely electronic markets. As markets of interbank trading, currency markets rely on electronic technologies that enable the dealer-to-dealer contacts and trading services across borders and continents. The news and service provider firms Reuters, Bloomberg, and Telerate wire together these markets, as do intranets that internally connect the trading room terminals and other facilities of particular banks and groups of banks in global cities. In the year 2001, Reuters had more than 300,000 terminals installed worldwide in all markets and facilities, and Bloomberg more than 150,000. Revenue from leases of their systems amounted to approximately $2.5 billion each at the end of 2001.[4] With the terminals comes a sophisticated software; dealing and information systems, worksheet, email and customization capabilities, electronic brokerage and accounting services, some of which—like EBS—have been developed by the banks themselves. The connections, and the intricate and expensive hardware and software delivered by providers and the banking institutions themselves constitute the material infrastructure of financial markets.

How does this bear on the difference between a network form of coordination and the reflexive, global form of coordination discussed in this chapter? First, it will be obvious from the description thus far that the material infrastructure of financial markets includes much more than electronic networks, the cable and satellite connections between banks and continents. It includes trading floors in the global cities that are the financial centers in the three major time zones: London, New York, Tokyo, Zurich, Singapore, and a few others (see Leyshon and Thrift 1997; Sassen 2001: ch.7). The trading floors are the bridgehead centers for a global market that moves from time zone to time zone with the sun. The centerpieces of the interconnected floors are their federations of terminals that feature the sophisticated hardware and software capabilities discussed. When talking about the electronic infrastructure of financial markets, we should not lose sight of the hardware and software of the trading floors themselves and the terminal structures that 'ready' these floors for trading. Second, the electronic interconnections which are part of this federation and link all participating institutions, including the service provider firms, are not simply coextensive with social networks through which transactions flow. As electronic networks they correspond to different construction criteria, involve electronic nodes and linkages irrelevant to social relationships, and what flows through them frequently does not derive from social and financial relationships; an example are EBS deals, which are traders' responses to anonymous buying or selling offers provided by an automated EBS. Third and most importantly, the terminals deliver much more than just windows to physically distant counterparties. In fact, they deliver the reality of financial markets—the referential whole to which 'being in the market' refers, the ground on which traders step as they make their moves, the world which they literally share through their shared technologies and systems. The thickly layered screens laid out in front of traders provide the core of the market and most of the context. They come as close as one can get to delivering a stand-alone world that includes 'everything' (see below) for its existence and continuation: at the center the actual dealing prices and incoming trading conversations, in a second circle the indicative prices, account information and some news (depending on the current market story), and further headlines and commentaries providing a third layer of information. It is this delivery of a world assembled and drawn together in ways that make sense and allow navigation and accounting which suggests the globally reflexive character of this form of coordination—and the scopic nature of traders' screens. The dealing and information systems on screen visually 'collect' and present the market to all participants.

Two aspects of the system need to be emphasized. One is that the GRS in currency markets assembles not only relevant information about, for example, political events, economic developments, and prices, but 'gathers up' the activities themselves—it affords the possibility of performing the market transactions and other interactions through its technological and software capabilities. In other words, the system is reflexive *and* performative. In fact, it not only affords these possibilities as an option but has drawn market activities in completely. With the exception perhaps of situations where there has been an electronic breakdown, when traders may resort to dealing via the telephone, nearly all dealing transactions—trades of financial instruments—and other interactions are performed on computer screens. This system effectively eliminates the pre-reflexive reality by integrating within its framework all relevant venues of the specialized lifeworld of financial markets. It also offers, in addition to anonymous venues of trading through the electronic broker, relational dealing systems—for example, the previously mentioned Reuters conversational dealing, where one trader contacts another and deals with him or her in what natives call a 'dealing conversation'. This window can also be used for conversing with a financial market friend connected to the system about anything of mutual interest; for example, it is used extensively for soliciting and offering and co-analyzing information. In sum, the GRS of financial screens integrates within its framework the conduits for building and maintaining relationships. Should we therefore conclude that this GRS is nothing more than an electronic facilitating device for markets that run through networks? Surely not. Roughly 80% of trades, if not more, according to traders' estimates, are conducted through the electronic broker, which is an anonymous dealing system, as indicated. Even if some of these deals involve parties with whom one entertains a business (or personal) relationship, these relationships remain interactionally irrelevant since the deal-offering parties are not disclosed in advance on the EBS. Among the 20% maximum of the trades conducted through conversational dealing systems, relationship deals are more likely, but they need not be dominant. Any bank accredited for certain dealing limits and electronically connected to the system can approach any other bank through the conversational dealing without a preexisting or ongoing relationship. Traders also differentiate between 'their networks' of contacts, those dealers and clients with whom they interact frequently and consider a subset of the market; their circle of closer 'friends' comprising perhaps up to five or ten people with whom they talk almost daily and sometimes extensively via the conversational dealing system and the telephone, and the market, which has a large anonymous component. As one trader put it, '(the market on screen) is probably like 99.99999% anonymous'.

The second aspect to be emphasized follows from the description thus far. The mirrored market that is comprehensively projected on computer screens acquires a presence and profile of its own, with its own properties. Traders are not simply confronted with a medium of communication through which bilateral transactions are conducted, the sort of thing the telephone stands for. They are confronted with a market that has become a 'life form' in its own right, a 'greater being', as one of our respondents, a proprietary trader in Zurich, put it—a being that is sometimes coherent but at other times dispersed and fragmented:

LG:  You know it's an invisible hand, the market is always right, it's a life form that has being in its own right. You know, in a sort of Gestalt sort of way ( ) it has form and meaning.
KK:  It has form and meaning which is independent of you? You can't control it, is that the point?
LG:  Right. Exactly, exactly!
KK:  Most of the time it's quite dispersed, or does it gel for you?
LG:  A-h, that's why I say it has life, it has life in and of itself, you know, sometimes it all comes together, and sometimes it's all just sort of, dispersed, and arbitrary, and random, and directionless and lacking cohesiveness.
KK:  But you see it as a third thing? Or do you mean the other person?
LG:  As a greater being.
KK:  ( )
LG:  No, I don't mean the other person; I mean the being as a whole. And the being is *the* foreign exchange market—and we are a sum of our parts, or it is a sum of its parts

The following quote also gives an inclusive definition of the market which brings out its life-like depth. The territorial disputes between economics, sociology, and psychology over market definitions all *melt* into a sort of '*markets are everything*' in which the focus can shift from aspect to aspect:

KK:  What is the market for you, is it the price action, or is it individual participants, or?
RG:  Everything. Everything.
KK:  Everything? The information?
RG:  Everything. Everything. How loudly he's screaming, how excited he gets, who's selling, who's buying, where, which centre, what central banks are doing, what the large funds are doing, what the press is saying, what's happening to the CDU (a political party in Germany), what the Malaysian prime minister is saying, it's everything—everything all the time.

All of these represent the market: who the buyers and sellers are, what significant actors and observers both in the market and outside it do and say, all the agents, activities, and contextual events indicated in the above quote, as well as all of the reactions of market observers and participants to these events. The quote comes from an experienced trader who had worked in several countries, including ones in the Far East before coming to Zurich. Note that his 'the market is everything' refers to the manifold things that one finds on financial screens, the news and news commentary, the confidential information about what some major players are doing, and the prices. The screens, or perhaps we should say the availability of a projection plane for financial markets, appear to have enlarged rather than reduced the world of this market. It has undeniably enlarged the world beyond that which ordinarily flows through trading networks, which, as we shall see in the next section, historically was to a large extent price information.

From the traders' perspective, and from the perspective of the observer of traders' lifeworld, the dominant element in the installation of trading floors in globally interconnected financial institutions are not the electronic infrastructural connections—the 'pipes' (Podolny 2001: 33) or arteries through which transactions flow—but the computer screens and the dealing and information capabilities which instantly reflect, project, and extend the reality of these markets *in toto*. They give rise to a form of coordination that includes networks but also vastly transcends them, projecting an aggregate and contextualized market. The screens on which the market is present are identically replicated in all institutions and on all trading floors, forming, as it were, one huge compound mirroring and transaction device to which many contribute and on which all draw. As an omnipresent complex 'Other', the market on screen takes on a presence and a profile in its own right with its own self-assembling and self-integrating features (e.g. the best prices worldwide are selected and displayed), its own calculating routines (e.g. accounts are maintained and prices may be calculated), and self-historicizing properties (e.g. price histories are displayed, and a multiplicity of other histories can be called up). The electronic programs and circuits which underlie this screen world assemble and implement on one platform the previously dispersed activities of different agents; of brokers and bookkeepers, of market-makers (traders) and analysts, of researchers and news agents. In this sense, the screen is a building site on which a whole economic and epistemological world is erected. It is not simply a 'medium' for the transmission of pre-reflexive interactions.

## How Did the Market Get on Screen? The Move Away from Network Markets

The market has of course not always been on screen. The history of foreign exchange markets since the 1970s instantiates and exemplifies the transition from a network market to a flow market utilizing a central, compound space. Let us start with the breakdown of the Bretton Woods Agreement, which had hitherto effectively fixed exchange rates. In the 1970s, first the United States abolished exchange controls (1971), then major European countries, including Britain by 1979, and finally Japan in the early 1980s, thereby effectively eliminating the Bretton Woods Agreement of fixed exchange rates in place since 1944. This allowed foreign exchange trading for purposes of speculation. Before the breakdown, foreign exchange markets also existed: foreign exchange deals are cross-border exchanges of currencies. Such exchanges were born with the dawn of international trade and persisted through all ages. But in the 30 years of the Bretton Woods Agreement, foreign exchange deals reflected by and large the real requirements of companies and others that needed foreign exchange to settle bills and pay for goods. When exchange controls were removed, currency trading itself became possible as a market where exchange reflected anticipation of price movements. In 1986, the dealing rooms of the world had taken off, with an average of US$150 billion and as much as $250 billion being traded around the globe, double the volume of five years before (Hamilton and Biggart 1993). In April 1998, according to the Bank of International Settlement's Triennial Survey (1998), the average daily turnover in traditional global foreign exchange instruments had risen from $36.4 billion in 1974 to $1.5 trillion. Two-thirds of this volume derives from speculation, that is, from inter-dealer transactions in a global banking network of institutions. Banks had responded quickly to the business opportunities which arose with the freedom of capital that the breakdown of the Bretton Woods system initiated. They also responded to an increasing demand stimulated by volatile exchange and interest rates reflecting various crises (e.g. the energy crisis of 1974) and to the tremendous growth in pension fund and other institutional holdings that needed to be invested. Though the volume of trading has since receded to approximately $1.2 trillion with the economic downturn and the elimination of some currencies (Bank for International Settlements 2002), the foreign exchange market is still by far the largest market in daily turnover worldwide.

When exchange controls were removed in 1971, the current foreign exchange market was born. Traders, however, had no computers, and trading was a question of finding and negotiating this market, which lay hidden within geographical space. A trading room, in the early beginnings, was a room with desks and phone lines and a calculating machine. It may also have had a central phone booth installed in the middle of the room, originally serving as a quiet place to take international phone calls which, early on, still had to be ordered through the phone company; only national calls could be dialed directly. A most important device was the 'ticker', a device which churned out '50 meters a day' of news headlines and price pointers, as a former participant put it (see Preda 2004 for its specific history). Activities on

*Karin Knorr Cetina*

the floor centered around 'finding the market', that is finding out what the price of a currency was and who wanted to deal. In the following quote, a former chief of trading recalls how he continually chased after the market:

P:    So you had to constantly find out what the rates were in countries.
KK:   And you did this by calling up banks?
P:    By, yes. And there were also calls on the telex by other banks who either wanted to trade or wanted to know, simply wanted to know where dollar-Swiss was.
KK:   ( )
P:    Yes, you were a broker for traders, every morning you had to fetch all the prices in Europe, Danish crowns, Swedish crowns, Norwegian crowns, and such, national currencies every morning, the opening rates. You gave them to traders, they calculated them in Swiss francs, and wrote them down on big sheets.
B:    And you offered two-way prices already?
P:    In Swiss banks exchange rates were determined by negotiation, like in a bazaar (etc.).

I use the notion presencing (see also Dreyfus 1991: 337) to refer to the creation of a reality that is inherently a reality in time, a timeworld as I shall say later. A presenced market requires the transport of details from different time zones and geographical locations. A partial attempt at making markets present occurred before the introduction of screens: the prices written down by hand on the 'big sheets' to which P. refers in the above quote were displayed on wall boards and can be seen as early attempts at market presencing. When screens appeared, they were at first no more than substitutes for the 'big sheets': displays on which the handwritten price sheets put together by female clerks were projected on the basis of pictures taken of the sheets on the floor. This form of present-making rested upon a chain of activities that was in important respects indistinguishable from the one that fetched prices in pre-screen times: it involved narrowing down where the market was by calling up or telexing banks, writing down the responses by hand (and perhaps recalculating prices in national currencies), and making this information available for internal purposes through a form of central presentation. Screens began to make present a dispersed and dissociated matrix of interests more directly only in 1973, when the British news provider Reuters first launched the computerized foreign exchange system 'Monitor', which became the basis for this electronic market (Read 1992). Monitor still rendered the market present only partially, however, since it, too, only provided indicative prices. Nonetheless it did, from the beginning, include news. Actual dealing remained extraneous to screen activities and was conducted over the phone and telex until 1981, when a new system also developed by Reuters that included dealing services went live to 145 institutional customers in nine countries. The system was extended within a year to Hong Kong, Singapore, and the Middle East, resulting in a market with a worldwide presence (Read 1992: 283 ff., 310–11). From that point onward, deals could be concluded on screen within 2–4 s, and dealers could communicate via the screen. Yet even before this system went live, the first system, Monitor, from its launch onward, radically changed one aspect of dealing: it answered the question of *where the market was*, that is, what the prices of currencies were and who might be ready to deal.

Before the market-on-screen, prices differed from place to place and had to be ascertained afresh for every deal through long and painful processes of phoning up banks and waiting for lines from operators for overseas calls. After the introduction of Monitor, prices suddenly became available globally to everyone connected by the system, in a market that functioned between countries and between continents. Before the market-on-screen, there were dispersed networks of trading parties entertaining business relationships. After the introduction of the computerized screen quotes in 1981, 'the market' no longer resided in a network of many places, but only in one, the screen, which could be represented identically in all places. The economic counterpart to this coming together of all market fragments in one location was the declining importance of arbitrage. Price differences between locations made visible on screen, even if they involve only indicative prices, will quickly be eliminated, as the information about them is available to all traders connected and traders try to take advantage of these differences. The sociological counter part of Monitor and its successor systems is the emergence of the GRS as a mechanism of coordination. Not only were markets recast with the coming together and expansion of all their functions and contexts on financial screens, but forms of social coordination were also reconfigured.

## The Market as a Moving Timeworld and the Flow Architecture of this Timeworld

I now want to address the flow architecture of foreign exchange markets which has been made possible by the GRS. The notion of a flow, as I shall use the term, responds to the aggregate properties the market acquired after being put on screens and to the processual qualities of this market. To start things off, consider the continuation of the conversation reported before with the proprietary trader who defined the market on screen as a life form. He also pointed to the continuously changing shape of the market:

KK:  I want to come back to the market, what the market is for you. Does it have a particular shape?
LG:  No, it changes 'shape' all the time.

Traders perform their activities in a moving field constituted by changing dealing prices, shifting trading interests (the indicative prices), scrolling records of the immediate past that are continually updated, incoming conversational requests, newly projected market trends, and emerging and disappearing headline news, comments and economic analyses. In other words, they perform their activities in a temporal world; the market itself is intrinsically dynamic and processual and the GRS of financial screens displays, enhances and accelerates the market process and its dynamic properties. As the information scrolls down the screens and is replaced by new information, a new market reality continually projects itself. The constantly emerging lines of text at times repeat the disappearing ones, but they also add to them and replace them, updating the reality in which traders move. The market as a 'greater being', as an empirical object of ongoing activities and effects, continually transforms itself like a bird changing direction in mid-flight, creating the anticipation problem traders confront. From one point of view, a defining characteristic of a financial market is its nonidentity with itself. Markets are always in the process of being materially defined, they continually acquire new properties and change the ones they have. It is this ontological liquidity of financial markets that contributes to their perception as a reality in flux. The flow of the market reflects the corresponding stream of activities and things: a dispersed mass of market participants continues to act, events continue to occur, policies take hold and have effects. Markets are objects of observation and analysis because they change continually; and while they are clearly defined in terms of prices, news, relevant economic indicators, and so on at any given moment, they are ill-defined with respect to the direction they will take at the next moment and in the less immediate future.

Historically, markets were marketplaces, physical locations where buyers and sellers were able to meet and coordinate their interests (e.g. Agnew 1986: 18). Likewise, our concepts of an everyday reality tend to be spatial concepts. We see reality as an environment that exists independently of us and in which we dwell and perform our activities. The very notions of a lifeworld and of a world on screen as used in this chapter also suggest spatiality; they suggest that the idea of a spatial environment can be extended to electronic domains as these become—for some of us—a place to work and live. The problem with these notions in regard to time is that they imply that time is something that passes in these spatial environments but is extraneous to the environment itself. We relate the existence of a lifeworld, of an environment, or of everyday reality more to the physical materiality of a spatial world than to any temporal dimension. We also express, one assumes, the durability of the physical world compared with the human lifespan through spatializing concepts. The point is that the screen reality discussed has none of this durability. It is more like a carpet of which small sections are rolled out in front of us. The carpet grounds experience; we can step on it, and change our positioning on it. But this carpet only composes itself as it is rolled out; the spatial illusions it affords hide the intrinsic temporality of the fact that its threads (the lines of text appearing on screen) are woven into the carpet only as we step on it and unravel again behind our back (the lines are updated and disappear). Thus the screen reality—the carpet—is a process, but it is not simply like a river that flows in the sense of an identical mass of water transferring itself from one location to another. *Rather, it is processual in the sense of an infinite succession of nonidentical matter projecting itself forward as changing screen.* This is what one may call the flow character of this reality.

This formulation suggests that what I have called the GRS—and particularly its screen component—is necessary for this flow reality to emerge: it is through the performative and presentational capabilities of the GRS mechanism and its information feeds that the market acquires the properties of an aggregate entity and, while being performed and reflexively analyzed and projected, takes on the character of a stream of things moving forward as a whole. We also need to distinguish here between participating financial flows and the composite reality of a flowing market. Traders sometime contrast 'taking a view' of a market development, which is subjective, with having concrete information about what they call 'orders' and 'flows', which is objective, since orders and flows are constitutive components of financial markets. Financial orders refer to requests for trades once the price of a financial instrument reaches a certain level; when an order is executed, it becomes a flow. Financial flows refer to volumes of a financial instrument changing positions and accounts; in accounting terms, flows are distinguished from 'non-changing' objects in that they must be expressed in terms of a time interval (Houthakker and Williamson 1996: 9). In foreign exchange, large flows are large amounts of currencies being bought or sold. The sales may arise from mergers and acquisitions of firms that require large cross-border payments, from central bank transactions in support of a particular currency, etc. Advance and concurrent knowledge of large orders and flows is important to traders because these orders and flows may 'move the market'—they may change price levels. They may also potentially set in motion new market trends and reverse upward or downward tendencies in currency prices. To participants, orders and flows are part of the market as an independent reality and they are at the same time forces that drive the market.

Participants' understandings of flows can be related to common notions of flow which we should briefly consider. Social scientists tend to associate the term flow either directly with (1) things traveling or (2) with fluidity. The first idea responds to the increased mobilities of contemporary life (Urry 2000: 15–16, 36–7). It gives expression to the phenomenon that it is not only people that commute, travel, and migrate in seemingly ever-increasing numbers, but that messages and information also move. It is particularly the traveling of communications that underpins the idea of a network society as one based on flows of information (e.g. Castells 1996). This idea is important, but it does not quite capture what happens in the case of financial flows. In currency trading, financial flows refer to payments that imply adjustments of accounts. No physical transfers of money need take place for this purpose; what flows in the sense of something being transferred is financial (market-, payment-, etc.) power as an abstract capacity rather than actual money.

The payments are important to market participants because they influence price levels, as indicated. The changes that occur and concern participants in response to financial flows pertain to the market as centrally composed of price levels. Also changing in conjunction with large financial flows may be market stories, commentaries, and analyses, headline news, trend extrapolations, and the like—all belonging to the level of the market as presented on screen. This level of the market is what the notion of a flow market as used in this chapter targets.

The second meaning of flow found in the literature is that of fluidity; it draws on the distinction between liquids and solids. For example, analysts who emphasize fluidity conceptualize the current stage of modernity as marked by a transition from more solid forms of order and tradition to structures that are more liquid and fluid, or that are melting, as in Marx's famous phrase that 'all that is solid melts into air' (e.g. Berman 1982; Bauman 2000). The liberalization of traditional education exemplifies this trend, as does the deregulation of markets, the flexibilization of labor, and the breakdown and replacement of traditional family relations (e.g. Lasch 1978). This idea of the 'melting of the solid' comes closer to the one used here, but the point about the screen reality as a flow is not that it is nomadic (without itinerary) and unmarked by the traces of social and economic structure. The point is the projection and reconstitution of this reality as one that is continually emerging in a piecemeal fashion. One can compare it to a text that is in the process of being written simultaneously by many authors, that is composed in the process of writing out numerous different components, and that reaches no further than the contributor's pen. It is the emergence of this market text in episodic pieces contemporaneously with the agent's activity and the short duration of the text that the notion of a flow as used here is intended to capture. I also suggest that it is possible to retain notions such as that of a world while remaining aware of the scrolling change of this particular world. The screen that rolls out the lifeworld in which traders move nonetheless presents such a lifeworld; it presents a complex environment composed of 'walkable' regions and horizons that ground activities. The ground may be shifting continually and the lifeworld is 'in flight'. But traders are able to deal with this flux; their ways of 'inhabiting' it are adapted to the timeworld they confront. An example of this adaptation is the traders' tendency to keep pace with their world-in-flight by following market movements in their trading, and by developing a 'feeling' for these movements. Traders also analyze the short-term and long-term tendencies of their lifeworld's movements in terms of stories and 'big pictures' that give duration to particular states.

If markets are continually changing processes with variable time attributes they can also be viewed as time contexts that move across space, or to be precise, across time zones. Here the global character of financial markets, particularly of currency markets, becomes important. One can see these markets as moving in and out of time zones continually with the sun, and as they do, of taking on different features and updating their positions. As global entities, markets have their own instrument- and clock-related characteristics that characterize them in the aggregate. For example, markets have characteristic 'speeds' indicated by the price movements which are at the center of a changing market process. In currency spot trading, which is the direct exchange of currencies, prices tend to change within split seconds during periods of average activity. As a consequence, the currency trading timeworld moves forward at a breath-taking pace. Another attribute is the liquidity of a market, which in this context indicates the speed with which a financial instrument *can* be bought or sold, without significant price changes. Markets will be 'thin' (have few participants willing to trade) at certain times and 'deep' at others, with market liquidity varying over time. Markets also undergo seasonal variations, for example, periods of low trading volume during the holiday season in December, when the accounting end of the year draws close. When markets are conceived as moving across time zones, additional features become relevant, underscoring their character as moving entities and timeworlds. To make this character plausible I want to consider the following aspects of global markets, focusing again on the foreign exchange market as the most developed global market. A first set of characteristics refers to the temporal unity of these markets: they keep their own clock and times and they have their own global schedules and calendars. A second characteristic of these markets is that they are globally 'exclusive' systems that have left behind their natural embeddedness in local and physical settings. This point will allow me to address the architecture of these markets as based on bridgehead centers in the three major time zones. My final point illustrates the working of a flow architecture as one where such centers play 'bridging' and mediating roles in giving support to a moving market and in updating and forwarding the market on a time zone trajectory.

A first feature that ties into the view of global foreign exchange markets as moving time contexts is that they follow their own time, which is Greenwich Mean Time (GMT). GMT, the time and date of the zero meridian which runs through Greenwich, England was adopted as a universal standard in November 1884 during the meeting of the International Meridian Conference in Washington, DC, United States. This conference drew up an international date line and created twenty-four time zones. Prior to that, the United States alone had over 300 local times (see Zerubavel 1982: 12–13 for its interesting historical origin). Since these markets have no central location, time is fixed to a particular coordinate of the globe to assure global identification of the correct transaction date. If this were not the case, a transaction in New York requiring delivery in Sydney two days later and the receiving side in Sydney might not register the same delivery date. But this also means that the respective markets carry their own time reckoning with them. As an aggregate of positions, orders, flows, and traveling 'books' (accounts), they remain independent of local time zones. A further aspect of the temporality of global markets is 'calendars' and schedules: dates and hours set for important economic announcements and for the release of periodically calculated economic indicators and data. These calendars and schedules structure and pace participants' awareness and anticipation. They originate in a particular world region and the respective time zones; for example, the data might be released in the Unites States at Eastern standard time and they will consist of national statistics referring, for example, to the United States, or of aggregate statistics referring to a group of nations, as with European Union data. But calendars and schedules from all three major time zones are relevant and will be listed in daily and weekly market 'schedules'. These schedules 'anchor' market developments in national or regional economies' fundamental characteristics. Yet as transnationally relevant time points that punctuate and dramatize the ordinary temporal flow of market events and observations, they also belong to the disembedded timeworld of global markets.

This disembedding is the second feature I want to discuss. It too sustains the notion of global markets as moving timeworlds. Giddens uses the notion of disembedding to refer to the 'lifting out of social relations from local contexts' (1990: 21–9). I use the term to refer to the phenomenon that the markets observed appear removed from their local context in terms of participants' orientation, their inherent connectivity and integration as the key to overcoming the geographical separation between participants, their rules of trading practices, their forms of compensation, and the like (see Knorr Cetina and Bruegger 2002*a, b* for an overview of these characteristics). To give some examples, market participants (e.g. traders) are disembedded in the sense that they are oriented toward one another across time zones rather than toward the local environment. They remain oriented to the translocal environment even after their working hours, continuing to watch the market that has moved on to another time zone through hand-held Reuters' instruments and TV-channels. An important feature that points beyond this global orientation is what has been called elsewhere the reciprocal interlocking of time dimensions among traders as a means for achieving a level of intersubjectivity in global fields. What holds participants together across space is a 'community of time' rather than a community of space, as in traditional societies. This community of time comes about, for example, by market participants on dispersed trading floors watching the market virtually continuously in synchronicity and immediacy for the duration of their working (and waking) hours.[5] All three aspects are important here: synchronicity refers to the phenomenon that traders and salespeople observe the same market events simultaneously over the same time period; continuity means they observe the market virtually without interruption, having lunch at their desks and asking others to watch when they step out; and temporal immediacy refers to the immediate real time availability of market transactions and information to participants within the appropriate institutional trading networks. Traders may also see themselves as belonging to global professional communities and they exhibit similar lifestyles across continents. Another disembedding feature are the rules of trading practice which are not covered by national law but correspond to a *lex mercatoria* holding among participants on a global level, and reinforced in trading interactions without recourse to formal law.

Going beyond disembeddedness and asking what 'supports' a market that moves freely across time zones, one can point to the trading floors in global cities where the moving market resides during time zone hours, becomes further articulated and defined, and then moves on to the next time zone. To begin, let me draw a distinction between a globally inclusive and a globally exclusive cultural form. A globally inclusive financial marketplace would be one where individual investors in any country are able to trade assets freely across national boundaries. Such a system requires, among other things, the computer penetration of investor locations (e.g. households), language capabilities or unification, Web architectures, payment and clearing arrangements between exchanges, regulatory approvals, and national pension and insurance systems that support individual financial planning. Such systems are in the process of being created in some regions, but they are far from being in place on a worldwide basis. On the other hand, in the area of institutional trading considered in this chapter, a global market of a different kind has been in evidence for some time. This form of globality is not based upon the penetration of countries or of individual behavior. Instead, it rests on the establishment of bridgehead centers of institutional trading in the financial hubs of the three major time zones: in New York, London, Tokyo, and Zurich, Frankfurt or Singapore. The moving market 'rests' in these centers where it becomes articulated and revised. The bridgehead centers contribute to the markets' continuation by the trading activities of their 'market makers' (the traders who take their own positions in the market), the activities of their salespersons, and others. These activities support the market, which becomes anchored in the time-zone-specific GRSs of trading floors. The activities also change the market, and this contributes to the notion of the market as a flow in the sense introduced before, and as a moving timeworld. Participants coming to work in New York in the morning will not be confronted with the same market they left at the end of their previous working day. They will see an updated version of this market, one that bears the mark of the events happening in the intermediate time zones of Asia and Europe. In addition, these markets will arrive 'whole', at every new time zone and take off 'whole' to the next one. This is somewhat simplified, but let us see what one might mean by such a statement. When traders arrive at their desks in the morning in Tokyo and open their screens they will find summary accounts of what happened before in the New York time zone—these accounts are encapsulated in closing rates, index values, volume statistics, intraday trading trends, etc. They will also find more qualitative summaries relayed to them by their contacts in the earlier time zone in their conversational dealing screens. In addition, traders

themselves will make efforts to find out more about market developments in
the earlier time zone by listening to relevant news services at home, calling
friends, or contacting them via the conversational dealing system before
and while they begin dealing. Most major institutional trading floors
also have morning meetings where such information is reported, analysts'
summaries prepared in another time zone are transmitted over intercoms,
and on-floor analysts and economists relate their assessment of the situation.
Similarly, at Tokyo closing time traders and analysts in this time zone will
transmit summary information to contacts, bulletin boards, and other outlets
in the next (European) time zone, and they may be contacted by those working there via phone or electronic mail for specific and concrete information.
The European (London, Zurich, Frankfurt) and American (New York) time
zones overlap by several hours (New York institutional trading starts at 8 AM,
which is 2 PM Central European Time). In response to the overlap between
the European and North American opening hours, the markets will not
'move on' immediately but will trade simultaneously until Europe closes—the
markets tend to get 'hectic' at these times just as they will be 'silent' when
Tokyo is not yet very active and New York has closed. When the European
closing time approaches, the same sort of summarizing and forwarding
described earlier will take place. The overlap between Europe and the United
States corresponds to a 'time gap' between the United States (New York) and
Japan (Tokyo) provoked by the larger time difference between these cities
where no or little trading takes place in both time zones. Traders in the same
institution dealing in the same instrument (say currency options) may cooper-
ate across time zones when longer-term contracts are involved (e.g. options)
and positions cannot be closed at the end of a trading day. In this case the
market's move to the next time zone may involve the transfer of a 'global
book'—an electronic record of all contracts entered, including those added
and structured in the forwarding time zone. Global books incorporate particular philosophies of trading whose content and adaptation to time-zone-
specific circumstances will be discussed in similar beginning- and end-of-day
global conversations between traders in different zones.

## Conclusion

The market 'flow' refers to these forwarded features as well as the aggregate
positions and accounts that circle the globe while changing continuously with
activities and events. A flow 'architecture' refers to the support systems of
these flows, which I take to be the time-zone-specific trading floor settings
with their GRSs. The GRSs provide for the market's unity and movement
across space. They also suggest a form of coordination of global fields that
is to be distinguished from spatially embedded network structures. As the above
examples show, the market's movement across the globe has an accomplished

sense; it cannot be detached from the activities of market participants who sustain the market in a particular time zone and then 'compute' and discursively summarize a market's features over time zone intervals as they forward these features to the next time zone. By the same token, participants provide for the continuation of global markets, but their activities are not the focus of this chapter. Also left unconsidered, given space constraints, are the activities of the information and service provider firms that develop and service the GRSs and assume much of the function of presencing the market.

## Notes

1. So far, however, economists have not been satisfied with attempts to model the determinants and movements of these rates (e.g. Koundinya 1997: 185).
2. For a more general use of the term 'architecture' in relation to market institutions approached from the angle of a theory of fields see Fligstein (2001).
3. The study is based on ethnographic research conducted from 1997 onward on the trading floor of a major global investment bank in Zurich and in several other banks. For a description of this research, see Knorr Cetina and Bruegger (2002a). See also Bruegger (1999) for an extensive description of currency trading in all its aspects.
4. These figures were reported in Barringer (2002).
5. As Harvey has argued (1989: 239–59), increasing time-compression is a characteristic of the whole process of modernity and of post-industrialization. A similar argument had been advanced by McLuhan (1964: 358), who proposed that electricity establishes a global network of communication that enables us to apprehend and experience media-transmitted events nearly simultaneously, as in a common central nervous system. To date, however, few media events are 'simultaneously' transmitted across time zones, and media content is adapted to local cultures and locally reinterpreted. I argue that many other mechanisms and infrastructures and in fact a secondary economy of information collection and transmission need to be in place to create a global social form.

## References

Abolafia, M. 1996. *Making Markets: Opportunism and Restraint on Wall Street.* Cambridge, MA: Harvard University Press.

Agnew, J.-C. 1986. *Worlds Apart. The Market and the Theater in Anglo-American Thought, 1550–1750.* Cambridge: Cambridge University Press.

Baker, W. E. 1981. *Markets as Networks: A Multimethod Study of Trading Networks in a Securities Market.* Ph. D. Dissertation, University of Chicago.

Baker, W. E., Faulkner, R. R., and Fisher, G. A. 1998. 'Hazards of the Market: The Continuity and Dissolution of Interorganizational Market Relationships', *American Sociological Review* 63: 147–77.

Bank for International Settlements. 1998. *Triennial Central Bank Survey of Foreign Exchange and Derivatives Market Activity in April 1998: Preliminary Global Data.* Basle: BIS.

Bank for International Settlements. 2002. *Triennial Central Bank Survey of Foreign Exchange and Derivatives Market Activity in March 2001—Final Results. Preliminary Global Data*. Basel: BIS.

Barringer, F. 2002. 'Bloomberg, Without Bloomberg, Faces an Industry in Retreat', *New York Times* September 2: BU 5.

Baumann, Z. 2000. *Liquid Modernity*. Cambridge: Polity Press.

Berman, M. 1982. *All That is Solid Melts Into Air: The Experience of Modernity*. London: Verso.

Bruegger, U. 1999. *Wie handeln Devisenhändler? Eine Ethnographische Studie über Akteure in einem globalen Market*. Ph.D. dissertation, University of St. Gallen.

Burt, R. 1992. *Structural Holes: The Social Structure of Competition*. Cambridge, MA: Harvard University Press.

Castells, M. 1996. *The Rise of the Network Society*. New York, NY: Harper & Row.

Clough, P. 2000. *Autoaffection. Unconscious Thought in the Age of Teletechnology*. Minneapolis, MN: University of Minnesota Press.

DiMaggio, P. and Louch, H. 1998. 'Socially Embedded Consumer Transactions: For What Sorts of Purchases do People Use Networks Most?', *American Sociological Review* 63(5): 619–37.

Dreyfus, H. 1991. *Being-in-the-world. A Commentary on Heidegger's Being and Time, Division I*. Cambridge, MA: MIT Press.

Fligstein, N. 2001. *The Architecture of Markets. An Economic Sociology of 21$^{st}$ Century Capitalist Societies*. Princeton, NJ: Princeton University Press.

Giddens, A. 1990. *The Consequences of Modernity*. Stanford, CA: Stanford University Press.

Granovetter, M. 1985. 'Economic Action and Social Structure: The Problem of Embeddedness', *American Journal of Sociology* 91(3): 481–510.

Hamilton, G. and Biggart, N. 1993. 'Market, Culture and Authority: A Comparative Analysis of Management and Organization in the Far East', in *The Sociology of Economic Life*, Granovetter, M. and Swedberg, R. (eds.). Boulder, CO: Westview Press.

Harvey, D. 1989. *The Condition of Postmodernity*. Cambridge: Blackwell.

Hertz, E. 1998. *The Trading Crowd. An Ethnography of the Shanghai Stock Market*. Cambridge: Cambridge University Press.

Houthakker, H. and Williamson, P. 1996. *The Economics of Financial Markets*. New York, NY: Oxford University Press.

Knorr Cetina, K. and Bruegger, U. 2002a. 'Global Microstructures: The Virtual Societies of Financial Markets', *American Journal of Sociology* 107(4): 905–50.

——2002b. 'Traders' Engagement with Markets: A Postsocial Relationship', *Theory, Culture & Society* 19(5/6): 161–85.

Koundinya, R. S. 1997. 'Exchange Rate Theories and the Behavior of Exchange Rates: The Record since Bretton Woods', in *The Global Structure of Financial Markets: An Overview*, Ghosh, D. K. and Ortiz, E. (eds.). London: Routledge, 182–91.

Lasch, C. 1978. *The Culture of Narcissism*. New York, NY: W.W. Norton.

Leyshon, A. and Thrift, N. 1997. *Money–Space: Geographies of Monetary Transformation*. London: Routledge.

McLuhan, M. 1964. *Understanding Media*. London: Routledge.

Podolny, J. 2001. 'Networks as the Pipes and Prisms of the Market', *American Journal of Sociology* 107(1): 33–60.

Preda, A. 2004. 'Informative Prices, Rational Investors: The Emergence of the Random Walk Hypothesis and the Nineteenth-Century "Science of Financial Investments"', *History of Political Economy*, 36(2): 351–86.

Read, D. 1992. *The Power of News. The History of Reuters*. Oxford: Oxford University Press.

Sassen, S. 2001. *The Global City*. Princeton, NJ: Princeton University Press.

Schutz, A. and Luckmann, T. 1973. *The Structures of the Life-World*. Evanston, IL: Nortwestern University Press.

Swedberg, R. 1997. 'New Economic Sociology. What Has Been Accomplished? What is Ahead?', *Acta Sociologica* 40: 161–82.

Urry, J. 2000. *Sociology Beyond Societies. Mobilities for the Twenty-First Century*. London: Routledge.

Uzzi, B. 1997. 'Social Structure and Competition in Interfirm Networks: The Paradox of Embeddedness', *Administrative Science Quarterly* 42(1): 35–67.

White, H. 1981. 'Where do Markets Come From?', *American Journal of Sociology* 87(3): 517–47.

——2002. *Markets from Networks. Socioeconomic Models of Production*. Princeton, NJ: Princeton University Press.

Zerubavel, E. 1982. 'The Standardization of Time: A Sociohistorical Perspective', *American Journal of Sociology* 88(1): 1–23.

# 3

# How a Superportfolio Emerges: Long-Term Capital Management and the Sociology of Arbitrage

DONALD MACKENZIE

## Introduction

Of all the contested boundaries that define the discipline of sociology, none is more crucial than the divide between sociology and economics. Despite his synthesizing ambitions, Talcott Parsons played a critical role in reinforcing this divide. The economy, argued Parsons and Smelser (1956: 7) is a 'differentiated subsystem of a more inclusive social system'. Conventional neoclassical economics could, Parsons believed, quite appropriately be applied to that subsystem. The technical core, so to speak, of the workings of market economies was the business of economists, not of sociologists.

In more recent years, a revived economic sociology has rebelled against this intellectual division of labor, which Stark (2000) calls 'Parsons' Pact'. A range of authors—amongst them White, Granovetter, Fligstein, Podolny, and Callon—have proposed a variety of ways of conceptualizing social processes not as 'surrounding' economic life but as being at its core (White 1981, 2001; Granovetter 1985, 1990; Podolny 1993, 2001; Fligstein 1996, 2001; Callon 1998). This chapter seeks to contribute to this post-Parsonian economic sociology not by proposing a new approach but a new (or almost new) topic for sociological investigation: arbitrage.

Arbitrage is trading that exploits price discrepancies, for example differences between the prices of the same asset at different geographical locations, or between the prices of similar assets at the one location. There is a sense in which arbitrageurs are the border guards, in economic practice, of the Parsonian boundary between economics and sociology. Suppose that the prices of two similar financial assets temporarily diverge for reasons that

This chapter is a revised version of a paper (MacKenzie 2003) published in *Economy and Society*. The case study of LTCM was supported financially by DIRC, the Interdisciplinary Research Collaboration on the Dependability of Computer-Based Systems (UK Engineering and Physical Sciences Research Council grant GR/N13999), and my ongoing research in social studies of finance is being supported by a professorial fellowship from the United Kingdom Economic and Social Research Council (RES-051-27-0062).

are 'sociological' rather than 'economic'; investors' irrational preferences, enthusiasms, or fears; legal constraints (often ultimately moral in their roots: see Zelizer 1979) on market participants such as insurance companies; regulatory impositions (perhaps driven by political ideologies); and so on. Arbitrageurs can then profit by buying the cheaper of the assets, and short selling the dearer (financial terminology such as 'short selling' is defined in the glossary in Table 3.1). Their purchases tend to raise the price of the

TABLE 3.1. Financial Terminology

| | |
|---|---|
| Arbitrage | Trading that seeks to profit from price discrepancies |
| Basis point | A hundredth of a percentage point |
| Future | A standardized contract traded on an organized exchange in which one party undertakes to buy, and the other to sell, a set quantity of a particular asset at a set price on a given future date |
| Haircut | When money is borrowed to buy securities such as bonds, and these are pledged as collateral for the loan, the haircut is the difference between the amount of money lent and the market price of the securities |
| Implied volatility | The *volatility* of a stock or index consistent with the price of *options* on the stock or index |
| Libor (London interbank offered rate) | The average rate of interest at which banks with the highest credit ratings are prepared to lend each other funds |
| Option | A contract that gives its purchaser the right, but not the obligation, to buy (call) or to sell (put) an asset at a given price on, or up to, a given future date (the 'expiration') |
| Short selling | Selling an asset one does not own, for example by borrowing it, selling it, and later repurchasing and returning it |
| Swap | A contract to exchange two income streams |
| Swap spread | The difference between the fixed interest rate at which interest-rate *swaps* can be entered into and the *yield* of a government bond of equivalent maturity denominated in the same currency |
| Value-at-risk | A method of estimating the exposure of a portfolio of assets to potential losses |
| Volatility | The extent of the fluctuations of the price of an asset, conventionally measured by the annualized standard deviation of continuously-compounded returns on the asset |
| Yield | The yield of a bond is the rate of return it offers at its current market price |

cheaper asset, and their sales to lower that of the dearer, thus helping to restore equality. The consequently plausible assumption that pricing discrepancies will be eliminated by arbitrage allows the development of elegant and influential economic models of markets. Arbitrage-based reasoning is, for example, central to the work that has won Nobel Prizes in economics for three of the five finance theorists so far honored: Merton H. Miller, Robert C. Merton, and Myron S. Scholes.

Arbitrage is thus seen by economists as making it possible for financial markets to be efficient even in the presence of investor irrationality and other social or psychological 'factors':

Neoclassical finance is a theory of sharks [i.e. arbitrageurs] and not a theory of rational homo economicus ... [A]rbitrageurs spot [price discrepancies], pile on, and by their actions they close aberrant price differentials ... Rational finance has stripped the assumptions [about the behaviour of investors] down to only those required to support efficient markets and the absence of arbitrage, and has worked very hard to rid the field of its sensitivity to the psychological vagaries of investors (Ross 2001: 4).

Furthermore, finance theory is itself drawn on by modern arbitrageurs, so arbitrage is a key issue for the 'performativity' of economics: the thesis that economics creates the phenomena it describes, rather than describing an already existing 'economy' (Callon 1998).[1] To the extent that arbitrageurs can eliminate the price discrepancies that finance theory helps them to identify, they thereby render the theory performative: price patterns in the markets become as described by the theory.

Despite the centrality of arbitrage, there has been little empirical study of it by economists and, for all the flowering in recent years of the sociology of the financial markets, almost none by sociologists. The only extant sociological study focusing directly on arbitrage is by Beunza and Stark (see Chapter 4, this volume), which is primarily descriptive: it does not, for example, investigate the capacity of arbitrage to eliminate price discrepancies and thus maintain the boundary between 'the social' and 'the economic'. That investigation, in contrast, is the goal of this chapter. It focuses on the hedge fund, Long-Term Capital Management (LTCM).[2] LTCM was highly skilled: it emerged from the celebrated arbitrage group at the investment bank Salomon Brothers, a group headed by John Meriwether, by common consent the most talented bond trader of his generation. LTCM, set up and led by Meriwether, had available to it the best of finance theory: amongst its partners were the Nobel laureates Merton and Scholes. It was hugely successful: at its peak, it deployed what is almost certainly the largest single concentration of arbitrage positions ever. And yet, in August and September 1998, in one of the defining moments of the economic history of the 1990s, adverse price movements drove LTCM to the brink of bankruptcy (it was recapitalized by a consortium of the world's leading banks, coordinated by the Federal Reserve Bank of New York).

The crisis of LTCM has provoked widespread comment—for example, books by Dunbar (2000) and Lowenstein (2000)—and even features in a novel (Jennings 2002). Typically, popular commentary advances two accounts:

1. The partners in LTCM were guilty of greed and gambling (consciously reckless risk-taking).
2. The partners in LTCM had blind faith in the accuracy of finance theory's mathematical models.

More informed discussion (e.g. President's Working Group on Financial Markets 1999) avoids blaming individuals' alleged character flaws, and instead advances a third hypothesis:

3. LTCM was over-levered—too high a proportion of its positions were financed by borrowing, rather than by LTCM's own capital.

This third hypothesis, however, explains at most LTCM's vulnerability to the events of August and September 1998: it does not explain those events. The most common explanation of them is:

4. On August 17, 1998, Russia defaulted on its ruble-denominated bonds and devalued the ruble. This triggered a 'flight-to-quality' in the financial markets—a sudden greatly increased preference for financial assets that were safer (less prone to default) and more liquid (more readily bought and sold).

That there was a flight-to-quality in August and September 1998, and that the Russian default triggered it, cannot be denied. The hypothesis of this chapter, however, is that superimposed on the flight-to-quality, and sometimes cutting against it, was a process of a different, more directly sociological kind:

5. The success of LTCM led to widespread imitation (White 1981, 2001; Fligstein 1996, 2001), and the imitation led to a 'superportfolio' of partially overlapping arbitrage positions. Sales by some holders of the superportfolio moved prices against others, leading to a cascade of self-reinforcing adverse price movements.

This chapter draws upon sources of information of four kinds. First is a set of 'oral history' interviews conducted by the author with partners in and employees of LTCM. These initial interviews were then followed up by further exchanges in person, by electronic mail, and by telephone. The second source of information is interviews conducted with other key individuals, not affiliated with LTCM, who were also active in the markets within which LTCM operated. These interviews give additional insight into the market processes surrounding LTCM, and make it possible to check for any 'exculpatory' bias in the views of LTCM insiders. These first two sources then permit reliable published sources on LTCM to be distinguished from unreliable ones (the only consistently reliable, detailed source is Perold 1999), and these form the third source of data drawn on here. The fourth source is the price movements of key parts of LTCM's portfolio in the months of its crisis, August and September 1998: readers interested in how these movements serve as a quantitative test of this chapter's hypothesis should consult MacKenzie (2003: 367–70).

An economist might object that a study of LTCM is not really a study of arbitrage. In finance theory, arbitrage is conceived as involving no risk and demanding no capital (it can be performed entirely with borrowed cash and/or securities). These are, indeed, precisely the assumptions that make arbitrage's capacity to close price discrepancies unlimited. LTCM's activities, in contrast, involved risk (even in 'normal' times, not just in 1998), and demanded at least modest amounts of capital. The response to this economist's objection is simple (Shleifer and Vishny 1997): much 'real-world' arbitrage involves risk and demands capital. Certainly, there is a spectrum in this respect—there are some arbitrages, typically of evanescent 'mispricings', that are very low risk—but LTCM's activities are reasonably characteristic, in terms of their risks and their capital demands, of a large class of arbitrage trades, including some of great theoretical significance, such as the arbitrage that enforces Black–Scholes–Merton option pricing, the single most influential model in finance theory (MacKenzie and Millo 2003).

This chapter has four parts. After this introduction comes a section describing LTCM's arbitrage trading and its risk management. Then comes a section on LTCM's 1998 crisis, which, after briefly discussing the other explanations, draws on the interview data to flesh out the 'superportfolio' explanation. In the conclusion, I return to more general issues of the sociology of arbitrage and its bearing upon the relations of 'economy' and 'society'.

## Long-Term Capital Management

LTCM, which began trading in February 1994, was a hedge fund based in Greenwich, Connecticut. It also had an office in London and a branch in Tokyo, and its primary registration was in the Cayman Islands. Its offices were not ostentatious (its Greenwich head office, for example, was a modest, low-rise suburban office block), and in terms of personnel, LTCM was of limited size: by September 1997, 15 partners and around 150 employees. These people, however, managed a considerable body of assets: in August 1997, LTCM's assets totalled $126 billion, of which $6.7 billion was the fund's own capital. While most hedge funds cater for rich individuals, they were the source of less than 4% of LTCM's capital, which came mostly from financial institutions, particularly banks (Perold 1999: A2, A22).

LTCM's basic strategy was 'convergence' and 'relative-value' arbitrage: the exploitation of price differences that either must be temporary or that have a high probability of being temporary. Typical were its many trades involving swaps: by the time of LTCM's crisis, its swap book consisted of some 10,000 swaps with a total notional value of $1.25 trillion (Anon 2000). A swap is a contract to exchange two income streams, for example fixed-rate and floating-rate interest on the same notional sum. The swap spread is the difference between the fixed interest rate at which swaps can be entered into and the yield of a government bond with a similar maturity denominated in the same currency. Swap spreads can indicate arbitrage opportunities because the party to a swap which is paying a floating rate of interest while receiving a fixed rate is in the same situation as someone who has borrowed money at a floating rate and used it to buy a bond which pays a fixed amount of interest. If there is sufficient discrepancy between the terms on which swap contracts can be entered into and on which positions in bonds in the same currency and of similar maturities can be financed, arbitrage may be possible.

Several features of swap-spread arbitrage go to the heart of LTCM's strategy. First is leverage. LTCM swap-spread trades were highly levered: that is, were constructed largely with borrowed capital. High levels of leverage were necessary if the small price discrepancies LTCM was exploiting were to yield adequate profits, and did not necessarily imply huge risk (as much subsequent commentary suggested). The risks of swap-spread trades, for example, are rather limited. Bond prices and the terms upon which swaps are offered fluctuate considerably, particularly as interest rates vary. LTCM, however, almost always neutralized that latter risk by constructing 'two-legged' trades, in which the effects on one leg of a change in interest rates would be cancelled out by its equal-but-opposite effect on the other leg. The chief market risk of swap-spread trading is of the spread temporarily moving in an unfavorable direction, but if that were to happen the arbitrageur can simply continue to hold the position and wait until such time as it became profitable to liquidate it. Indeed, if necessary the position can be held until the bond matures and the swap expires. That feature was the essence of convergence arbitrage: if held to maturity, a convergence arbitrage position *has* to make a profit, whatever the market fluctuations along the way.

If the risks were limited, the profits from LTCM's swap-spread and similar arbitrage trading were impressive. Between February and December 1994 LTCM's returns before fees were 28.1% (unannualized); after management and incentive fees were deducted, investors received 19.9% (unannualized). Gross returns in 1995 were 59.0%, and returns after fees 42.8%; in 1996, the corresponding figures were 61.5% and 40.8%.[3]

Although LTCM was active in the US and Japanese markets, it also had particularly heavy involvement in European markets. In the 1990s, financial deregulation in Europe proceeded apace, but arbitrageurs such as LTCM initially found much less competition than in the United States or Japan: 'the Japanese banks...were the ones who were terribly interested in setting up proprietary desks. The European banks were still a bit hesitant' (Kaplanis interview). LTCM scrutinized the 'yield curves' for European government bonds (see Figure 3.1), along with the corresponding swap curves, looking for the 'bulges' and other anomalies that might indicate arbitrage opportunities. If LTCM was confident it understood the reasons for anomalies—frequently

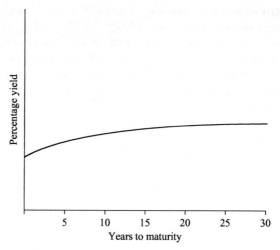

FIGURE 3.1. A Hypothetical Example of a Yield Curve (highly schematic). Yield curves usually (but not always) have the upward slope shown here

they were matters such as regulatory requirements on insurance companies to purchase bonds of particular maturities—it would seek to exploit them by trades carefully constructed to neutralize the risks of interest-rate fluctuations or of changes in the overall steepness of the yield curve.

As well as diversifying geographically, LTCM also diversified from bonds and interest-rate swaps into other asset classes. Some relative-value trades involved pairs of shares, such as Royal Dutch and Shell Transport (Perold 1999: A9). Shares of Royal Dutch are traded in Amsterdam and the corresponding American Depository Receipts trade in New York, while shares of Shell trade in London, but the two sets of shares represent equivalent rights of ownership of what is essentially a single company (Royal Dutch/Shell) and thus equivalent claims on a single income stream. However, they often trade at different prices, for example, because the way dividends are taxed leads investors to prefer one or the other. In a situation like this, arbitrage can be attractive if the difference between the prices of the two sets of shares is expected to narrow, to widen, or to change direction. LTCM could profit from an expected change in relative value while being protected from fluctuations either in the overall stock-market or in the performance of Royal Dutch/Shell.

Another equity-related position, taken on in 1997, responded to an anomaly developing in the market for equity index options with long expirations (see Table 3.1 for the meaning of 'option'). Increasingly, banks and other financial companies were selling investors products with returns linked to gains in equity indices but also a guaranteed 'floor' to losses. Long-maturity

options were attractive to the vendors of such products as a means of hedging their risk, but such options were in short supply. The price of an option
is dependent upon predictions of the volatility of the underlying asset, and
market expectations of that volatility (implied volatility) can be deduced
from option prices using option pricing theory. In 1997, however, the demand
for long-expiry options had pushed the volatilities implied by their prices to
levels that seemed to bear little relation to the volatilities of the underlying
indices. Five-year options on the S&P 500 index, for example, were selling
at implied volatilities of 22% per annum and higher, when the volatility of the
index itself had for several years fluctuated between 10% and 13%, and the
implied volatilities of shorter-term options were also much less than 20% per
annum. LTCM therefore sold large quantities of five-year index options,
while hedging the risks involved with index futures and sometimes short-
expiry options (Perold 1999: A7, A8).

Not all LTCM's trades were successful: 'We lost a lot of money in France
in the front end [of the bond yield curve]', says LTCM's Eric Rosenfeld
(interview). Nevertheless, as noted above, extremely attractive overall returns
were earned, and the volatility of those returns was reassuringly low. Most of
LTCM's positions were almost completely insulated from broad market
movements. The firm had only limited involvement in areas where the chance
of default was high, such as in high-yield (junk) corporate bonds or 'emerging markets', such as Russia, Thailand, and Argentina. Risks were carefully
calculated and controlled using the 'value-at-risk' approach standard in the
world's leading banks (Meriwether interview). In the case of the dollar swap
spread, for example, historical statistics and judgements of likely future
values led LTCM to estimate that the spread had an 'equilibrium value' of
around 30 basis points, with a standard deviation of about 15 basis points per
annum (Rosenfeld interview). Using those estimates, it was then possible to
work out the relationship between the magnitude of possible losses and their
probabilities, and thus the 'value-at-risk' in the trade.

When a firm holds a large number of positions, the estimation of the probabilities of loss in individual positions is less critical to overall value-at-risk
than estimates of correlation between positions. If correlations are low,
a large loss in one position is unlikely to be accompanied by large losses in
others, so aggregate value-at-risk levels will be modest. In contrast, if correlations are high, then when one position goes bad, it is likely that other positions will also do so, and overall value-at-risk will be high. LTCM's positions
were geographically dispersed, and in instruments of very different kinds.
At the level of economic fundamentals, little if anything connected positions
such as on the spread between US government bonds and mortgage-
backed securities, on the difference between the prices of the shares of pairs
of companies such as Royal Dutch and of Shell, on the bulges in the yen yield
curve, on the chances of specific mergers failing, and so on. LTCM was aware
that its own and other arbitrageurs' involvement in these diverse positions

would induce some correlation, but nevertheless the observed correlations, based on five years of data, were very small: typically of the order of 0.1 or lower.

The standard deviations and correlations that went into LTCM's aggregate risk model were, however, not simply the empirically observed figures but deliberately conservative estimates of their future values. The observed standard deviation of the US dollar swap spread, for example, was around 12 basis points a year, while, as noted above, the risk model assumed it would be 15 (Rosenfeld interview). Past correlation levels, likewise, were 'upped' (Meriwether interview) to provide a safety factor: despite observed correlations being 0.1 or less, LTCM was 'running analyses at correlations at around 0.3'. The consequence of this conservatism was that while the firm's risk model suggested that the annual volatility (standard deviation) of its net asset value would be 14.5%, in actuality it was only 11% (Meriwether interview). Both figures were considerably less than the risk level of 20% that investors had been told to expect (Perold 1999: A11).

Of course, such statistical analyses of risk assumed the absence of catastrophic events in the financial markets. LTCM's key members were well aware of the possibility of such events. So LTCM also 'stress tested' its portfolio, investigating the consequences of hypothetical events too extreme to be captured by statistical value-at-risk models, events such as a huge stock market crash or failure of European economic and monetary union (EMU). As well as investigating the consequences of such events for market prices and for LTCM's risk capital, it also calculated—and set aside—the funds necessary to cope with a sudden increase in 'haircuts' (see Table 3.1) in a situation of stress. When an event could have particularly catastrophic consequences, LTCM either turned to insurance—it bought insurance against bond default by the government of Italy—or balanced its portfolio to minimize consequences, as in the case of EMU failure.

## The Crisis of 1998

The partners in LTCM, therefore, believed themselves to be running the fund conservatively, and in the modest volatility of its returns they had evidence for the correctness of this belief. After the fund's crisis, it was commonly portrayed as wildly risk-taking, but I have found almost no one inside or outside LTCM who can be proved to have expressed that view prior to the crisis. Gambling—consciously reckless risk-taking—does not explain LTCM's 1998 disaster. Nor does the second hypothesis advanced in the commentary: blind faith in mathematical models. Models were much less critical to LTCM's trading than commonly thought. Many of the pricing anomalies it sought to exploit could be identified without sophisticated modeling, and although models were important in how its trades were implemented and in assessing the risks involved, all those involved knew that models were approximations to reality and a guide to strategy rather than a determinant of it. LTCM's traders had often themselves developed the models they used: no one was more aware than they of the models' likely deficiencies. The way in which the standard deviations and correlations in the most important model of all—LTCM's overall risk model—were increased by explicitly judgement-based 'safety factors' is indicative of that.

The third posited explanation of LTCM's crisis—over-leverage—is almost tautologically correct. If LTCM had been operating without leverage, or at lower levels of leverage, the events of August and September 1998 would have placed it under much less strain. However, LTCM's levels of leverage were comparable to those of the leading global investment banks (Perold 1999: C11, C12; President's Working Group on Financial Markets 1999: 29) and, in any case, blaming LTCMs crisis on leverage is like attributing a plane crash to the fact that the aircraft was no longer safely in contact with the ground: it identifies the source of overall vulnerability but not the specific cause. That cause was the financial crisis of August and September 1998, and in particular the way in which the adverse price movements of those months exceed LTCM's, or anyone else's, expectations. Conventionally, the 1998 crisis is regarded as a 'flight-to-quality': an increased relative preference for assets with low risk of default, and/or an increased preference for more liquid assets, in other words those that can more readily be bought and sold at or near prevailing market prices.[4] The interviews drawn on here, however, suggest a rather different, more directly sociological process. Meriwether's group at Salomon and at LTCM earned remarkable profits, and were *known* to have earned those profits. This encouraged others—in other investment banks, and increasingly in other hedge funds—to follow similar arbitrage strategies. Others were being told: 'LTCM made $2 billion last year. Can't you?' (Meriwether interview). For example, LTCM's success meant that it rapidly became largely closed to new investors, and in January 1998 a new fund, Convergence Asset Management, 'raised $700 million in a single month purely from disgruntled investors denied a chance to buy into LTCM' (Dunbar 2000: 197).

LTCM tried hard not to reveal its trading positions. For example, it would avoid using the same counterparty for both legs of an arbitrage trade. However, as one trader and manager not connected to LTCM put it: '(t)he arbitrage community ... are quite a bright lot, so if they see a trade happening—and the market gets to find out about these trades, even if you're as secretive as Long-Term Capital Management—they'll analyze them and realize there's an opportunity for themselves' (Wenman interview).

LTCM's basic strategy—convergence and relative-value arbitrage—had to be disclosed to potential investors and thus could not be hidden, and others seeking to follow that strategy would often be led to take similar positions to LTCM's. It 'doesn't take a rocket scientist' to discover the kinds of arbitrage opportunities being pursued (Rosenfeld interview), especially when discovering one leg of an LTCM trade through being a counterparty to it would greatly narrow the range of possible other legs. Some of LTCM's trades were well-known to market insiders before LTCM became involved: the Royal Dutch-Shell trade, for example, was the 'classic European arbitrage trade' (Wenman interview), and the relationship between Royal Dutch and Shell shares had even been discussed in the academic literature (Rosenthal and Young 1990).

As a result of conscious and unconscious imitation, many of LTCM's positions became 'consensus trades' (Kaplanis interview). Of course, the growing number of arbitrage traders in investment banks and hedge funds did not sit down together in a room to identify good arbitrage opportunities. Rather, 'the arbitrage philosophy ... had been disseminated, well disseminated by August 98; it was there in quite a few hedge funds, it was there in quite a few firms. So Salomon [and LTCM] lost their uniqueness in doing these things. There were many, many others that could do them'. There was *some* communication: if you talk[ed] to another arb trader in the street they'd say, "Oh yes, I have this as well, I have that as well"' (Kaplanis interview). But even had there not been communication, many traders would still have identified the same opportunities. 'And what happened by September '98 is that there was a bunch of arb trades that became consensus. People knew that the UK swap spreads was a good trade, people knew that US swap spreads was a good trade' (Kaplanis interview). No other market participant had the same portfolio as LTCM—many arbitrageurs were restricted to particular portions of the spectrum of arbitrage trades—but, collectively, much of LTCMs portfolio of positions was also being held by others.

The initial effect of imitation was probably to LTCM's benefit. If others are also buying an underpriced asset and short selling an overpriced one, the effect will be to cause prices to converge more rapidly. However, imitation also meant that when existing trades *had* been liquidated profitably, replacing them was more difficult:

Author: Did you find that, as the years went by with LTCM—'94, '95, '96, '97 and so on—did you find ... that the opportunities were drying up a bit?
Rosenfeld: Yes, big.

In the summer of 1998, imitation switched to become a disastrously negative factor because of two decisions, neither of which had anything directly to do with LTCM. In 1997, Salomon Brothers was taken over by the Travelers Corporation, whose famously risk-averse chair, Sandy Weill, was building the world's largest financial conglomerate, Citigroup (Booth 1998). According to Kaplanis, Salomon's US arbitrage desk had not been consistently successful since the departure of Meriwether and his group, and in the first half of 1998 it was loss-making. Though Kaplanis, promoted to head of global arbitrage for Salomon, advised against it, the decision was taken to liquidate the US arbitrage desk's portfolio as quickly as possible, and responsibility for the liquidation was passed to Salomon's US customer desk. Since the latter was 'not accountable for the losses generated as a result of the liquidation, the speed of the latter was faster than would otherwise have been the case'. This caused losses not just to Travelers/Citicorp but also to all of those who had similar positions: 'not only did we lose money as the positions went against us as we were selling them, but all the other funds that also had these consensus trades also started losing money' (Kaplanis interview).

If the liquidation of Salomon's arbitrage positions was a background factor in the problems of the summer of 1998, the immediate cause of the 1998 crisis was Russia's August 17 default on its ruble-denominated debt. That Russia was in economic trouble was no surprise: what was shocking was that it (unlike most previous debtor governments) should default on debt denominated in domestic currency. 'I was expecting them [the Russian government] to just print money' to meet their ruble obligations, says Kaplanis, and he was not alone in this expectation. Initially, the default seemed to be an event of only modest significance for firms, such as LTCM, that had little exposure to Russia or similar 'emerging markets': on August 17, the Dow Jones rose nearly 150 points (Lowenstein 2000: 144). In the days that followed, however, it became increasingly clear that the default had triggered what Kaplanis calls an 'avalanche'. The default was combined with a devaluation of the ruble and a month's ban on Russian banks complying with forward contracts in foreign exchange (Dunbar 2000: 200–1). Since western investors used these contracts to hedge against the declining value of the ruble, widespread losses were incurred. LTCM's losses in the Russian market were limited, but other arbitrageurs carrying losses began liquidating positions elsewhere to meet the demands of their counterparties. A hedge fund called High-Risk Opportunities, which had a large position in ruble-denominated bonds, was forced into bankruptcy, owing large sums to Bankers Trust, Credit Suisse, and the investment bank Lehman Brothers. Rumours began to circulate that Lehman itself faced bankruptcy. For weeks, Lehman 'went bankrupt every Friday' according to the rumour mill. Though the bank survived, its stock price suffered badly.

In a situation in which the failure of a major investment bank was conceivable, there was indeed a flight-to-quality. Though there are exceptions, convergence and relative-value arbitrage typically involves holding the less liquid of a pair of similar assets. In August and September 1998 the prices of illiquid assets fell sharply and those of liquid ones rose, causing losses to convergence and relative-value arbitrageurs. LTCM had known perfectly well that a flight-to-quality could happen and that this would be its consequence. Indeed, it was of the very essence of convergence and relative-value arbitrage that spreads could widen—prices could move against the arbitrageur—before a trade finally converged. For that reason, LTCM had required investors to leave their capital in the fund for a minimum of three years: it was this restriction that made the fund *Long-Term* Capital Management. If spreads widened, however, it was assumed that arbitrage capital would move in to exploit them, and in so doing restrict the widening (Rosenfeld interview). Indeed, once spreads had become wide enough, the actions of ordinary investors were expected to reduce them.

The configuration of the markets by August 1998, however, was that the widening of spreads was self-feeding rather than self-limiting. As arbitrageurs began to incur losses, they almost all seem to have reacted by seeking to reduce their positions, and in so doing they intensified the price pressure that had caused them to make the reductions. In some cases, senior management simply became 'queasy' (Rosenfeld interview) at the losses that were being incurred, and unwilling to incur the risk of further, possibly larger, losses before trades turned profitable. In the United Kingdom, for example, Salomon, LTCM, a large British clearing bank, and others had all taken positions in the expectation of a narrowing of sterling swap spreads. As those spreads widened, the senior management of the clearing bank decided to exit. Such a decision by management might even be anticipated by the traders: 'you know that if your manager sees that you're down $10 million... the likelihood that he will ask you to get out of this position is very high. It's not a formal stop-loss but... it's there' (Kaplanis interview).

Another factor may paradoxically have been modern risk management practices, particularly the 'value-at-risk' method of measuring and managing the exposure of a portfolio of assets to losses. This statistical technique allows senior management to control the risks incurred by trading desks by allocating them a risk limit, while avoiding detailed supervision of their trading. When a desk reaches its value-at-risk limit, it must start to liquidate its positions. Says one trader: 'a proportion of the investment bank[s] out there... are managed by accountants, not smart people, and the accountants have said, "well, you've hit your risk limit. Close the position"' (Wenman interview). An international change in banking supervision practices increased the significance of value-at-risk. Banks are required to set aside capital to meet the various risks they face, and in 1996 they began to be allowed to use value-at-risk models to calculate the set-aside required in respect to fluctuations in the market value of their portfolios (Basle Committee on Banking Supervision 1996). The change was attractive to banks because it reduced capital requirements, but it had the consequence that as market prices move against a bank and become more volatile, it has either to raise more capital to preserve its trading positions, a slow and often unwelcome process, or to try to liquidate those positions.

The consequences for LTCM of these processes went beyond losses on individual trades. '[A]s people were forced to sell, that drove the prices even further down. Market makers quickly became overwhelmed, where the dealers, who would [normally] be willing to buy or sell those positions were simply unwilling to do it, and they either said, "Just go away. I'm not answering my phone" or set their prices at ridiculous levels' (Shaw interview). The simple fact that the crisis occurred in August, the financial markets' main holiday month and thus typically the worst time to try to sell large positions, may have exacerbated the effects on prices. Crucially, correlations between the different components of LTCM's portfolio leapt upward from their typical level of 0.1 or less to around 0.7 (Leahy interview). Suddenly, a whole range of positions—hedged, and with little or nothing in common at the level of economic fundamentals—started to incur losses virtually across the board. LTCMs losses were stunning in their size and rapidity: in August 1998, it lost 44% of its capital. However, though massive, and far greater than had seemed plausible on the basis of LTCM's risk model, this loss was not in itself catastrophic. LTCM was, it seemed, a long way from being bankrupt, and indeed, the widening of spreads meant that the arbitrage positions it held had become more attractive. Spreads could be expected to fall—indeed, they *have* subsequently fallen—and as they did LTCM's losses could be recouped and profits made.

This would happen, however, only if LTCM survived to make those profits. At this point a social process of a different kind intervened: in effect, a run on the bank. 'If I had lived through the Depression', says Meriwether: 'I would have been in a better position to understand events in September 1998' (Meriwether interview). Unlike investment banks, which report their results quarterly, LTCM and other hedge funds report monthly. On September 2, Meriwether faxed LTCM's investors its estimate of the August loss. His fax, intended to be private to LTCM's investors, became public almost instantly: 'Five minutes after we sent out first letter . . . to our handful of shareholders, it was on the Internet' (Merton interview). In an already febrile atmosphere, news of LTCM's losses fed fears of the fund's imminent collapse. These fears had two effects. First, they had an immediate effect on the prices of assets LTCM was known or believed to hold in large quantities. Such assets became impossible to sell at anything other than distressed prices. Beliefs about LTCM's portfolio were sometimes far from accurate: after the crisis LTCM was approached with an offer to buy six times the position it actually held in Danish mortgage-backed securities (Meriwether interview). Nevertheless, presumptions about its positions were accurate enough to worsen its situation considerably.

The second effect upon LTCM of fears of its collapse was even more direct. Its relationship to its counterparties typically was governed by 'two-way mark-to-market': as market prices moved in favour of LTCM or its counterparty, solid collateral, such as government bonds, flowed from one to the other. In normal times, in which market prices were reasonably unequivocal, it was an eminently sensible way of controlling risk by minimizing the consequences of default. In September 1998, however, the markets within which LTCM operated had become illiquid. There was 'terror' that LTCM was going to liquidate, says Meriwether (interview). The loss caused to a counterparty if that happened could be mitigated by it getting as much collateral as possible from LTCM before liquidation, and this could be achieved by 'marking against' LTCM: by choosing, out of the wide spectrum of plausible market prices, a price unfavourable to LTCM, indeed predicated upon the latter's failure (Merton interview; Meriwether interview). LTCM had the contractual right to dispute unfavourable marks: in its index options contracts, for example, such a dispute would have been arbitrated by getting price quotations from three dealers not directly involved. These dealers, however, would also be anticipating LTCM's failure, so disputing marks would not have helped greatly. The outflows of capital resulting from unfavourable marks were particularly damaging in LTCM's index option positions, where they cost the fund around $1 billion, nearly half of the September losses that pushed it to the brink of bankruptcy (Rosenfeld interview).

LTCM kept its counterparties and the Federal Reserve informed of the continuing deterioration of its financial position. On September 20, 1998, staff from the Federal Reserve Bank of New York and Assistant Secretary of the Treasury Gary Gensler met with LTCM. By then, it was clear that without outside intervention bankruptcy was inevitable. In the words of William J. McDonough, President of the Federal Reserve Bank of New York:

Had Long-Term Capital been suddenly put into default, its counterparties would have immediately 'closed out' their positions...[I]f many firms had rushed to close out hundreds of billions of dollars in transactions simultaneously...there was a likelihood that a number of credit and interest rate markets would experience extreme price moves and possibly cease to function for a period of one or more days and maybe longer (McDonough 1998: 1051–2).

Although not everyone agreed just how serious a threat LTCM's bankruptcy would pose to the financial system, Alan Greenspan's judgement was that if 'the failure of LTCM triggered the seizing markets,' it 'could have potentially impaired the economies of many nations, including our own' (Greenspan 1998: 1046).

McDonough brokered a meeting of LTCM's largest counterparties, which concluded that a recapitalization of LTCM would be less damaging to them than a fire sale of its assets. Fourteen banks contributed a total of $3.6 billion, in return becoming owners of 90% of the fund. LTCM's investors and partners were not bailed out: they were left with only $400 million, a mere tenth of what their holdings were worth not long previously. The recapitalization did not immediately end the crisis: many feared that the consortium that now owned LTCM might still decide on an abrupt liquidation. On October 15, 1998, however, the Federal Reserve cut interest rates without waiting for its regular scheduled meeting, and the emergency cut began to restore confidence. It also gradually became clear that the consortium was intent on an orderly, not a sudden, liquidation of LTCM's portfolio, which was achieved by December 1999.

## Conclusion

What, then, might a sociology of arbitrage consist in, and how does the case of LTCM bear upon it? Three key points emerge. First, arbitrage has a 'Granovetterian' sociology (Granovetter 1985, 1990): it is an activity conducted not by anonymous, atomistic economic agents, but by people who are often personally known to each other. Second, included in the possible forms of interaction amongst these people is imitation, and this has particularly dangerous consequences (as in the more general economic sociology models of White and Fligstein). Third, for this and other reasons the capacity of arbitrage to insulate 'the economic' from 'the social' is limited: indeed, the interweaving of the economic and the social is too intimate to be captured even by notions of imperfect insulation.

Interviewee David Wenman's use of the phrase 'arbitrage community' is not happenstance: arbitrageurs often know each other and are affected by each other. 'Community' does not imply harmony. For example, one interviewee at LTCM suggested that it had generated resentment amongst Wall Street investment banks (for instance by pressing hard to reduce 'haircuts') and that others 'were, I think, jealous of the money we made'. Resentment and jealousy, however, are indicative that those involved were not atomistic individuals, but mutually aware and mutually susceptible. Positive forms of this awareness and susceptibility were also evident: I was struck, especially during the process of getting interviewees' permission for quotation, how exercised they often were not to give offence to each other.

These issues of mutual susceptibility are not matters incidental to the real business of arbitrage, because that real business depends upon mundane forms of social interaction with personally known others. To perform its arbitrages, the Salomon/LTCM group had to borrow money (via what participants call 'repo', in which the borrowed money is used to buy securities that are pledged as collateral for the loan) and also had to borrow bonds (for short sale). Others of its trades, for example the Royal Dutch/Shell arbitrage, were implemented by arranging 'total return swaps' with banks. All these were wholly legitimate activities, but getting the best possible repo, bond borrowing and swap terms was critical to the profitability of arbitrage exploiting small price discrepancies. It could be done better amongst personally-known people, rather than by anonymous commercial interaction. In the 1970s and 1980s, for example, 'repo ... wasn't done by the top people at the firm: it was almost like a clerk's job', and Rosenfeld and his Salomon and future LTCM colleagues 'always spent a lot of time with those guys and that was very important to us' (Rosenfeld interview).

The emphasis in commentary on LTCM on its use of mathematical models has diverted attention from the extent to which its arbitrage activities (and also those of its predecessor group at Salomon) rested upon a Granovetterian, institutional understanding of the embedded nature of markets. Meriwether's reputation as a trader in the US bond market rested less on mathematical sophistication than on his understanding of matters like who held which bonds and why. 'Mathematics was helpful', he says, but understanding the institutional structure of the bond market was 'more important' (Meriwether interview).

As Salomon's arbitrage activities began to expand overseas, Meriwether realized that it would not be enough simply to send Americans, however sophisticated mathematically, into overseas markets. 'Knowing the culture was more important than just quantitative knowledge', he says. Typically, Salomon would seek to recruit people brought up overseas, train them in New York, and then send them back to the markets in the countries in which they were raised. The head of Salomon's trading activities in Japan, the legendarily-successful Shigeru Miyojin is an instance. Someone who did not know Japanese would be at a disadvantage, and in Japan (as elsewhere) the price discrepancies that were of interest to arbitrage would typically be 'driven by the tax and regulatory framework'. An outsider would often find that framework hard to comprehend in sufficient depth (Meriwether interview).

The Granovetterian sociology of market embedding is thus evident in the normal practice of arbitrage. In the case of LTCM, however, that embedding took a very specific form, imitation, and this is the second aspect of the sociology of arbitrage that needs emphasizing. The underlying general point is well-known to economic sociology, and has been emphasized, for example, by White (1981, 2001) and Fligstein (1996, 2001). Firms do not choose courses of action in isolation: they monitor each other, and make inferences about the uncertain situation they face by noting the success or failure of others' strategies. When this leads to diversity—to firms selecting different strategies and coming to occupy different niches—a stable market structure can result. But if firms imitate, each choosing the same strategy, disastrous crowding (White 2001: 139–44) can occur. That is what took place in global arbitrage in the 1990s.

The effects of imitation run deep: it can, for example, affect the statistical distributions of price changes, causing distributions to become dangerously 'fat-tailed' (i.e. the probability of extreme events is far higher than implied by standard normal or log-normal distributional assumptions). That imitation can affect statistical distributions in this way was shown in theoretical work by Lux and Marchesi (1999); the case of LTCM appears to show it happening in practice. The unraveling of the imitative superportfolio caused 'fat tailed' price changes far beyond those anticipated on standard models.[5]

Imitation led to extreme price movements and to disaster because of a third feature of the sociology of arbitrage: the possibility of 'arbitrage flight', the risk that arbitrage positions that, if held for long enough, have to be profitable may nevertheless have to be abandoned.[6] (LTCM's arbitrage positions *were* eventually profitable: the consortium that recapitalized the fund not only recouped its investment but made a modest profit on it, and would have made a larger profit had its goal not been to liquidate LTCM's positions in an orderly but rapid fashion.) This possibility was expressed to me, separately, by two partners in LTCM who used the same analogy. Suppose they had been vouchsafed a little peek into the future: that they knew, with absolute certainty, that at a particular point in time the stock price of company X would be zero (these conversations took place during the dot.com bubble). Could they, they asked me, make money with certainty from this knowledge? Their question was rhetorical: they knew the answer to be no. Of course, they could sell the stock short (see the glossary in Table 3.1). *If* they could hold their position until the stock price became zero, they could indeed profit handsomely. But a rise in price in the interim could still exhaust their capital and thus force them to liquidate at a loss.

The consequence of this third feature of arbitrage, when conjoined with the second feature (imitation),[7] is that arbitrage's capacity to 'insulate' the economic from the social is limited. This constitutes, for example, a limit on the performativity of economics: under some circumstances, arbitrage may be unable to eliminate what economic theory regards as pricing discrepancies. Ultimately, the metaphor of 'insulation', the Parsonian view of the economy as a differentiated subsystem, is itself inadequate. The financial markets are not an imperfectly insulated sphere of economic rationality, but a sphere in which the economic and the social interweave seamlessly. In respect to arbitrage, the key risks may be social risks from patterns of interaction within the financial markets, rather than shocks from the real economy or from events outside the markets. That, at least, is what seems to be suggested by the contrast between August 17, 1998 (the Russian default, a relatively minor economic event, triggered a disastrous unravelling of an imitative superportfolio) and September 11, 2001 (a dramatic external shock that failed to trigger dangerous internal social processes).[8]

The interweaving of the economic and the social is not simply a matter of analytical interest. It affects the technical practices of risk management, because imitation of the kind evident in 1998 can undermine the protection flowing from the basic precept of such management: diversification. The most important way in which LTCM's successor, JWM Partners, has altered its predecessor's risk model to take account of the lessons of 1998 is that all the fund's positions, however well diversified geographically and unrelated in asset type, are now assumed to have correlations of 1.0 'to the worst event' (Meriwether interview). In an extreme crisis, it is assumed that diversification may fail completely: all the fund's positions may move in lock-step and adversely, even those positions where the fund holds assets that should rise in relative value in a crisis.

One way of expressing the forms currently taken by the inextricable interweaving of the economic and the social is via Knorr Cetina and Bruegger's notion of global microstructure. The financial markets are now global in their reach, but interaction within them still takes the form of 'patterns of relatedness and coordination that are microsocial in character and that assemble and link global domains' (Knorr Cetina and Bruegger 2002: 907). In a sense, it was globalization that undid LTCM: 'Maybe the error of Long-Term was that of not realizing that the world is becoming more and more global over time', says Myron Scholes (interview). Of course, no one was more aware than LTCM's principals of globalization *as a general process* (they had surfed globalization's wave, so to speak), but what caught them unawares were the consequences of the global microstructure created by imitative arbitrage. What happened in August and September 1998 was not simply that international markets fell in concert (that would have had little effect on LTCM), but that very particular phenomena, which at the level of economic fundamentals were quite unrelated, suddenly started to move in close to lock-step: swap spreads, the precise shape of yield curves, the behaviour of equity pairs such as Royal Dutch/Shell, and so on. The 'nature of the world had changed', says Meriwether, 'and we hadn't recognised it'. LTCM's wide diversification, both internationally and across asset classes, which he had thought kept aggregate risk at acceptably modest levels, failed to do so, because of the effects of a global microstructure.

Since September 1998, this particular microstructure has dissipated as arbitrage capital has withdrawn from the markets. The failure of the shock of September 11, 2001, to ramify and amplify through the markets is testimony to the way in which market linkages driven by imitative arbitrage have been very much weaker subsequently. LTCM's successor fund, JWM Partners, was active then too, but its capital base was smaller and its leverage levels lower, so its arbitrage positions were considerably smaller (Silverman and Chaffin 2000). The amount of capital devoted to convergence and relative value arbitrage by other market participants such as investment banks was also much smaller (interviewees estimate possibly only a tenth as large in total). There was thus no significant superportfolio in 2001. September 11 sparked another flight-to-quality, but there was no equivalent crisis. While LTCM had been devastated in 1998, JWM Partners' broadly similar, but much smaller, portfolio emerged unscathed from September 2001: the partnership's returns in that month were 'basically flat'. Of course, the linkages manifest in 1998 may well return, albeit most likely in different forms. But that, indeed, may precisely be the point. Globalization is not a once-and-for-all event, not a unidirectional process, not something that can be stopped, but a composite of a myriad microstructures, often contradictory, waxing, and waning.

## List of interviews

*Partners in and employees of LTCM*:
Haghani, Victor, Gérard Gennotte, Fabio Bassi, and Gustavo Lao, London, February 11, 2000.
Leahy, Richard F., Greenwich, Conn., October 31, 2000.
Meriwether, John W., Greenwich, Conn., November 14, 2000.
Merton, Robert C., Cambridge, Mass., November 2, 1999.
Rosenfeld, Eric, Rye, NY, October 30, 2000.
Scholes, Myron S., San Francisco, June 15, 2000.

This article also draws on a wider set of interviews (numbering 60 in total) conducted by the author with finance theorists and market practitioners, of which those drawn on most directly here are:

Kaplanis, Costas, London, February 11, 2000.
Shaw, David E., New York, November 13, 2000.
Wenman, David, London, June 22, 2001.

Not all interviewees were prepared to be identified, and some quotations and interview material are therefore anonymous.

## Notes

1. See Barry and Slater (2002) and the subsequent papers in the May 2002 issue of *Economy and Society*.
2. Strictly, the fund was the investment vehicle (Long-Term Capital Portfolio) that LTCM managed, but to avoid complication I shall refer to both as LTCM.
3. Figures for total returns are calculated from the data in Perold (1999: A19); the figures for returns net of fees are taken from Perold (1999: A2).
4. See Scholes (2000) for an interpretation of the crisis in terms of the 'liquidity premium'.
5. The dollar swap spread, for example, has a daily volatility (standard deviation) of around 0.8 basis points. Perhaps the single most dramatic event in the crisis of August and September 1998 was the widening of the dollar swap spread in half a day (the morning of Friday, August 21, five days after the Russian default) of 19 basis points (Perold 1999: C2): a $35\sigma$ event. Of course, nothing can safely be inferred from a single event plucked from amongst many, but it is worth noting that the aggregate movement in price of LTCMs positions in August 1998 (a 44% loss) was a $-14\sigma$ event in terms of the 3.2% historical monthly volatility of the fund's portfolio and a $-10.5\sigma$ event on its risk model's 4.2% monthly volatility. Either is wildly unlikely on standard distributional assumptions.
6. This feature has been modelled by behavioral finance specialist Andrei Shleifer (Shleifer and Vishny 1997; Shleifer 2000). Shleifer's work is prescient: the Shleifer and Vishny model captures well one key aspect of 1998, the arbitrage flight that occurs when those who invest capital in arbitrageurs withdraw it prematurely in response to adverse price movements. But in another respect even Shleifer preserves the Parsonian boundary around the 'economic'. The Shleifer–Vishny model's arbitrageurs are not influenced by each other, and each has perfect individual knowledge of the true value of the asset they trade. As we have seen, however, a key dynamic leading to the crisis of 1998 was imitation amongst arbitrageurs. The resultant correlation of prices that were otherwise essentially unrelated economically— the second key aspect of 1998—is not captured by the Shleifer–Vishny model's single asset market and non-imitative arbitrageurs.
7. Were it not for the risk of imitation-induced correlation, the dangers posed by arbitrage flight could be reduced greatly by holding a large portfolio of diverse arbitrage positions.
8. 2002 saw sharp falls in global stock markets, but these were not the direct effect of September 11. After recovering quickly from the initial shock of September 11,

stock markets continued to rise for several months before succumbing to the effects of events such as the Enron and WorldCom scandals.

# References

Anon. 2000. 'Risk Managers of the Year: LTCM Oversight Committee', *Risk* 13: 32–3.

Barry, A. and Slater, D. 2002. 'Introduction: The Technological Economy', *Economy and Society* 31: 175–93.

Basel Committee on Banking Supervision. 1996. *Amendment to the Capital Accord to Incorporate Market Risks*. Basel: Bank for International Settlements.

Booth, T. 1998. 'Why Costas Kaplanis had to sell', *Institutional Investor* 23(10): 12–6.

Callon, M. (ed.). 1998. *The Laws of the Markets*. Oxford: Blackwell.

Dunbar, N. 2000. *Inventing Money: the Story of Long-Term Capital Management and the Legends Behind it*. Chichester, West Sussex: Wiley.

Fligstein, N. 1996. 'Markets as Politics: A Political–Cultural Approach to Market Institutions', *American Sociological Review* 61: 656–73.

—— 2001. *The Architecture of Markets*. Princeton, NJ: Princeton University Press.

Granovetter, M. 1985. 'Economic Action and Social Structure: The Problem of Embeddedness', *American Journal of Sociology* 91: 485–510.

—— 1990. 'The Old and the New Economic Sociology: A History and an Agenda', in *Beyond the Marketplace: Rethinking Economy and Society*, Friedland, R. and Robertson, A. F. (eds.). New York, NY: De Gruyter, 89–112.

Greenspan, A. 1998. 'Statement before the Committee on Banking and Financial Services, U.S. House of Representatives, October 1', *Federal Reserve Bulletin* 84: 1046–50.

Jennings, K. 2002. *Moral Hazard*. London: Fourth Estate.

Knorr Cetina, K. and Bruegger, U. 2002. 'Global Microstructures: The Virtual Societies of Financial Markets', *American Journal of Sociology* 107: 905–50.

Lowenstein, R. 2000. *When Genius Failed: The Rise and Fall of Long-Term Capital Management*. New York, NY: Random House.

Lux, T. and Marchesi, M. 1999. 'Scaling and Criticality in a Stochastic Multi-Agent Model of a Financial Market', *Nature* 397: 498–500.

MacKenzie, D. 2003. 'Long-Term Capital Management and the Sociology of Arbitrage', *Economy and Society* 32: 349–80.

—— and Millo, Y. 2003. 'Constructing a Market, Performing Theory: The Historical Sociology of a Financial Derivatives Exchange', *American Journal of Sociology* 109(1): 107–46.

McDonough, W. J. 1998. 'Statement before the Committe on Banking and Financial Services, U.S. House of Representatives, October 1', *Federal Reserve Bulletin* 84: 1050–4.

Parsons, T. and Smelser, N. J. 1956. *Economy and Society: A Study in the Integration of Economic and Social Theory*. London: Routledge & Kegan Paul.

Perold, A. 1999. *Long-Term Capital Management, L.P.* Boston, MA: Harvard Business School Publishing.

Podolny, J. M. 1993. 'A Status-Based Model of Market Competition', *American Journal of Sociology* 98(4): 829–72.

—— 2001. 'Networks as the Pipes and Prisms of the Market', *American Journal of Sociology* 107(1): 33–60.

President's Working Group on Financial Markets. 1999. 'Hedge Funds, Leverage and the Lessons of Long-Term Capital Management'. www.treas.gov/press/releases/reports/hedgfund.pdf. Downloaded on February 4, 2004.

Rosenthal, L. and Young, C. 1990. 'The Seemingly Anomalous Price Behavior of Royal Dutch/Shell and Unilever N.V./Plc', *Journal of Financial Economics* 26: 123–41.

Ross, S. A. 2001. 'Neoclassical and Alternative Finance', EFMA Meetings, keynote address.

Scholes, M. S. 2000. 'Crisis and Risk Management', *American Economic Review* 90: 17–21.

Shleifer, A. 2000. *Inefficient Markets: An Introduction to Behavioral Finance.* Oxford: Oxford University Press.

—— and Vishny, R. L. 1997. 'The Limits of Arbitrage', *Journal of Finance* 52: 35–55.

Silverman, G. and Chaffin, J. 2000. 'Hedge Fund Guru Back in the Game', *Financial Times* August 21: 9.

Stark, D. 2000. 'For a Sociology of Worth', European Association of Evolutionary Political Economy, Berlin, November 1–4, 2000.

White, H. C. 1981. 'Where Do Markets Come From?', *American Journal of Sociology* 87: 517–47.

—— 2001. *Markets from Networks.* Princeton, NJ: Princeton University Press.

Zelizer, V. A. R. 1979. *Morals and Markets: The Development of Life Insurance in the United States.* New York, NY: Columbia University Press.

# 4

# How to Recognize Opportunities: Heterarchical Search in a Trading Room

## DANIEL BEUNZA AND DAVID STARK

### Introduction

In Novum Organum, one of the founding documents of modern science, Francis Bacon (1960 [1620]) outlined a new course of discovery. Writing in an age when the exploration, conquest, and settlement of territory was enriching European sovereigns, Bacon proposed an alternative strategy of exploration. In place of the quest for property, for territory, Bacon urged a search for properties, the properties of nature, arguing that this knowledge, produced at the workbench of science, would prove a yet vaster and nearly inexhaustible source of wealth.[1]

Three centuries later, several recent innovations hold a similarly alluring promise for Wall Street traders and modern economies. The creation of the NASDAQ in 1971 and of Bloomberg terminals in 1980 has given Wall Street an electronic exchange three decades before the appearance of the commercial Internet. The development of formulas for pricing derivatives such as the Black–Scholes in 1973 has given traders precision tools previously reserved for engineers. And the dramatic growth in computing power since the introduction of the PC has given traders the possibility to combine these equations with powerful computational engines. The mix of formulas, data to plug into them, computers to calculate them, and electronic networks to connect it all has been explosive, leading to a decisive shift to 'quantitative finance' (Bernstein 1993; Dunbar 2000; MacKenzie and Millo 2003). As a result, finance is today mathematical, networked, computational, and knowledge-intensive.

Just as Bacon's experimentalists at the beginnings of modern science were in search of new properties, so our quantitative traders have, in their quest for

Our thanks to Pablo Boczkowski, Karin Knorr Cetina, Paul Duguid, Geoff Fougere, Vincent Lepinay, Fabian Muniesa, Alex Preda, Benjamin Stark, and especially Monique Girard for helpful comments and suggestions on a previous draft. We are grateful to Oxford University Press for permission to reprint material from 'Tools of the Trade', *Industrial and Corporate Change* 2004, 13(2).

profits, gone beyond traditional properties of companies such as growth, solvency, or profitability. Their pursuit has taken them to abstract financial qualities such as volatility, convertibility, or liquidity, as different from accounting-based measures as Bacon's search was from the conquest of new territory.

But, how are the new properties to be found? Bacon's radical proposal, at least in the more standard reading, came with an equally novel strategy for its fulfillment, a program of inductive, experimentalist science that contrasted sharply with the method of logical deduction prevailing at the time. Is there a financial counterpart to Bacon's program of experimentation?

Our task in this chapter is to analyze how a Wall Street trading room is organized for this process of discovery. A trading room, as we shall see, is a kind of laboratory in which traders are engaged in a process of search and experimentation. At one level it would seem that their search is straightforward: they are searching for value. And it would seem that the means for this search are similarly obvious: use channels of high-speed connectivity to gather as much timely information as possible and take advantage of sophisticated mathematical formulae to process that information. At the very elite of the profession, however, these means, in themselves, do not give advantage. You must have them to be a player, but your competitors are likely to have them as well. That is, the more that timely information is available simultaneously to all market actors, the more advantage shifts from economies of information to processes of interpretation. Moreover, what seems straightforward—value—is exactly what is at issue.

The challenge of search and experimentation must thus be re-specified: how do you recognize an opportunity that your competitors have not already identified? At the extreme, therefore, you are searching for something that is not yet named and categorized. The problem confronting our traders, then, is a problem fundamental to innovation in any setting: how do you search—when you do not know what you are looking for but will recognize it when you find it?

To explore this challenge, we conducted ethnographic field research in the Wall Street trading room of a major international investment bank. Pseudonymous International Securities is a global bank with headquarters outside the United States. It has a large office in New York, located in the World Financial Center in Lower Manhattan. With permission from the manager of the trading room we had access to observe trading and interview traders. Our observations extended to sixty half-day visits across more than two years. During that time, we conducted detailed observations at three of the room's ten trading desks, sitting in the tight space between traders, following trades as they unfolded and sharing lunches and jokes with the traders. We complemented this direct observation with in-depth interviews. In the final year of our investigation, we were more formally integrated into the trading room—provided with a place at a desk, a computer, and a telephone. The time span of our research embraced the periods before and after the September 11 attack on the World Trade Center (for accounts of the trading room's response and recovery, see Beunza and Stark 2003, 2004).

To anticipate the major lines of our argument and provide a road map of the sections of the chapter: in the following section we introduce the practices of modern arbitrage—the trading strategy that best represents the distinctive combination of connectivity, knowledge, and computing that are the defining features of the quantitative revolution in finance. Arbitrageurs locate value by making associations among securities. At the sophisticated level of trading at International Securities there is a sharp premium on making novel, unexpected, and innovative associations. In subsequent sections, we examine how such associations are made at International Securities through heterarchical organization, a form whose features we elaborate in more detail below.

The cognitive challenge facing our arbitrage traders is the problem of recognition. On one hand, they must be adept at pattern recognition (e.g. matching data to models, etc). But if they only recognize patterns familiar within their existing categories, they would not be innovative (Brown and Duguid 1998; Clippinger 1999). Innovation requires another cognitive process that we can think of as re-cognition (making unanticipated associations, re-conceptualizing the situation, breaking out of lock-in).

The trading room is equipped to meet this twin challenge of exploiting knowledge (pattern recognition) while simultaneously exploring for new knowledge (practices of re-cognition). Each desk (e.g. merger arbitrage, index arbitrage, etc.) is organized around a distinctive evaluative principle and its corresponding cognitive frames, metrics, 'optics', and other specialized instrumentation for pattern recognition (Hutchins 1995). That is, the trading room is the site of diverse, indeed rival, principles of valuation. And it is the interaction across this heterogeneity that generates innovation. Rather than bureaucratically hierarchical, the trading room is heterarchical (Stark 1999; Girard and Stark 2002). In place of hierarchical, vertical ties, we find horizontal ties of distributed cognition; in place of a single metric of valuation, we find multiple metrics of value; and in place of designed and managed R&D, we find innovations as combinatorics (Kogut and Zander 1992) that emerge from the interaction across these coexisting principles and instruments. The trading room distributes intelligence and organizes diversity.

## Arbitrage, or the Recombinant Properties of Modern Finance

Arbitrage is defined in finance textbooks as 'locking in a profit by simultaneously entering into transactions in two or more markets' (Hull 1996: 4). If, for instance, the prices of gold in New York and London differ by more than the transportation costs, an arbitrageur can realize an easy profit by buying in the market where gold is cheap and selling it in the market where it is expensive. But reducing arbitrage to an unproblematic operation that links the obvious (gold in London, gold in New York), as textbook treatments do, is doubly misleading, for modern arbitrage is neither obvious nor unproblematic. It provides profit opportunities by associating the unexpected, and it entails real exposure to substantial losses.

Arbitrage is a distinctive form of entrepreneurial activity that exploits not only gaps across markets but also the overlaps among multiple evaluative principles. Arbitrageurs profit not by having developed a superior way of deriving value but by exploiting opportunities exposed when different evaluative devices yield discrepant pricings at myriad points throughout the economy.

As a first step to understanding modern arbitrage, consider the two traditional trading strategies, value and momentum investing, that arbitrage has come to challenge.[2] Value investing is the traditional 'buy low, sell high' approach in which investors look for opportunities by identifying companies whose 'intrinsic' value differs from its current market value. Value investors are essentialists: they believe that property has a true, intrinsic, essential value independent from other investors' assessments, and that they can attain a superior grasp of that value through careful perusal of the information about a company.

In contrast to value investors, momentum traders (also called chartists) turn away from scrutinizing companies toward monitoring the activities of other actors on the market (Malkiel 1973). Like value investors, their goal is to find a profit opportunity. However, momentum traders are not interested in discovering the intrinsic value of a stock. Instead of focusing on features of the asset itself, they turn their attention to whether other market actors are bidding the value of a security up or down. Like the fashion-conscious or like nightlife socialites scouting the trendiest clubs, they derive their strength from obsessively asking, 'where is everyone going?' in hopes of anticipating the hotspots and leaving just when things get crowded.

As with value and momentum investors, arbitrageurs also need to find an opportunity, an instance of disagreement with the market's pricing of a security. They find it by making associations. Instead of claiming a superior ability to process and aggregate information about intrinsic assets (as value investors do) or better information on what other investors are doing (as momentum traders do), the arbitrage trader tests ideas about the correspondence between two securities. Confronted by a stock with a market price, the arbitrageur seeks some other security or bond, or synthetic security such as an index composed of a group of stocks, etc.—that can be related to it, and prices one in terms of the other. The two securities have to be similar enough so that their prices change in related ways, but different enough so that other traders have not perceived the correspondence before. As we shall see, the posited relationship can be highly abstract. The tenuous or uncertain strength of the posited similarity or co-variation reduces the number of traders that can play a trade, hence increasing its potential profitability.

Arbitrage hinges on the possibility of interpreting securities in multiple ways. Like a striking literary metaphor, an arbitrage trade reaches out and associates the value of a stock to some other, previously unidentified security.

By associating one security to another, the trader highlights different properties (qualities) of the property he is dealing with.

Like Bacon's experimentalists, arbitrage traders have moved from exploring for territory (traditional notions of *property*) to exploring for the underlying *properties* of securities. In contrast to value investors who distill the bundled attributes of a company to a single number, arbitrageurs reject exposure to a whole company. But in contrast to corporate raiders, who buy companies for the purpose of breaking them up to sell as separate properties, the work of arbitrage traders is yet more radically deconstructionist. The unbundling they attempt is to isolate, in the first instance, categorical attributes. For example, they do not see Boeing Co. as a monolithic asset or property, but as having several properties (traits, qualities) such as being a technology stock, an aviation stock, a consumer-travel stock, an American stock, a stock that is included in a given index, and so on. Even more abstractionist, they attempt to isolate such qualities as the volatility of a security, or its liquidity, its convertibility, its indexability, and so on.

Thus, whereas corporate raiders break up parts of a company, modern arbitrageurs carve up abstract qualities of a security. In our field research, we find our arbitrageurs actively shaping trades. Dealing with the multiple qualities of securities as narrow specialists, they position themselves with respect to one or two of these qualities, but never all. Their strategy is to use the tools of financial engineering to shape a trade so that exposure is limited only to those equivalency principles in which the trader has confidence. Derivatives such as swaps, options, and other financial instruments play an important role in the process of separating the desired qualities from the purchased security. Traders use them to slice and dice their exposure, wielding them in effect like a surgeon's tools—scissors and scalpels to give the patient (the trader's exposure) the desired contours.

Paradoxically, much of the associative work of arbitrage is therefore for the purpose of 'disentangling' (see Callon 1998 for a related usage)—selecting out of the trade those qualities to which the arbitrageur is not committed. The strategy is just as much not betting on what you do not know as betting on what you do know. In merger arbitrage, for example, this strategy of highly specialized risk exposure requires that traders associate the markets for stocks of the two merging companies and dissociate from the stocks everything that does not involve the merger. Consider a situation in which two firms have announced their intention to merge. One of the firms, say the acquirer, is a biotech firm and belongs to an index, such as the Dow Jones (DJ) biotech index. If a merger arbitrage specialist wanted to shape a trade such that the 'biotechness' of the acquirer would not be an aspect of his or her positioned exposure, the arbitrageur would long the index. That is, to dissociate this quality from the trader's exposure, the arbitrageur associates the trade with a synthetic security ('the index') that stands for the 'biotechness'. Less categorical, more complex qualities require more complex instruments.

Arbitrageurs, do not narrow their exposure for lack of courage. Despite all the trimmings, hedging, and cutting, this is not a trading strategy for the faint-hearted. Arbitrage is about tailoring the trader's exposure to the market, biting what they can chew, betting on what they know best, and avoiding risking their money on what they do not know. Traders expose themselves profusely—precisely because their exposure is custom-tailored to the relevant deal. Their sharp focus and specialized instruments gives them a clearer view of the deals they examine than the rest of the market. Thus, the more the traders hedge, the more boldly they can position themselves.

Arbitrageurs can reduce or eliminate exposure along many dimensions but they cannot make a profit on a trade unless they are exposed on at least one. In fact, they cut entanglements along some dimensions precisely to focus exposure where they are most confidently attached. As Callon (1998; Callon and Muniesa 2002; Callon, Méandel, and Rabeharisoa 2002) argues, calculation and attachment are not mutually exclusive. To be sure, the trader's attachment is distanced and disciplined; but, however emotionally detached, and however fleeting, to hold a position is to hold a conviction.[3] In the field of arbitrage, to be opportunistic you must be principled, that is, you must commit to an evaluative metric. And, as we shall see, to engage in complex, high-stakes trading, you must also be able to collaborate with those who are attached to different metrics.

## Heterarchy

How do unexpected and tenuous associations become recognized as opportunities? How could the traders at International Securities exploit the knowledge they had (to recognize patterns that it had identified) while also exploring for new opportunities (if you like, re-cognizing properties)?[4] To do so, the trading room adopted an organizational form that we characterize as heterarchy. As the term suggests, heterarchies are characterized by minimal hierarchy and by organizational heterogeneity. Heterarchies involve a distributed intelligence (lateral accountability) and the organization of diversity (coexisting evaluative principles).

Mid-twentieth century, there was general consensus about the ideal attributes of the modern organization: it had a clear chain of command, with strategy and decisions made by the organizational leadership; instructions were disseminated and information gathered up and down the hierarchical ladder of authority; design preceded execution; the latter was carried out with the time-management precision of a Taylorist organizational machine. By the end of the century, the main precepts of the ideal organizational model would be fundamentally rewritten. The primacy of relations of hierarchical dependence within the firm and the relations of market independence between firms became secondary to relations of interdependence among networks of firms and among units within the firm (Kogut and Zander 1992; Powell 1996; Grabher and Stark 1997).

To cope with radical uncertainties, instead of concentrating its resources for strategic planning among a narrow set of senior executives or delegating that function to a specialized department, heterarchical firms embark on a radical decentralization in which virtually every unit becomes engaged in innovation. That is, in place of specialized search routines in which some departments are dedicated to exploration while others are confined to exploiting existing knowledge, the functions of exploration are generalized throughout the organization. In place of vertical chains of command, intelligence is distributed—laterally. With its flattened hierarchy, the absence of separate offices for the room's few managers, its open architectural plan, and its collegial culture, the trading room at International Securities shows collaborative features of such distributed intelligence.

Heterarchies, however, are not simply non-bureaucratic. Heterarchies interweave a multiplicity of organizing principles. The new organizational forms are heterarchical not only because they have flattened hierarchy, but also because they are the sites of competing and coexisting value systems. They maintain and support an active rivalry of multiple evaluative principles. A robust, lateral collaboration flattens hierarchy without flattening diversity. The coexistence of more than one evaluative principle produces a creative friction (Brown and Duguid 1998) and fosters cross-fertilization. It promotes organizational reflexivity, the ability to redefine and recombine resources. Heterarchies are not simply tolerant of diversity among isolated and non-communicating factions; the organization of diversity is not a replicative redundancy but a generative redundancy. It is the friction at the interacting overlap that generates productive recombinations. The challenge is to create a sufficiently common culture to facilitate communication among the heterogeneous components without suppressing the distinctive identities of each. Heterarchies create wealth by inviting more than one way of evaluating worth.

This aspect of heterarchy builds on Knight's (1921) distinction between risk, where the distribution of outcomes can be expressed in probabilistic terms, and uncertainty, where outcomes are incalculable. Whereas in neoclassical economics all cases are reduced to risk, Knight argued that a world of generalized probabilistic knowledge of the future leaves no place for profit (as a particular residual revenue that is not contractualizable because it is not susceptible to measure ex ante) and hence no place for the entrepreneur. Properly speaking, the entrepreneur is not rewarded for risk-taking but, instead, is rewarded for an ability to exploit uncertainty. The French school of the 'economics of conventions' (Boltanski and Thévenot 1991, 1999; Thévenot 2001) demonstrates that institutions are social technologies for transforming uncertainty into calculable problems; but they leave unexamined the incidence of uncertainty about which institution ('ordering of worth') is operative in a given situation. In this light, Knight's conception of entrepreneurship can be re-expressed: entrepreneurship is the ability to keep multiple evaluative principles in play and to exploit the resulting ambiguity (Stark 2000). Restated, entrepreneurship in this view is not brokerage across a gap but facilitating productive friction at the overlap of coexisting principles.

## Distributing Intelligence and Organizing Diversity in the Trading Room

### A Desk with a View of the Markets

The trading room at International Securities offers a sharp contrast to the conventional environment of corporate America. Unlike a standard corporate office with cubicles and a layout meant to emphasize differences in hierarchical status, the trading room is an open-plan arrangement where information roams freely. Instead of having its senior managers scattered at window offices along the exterior of the building, the bank puts managers in the same desks as their teams, accessible to them with just a movement of the head or hand. Underscoring the importance of sociability, the bank has limited the number of people in the room to 150 employees and has a low monitor policy so people can see each other. Computer programmers and other critical, technical support staff are not separated but have desks right in the trading room.

Whereas the traders of the 1980s, acutely described by Tom Wolfe (1987) as Masters of the Universe, were characterized by their riches, bravado, and little regard for small investors, the quantitative traders at International Securities have MBA degrees in finance, Ph.D.s in physics and statistics, and are more appropriately thought of as engineers. None of them wears suspenders.

The basic organizational unit of the trading room is a 'desk', and it is here that the organization of diversity in the trading room begins by demarcating specialized functions. The term 'desk' not only denotes the actual piece of furniture where traders sit, but also the actual team of traders—as in 'Tim from the equity loan desk'. Such identification of the animate with the inanimate is due to the fact that a team is never scattered across different desks. In this localization, the different traders in the room are divided into teams according to the financial instrument they use to create equivalencies in arbitrage: the merger arbitrage team trades stocks in companies in the process of consolidating, the options arbitrage team trades in 'puts' and 'calls',[5] the derivatives that lend the desk its name, and so on. The extreme proximity of the workstations enables traders to talk to each other without lifting their eyes from the screen or interrupting their work. The desk is an intensely social place where traders work, take lunch, make jokes, and exchange insults in a never-ending undercurrent of camaraderie that resurfaces as soon as the market gives a respite.

Each desk has developed its own way of looking at the market, based on the principle of equivalence that it uses to calculate value and the financial instrument that enacts its particular style of arbitrage trade. Merger arbitrage traders, for example, keen on finding out the degree of commitment of two merging companies, look for a progressive approximation in the stock prices of two companies. They probe commitment to a merger by plotting the 'spread' (difference in price) between acquiring and target companies over time. As with marriages between persons, mergers between companies are scattered with regular rituals of engagement intended to persuade others of the seriousness of their intent. As time passes, arbitrage traders look for a pattern of gradual decay in the spread as corporate bride and groom come together—that is, a descending diagonal curve on their Bloomberg screens, not unlike the trajectory of a landing airplane.

Convertible bond arbitrageurs, by contrast, do not obsess about whether the spread between two merging companies is widening or narrowing. Instead, they specialize in information about stocks that would typically interest bond-holders, such as their liquidity and likelihood of default. At yet another desk, index arbitrageurs, in their attempt to exploit minuscule and rapidly vanishing misalignments between S&P 500 futures and the underlying securities, specialize in technology to trade in high volume and at a high speed. Thus, within each team there is a marked consistency between its arbitrage strategy, its visual displays, its mathematical formulae, and its trading tools.

Such joint focus on visual and economic patterns forges each desk into a distinctive community of practice, with its own evaluative principle, tacit knowledge, social ties, and shared forms of meaning (Lave and Wenger 1990). This includes a common sense of purpose, a real need to know what each other knows, a highly specialized language, and idiosyncratic ways of signaling to each other. It even translates into friendly rivalry toward other desks. A customer sales trader, for example, took us aside to denounce statistical arbitrage as 'like playing video games. If you figure out what the other guy's program is, you can destroy him. That's why we don't do program trades', he explained, referring to his own desk. Conversely, one of the statistical arbitrage traders, told us, in veiled dismissal of manual trading, that the more he looks at his data (as opposed to letting his robot trade) the more biased he becomes.

Homogeneity within a desk facilitates speed and sophistication to navigate crowded and fast-moving capital markets. But the complex trades that are characteristic of our trading room, however, seldom involve a single desk/team in isolation from others. It is to these collaborations that we turn.

### Distributed Cognition across Desks

The desk, in our view, is a unit organized around a dominant evaluative principle and its arrayed financial instruments (devices for measuring, testing, probing, cutting). This principle is its coin; if you like, its specie. But the trading room is composed of multiple species. It is an ecology of evaluative principles.

Complex trades take advantage of the interaction among these species. To be able to commit to what counts, to be true to your principle of evaluation, each desk must take into account the principles and tools of other desks. Recall that shaping a trade involves disassociating some qualities in order to give salience to the ones to which your desk is attached. To identify the relevant categories along which exposure will be limited, shaping a trade therefore involves active association among desks. Co-location, the proximity of desks, facilitates the connections needed to do the cutting.

Whereas in most textbook examples of arbitrage the equivalence-creating property is easy to isolate, in practice, it is difficult to fully disassociate. Because of these difficulties, even after deliberate slicing and dicing, traders can still end up dangerously exposed along dimensions of the company that differ from the principles of the desired focused exposure. We found that traders take into account unintended exposure in their calculations in the same way as they achieve association—through co-location. Physical proximity in the room allows traders to survey the financial instruments around them and assess which additional variables they should take into account in their calculations.

For example, the stock loan desk can help the merger arbitrageurs on matters of liquidity. Merger arbitrage traders lend and borrow stock as if they could reverse the operation at any moment of time. However, if the company is small and not often traded, its stock may be difficult to borrow, and traders may find themselves unable to hedge. In this case, according to Max, senior trader at the merger arbitrage desk, 'the stock loan desk helps us by telling us how difficult it is to borrow a certain stock'. Similarly, index arbitrageurs can help merger arbitrageurs trade companies with several classes of shares. Listed companies often have two types of shares, so-called 'A-' and 'K-class' stock. The two carry different voting rights, but only one of the two types allows traders to hedge their exposure. The existence of these two types facilitates the work of merger arbitrageurs, who can execute trades with the more liquid of the two classes and then transform the stock into the class necessary for the hedge. But such transformation can be prohibitively expensive if one of the two classes is illiquid. To find out, merger arbitrageurs turn to the index arbitrage team, which exploits price differences between the two types.

In other cases, one of the parties may have a convert provision (i.e. its bonds can be converted into stocks if there is a merger) to protect the bondholder, leaving merger arbitrageurs with questions about how this might affect the deal. In this case, it is the convertible bond arbitrage desk that helps merger arbitrage traders clarify the ways in which a convertibility provision should be taken into account. 'The market in converts is not organized', says Max, in the sense that there is no single screen representation of the prices of convertible bonds. For this reason: 'We don't know how the prices are fluctuating, but it would be useful to know it because the price movements in converts impacts mergers. Being near the converts desk gives us useful information'.

In any case, according to Max, 'even when you don't learn anything, you learn there's nothing major to worry about'. This is invaluable because, as he says, 'what matters is having a degree of confidence'. By putting in close proximity teams that trade in the different financial instruments involved in a deal, the bank is thereby able to associate different markets into a single trade. As a senior trader observed: 'While the routine work is done within teams, most of the value we add comes from the exchange of information between teams. This is necessary in events that are unique and non-routine, transactions that cross markets, and when information is time-sensitive'.

Thus, whereas a given desk is organized around a relatively homogeneous principle of evaluation, a given trade is not. Because it involves hedging exposure across different properties along different principles of evaluation, any given trade can involve heterogeneous principles and heterogeneous actors across desks. If a desk involves simple teamwork, a (complex) trade involves collaboration. This collaboration can be as formalized as a meeting (extraordinarily rare at International Securities) that brings together actors from the different desks. Or it might be as primitive as an un-directed expletive from the stock loan desk which, overheard, is read as a signal by the merger arbitrage desk that there might be problems with a given deal.

### Reflexivity

To see opportunities, traders use the mathematics and the machines of market instruments. We can think of traders as putting on the financial equivalent of infrared goggles that provide them with the trader's equivalent of night-vision. The traders' reliance on such specialized instruments, however, entails a serious risk. In bringing some information into sharp attention, the software and the graphic representations on their screens also obscure. In order to be devices that magnify and focus, they are also blinders. According to a trader, 'Bloomberg shows the prices of normal stocks; but sometimes, normal stocks morph into new ones', such as in situations of mergers or bond conversions. If a stock in Stan's magnifying glass—say, an airline that he finds representative of the airline sector—were to go through a merger or bond conversion, it would no longer stand for the sector.

An even more serious risk for the traders is that distributing calculation across their instruments amounts to inscribing their sensors with their own beliefs. As we have seen, in order to recognize opportunities, the trader needs special tools that allow him to see what others cannot. But the fact that the tool has been shaped by his theories means that his sharpened perceptions can sometimes be highly magnified misperceptions, perhaps disastrously so. For an academic economist who presents his models as accurate representations of the world, a faulty model might prove an embarrassment at a conference or seminar. For the trader, however, a faulty model can lead to massive losses. There is, however, no option not to model: no tools, no trade. What the layout of the trading room—with its interactions of different kinds of traders and its juxtaposition of different principles of trading—accomplishes is the continual, almost minute-by-minute, reminder that the trader should never confuse representation for reality.

Instead of reducing the importance of social interaction in the room, the highly specialized instruments actually provide a rationale for it. 'We all have different kinds of information', Stan says, referring to other traders, 'so I sometimes check with them'. How often? 'All the time'.

Just as Francis Bacon advocated a program of inductive, experimentalist science in contrast to logical deduction, so our arbitrage traders, in contrast to the deductive stance of neoclassical economists, are actively experimenting to uncover properties of the economy. But whereas Bacon's New Instrument was part of a program for 'The Interpretation of Nature',[6] the new instruments of quantitative finance—connectivity, equations, and computing— visualize, cut, probe, and dissect ephemeral properties in the project of interpreting markets. In the practice of their trading room laboratories, our arbitrage traders are acutely aware that the reality 'out there' is a social construct consisting of other traders and other interconnected instruments continuously reshaping, in feverish innovation, the properties of that recursive world. In this coproduction, in which the products of their interventions become a part of the phenomenon they are monitoring, such reflexivity is an invaluable component of their tools of the trade.

## Innovation as Recombination

Just as Latour (1987) defined a laboratory as 'a place that gathers one or several instruments together', trading rooms can be understood as places that gather diverse market instruments together. Seen in this light, the move from traditional to modern finance can be considered as an enlargement in the number of instruments in the room, from one to several. The best scientific laboratories maximize cross-fertilization across disciplines and instruments. For example, the Radar Lab at MIT in the 1940s made breakthroughs by bringing together the competing principles of physicists and engineers (Galison 1997; Galison and Thompson 1999). Similarly, the best trading rooms bring together heterogeneous value frameworks for creative recombination.

How do the creativity, vitality, and serendipity stemming from close proximity in the trading room yield new interpretations? By interpretation we refer to processes of categorization, as when traders answer the question, 'what is this a case of'? but also to processes of re-categorization such as making a case for. Both work by association—of people to people, but also of people to things, things to things, things to ideas, etc.

We saw such processes of recognition at work in the following case of an announced merger between two financial firms. The trade was created by the

'special situations desk', its name denoting its stated aim of cutting through
the existing categories of financial instruments and derivatives. Through
close contact with the merger arbitrage desk and the equity loan desk, the
special situations desk was able to construct a new arbitrage trade, an 'election trade', that recombined in an innovative way two previously existing
strategies, merger arbitrage and equity loan.

The facts of the merger were as follows: on January 25, 2001, Investors
Group announced its intention to acquire MacKenzie Financial. The
announcement immediately set off a rush of trades from merger arbitrage
desks in trading rooms all over Wall Street. Following established practice,
the acquiring company, Investors Group, offered the stockholders of the target company to buy their shares. It offered them a choice of cash or stock in
Investors Group as means of payment. The offer favored the cash option.
Despite this, Josh, head of the special situations desk, and his traders rea-
soned that a few investors would never be able to take the cash. For example,
board members and upper management of the target company are paid
stocks in order to have an incentive to maximize profit. As a consequence, 'it
would look wrong if they sold them' John said. In other words, their reasoning
included 'symbolic' value, as opposed to a purely financial profit-maximizing
calculus.

The presence of symbolic investors created, in effect, two different
payoffs—cash and stock. The symbolic investors only had access to the
smaller payoff. As with any other situation of markets with diverging local
valuations, this could open up an opportunity for arbitrage. But how to
connect the two payoffs?

In developing an idea for arbitraging between the two options on election
day, the special situations desk benefited crucially from social interaction
across the desks. The special situations traders sit in between the stock loan
and merger arbitrage desks. Their closeness to the stock loan desk, which
specialized in lending and borrowing stocks to other banks, suggested to the
special situations traders the possibility of lending and borrowing stocks on
election day. They also benefited from being near the merger arbitrage desk,
as it helped them understand how to construct an equivalency between cash
and stock. According to Josh, head of the special situations desk:

[The idea was generated by] looking at the existing business out there and looking at
it in a new way. Are there different ways of looking at merger arb?... We imagined
ourselves sitting in the stock loan desk, and then in the merger arbitrage desk.
We asked, is there a way to arbitrage the two choices, to put one choice in terms of
another?

The traders found one. Symbolic investors did not want to be seen
exchanging their stock for cash, but nothing prevented another actor such as
International Securities from doing so directly. What if the special situation
traders were to borrow the shares of the symbolic investors at the market

price, exchange them for cash on election day (i.e. get the more favorable terms option), buy back stock with that cash and return it to symbolic investors? That way, the latter would be able to bridge the divide that separated them from the cash option.

Once the special situation traders constructed the bridge that separated the two choices in the election trade, they still faced a problem. The possibilities for a new equivalency imagined by Josh and his traders were still tenuous and untried. But it was this very uncertainty—and the fact that no one had acted upon them before—that made them potentially so profitable. The uncertainty resided in the small print of the offer made by the acquiring company, Investors Group: how many total investors would elect cash over stock on election day?

The answer to that question would determine the profitability of the trade: the loan and buy-back strategy developed by the special situations traders would not work if few investors chose cash over stocks. IG, the acquiring company, intended to devote a limited amount of cash to the election offer. If most investors elected cash, IG would prorate its available cash (i.e. distribute it equally) and complete the payment to stockholders with shares, even to those stockholders who elected the 'cash' option. This was the preferred scenario for the special situation traders, for then they would receive some shares back and be able to use them to return the shares they had previously borrowed from the 'symbolic' investors. But if, in an alternative scenario, most investors elected stock, the special situations desk would find itself with losses. In that scenario, IG would not run out of cash on election day, investors who elected cash such as the special situations traders would obtain cash (not stocks), and the traders would find themselves without stock in IG to return to the original investors who lent it to them. Josh and his traders would then be forced to buy the stock of IG on the market at a prohibitively high price.

The profitability of the trade, then, hinged on a simple question: would most investors elect cash over stock? Uncertainty about what investors would do on election day posed a problem for the traders. Answering the question, 'what will others do?' entailed a highly complex search problem, as stock ownership is typically fragmented over diverse actors in various locations applying different logics. Given the impossibility of monitoring all the actors in the market, what could the special situation traders do?

As a first step, Josh used his Bloomberg terminal to list the names of the twenty major shareholders in the target company, MacKenzie Financial. Then he discussed the list with his team to determine their likely action. As he recalls: 'What we did is, we [would] meet together and try to determine what they're going to do. Are they rational, in the sense that they maximize the money they get?'

For some shareholders, the answer was straightforward: they were large and well-known companies with predictable strategies. For example, Josh would note: 'See ... the major owner is Fidelity, with 13%. They will take cash, since they have a fiduciary obligation to maximize the returns to their shareholders'.

But this approach ran into difficulties in trying to anticipate the moves of the more sophisticated companies. The strategies of the hedge funds engaged in merger arbitrage were particularly complex. Would they take cash or stock? Leaning over, without even leaving his seat or standing up, Josh posed the question to the local merger arbitrage traders: ' "Cash or stock?" I shouted the question to the merger arbitrage team here who were working [a different angle] on the same deal right across from me. "Cash! We're taking cash", they answered'.

From their answer, the special situations traders concluded that hedge funds across the market would tend to elect cash. They turned out to be right. The election trade illustrates the ways in which co-location helps traders innovate and take advantage of the existence of multiple rationalities among market actors. The election trade can be seen as a re-combination of the strategies developed by the desks around special situations. Proximity to the stock loan desk allowed them to see an election trade as a stock loan operation, and proximity to risk arbitrage allowed them to read institutional shareholders as profit maximizers, likely to take cash over stock.

## Sociology of Finance as a Sociology of Value

At mid-century, organizational analysts at Columbia University led by Robert Merton and Paul Lazarsfeld launched two ambitious research programs. On one track, Merton and his graduate students examined the origins and functioning of bureaucracy; on a second, parallel track Merton and Lazarsfeld established the Bureau of Radio Research to examine the dynamics of mass communication. Whereas our Columbia predecessors charted the structure of bureaucratic organizations in the era of mass communication, the research challenge we face today is to chart the emergence of collaborative organizational forms in an era of new information technologies.

Trading rooms provide an opportunity to explore the terms of that research challenge (Knorr Cetina and Bruegger 2002). Electronically connected to markets of global reach, the traders at International Securities reach out to colleagues only a few paces away to calibrate the tools of their trade. The trading room is an ecology of knowledge in which heterarchical collaboration is the means to solve the puzzle of value.

If trading rooms offer an opportunity for the sociology of finance to make contributions to organizational theory, the problem of value that is at the core of finance means that the sociology of finance can make a fundamental contribution to economic sociology as well. In its contemporary form, economic sociology arguably began when Talcott Parsons made a pact with economics. You, the economists, study value; we sociologists study values. You study the economy; we study the social relations in which economies are embedded. But the sociology of finance can ally with others who did not sign that pact (White 1981, 2001; Boltanski and Thevenot 1991; Stark 2000; Thévenot 2001; Callon and Muniesa 2002; Girard and Stark 2002). In doing so, we should put problems of valuation and calculation at the core of our research agenda. Just as post-Mertonian studies of science moved from studying the institutions in which scientists were embedded to analyze the actual practices of scientists in the laboratory, so a post-Parsonsian economic sociology must move from studying the institutions in which economic activity is embedded to analyze the actual calculative practices of actors at work.

## Notes

1. We owe this insightful reading of Bacon's writings, including *Novum Organum* and his (often unsolicited) 'advices' to his sovereigns, Elizabeth I and James I, to Monique Girard.
2. See especially Smith (2001), who refers to these strategies as *fundamentalist* and *chartist*.
3. Zaloom (2002, 2003) correctly emphasizes that, to speculate, a trader must be disciplined. In addition to this psychological, almost bodily, disciplining, however, we shall see that the arbitrage trader's ability to take a risky position depends as well on yet another discipline—grounding in a body of knowledge.
4. We are re-interpreting March's (1991) exploitation/exploration problem of organizational learning through the lens of the problem of recognition. On a separate but related challenge in a new media startup, see Girard and Stark (2002).
5. A put is a financial option that gives its holder the right to sell. A call gives the right to buy.
6. *Novum Organum* translates as 'New Instrument'. Bacon contrasts the deductive method of 'Anticipation of the Mind' to his own method of 'Interpretation of Nature' (Bacon 1960 [1620]: 37).

## References

Bacon, F. 1960 [1620]. *Novum Organum*. Indianapolis: Bobbs-Merrill.

Bernstein, P. L. 1993. *Capital Ideas: The Improbable Origins of Modern Wall Street.* New York, NY: Free Press.

Beunza, D. and Stark, D. 2003. 'The Organization of Responsiveness: Innovation and Recovery in the Trading Rooms of Wall Street', *Socio-Economic Review* 1(1): 135–46.

——2004. 'A Desk on the 20th Floor: Survival and Sense-Making in a Trading Room', in *Recovering from September 11th: The Social Effects of the World Trade Center Tragedy on the New York Area*, Foner, N. (ed.). New York, NY: Russell Sage Foundation.

Boltanski, L. and Thévenot, L. 1991. *De la Justification: Les Économies de la Grandeur*. Paris: Gallimard.

Boltanski, L. and Thévenot, L. 1999. 'The Sociology of Critical Capacity', *European Journal of Social Theory* 2(3): 359–77.

Brown, J. S. and Duguid, P. 1998. 'Organizing Knowledge', *California Management Review* 40(1): 90–111.

Callon, M. 1998. 'An Essay on Reframing and Overflowing: Economic Externalities Revisited by Sociology', in *The Laws of The Markets*, Callon, M. (ed.). Oxford: Blackwell, 244–69.

—— and Muniesa, F. 2002. 'Economic Markets as Calculative and Calculated Collective Devices', Manuscript, Centre de Sociologie de l'Innovation, École des Mines de Paris.

——, Méandel, C., and Rabeharisoa, V. 2002. 'The Economy of Qualities', Manuscript, Centre de Sociologie de l'Innovation, École des Mines de Paris.

Clippinger, J. H. 1999. 'Tags: The Power of Labels in Shaping Markets and Organizations', in *The Biology of Business: Decoding the Natural Laws of Enterprise*, Clippinger (ed.). San Francisco: Jossey-Bass, 67–88.

Dunbar, N. 2000. *Inventing Money: The Story of Long Term Capital Management and the Legends Behind It*. New York: John Wiley & Sons.

Galison, P. L. 1997. *Image and Logic: A Material Culture of Microphysics*. Chicago, IL: University of Chicago Press.

—— and Thompson, E. 1999. *The Architecture of Science*. Cambridge, MA: MIT Press.

Girard, M. and Stark, D. 2002. 'Distributing Intelligence and Organizing Diversity in New Media Projects', *Environment and Planning A* 34(11): 1927–49.

Grabher, G. and Stark, D. 1997. 'Organizing Diversity: Evolutionary Theory, Network Analysis, and the Postsocialist Transformations', *Regional Studies* 31(5): 533–44.

Hull, J. C. 1996. *Options, Futures, and Other Derivative Securities*. Englewood Cliffs, NJ: Prentice Hall.

Hutchins, E. 1995. *Cognition in the Wild*. Cambridge, MA: MIT Press.

Knight, F. H. 1921. *Risk, Uncertainty, and Profit*. Boston, MA: Houghton Mifflin Company.

Knorr Cetina, K. and Bruegger, U. 2002. 'Global Microstructures: The Virtual Societies of Financial Markets', *American Journal of Sociology* 107(4): 905–950.

Kogut, B. and Zander, U. 1992. 'Knowledge of the Firm: Combinative Capabilities, and the Replication of Technology', *Organization Science* 3(3): 383–98.

Latour, B. 1987. *Science in Action: How to Follow Scientists and Engineers Through Society*. Cambridge, MA: Harvard University Press.

Lave, J. and Wenger, E. 1990. *Situated Learning: Legitimate Peripheral Participation*. Cambridge: Cambridge University Press.

MacKenzie, D. and Millo, Y. 2003. 'Negotiating a Market, Performing Theory: The Historical Sociology of a Financial Derivatives Exchange', *American Journal of Sociology* 109(1): 107–46.

Malkiel, B. G. 1973. *A Random Walk Down Wall Street*. New York, NY: Norton.

March, J. G. 1991. 'Exploration and Exploitation in Organizational Learning', *Organization Science* 2(1): 71–87.

Powell, W. 1996. 'Inter-organizational Collaboration in the Biotechnology Industry', *Journal of Institutional and Theoretical Economics* 152: 197–215.

Smith, C. 2001. *Success and Survival on Wall Street: Understanding the Mind of the Market*. New York, NY: Rowman and Littlefield.

Stark, D. 1999. 'Heterarchy: Distributing Intelligence and Organizing Diversity', in *The Biology of Business: Decoding the Natural Laws of Enterprise*, John Clippinger (ed.). San Francisco: Jossey-Bass, 153–79.

——2000. 'For a Sociology of Worth', Working Paper, Columbia University, Center on Organizational Innovation, www.coi.columbia.edu/workingpapers.html#fsw. Downloaded 4 February, 2004.

Thévenot, L. 2001. 'Organized Complexity: Conventions of Coordination and the Composition of Economic Arrangements', *European Journal of Social Theory* 4(4): 405–25.

White, H. C. 1981. 'Where Do Markets Come From?', *American Journal of Sociology* 87: 983–1038.

——2001. *Markets From Networks: Socioeconomic Models of Production*. Princeton, NJ: Princeton University Press.

Wolfe, T. 1987. *The Bonfire of the Vanities*. New York, NY: Farrar, Straus and Giroux.

Zaloom, C. 2002. 'The Discipline of the Speculator', Paper prepared for the Social Science Research Council Workshop on the Corporation as a Social Institution. Berkeley: University of California.

——2003. 'Ambiguous Numbers: Trading and Technologies in Global Financial Markets', *American Ethnologist* 30(2): 258–72.

# 5

# Emotions on the Trading Floor: Social and Symbolic Expressions

## JEAN-PIERRE HASSOUN

## Introduction

In *The Passions and the Interests* (1977), Albert O. Hirschman surveyed the history of ideas in an effort to understand how lucrative activities such as commerce, banking, and speculation could, at different times in the same places, be either stigmatized and counted among the worst social defects, such as greed and avarice, or become legitimate, and ultimately come to stand as behavior models. In his view, this long evolution of ideas crystallized around the paradigmatic opposition between passions and interests. Thinkers as diverse as Saint Augustine, Thomas Aquinas, Calvin, Pascal, La Rochefoucauld, Montesquieu, Vico, Hobbes, Adam Smith, Max Weber, and though only alluded to, Freud, dissected human nature to find answers to the question of how to handle the harmful passions, of which greed was one of the most recurrent manifestations. Should such passions be censored or repressed? Should the passions be allowed to play themselves against each other, thereby canceling each other out? Should they instead be channeled, sublimated, used, even valued and praised? The question runs all through Western thought, concerned as it has been to reconcile 'moral' imperatives generally rooted in Christian tradition with the imperatives of economic development.

But if we change the focus, leaving aside ideas understood as guides to human action during a given period and conceiving the market act as what I will call a 'total market action' occurring within a specific institutional arrangement that has its own social dynamic and time frame, the moral and normative paradigms assumed to legitimate the field of economic activity come to seem rather abstract. What reason is there to think that in action the passions fade away, yielding to cold calculation and control? Do passion-fueled emotions become 'disenchanted' in that, as we understand it, the ultimate function and goal of the passions is rational? Are they destined to

Translation by Amy Jacobs. I first touched on the subject of this chapter at a conference of the Social Studies of Finance Association (SSFA), 17 May 2002, entitled 'Paris, place financière.' My thanks to Marie Buscatto, Jérome Gautié, Karin Knorr, Paul Lagneau-Ymonet, Alex Preda, and Florence Weber for their comments on previous versions of this text.

be 'instrumentalized' in the service of higher moral and collective interests? The concept of a 'metamorphosis' of the passions seems to partake more of an opaque moral, even transcendental alchemy than of analysis in terms of social uses and symbolic issues? As I see it, while these ideas may refer to an ideological and normative transformation that occurred within the history of ideas, they diminish or leave unexplored the social mechanisms by which it is possible to *manage* the passions in action, rather than transform them.

My purpose here is to take up the classic question of relations between passions and interests without being boxed into a paradigmatic opposition between the two terms and without giving privilege of place to the idea that passions are transformed into interests.

Rather than 'dissect the human soul' atopically, I propose to examine the problem from a vantage point firmly anchored in both place and time: the financial market trading floor during intense moments of market action and the intense emotions such action causes and brings to the surface.

## Market Emotions

I define market emotions as those moments in market activity when increased intensity in trading activity provokes intense affective states characterized by (1) physical and mental disturbance or excitement and (2) the individual production of metaphors that fleetingly transfigure the relation of market actor to market activity. In contrast to the usual definition of emotion, I do not establish a correlation between emotion and disturbance or abolition of appropriate reactions for adapting to events. On the contrary, I am interested in situational emotion within the market process and in how that emotion is expressed by market actors.

Studies of financial trading floors have focused on the physical morphology of 'the crowd' and its effects on volatility (Baker 1984*a*, *b*), the ambiguities of trader behavior (Marks 1988), the effects of computerization on the physical market (Jorion 1994), and relations among market strategies, institutional frameworks, and social norms (Abolafia 1996, 1998; Hassoun 2000*a*, 2002). While these authors agree that such markets constitute oversocialized worlds, they have not studied the human passions expressed in them as a research object. It is true that emotions are of marginal interest to economic theory, and when they are taken into account, the focus tends to be exclusively on their possible effects on individual behavior (Elster 1998). In theoretical thinking on financial markets, 'emotional reactions' are most often associated with investors' 'irrational exuberance', a notion used to explain how speculative bubbles happen (Shiller 2001).

And yet anyone who has directly observed financial market actors knows that emotions and their verbal and physical expression are a daily part of these activities. I had repeated opportunities to realize this during the year-long ethnographic study I conducted (1997–8) at the Palais Brongniart, site of the Paris Stock Exchange or Bourse. In addition to daily observation, I spoke with approximately fifty persons, all present and officially working there, in both formal recorded interviews and ordinary conversation. I also regularly spent time with some in the Palais de la Bourse cafeteria, and lunched with them several times in nearby restaurants. After the markets were computerized in May 1998 (see Godechot, Hassoun, and Muniesa 2000), I remained in contact with approximately twenty professionals, thereby collecting retrospective views on this development. Given that language was one of the 'pillars' of open-outcry trading-floor activity, somewhat as networks, mathematical formulas, and computers are of electronic financial markets (Beunza and Stark 2004, Chapter 4, this volume), actors' accounts and vocabulary occupy an important place in this article.[1]

Emotions on the trading floor are to be read first of all on faces, where strong tension and concentration may be perceived, but also at those moments when facial muscles, and the body with them, suddenly go loose. Emotions are perceptible in the interaction rites of a place where physical proximity dominates (Hassoun 2000*b*); they are on daily display in the form of angry verbal outbursts, shoving, friendly, ambiguous, or aggressive back-slapping, complicitous hand taps, hateful or empathetic looks, yelling, swearing, and insults. Financial market actors' behavior openly expresses such varied emotions as sympathy, admiration, anger, aggressiveness, feelings of rivalry, shame, and humiliation. And generally, these emotional phenomena are fully verbalized, either at the moment the feelings are felt, or in the discussion and reminiscing that fuel daily life in these places, which, whatever else they are, are places of work.

Before considering more closely the contexts in which such emotions emerge, it is useful to specify the different types of market actors exposed to feeling them.

Brokers regularly employed by Bourse brokerage firms execute buying and selling orders for off-the-floor clients, but they also develop sophisticated know-how for attaining their ends and in this sense are directly involved in the market performance.

Brokers also engage in *spieling* (from German 'game to play') with the firm's *compte maison* (house account); that is, buying and selling with the firm's money independently of client orders. All spieling profits are divided up as bonuses among employees on the relevant trader team. The *compte maison* can of course show a negative balance (in which case it is called the *compte erreur*) from losses due to trading errors, disputes among traders, or losing spiels, all potential sources of what I am calling market emotions since, even though personal funds are not at stake, spieling involves hope of gain in the form of bonuses.

Independent floor traders (IFT) were established by the Marché à Terme International de France, Société Anonyme (Matif SA) to create liquidity.[2]

IFTs sometimes called speculators, work for themselves and generally act as 'scalpers', initiating positions that they then 'turn around' as quickly as possible for immediate profit.[3] They risk their own money, along with their professional existence since they can 'get blown off' the market at any moment.

*Boxemen* provide live 'market commentary' by telephone to the desks; *flashers* gesture information between traders and boxemen. Couriers run in all directions transmitting time-stamped orders to computer operators for registration. Employees in these categories are also fully exposed to market emotions through their participation in collective performances and the general hub–bub and excitement.

The intensity and frequency of emotion are of course unequally distributed among these groups, but to construct the research object it seems reasonable to adopt a transversal perspective rather than emphasizing social or functional differentiation. Observation, interviews, and conversations all suggest that market action—buying and selling, winning and losing—is likely to produce emotions among those who engage in it, whatever their occupational status or financial means.

Though market emotion is never fully disconnected from monetary gain or loss, this directly utilitarian relation hardly exhausts the phenomenon. Here I wish to explore its other component—the passions—without effacing or neglecting the question of financial profit or loss, i.e. interests.

## A Typology of Market Emotions and Their Social Effects

### Performance and Competition

The emotional phenomena discussed here can only be approached sociologically if we are careful not to dissociate what causes the emotion from what the emotion itself may bring about in the immediate social environment. The following interview excerpts provide a means of examining the connections between situations in which emotions are experienced and the effects of those emotions on local social surroundings.

One day I bought 5600 contracts in one hour. For the same client. He's THE client, you use the formal with him...I once sold 4000 contracts with him, another time 4800; once I bought 3000. But [that one] was the biggest [trade] I've done...You've got everybody watching you, they can't believe their eyes. And it *was* unbelievable—you'd've thought we were on the Notionnel.[4] In the space of a minute he's going, 'Buy 200', 'You got it!' 'Buy 300', 'I'll give ya 200!'. The NIPs were staring at us, it showed up on the CAC[5] —we were creatures from outerspace, there's no other word for it. (Head of a trader team)

Keep in mind that the CAC [Futures] record is 73 000 contracts in one day. Once, at the Sirap, we did 43 000 contracts on the CAC in a single day. We were way over 50% [of pit volume]—we were the kings of the universe! There was nobody but us. You couldn't do a trade without going to see the Sirap—impossible! I was all over the

place. In all the commentaries it was 'Sirap, Sirap' all day long. That evening all
the boxemen came to me saying, 'What a hard-on you musta had!'....(Head of a
boxemen team)

The emotions here narrated were produced by accomplishing a trading
performance that consists, in the case of a broker–client relation, of buying
or selling a high number of contracts at the rate the client demands, or, for
independent traders, selling or getting extraordinarily high volumes of
orders. This type of performance is measured in comparison to either a single
*deal* or a trading day and may be either individual or collective. It can take
the form of a 'record', and thus shows that market activity involves internalized social experience that produces local memory disconnected from economic functions and goals, since thinking of number of contracts sold in a
day as a record creates a symbolic function that then coexists with the economic goal implied in thinking of each trade as separate from all others.

This type of emotion has multiple social meanings and effects. It can bring
about territorial polarization: 'You've got everybody watching you', 'I was all
over the place; In all the commentaries', 'way over 50%'. It allows for explicitly establishing a symbolic hierarchy among the different exchanges operating at the Palais de la Bourse: 'You'd've thought we were on the Notionnel'.
It reflects and intensifies competition between the different status groups
('The NIPs were staring at us'), and it underlines the social feeling of having
had an exceptional experience ('we were creatures from outer space').

Territorialization, competition, exceptional experience all work together to
infuse actors with the feeling they are participating in a contest:

The biggest moment I think, or that I remember, was when interests rates were
changed in '93...We were at around 130 on the Notionnel and had an order to sell a
block of 1000 contracts every 5 centimes. No one saw me move, and we sold 25 or
30 000 contracts in under three hours. I'd say we really *made* the market that day—we
brought it down two points...It was a massacre, it went from 130 to 115. At closing
I didn't even know my name...When you've lived through that, you're almost a vet-
eran, you relativize, 4 points doesn't seem like such a big deal anymore...You sweat
all over the place saying it can't be true, and it wears you out a little, but those are
good memories—real moments. (Desk sales, in touch with the floor)

The competition here is among contestants struggling against each other
to find the desired buyer or seller, to be the fastest to find a buyer or seller, to
move at the right moment ('no one saw me move'). But these same contestants will come together immediately afterward as complementary parties to
strike the next deal. The competitive relations uniting exchange members are
paradoxical, involving both market competition and market alliance. And
their twofold nature goes together with an informal symbolic struggle among,
on the one hand, individuals following largely male norms and holding
largely male values which are only strengthened by working in a place
from which women are virtually absent, and on the other, the various Bourse
brokerage firms, whose names, like the colors of the jackets worn by their

brokers, are coded in terms of prestige. The twofold symbolic competition is accentuated by the fact that the trading floors are also labor markets where one can change employers easily, thereby converting accumulated prestige into supplementary financial income. But once again, prestige accumulation can never be conceived exclusively in terms of monetary convertibility. It must be seen in relation to professional self-valuing, in turn heightened by this type of emotion. Emotion is an active principle in the hands-on, in-the-pit professional self-construction process.

The emotions provoked by successful 'performance', and the accounts of those emotions, recall the 'cult of performance' described by Alain Ehrenberg (1991) at a much broader social scale with regard to 'extreme sports' (bungie-jumping, car and motorcycle racing, etc.). In France, people began practising such sports at the same time the financial markets were taking off, and some trading-floor actors I met did extreme sports on the weekend or during vacation.

More generally, this type of emotion partakes in the social fabric of open-outcry markets, contributing to actors' on-the-job internalization of a few specific social principles: the pit is a territory; the different futures markets are hierarchically ordered; the activity involves the staging of a social, inter- and intraprofessional contest; prestige should be accumulated to develop professional renown.

## Violence

Emotions can also arise following abrupt, violent market movements that accentuate the uncertainty consubstantial with these activities; and in response to events external to the trading floor that upset market equilibrium: wars, conflicts, or political decisions.

The Gulf War was hell...the most torrid, turn-on moments I've ever known on the Bourse, the headiest, the most destructive, too. We were at the farthest extremes...I'm amazed that not everyone tells you about it because we and everybody's still talking about it today...For us it's THE reference. In terms of activity, the market exploded. It could lose 150 points, then lose them again in another 20 minutes. It was going every which way. One day you lost 30 000 francs, the next you made 40 000.[6] You were always in the air, you didn't know your own name. August 2, Iraqi troops enter Kuwait. We felt immediately something really serious had happened—from the nervousness of the market. I've never seen such panicky order-giving in all my time at the Bourse...Ten times more orders than we could handle, with outrageous quantities and price spreads. You could feel panic in everyone. I got the chills, felt incredibly cold all over—then the sweats. 'What's going on?!' I said. Because when it started, we didn't know what it was. All we knew was that it was total panic. And panic scares people. All the guys who come onto the Bourse now, when we tell them about it they say, 'I'd sure like to experience that! Damn, that must've been something!'. (Boxeman–seller, later head of a broker team and client manager)

I don't know how to explain it. It's so wild. If a guy sees it who's not in it, all he could say is, 'They should be locked up!' It's so violent when it takes off. It's violent, the power of the market... when it starts moving. When we were in the Gulf War, it was 300 000, 400 000 contracts a day for six months, it was opening and closing.[7] You've gotta be in it... It's all that counts, you clear out your head, you don't hear anything anymore. I was in it all that time, that's why I spieled, because when you've got a position, you've got to be in it. Then you're not surprised when an order comes in, you know the rates, you know who's doing what, who's buying, who's selling... You've got to be in it all the time to know where the market is, you've got to have a position and know where to strike. (IFT)

The day Buba [Bundesbank] rates went up, I lost 4000 ticks on my first operation.[8] My first operation! I was long for 300 contracts,[9] at around 40 on average, and I cut at 10. I lost 400 000 francs. But afterwards I re-initiated, and at the end of the day I'd only lost 700 ticks. Losing 400 000 francs didn't paralyze me. I went back in and... no, what's good about me is that when I get slapped down, I'm already raging to get back in. Because, I say to myself, they're not going to take that away from me—C'mon, back to the front. I take five minutes out from the exchange, smoke a cigarette, clear my head, and charge back in. (Broker, later IFT)

One of the social effects of such heady moments is the production of something resembling collective memory, itself given strong verbal expression. Even though the market actors I spoke with tended to cite the same events (primarily the 1990–1 Gulf War, the 1991 putsch in Russia, the 1992 French referendum on the Maastricht Treaty, and the European Central Bank's 1993 interest rate decision) and present them similarly, I would hesitate to qualify this as full-fledged collective memory because it has not been stabilized within a 'social framework', either patrimonial, associative, or around a trade union (Halbwachs 1922 [1924]).

Can what I am calling market action be stabilized within a similar official, legitimate social framework, thereby allowing diffuse, atomized professional memories to be shaped into legitimate collective memory? A partial answer to this question may be found in the City of London. In the street of the London International Financial Futures Exchanges (Liffe) stands a statue of a floor trader, unveiled at a public ceremony by the Mayor of London. Thus encompassed in a positive public discourse, the statue confers a degree of social value on financial trading and speculation professionals, and hence, indirectly, on their emotions, inscribing them in lasting urban memory. In Paris, on the contrary, a lack of institutional links, combined with an ideology which keeps market activities in shadow, explains why these memory fragments cannot be aggregated into a collective narrative and thus seem more atomized than truly collective memory. But atomization does not prevent individuals from making retrospective social use of remembered emotions.

The second social and ideological meaning of this type of emotion has to do with the extremely ambivalent attitude these actor-speakers have toward violence. This is suggested by the 'heady/destructive' opposition. Once market shock and the strong, unpleasant emotion accompanying it have been felt ('it was a massacre'; 'it's violent, the power of the market') or once a blow has been taken, the trader, either broker or independent, can only return to the violence of the market ('I charge back in'; 'know where to strike'). Such objective movements of violence and counterviolence can only strengthen the ambient male norm and transform it into a social value. 'I'd sure like to experience that!' say the newcomers, who have to become integrated and who understand that the violence of the market also serves an initiation function. The 'heady/destructive' pair can also reflect a will to power, as when traders feel or imagine that their moves can make the market itself move or change significantly. It did occasionally happen that a sufficient number of independent traders joined together to 'push' the market up or down after a moment of relative price calm, flooding it with orders either to buy or sell. At such times, they were openly pleased to have successfully, if only momentarily, gotten on top of the 'movement' they had to confront and cope with in both real and symbolic terms every day.

Such counterviolence or will to power can also be observed when trading is experienced as a kind of show-down with The Market, in which case it is generally designated by means of the third-person singular pronoun *il* or more impersonally as *ça* (it or that). Here the necessarily human relations that trading involves are effaced and an imaginary, transcendental entity such as that presented in economic theory is constructed. But in actors' language, the market can also take on patently human (or animal) characteristics: 'The market is jumpy'; 'It was healthier'; 'It's barfing'.

General formulas of this type may also be used to refer to institutional actors that, while not physically present, 'shape' and 'direct' market orientations through the buy and sell orders they transmit to the boxcmen. This situation may also give rise to indirect references to the Matif SA market and produce utterances in which traders' ambiguous, often resentment-charged relation with the managing organization are symbolically staged, a relation which sometimes resembles that between boss (Matif) and employees (market actors): 'Matif... was set up to serve the interests of the big French brokers... and it uses them... When they can dip into the funds, they do so.... When they can get the rules to go in their favor, they apply them—that's how I see it' (IFT).

Lastly, some traders manage to reappropriate market violence, to make hedonistic use of sensations accompanying the emotions caused by it. This also means that there are diverse sources and springs of professional identity. Hedonistic use of violence may be likened to the uses made of the prestige linked to performance-related emotions (see above). It too arises when professional narcissism and the taste for competition are heightened and quickened.

But caution is in order here. Just as sociologists speak of a 'rationalization effect' in the interview context, so with market actors there may sometimes be a 'hedonization effect'. The 'heady/destructive' moments of their experience should be relativized, situated in the long term of their professional trajectories, which obviously do not consist in pure thrill, but a combination of thrill and routine. Nonetheless, actors' experience of these emotions, like their accounts of and reminiscing about them, are an integral part of the appraisal, in symbolic terms, that each of them makes of his social identity and/or the matter of presenting self outside the market sphere.

## A Game, Gaming, Gambling

The term *spiel* immediately establishes a connection between certain phases of market action and emotions associated with game-playing and gambling:

I've always spieled... on the house account. The biggest thrill ever was when I did 40 000 contracts by myself. You've gotta hold 'em, it's like sports, you've gotta be there physically, and that was my thing...[I discovered spieling] little by little, with the strike force I had[10]...Because when you do orders there're always a few contracts left over, it never comes out just right, and those extra contracts, you've either got to cut 'em [11] or handle 'em. And little by little, well, the lure of profit, money, grows, and it made me spiel a little to try to get back my losses, and that really pulled me into spieling... You realize that our profession is a game in a way. In some way, it's like a casino...[Today,] the bigger the volume... the more it moves in all directions, the happier I am. I really get off. It's like when I was a broker, the more they hit me over the head with orders, the happier I was. Like a game... It's a sport, too, because it's physical. A job, yeah, it's a job because a job makes you a living. But I'd say, you know, it's more a game. For a guy like me who's a gambler, it's a feast... It's kind of like roulette at the casino, when you put your chip on a number and the wheel spins and it hits your number—you get an adrenalin rush. I don't get the rush when I initiate, but right afterwards. It's when I'm in 'pose' [position] and it moves with me—or in the opposite direction. Win or lose. But the adrenalin rush comes then, when I'm already in pose and it takes off, for me or against me. If it's against you, you need the adrenalin for handling the 'pose', you've gotta have a clear head to get back in and try to bring it back to your prices. And when it rises, it's to try to bring it along with you, bring it into port. Then you say, hey, it's mine. It's then, in fact. It's not when you get in or when you get out, it's in between. (IFT on the Notionnel)

Using Roger Cailloix' categories for classifying games (1958), we can say that the emotions described here bring together the principles and instincts of the *agôn* characteristic of competitive sport ('it's like sports, you've gotta be there physically'); *alea* or chance, as in gambling ('It's kind of like roulette at the casino'); *ilinx* or the giddiness and intoxication associated with the desired adrenalin rush but also with emotional ambivalence ('win or lose'); and even *mimicry*, if we think of the role-playing suggested by the hesitation about personal identity reflected in the set of disparate terms traders use to designate their occupation: 'job', 'profession', 'a game'.

The social effect of this type of emotion is less clear and more ambivalent than for the other two, in that one characteristic of a 'gambler' is to be egocentric and to fantasize being disconnected from the surrounding social world. Obviously in the emotions described here, any sense of being disconnected is quite fleeting. However, the speaker's precision about the adrenalin-rush experience suggests that despite the oversocialization of the place, market action can generate a kind of violent—and very private—hedonism. The emphasis on sensations, indeed microsensations, shows how important bodily engagement and the heightening of the senses is in full professional engagement in the market.

It should be noted with regard to the gaming aspect, that trader hedonism is particularly ambiguous and ambivalent: it may underline the exceptional nature of what is experienced and strengthen professional identity, but it is also at the core of ever-potential occupational destabilization.

The aspects of market-actor experience constituted by performance and competition, violence, and gaming can thus generate emotions with various, often convergent social effects and meanings. Most importantly, they all show that market action can have 'other values' or 'rewards' than directly economic ones, as Roy (1953) showed for the context of industrial piece-work, describing the private strategies workers develop for meeting goals or production quotas, wherein they experience 'the pleasure of a game'. How closely can industrial piecework constraints be compared with the constraint on traders to 'produce' futures rates? Both worlds are subject to a pace set outside themselves. All traders, salaried and independent, are affected by market volatility, and the pace and volume of buying and selling orders produces strong constraints that, like industrial piecework, give rise to self-compensation strategies. These strategies are brought to light by the various types of emotion.

For those who are not eliminated from the trading-floor world by the pace and strong emotions, the 'heady', 'intense', 'real' moments, including the most aggressive and violent of them, can also be understood as a way of moment-arily turning the market's function to other uses. It is significant that when traders cease their activities, one of the things they say they miss most are the moments of intense emotion. Indeed, acceding to such moments is often presented as a kind of privilege, which suggests attribution of social value. For the least educated, this 'singularity' fuels their sense of the unpredictability of their social itinerary; they swing back and forth between a feeling of their own audacity and a sense of illegitimacy, a pattern often found among outsiders. For those with the most education, the relative social transgression that such 'freedoms' represent also distinguishes them in their own eyes from persons of the same generation who, after the same scholastic career, chose more normed, predictable professions or occupations.

Rather than indicating a way of using the passions that diverts or transforms them into interests, traders' behavior and experience suggests that they manage interests through hedonistic use of the passions.

### Vocabulary and Symbolic Representations of Market Emotions

For Marcel Mauss (1968 [1906]), the phenomena of acting in common and thinking in common in shared time and space (particularly in religious rituals) can only be explained by the existence of thought categories which, while not made explicit, nonetheless guide consciousness and are constantly present in language.

For my part, I have tried to deduce from the subjective meaning that traders attribute to their emotions some of the objective effects of those emotions in the social space of the trading floor. To further the initial investigation into relations between passions and interests, I will now try to identify categories of indigenous emotion (or passion) along the lines of Hubert and Mauss's categories of indigenous thought. My hypothesis here is that on trading floors, which can also be defined as a shared space and time, emotions can likewise be seen (above and beyond their social effects) as the most spontaneous type of individual symbolizing activity. To grasp the symbolic framework of market passions, I shall first identify the most frequently occurring signifiers used to express market emotions (Table 5.1).

Like the contexts emotions emerge in (performance, violence, gaming, and gambling), the boundaries of these lexical fields are not impermeable. Metaphor use here, which both establishes a protective distance and works to appropriate market action as a social activity, is not always limited to high-emotion situations, and may be found at less than exceptional moments, where the metaphors used have even stronger sexual connotations: 'feel up' or 'stroke' the market, 'touch [= get] a contract', be 'in the air',[12] 'screw an order', 'get the pussy',[13] 'give the market a screw'. Also to describe more routine market life, there is a series of metaphors related to eating—attack 'la fourchette',[14] 'the market is barfing', etc.—together with regular references to liquidity, which according to some symbolic grids goes with sexuality or bodily intimacy. Jean-François Barré (1991) has noted the recurrence of such terms in international finance writing and suggested possible symbolic meanings.

Though the financial transactions market actors conduct are real and inscribed in specific economic and social relations, could actors be said to momentarily disconnect them from reality when they change the (signified) of a difficult or perilous trade by using a signifier linked to a sports contest, a drive for power, or sexual acts?[15] The question is also raised by a comment that came up in various forms in the interviews: 'You can't think about what each trade represents financially . . . if you did, you couldn't last'. This suggests that the 'distancing' should be thought of as a kind of individual self-regulation, one that can only benefit the market and the market managing institution (Matif SA).

Passion and emotion bring about symbolic productions necessary for coping with the violence of the most extreme phases of market action

TABLE 5.1. The Panoply of Emotions

| Performance, competition, extremes | Violence, combat, fear, power | Gaming, pleasure, sexual activities |
|---|---|---|
| Everyone's watching you | Strike force | A game |
| Can't believe | So violent | Gambler |
| The kings of the universe | All the explosions | A feast |
| At the widest extremes | Ten times more than what we could handle | Roulette |
| All the extremes | The chills | Casino |
| Outrageous spreads | The sweats | Adrenalin rush |
| I didn't even know my name | Know where to strike | Great pleasure |
| Extravagant orders | Panic | Happy |
| | Fear | The greater the volume, the happier I am |
| | Incredibly cold | The more it moves, the happier I am |
| | Holding it all in your hands | Get off |
| | Do the market | Real moments |
| | Hit over the head with orders | Adrenalin rush: when it goes my way or against me |
| | Sweat all over the place | It's not when you get in or when you get out, it's in between |
| | Intense | To like that state |
| | Destructive | Explode |
| | Always in the air | Be moving |
| | | Have a hard-on |
| | | Torrid |
| | | Turn-on |

(temporal compression and thus intensity of actions and risk, and unpredictable volatility). But the need to symbolize is operative in everyday language also. Passions and emotions are fully present at this level, too, and interest logic does business with the symbolic logic of emotions.

## Expressing Emotion is Licit

As will surely have been noticed, market actors do not use euphemisms when expressing their emotions. They speak directly, boldly, do not mince words or water down expressions, have little regard for the proprieties. Restrictive social norms do not apply here and expression of the passions is an integral part of the interpersonal and linguistic environment.

On Matif trading floors in Paris and still today on the floors of Wall Street, the Chicago Mercantile Exchange, and the Chicago Board of Trade, there are no real sanctions or reprimands for externalizing feelings or showing aggressiveness (Marks 1988; Abolafia 1996). When emotions lead to serious insults or, on very rare occasions, physical aggression, these infractions are sanctioned by fines or temporary suspensions, but in general, it is socially permissible to express feelings. Here, sport (often evoked by actors to describe market social relations) seems the only relevant area of comparison.

Given the regulative frames for these activities, it would be too much to say that emotional expression is pacified, as Norbert Elias (1994 [1939]) wrote of sports arenas, conceived as pockets of tolerance and regulation within the 'civilizing process'. Financial markets too would seem to be temporal and spatial enclaves in which aggressiveness may be more freely expressed, spaces where 'discharge of affects' and 'the aggressive expression of pleasure' (pp. 165–6) are not only allowed to develop and prosper but are socially valued. It seems fair to think that an indirect effect of this is to personalize market relations a bit further, even though such relations are reputed to be neutral. In banks, for example, social relations are framed by reserve and discretion; expression of emotion is censured, repressed, kept in check because considered harmful to the proper functioning of this socioprofessional world. Why, then, is expression of emotion more readily tolerated on trading floors?

One part of the answer is that marking 'interpersonal distance' on the trading floor may prove counterproductive (Hassoun 2000a, 2002). Familiarity (limited use of polite expressions, generalized use of the familiar form, loud talking, etc.) is the norm; otherwise the pace of market relations would slow and each trader would have fewer trading partners. I used the term *interpersonal liquidity* to designate this relation between daily trading volume and the interpersonal norms and know-how that increase the likelihood of participants finding trading partners easily and quickly. Interpersonal liquidity, then, is akin to the liquidity of financial theory, an indigenous category evoked by traders not just regularly but almost obsessively. In financial theory, liquidity is exclusively quantitative, measured by volume of daily exchanges ensuring that investors will be able to buy or sell a contract rather than getting stuck on the market without a trading partner. Human relations in the pit have to be liquid too; that is, smooth enough for transactions to take place with the least possible disturbance or dysfunction.

Social relations on the Matif floor not only had to be familiar and smooth-running, but also had to be unstable; that is, capable of being made and unmade in an instant so that others could be made, and thereby capable of following price instability. The second normative injunction, then, the complement to interpersonal liquidity, can be conceptualized as relational volatility. This notion is a means of qualitatively assessing the tolerance of instability and dispersion so beneficial to market relations in that it enables everyone to multiply market opportunities as fast as possible. Relational volatility can be linked to the financial notion of volatility used to assess and measure price instability and spread. Along with the adjective liquid, the *vol*, as it is called, is part of the daily linguistic environment, and is used even by actors who have only the vaguest theoretical understanding of it.

Interpersonal liquidity and relational volatility are two sides of the same sociological coin. This somewhat paradoxical pair of normative injunctions— which says, in essence, be on good terms with the greatest possible number of people without being too closely tied to any of them—may be considered a sociological parallel to the liquidity and volatility of financial theory. It is as though the imperative to produce a high quantity of rates and trades in a short time had produced its own social norms.

It is within this framework that the relatively free and licit expression of emotion becomes understandable. In the continual search for relational and organizational efficiency, restricting expression of market-related affect could clog up the works, as is shown by how hard it was for the Matif SA through- out its history (1986–2000), and other organizers of open-outcry markets throughout the world, to impose strict dress codes or behavioral norms on members.

This is a case of necessity determining the law (or norm), an idea which might in turn explain why in economic practices as in sports there is a 'con- trolled decontrolling of affect' (Elias and Dunning 1986). The market, seen here as a social institution, could be said to tolerate and 'accompany' the expression of market emotions in implicitly functionalist fashion. Because pro- fessionals are able to let loose, they can handle the intense pace, liquidity vol- umes, and high financial and social risk that are integral parts of their work.

In this context, the passions and their expression are not transformed, nor do they evaporate. Instead they are liberated, and integrated into the social norms constructed and imposed by these markets. Like social relations, emotions need to be relatively liquid and volatile, and expression of emotion relatively free and unrestrained.

## Incomplete Sublimation?

Given the symbolic aspects and social and institutional uses of market emo- tion, the Freudian notion of sublimation seems relevant. It should be applied with great care, however. Freud specifies that in addition to modifying the object and aim, sublimation is linked to social evaluation or effect. Economic activities—in this case the series of market acts—are obviously not directly connected to sexuality. But when they are a source of intense emotion, and even when they are carried out more calmly and routinely, they are often spo- ken of and symbolized in sexual terms, as shown. This justifies thinking that at least one of their sources is related to sexual energy. The object has obviously been modified, but the sublimation process seems incomplete because the vocabulary used is explicitly sexual, while also having a variety of other connotations such as physical confrontation and sports competition, these too possibly related to libidinal energy. As for what Freud called 'social evaluation', it is to be found in the uses that can be made of emotions that have been converted into symbolic benefits (recognition and other narcissistic satisfactions, status and territorial appropriation, influence and domination, etc.).

The meaning and value of market emotions can also be grasped in the terms of classic economic reasoning. The emotions that traders seek out and experience could, it seems to me, be considered external to the primary goals of the market in two ways: (1) market movements give the trader or speculator the sought benefit of extreme emotions over and above (or next to or below) his potential financial gains, and (2) the individual's quest for emotion may simultaneously provide financial-market managing institutions with increased dynamism in terms of liquidity and volatility.

It is necessary to keep in mind that on these markets, an increase in activity is always beneficial to market managers because it generates business for *them*. The Matif SA actually encouraged fits of activity by handing out bonuses (in the form of discounts on every trade realized) and awards for best trader of the month. The winner's name was ritually announced over the microphone to the whole floor and the award was accompanied with luxury gifts (champagne, expensive ties or scarves). This attitude on the part of the market organizers corresponds to the behavior of some independent traders who, with no precise strategy, bought and sold as many contracts as possible, betting on the profitability of such frenetic behavior but also looking for strong emotions. 'Do the helicopter', 'turn over', or 'grind out' contracts are three expressions market members used to qualify behavior they viewed as 'extreme' or 'crazy'.

### Conclusion

In seeking an answer to the initial question, we should perhaps focus not on the transformation of passions into interests, which from Montesquieu, concerned with society at large, to Adam Smith directly concerned with the market, was presented as a virtue, but rather on emotions conceived in terms of their differentiated yet intertwined social and institutional uses. These may be situated on three levels or identified as three 'registers' of market action, ranging from macro to micro:

1. The overall functioning of the market, which burns or runs on the energy and apparent disorder of affect, stimulating, making licit, and integrating emotions and various expressions of them within the local normative framework that serves its informal regulation system (market as social institution).

2. The social construction of the professional market position, which requires a great number of distinctive experiences and prestige accumulation, especially since it is itself not firmly institutionalized. This includes phenomena of committing to memory and valuing (professional self-affirmation on a social stage).
3. The symbolic and linguistic productions necessary for taking on and appropriating the financial, social, and symbolic risks particular to the speculative act (the market individual).

## Total Market Action

Each of these levels or registers of action—institutional regulation and stimulation, prestige accumulation, symbolization—are closely linked at one moment or another to emotions. Some of their meanings or effects may be thought of as false notes, gaps, or contradictions with regard to the canonical conception of competitive markets. Indeed, such behavior (along with the personal dispositions it is rooted in) may contradict some of the basic theoretical principles of such markets. For example, the fact that the market managing institution (in this case the Matif SA) stands to profit financially from emotional excitement, and indeed at certain moments stimulates and rewards such emotion, may produce high risk-taking behavior, a phenomena that contradicts the theoretical claim that normal agents are risk-adverse. Similarly, the fact that the professional construction of market actors involves prestige-seeking, at least partially contradicts the theoretical atomized character of markets according to which agents are detached during market action from all reference to or dependence on a social group or symbolic reference. In other words, if competition—i.e. succeeding against others within a regulated framework— is a licit principle in economic theory, prestige-seeking would seem off topic for such theory. Lastly, the idea of taking on the market or making it move (if only for a moment) also clearly contradicts the market atomicity principle according to which no actor is strong enough to have an impact on prices and volumes. At times, one actor or group of actors is indeed strong enough.

But is pointing out hiatuses between economic theory and social practice heuristically effective? It would seem preferable to think of the market *act* microhistorically, in its specific time frame; that is, as a (market) *action* that can be broken down into qualitatively distinct but ultimately interdependent sequences (see the interview excerpt on the adrenalin rush). Once the paradigm of historicity has been introduced, we see that the three comprehensive explanatory levels suggest a melting of emotion into economic action.

These three levels or registers must be understood as linked if they are to explain both the repeated production of emotions and the social licitness of expressing them in the ways they are expressed. Taken together, they transcend common oppositions between economic and social facts, between rational action in the pursuit of self-interest and impassioned irrational action, generating instead an approach in terms of 'total market action' (along the lines of Mauss's 'total social fact'). Even if market actors, like those in many other parts of the social world, generally distrust emotion and say they try to hold it in check, citing either the necessary, almost mythic cool of calculation, the need for discipline, or the importance of ethics, such emotions are an integral part of trading-floor activity. They are not marginal, nor do they constitute aporia. Normative judgments of the type just cited can only make it difficult to take into account the market action as a complex whole. This is what market actors seemed to be saying in their own fashion when they laid claim to their role in 'making' the market and its history, including in that claim—while neither dissolving or mythicizing them—the taste and in some cases the quest for prowess, risk, and money. That triptych of values works to forge a kind of ethos from which emotions are not absent and in which they may even be practical and necessary.

## Notes

1. Though the trading floors of Paris and London no longer exist, open-outcry markets are of course still in operation in New York and Chicago. I have chosen to keep the greater part of this account and analysis in the present tense.
2. From 1986 to 2000, French futures markets were officially managed by the Matif SA, identified as a specialized financial institution (IFS). Its main shareholders were France's major banks and insurance companies. The Matif was a hybrid institution with somewhat difficult-to-reconcile functions; it was both a for-profit service provider materially running the market and charging brokerage firms a small fee for each deal, and the institution charged with overseeing activity and ensuring rule compliance. At the time, this configuration could be qualified as a French particularity, since British and American exchanges were and continue to be member-owned (the Liffe in London, the Chicago Board of Trade (CBOT) or Chicago Mercantile Exchange (CME)). Matif SA has since been absorbed by Euronext, itself a publicly traded company.
3. Initiating means starting a buying and selling cycle that invariably ends in exit from the market.
4. Futures contracts traded on the Notionnel were composed of a basket of French government bonds. Volumes were greatest here. With some awe, traders called it a market of 'big ones'.
5. CAC 40 Futures: market for futures contracts based on the CAC 40 (basket of forty weighted French firms representative of the national economy). The Matif also managed the Paris Interbank Offered Rate (Pibor), the interest rate futures market.

6. 30,000 francs ~ €4,573.17.
7. As agitated as for market openings and closings.
8. The tick (also *oreille*, 'ear', in French jargon) is the basic price change unit. It was 1 franc (approximately €0.15).
9. Long: selling.
10. Strike force: number of futures contracts a salaried broker was permitted to trade.
11. Cut a contract: sell regardless of price bought at.
12. 'S'envoyer en l'air' is the equivalent of 'screw' or 'have it off'.
13. 'Avoir la chatte' (= pussy) = 'avoir de la chance', be lucky.
14. *Fourchette*: the difference between asking and bidding prices. The word also means fork.
15. 'Fuck the market', 'get fucked by the market' are current expressions.

# References

Abolafia, M. Y. 1996. *Making Markets: Opportunism and Restraint on Wall Street.* Cambridge, MA: Harvard University Press.

—— 1998. 'Markets as Cultures: An Ethnographic Approach', in *The Law of the Markets*, Callon, M. (ed.). Oxford: Blackwell Publisher, 69–85.

Baker, W. 1984a. 'Floor Trading and Crowd Dynamics', in *The Social Dynamics of Financial Markets*, Adler, P. A. and Adler, P. (eds.). London: Greenwich.

—— 1984b. 'The Social Structure of a National Securities Market', *American Journal of Sociology* 89: 775–811.

Barré, J.-F. 1991. 'Images de la finance', *L'Homme* 119: 23–40.

Cailloix, R. 1961 [1958]. *Man, Play, and Games.* New York, NY: Free Press.

Ehrenberg, A. 1991. *Le Culte de la Performance.* Paris: Calmann-Lévy/Hachette.

Elias, N. 1994 [1939]. *The Civilizing Process.* Oxford: Blackwell

—— and Dunning, E. 1986. *Quest for Excitement. Sport and Leisure in the Civilizing Process.* Oxford: Basil Blackwell.

Elster, J. 1998. 'Emotions and Economic Theory', *Journal of Economic Literature* 36: 47–74.

Godechot, O., Hassoun, J. P., and Muniesa, F. 2000. 'La Volatilité des Postes. Professionnels des Marchés Financiers et Informatisation', *Actes de la Recherche en Sciences Sociales* 134: 45–55.

Halbwachs, M. 1992 [1924]. *Les Cadres Sociaux de la Mémoire.* Paris: Alcan/Albin Michel.

Hassoun, J. P. 2000a. 'Le Surnom et ses Usages sur les Marchés à la Criée du Matif. Contrôle Social, Fluidité Relationnelle et Représentations Collectives', *Genèses* 41: 5–40.

—— 2000b. 'Trois Interactions Hétérodoxes sur les Marchés à la Criée du Matif. Rationalité Locale et Rationalité Globale'. *Politix* 52: 99–119.

—— 2002. 'Autour de Notions Financières et Sociologiques Homologues: Liquidité des Marchés/Liquidité Relationnelle—Volatilité des Cours/Volatilité Relationnelle'. www.sciences-sociales.ens.fr/chap4/page2-1.htm.

Hirschman, A. O. 1977. *The Passions and the Interests. Political Arguments for Capitalism before its Triumph.* Princeton, NJ: Princeton University Press.

Jorion, P. 1994. 'La Queue qui Remue le Chien. Métamorphose de la Finance due à son Informatisation', *Techniques et Culture* 23–24: 307–49.

Marks, J. R. 1988. *Disguise and Display: Balancing Profit and Morality in the Pit of a Commodities Futures Exchange*. Unpublished PhD Dissertation, New York University.

Mauss, M. 1968 [1906]. 'Introduction à l'Analyse de Quelques Phénomènes Religieux', in *Oeuvres*, Karady, V. and Mauss, M. (eds.). Paris: Minuit.

Roy, D. 1953. 'Work Satisfaction and Social Reward in Quota Achievement: An Analysis of Piecework Incentive', *American Sociological Review* 18(5): 507–14.

Shiller, R. J. 2001. *Irrational Exuberance*. Princeton, NJ: Princeton University Press.

# 6

# Women in Financial Services: Fiction and More Fiction

BARBARA CZARNIAWSKA

## Introduction

At the peak of the 'new economy', the Swedish newspapers were reporting an interesting fact: women were entering financial services, joining not the old-fashioned occupational groups such as bank clerks, but the avant-garde: traders and analysts. A survey following these announcements (Renemark 2003) revealed that the claim was unverifiable. True, there were several financial service companies reporting the arrival of female traders and analysts, but these were very small companies, and the 'influx' often meant one new woman employee. The big companies, the most likely location of such change, either have not answered the questionnaire, or else admitted the impossibility of providing accurate data, as their personnel statistics, even if they showed gender distribution, did not indicate distribution among different employee categories.

But as discourses tend to create their own objects, a field study on work careers of men and women in financial services has been initiated in Sweden, inspired by Linda McDowell's *Capital Culture: Gender at Work in the City* (Renemark 2003). Awaiting its results, this chapter makes use of the material already in existence, namely a detective story *Star Fall*, written by David Lagercrantz (2001), a journalist with an analyst's past and the biographer of the Swedish inventor of a navigation system, Håkan Lans. His book came out on June 1, 2001, and its theme is the crash of the stock exchange and its impact on the Stockholm financial world. On the cover, the Editor-in-Chief of the Swedish *Stock Exchange Weekly* says: 'I have never read a better description of the frightening side of the world of finances'. Acknowledgments refer to many actors in financial services, several of them women. The reviews praise the correctness of the novel's factual basis. The background analysis of the global financial market and its operations owes much to John Kenneth Galbraith's *The Great Crash, 1929*, adds the author in the *Afterword*.

One of the main characters in the novel is a young woman analyst (in fact, women in financial services tend to be analysts, not traders), Elin Friman. The readers learn three things about Elin: she is brilliant (could have been the world's chess champion), she is heavily involved in sexual intrigues, and she is immoral.

This chapter begins with a presentation of this character, comparing her first to other women and men in the novel, and then to other fictitious or fictionalized characters. It proceeds by analyzing the case of a woman trader tried in Sweden for 'blanking' shares—as described in the newspapers, and ends by confronting these Swedish images with those in international literature on financial markets.

## The Construction of Elin

When the stock market crashes on the evening of January 26, a rumor says that two people have been murdered in Stockholm; General Bank's IT analyst Elin Friman, and the famous inventor André Borg [whose IT company has just become public]. It seems that the murders were committed one after the other, hours only after the rates started to fall at the New York Stock Exchange (NYSE), and the rumors increase anxiety and quicken the fall (Lagercrantz 2001: 1).

It is not advisable to reveal the whole plot of a detective story, so I will limit myself to saying that Elin is not only a victim, but also a perpetrator, a tool in the hands of the Russian mafia, and related to it by her relationship with her former chess teacher. The mystery is resolved by Daniel Mill, an amateur detective whose moral sensibility made him end his analyst's career, and turned him into an astute critic of the world of finances (apart from making him rich and therefore independent).

Elin is perceived by her male colleagues primarily as a sex object: 'her smile, at the same time uncertain and cool, which sometimes seems to be an erotic promise', and so on, through various parts of her body. She listens to men and appears to admire them:

She made him talk, made him elaborate long theories on economy, the company, love, human longing. Her presence intoxicated him ... When he noticed that she looked in the same way at all the male bosses, he began to dislike her willingness to serve, her incessant cleverness[1]. (Lagercrantz 2001: 11)

As an employee of the General Bank, she tends to exaggerate all the desirable traits:

He encouraged ambition and responsiveness to General Bank's corporate culture, but Elin went too far. The bank absorbed her totally, so that sometimes she seemed to lack a core. She could be anything: a mountain climber, a poet, an evening press reporter, a university lecturer but also a hippie. (Lagercrantz 2001: 11)

Lacking her own identity, she assumes that of the man she is (most) enchanted with at the moment. In love with sensitive leftist Daniel, she is against the world's injustice. When Daniel quits his analyst job, she fixes her adoring gaze on the bank's Managing Director and becomes a careerist. As it turns out, she is persistently faithful to one man and one ideology, in a way that is close to fanatic, as her colleagues reflect afterwards. This lack of an individual identity, muses the—neglected by Elin—Financial Deputy, could have been produced by a collision between her natural talents and her poor background, a contrast between nature and nurture, as it were:

What he sees as a weak self can have resulted from her youth and uncertainty. She is 27, her father is an unemployed bus driver who drinks... so she probably wanted to escape from it all, find another world, whatever the cost. She has an analytical talent. She immediately grasps the most complex situations and she remembers numbers— especially quotations—in a way that almost frightens him. (Lagercrantz 2001: 12)

The readers of Oliver Sachs will of course recognize the extraordinary capacity of the mechanical memory, usually accompanied by a complete inability to function in social life. Elin lies, she uses 'feminine cunning' and blackmail. But she is not evil: she helps her sister and wants to serve her men. If anything, she 'loves too much', as Robin Norwood's bestseller (1989) put it. She has masochistic tendencies, begs to be mistreated, and yet abhors the sexual exploitation of other women. She loves women but also ideologies: she cheats and exploits, but for a higher cause. A veiled Marxist, she condemns capitalism in general and her bank in particular, but sees no problem in manipulating the shareholders:

She always talked about the two rules of the shares market: faith and doubt[2]. There is no better way of making money, she used to say, especially as people need not believe or doubt long. A couple of minutes is enough. (Lagercrantz 2001: 134)

After her death, people wonder about her and her motives, as more surprising information is revealed. Her sister finds a photo where Elin looks like a member of *Hitlerjugend*, with a caption: 'Elin, 11, wants to be best in the world. Believes in hard discipline'. And her US super-boss says: 'She was complex. She wanted to serve and to be appreciated—no doubt. But she was also vengeful and angry... She was like a lion's paw: soft and pretty, but inside there was a claw that wanted to tear all of us to pieces' (Lagercrantz 2001: 225).

The novel's psychiatrist (a spokesperson for a Swedish woman writer, says the author in the *Afterword*) explains to the Financial Deputy: 'A person can be both innocent and wicked and equally genuine in both those roles' (Lagercrantz 2001: 209). The psychiatrist is a clearly positive female character, but then she has a suitable job for a woman; she tries to understand people and their problems. The other two women involved in finances are mentioned only briefly. Eva Björk is a top manager at Nordea, another bank, and will become the Financial Deputy at General Bank in the end. She speaks in public about shares in a 'folksy way', an allusion to the Swedish way of 'domesticating' the world of finances that became very prominent in the mass media (Ohlsson 2003). Teresa Granquist, another analyst at General Bank, returns several times, but mostly to deliver information. The only thing the readers learn about her is that she was 'tough and cool. Elin did not threaten the male self-esteem in the same way' (Lagercrantz 2001: 58).

Teresa was the only woman who had relatively close contacts with Elin. Elin lived among men, so she must be compared to men. Daniel Mill is every-thing she is not: he has a (moral) core that stabilizes him and makes him incorruptible ('Don Quijote', Lagercrantz 2001: 230). A mafia-related chess master[3] is of course evil and corrupt, but he knows what he is doing; Elin does not, and needs to be told. The chess master is the evil equivalent of the noble Daniel. Finally, the Financial Deputy is weak, but thoughtful; also, he lacks Elin's talents and therefore is not dangerous.

The detective story genre has its rules, and a dramatization of events and a demonization of characters belong to the most prominent. Nevertheless, the character thus created deserves attention, as its construction makes (often unintentional) use of the accessible cultural material. 'The construction of Elin' can be seen as highly significant, as it reflects both the received image of today's finances (inside and outside financial circles) and of people in finan-cial services. Extremely high intelligence (rather than formal education) is both assumed and claimed by traders and analysts. Elin is even more intelli-gent than most, thus reinforcing the conviction that, for the same job, women need to be twice as good as men. Her sexual intrigues also correspond to the image of a 'work hard, play hard', no-family oriented world; but while men are presented as ensnared in her sexual intrigues, Elin initiates them. Last but not least, lack of moral guidance is a trait supposedly prominent in financial dealings, but while young men seem to be *amoral*, Elin is *immoral*, actively contributing to evil. Less this characterization create an image of a Super-Woman, like Carol O'Connell's (1994) Mallory, it needs to be added that Elin performs all her evil deeds as instructed by a man, the true master-mind behind the plot. Female after all: a will-less tool in the hands of a purposeful man.

While there is no doubt about the fictitiousness of Elin's character, the message (perhaps unintended) is clear: the world of finances is no place for women. Those who made it there are 'unnatural'—twice everything else the men are, especially the vice, and not even aware of it. While the novel contains many thoughtful men, acutely aware of traps and dangers connected to this world, women, it seems, can only be the victims and the perpetrators in it.

## Between Fact and Fiction

Elin's character brings to mind another fictitious woman in the world of finances: the insurance investigator, played by Faye Dunaway in *The Thomas Crown Affair* (1968, director Norman Jewison). She was also extremely intel-ligent and played chess[4]; she was immoral and exploited sex in her business conduct. However, probably because it was a US movie, she was redeemed in the last scene, allowing herself to be—amorously—duped by Steve McQueen (a property tycoon turned robber).

Some other characters that could be compared and contrasted with Elin are half-fictitious. I have in mind, in the first place, the movie *Rogue Trader* (Granada Film, 1998, director James Dearden): the story of Nicholas Leeson[5] based on his own autobiography. Nick and Elin have two things in common: a working class background and a wish to ascend in life. Here the similarities end, though. The movie is developed around two theses. One concerns Leeson's psychological makeup; at least as portrayed in the film, he has all the traits of a gambler, as described in Dostoyevsky's *The Gambler* (1886): growing dependence and denial, diminishing capacity of foreseeing the consequences of his own actions, etc. Gamblers are not chess players, although they imagine themselves to be. The second thesis is sociological and has to do with a clash and misunderstanding between two sets of financial people: the old-fashioned bankers of Baring Ltd, whose world is still a gentlemen's club, generously open to the newcomers, and the nouveau-riches like Leeson, who are not even aware of the implicit rules of the club's game. Also, while Leeson brings Baring to bankruptcy, Elin has become a scapegoat for General Bank that, if anything, profits from her death, which permits covering up many other misdemeanors.

The US equivalent of Nick Leeson, at least as far as drama goes, is Michael Milken, 'the king of junk-bonds', the story that allegedly formed the basis of the movie *Boiler Room* (2000, directed by Ben Younger). As the link between the movie and the story is loose, and Milken's criminal actions are of a different type than those of Elin and Nick, I shall only quote Mitchell Y. Abolafia's comment on Milken's drama, as he, too, points to the role of dramatization in the accounts flowing in from the world of finance:

Like many dramatic heroes, Milken had a fatal flaw. Some saw it as greed. I think it was hubris. Milken had developed an exaggerated sense of himself in relation to the rules and norms of his community. His success was built on an escalating series of normative violations. There were no restraints for Michael Milken. The crimes for which he was imprisoned, all of which occurred during the take-over mania of the mid-1980s, reflect the recklessness of an overheated deal-maker. (Abolafia 1996: 163)

Abolafia speaks of a 'social drama'; this is an interesting way of combining the requirements of two genres. Social science accounts tend, by definition, toward sociological interpretations. Fiction is permitted a dramatization that factual literature usually avoids; drama tends to focus on characters, thus promoting psychological interpretations. Sociological novels (including a sociological movie, such as *Rogue Trader*) and a dramatist approach in sociology stand in-between: 'psychologizing' becomes a social act dictated by genre, to be studied. In such dramatizations women—possibly because they are fewer—tend to be portrayed either as 'characters' or as sociological tokens.

Michael Lewis' *Liar's Poker* stands on the 'Fact' shelf in bookstores, but is more stylized than research reports are permitted to be, and therefore midway between fiction and fact. It offers several interesting observations considering the role of women in international finance. The women he mentions are not at all like Elin, but they are very much like Teresa: 'tough and cool'. Here is Lewis going to be interviewed for a job at Lehman Brothers:

Good news. Lehman had sent to Princeton one man and one woman. I didn't know the man. But the woman was a Princeton graduate, an old friend I hadn't expected to see. Perhaps I would survive.

Bad news. As I walked into the cubicle, she didn't smile or otherwise indicate that she knew me. She later told me that such behaviour is unprofessional. We shook hands and she was about that chummy as a boxer before a fight. She then retired to her corner of the room as if waiting for the bell to ring. She sat silently in her blue suit and little bow tie. (Lewis 1999: 31)

Are they selected because they are tough and cool or do they learn to become so? Lewis suggests the latter, speaking of the same Princeton graduate:

One year on Wall Street and they have been transmogrified. Seven months earlier my friend could be seen on campus wearing blue jeans and a T-shirt that said dumb things. She drank more beer than was healthy for her. She had been, in other words, a fairly typical student. Now she was a bit-player in my Orwellian nightmare. (Lewis 1999: 31–2)

How is this transmogrification achieved? A snap from a trainee program explains it only too well:

Everyone wanted to be a Big Swinging Dick, even the women. Big Swinging Dickettes...A hand shot up (typically) in the front row. It belonged to a woman. She sat high in her regular seat, right in front of the speaker. The speaker had momentum... The speaker didn't want to stop now, especially for a front-row person. He looked pained, but he could hardly ignore a hand in his face. He called her name, Sally Findlay.

'I was just wondering', said Findlay, 'if you could tell us what you think has been the key to your success'.

This was too much. Had she asked a dry technical question, she might have pulled it off. But even the speaker started to smile...he knew he could abuse the front row as much as he wanted. His grin spoke volumes to the back row. It said, 'Hey, I remember what these brown-nosers were like when I went through the training programme, and I remember how much I despised speakers who let them kiss butt, so I'm going to let this woman hang out and dry for a minute, heh, heh, heh'. The back row broke out in its louder laughter yet. Someone cruelly mimicked Findlay in a high-pitched voice, 'Yes, *do* tell us why you're *sooooo* successful'. Someone else shouted, 'Down Boy'! as if scolding an overheated poodle. A third man cupped his hands together around his mouth and hollered, '*Equities in Dallas*'.

Poor Sally...Equities in Dallas became training-programme shorthand for 'just bury that lowest form of human scum where it will never be seen again'. Bury Sally, they shouted from the back of the room. (Lewis 1999: 53)

When doing a study of humiliation at work (Czarniawska 2004), I came across a homepage of the US Navy that contained a reminiscent passage in a description of the Navy Chiefs' training:

You are now the 'CHIEF'! So this, then, is why you were caused to experience these things. You were subjected to humiliation to prove to you that humility is good, a great, a necessary attribute which cannot mar you—in fact, it strengthens you—and, in your future as a Chief Petty Officer, you will be caused to suffer indignities, to experience humiliation far beyond those imposed upon you today. Bear them with the dignity, and with the same good grace, which you bore them today! It is our intention to prove these facts to you. It is our intention that you will never forget this day. It is our intention to test you, to try you, and to accept you. Your performance today has assured us that you will wear your hat with aplomb, as did your brothers in arms before you. We take a deep, sincere pleasure in clasping your hand, and accepting you as a Chief Petty Officer in the United States Navy. (www.NavyChief.com/creed.html, accessed 020515)

What would happen to Sally if she survived this humiliation, if she became tough and cool? There existed a range of possibilities, it seemed. Lowest in the ranks was Susan James:

Susan James... played a strange role. She was something between the baby-sitter and an organiser of the programme. Her reward for a job well done was, perversely, to be admitted to a future training programme. Like everyone else, she wanted to work on the trading floor, but she was one step further removed than us [the trainees] from realising her ambition. Her distance from the money-making machine reduced her credibility as a disciplinarian to zero. She had only the power to tattle on us, and really not even that. Because we were her future bosses, she wanted to be our friend. Once we had moved to the trading floor and she to the training programme, she would be pleading with us for a job. (Lewis 1999: 62–3)

Not all women trainees were lost and humiliated:

as I walked into the foyer that first morning, a female trainee was shouting into what must have been a fuzzy telephone connection. In the midst of a scorching July, the pudgy woman on the phone was stuffed into a three-piece beige tweed suit with an oversize bow tie, to which I probably would not have given a second thought, had she not herself called attention to it. She placed one hand over the receiver and declared to a tiny group of women: 'Look, I can do six full suits for seven hundred and fifty bucks. *These* are quality. And *that* is a good price. You can't get them any cheaper'.

That explained it. She was wearing tweed because she was selling tweed. She guessed rightly that her training class represented a market in itself: people with money to burn, eyes for a bargain, and space in their closets for the executive look. She had persuaded an oriental sweatshop to supply her with winter wear in bulk. When she saw me watching her she said that given a bit of time she could 'do men too'. She did not mean it as a bawdy joke. Thus the first words spoken to me by a fellow trainee were by someone trying to sell me something. It was a fitting welcome to Salomon Brothers. (Lewis 1999: 41)

For the woman, it was also a fitting training for her future job:

At Salomon Brothers men traded. Women sold. No one ever questioned the Salomon ordering of the sexes. But the immediate consequence of the prohibition of women in trading was clear to all: it kept women further from power. Traders required market savvy. Salesmen required interpersonal skills. (Lewis 1999: 79)

The crash of 1987 came, and women were its main victims:

Scribbled over the empty seat of a redundant saleswoman was her view that 'Men who call women sweetheart, baby or honey should have their tiny peckers cut off'.

These were no ordinary victims, though victims they were. Here in New York, as in London, a conspicuously large number of women were canned. It's not as if the women had been less astute in choosing their jobs; they just had less say in their destiny. For whatever reason, women coming out of the training programmes were assigned to loss leaders. For several years one of the sink-holes had been the money market department. Perhaps 10 percent of the trading floor professionals were women. But women were nearly half of money market's sales, and, therefore, a large number of the sackees. (Lewis 1999: 283)

Without her extraordinary intelligence and her fanaticism, these women shared Elin's victimhood because their destiny has been in the hands of others. Were there no women in the positions of power? Lewis describes one:

Syndicate managers on Wall Street and in the City of London are charged with the job of co-ordinating all deals; the London syndicate manager of Salomon, one of the few powerful women within the firm, had co-ordinated our German warrant. Syndicate managers are the investment banking equivalents of chiefs of staff in the White House, or general managers of professional sports teams... The role produces masters of realpolitik, Machiavellian in the original sense of the world. They see all. They hear all. They know all. You don't cross a syndicate manager. If you do, you get hurt.

The next day I told the London syndicate manager of my conversation the previous night [with Opportunist, who tried to bluff Lewis]. She knew the truth of the German warrant deal because she had played a role in its success. She was even angrier than I hoped. She was also extremely plugged in at Salomon Brothers, in the way that Opportunist was not. I mercilessly left his fate in her hand; it was like leaving a goldfish in the care of an alley cat. Only then, after it was too late to reverse the process, did I feel remorse. But not much... The woman I had spoken with was directly responsible for deciding what the Opportunist was paid. The Opportunist was expecting a lot of money and a promotion from vice-president to director. The promotion was critical to his future. This woman made five or six phone calls and squashed his plans. (Lewis 1999: 228–9)

Not a criminal, not a fanatic, not a sex maniac, an alley cat after the fish. A specialist in interpersonal relationship, but not in a 'feminine' way—no mothering instincts or 'feminine cunning'. Just 'one of the boys'.

## Lisa is Not Her Real Name

This is a four-year-long story, so I am going to render only its end phase, not just because of the lack of space, but also because the media—my source of material—have reached a certain narrative maturity during that time [6]. But let me quote the first press release on the matter:

February 2, 1999. Trader cheated Nordbank STOCKHOLM (*TT*) A trader at Merita-Nordbank is suspected of having swindled the bank out of millions—through illegal deals. The deals caused the bank a loss close to 300 million kronor. The trader was arrested on Monday, suspected of serious breach of trust and serious malversation...

The illegal deals continued for several months. The trader made so-called blanking deals, that is deals with borrowed shares similar to Leeson.

Only the next day (February 3) did the readers learn that the trader was a woman. *Dagens Industri* revealed it and ended its long article explaining what had happened in financial terms, saying: 'For this trader, as for all others who ended up in a dangerous spiral, it is a catastrophe. She is right now alone against the whole world and risks a prison sentence'.

The District Court freed the woman from both accusations and severely criticized the way the prosecutor's office handled the case. The prosecutor's office turned to the Appeals Court, and the trial took place January 14–15, 2003.

Two weeks before the trial, the weekend supplement to the regional newspaper where both the trader and I live published a portrait of the trader, giving her the fictitious name 'Lisa'. The title ran: 'Here vanished 269 million', and under this, in the mock soap opera advertising style, it said: 'A young woman who just became a mother. A quarter of a billion that got speculated away. An angry prosecutor, seeking revenge. A clumsy bank. On Wednesday a new installment of the drama *"Nordbank v. the trader"* in Svea Appeals Court. *Two Days* met the now 35-year-old Lisa from Kullavik, south of Gothenburg. A super-intelligent lass—who went astray'. This was followed by a drawing of a childish-looking girl in glasses at a computer, quotation list to her left, two men in the background, and a color drawing of a sailboat in a blue bay to the right. The caption says: 'TALENT. Lisa was not only a star trader. She has participated in the European Sailing Championship. And she talked three foreign languages fluently. When she spoke on the telephone, she often used French, so that her boss and her colleagues wouldn't understand' (the deals were done by Lisa with the help of a female friend at Credit Lyonnais in France).

Under the headline 'Clever in Most Things', the article sketched a portrait of Lisa:

Who was this 31-year-old woman who, exhausted, was taken to prison again (she was arrested at her parents' house where she took refuge after her deals were discovered by the bank) and would then be summoned for interrogation every two weeks, so that, after four months in an isolation cell, she felt so poorly that she couldn't participate in person?... She who speculated away 269 million—and her future.

And what a future it was. She finished the natural sciences high school with the highest grades. Her performance was equally outstanding at the Stockholm School of Economics [Elin's *alma mater*], where she was also active in the student association. She studied in Germany and France; she worked in Hamburg, London, and Paris. She wrote her thesis on share-index swapping using Credit Lyonnais as her case.

Lisa speaks fluent English, French, and German and can converse in Italian. She plays piano, guitar, and clarinet. She has had a traineeship at Sotheby's in London and did research on impressionism and modern art.

As a junior she participated in sailing championships but also skied, played tennis, squash, and golf, and she danced and practiced gymnastics.

A real 'A' child in other words. And yet it all went wrong. Not that she is in a bad spot. She recently married a man from West Sweden, who is the managing director of a small food company in a big corporation. He has moved from Masthugget in Gothenburg and she from Östermalm in Stockholm to a town in Scania. They live in an English-style terrace house bought for 2.4 million kronor.

But Lisa is on sick leave for 'reactive depression' and gets about 10,700 a month after taxes. Last year in the bank she earned about 1.5 million in salary and bonuses.

## Topped the Bank's Lists

She came to Nordbank in 1996 as an institutional investment trader. She quickly showed her talents and soon she was at the top of the earning list in the bank. Last year she earned 22.9 million for the bank, four times the targeted amount. In the police interrogations her colleagues present a long list of her merits as a trader: capable, ambitious, inspired, incredibly intelligent, great social competence, talented, good sense of the market, a star trader. Their opinions of her person are not worse: humble, never bossy, nice, helpful, easy to get on with, pleasant, kind, decent, happy, eager to please.

But there was also another side to her, according to her colleagues. She was a competitive person and always wanted to be best. Therefore she could be incredibly sensitive, especially at the beginning, when she could cry over the loss of a couple of thousand. Her friend at Credit Lyonnais, who was also taken to court (she did not have the right to approve the deal that she did), and who shared a flat with Lisa in London, says: 'She dramatized a lot and exaggerated. It always sounded worse than it was...She took on herself all the world's problems as if they were her fault. A peculiar personality trait'.

Lisa says of herself that she has a low self-esteem, and exaggerates the negative side—especially her own. Yet she claims that she did nothing wrong. Her clients and her bosses bluffed, cheated, erred, and betrayed—but not she. Her father shares her opinion: she has been made a scapegoat by the incompetent people at the bank. The prosecutor has another explanation: 'This, in his opinion, extraordinarily intelligent woman was understimulated in her job: therefore one can guess that she was hit by a gambling obsession. People in this profession have a certain tendency to suffer from gambling obsession'.

The District Court had concluded that Lisa acted incorrectly, but that the fault was the bank's: they did not train and control her properly. The Court was also very critical of the prosecutor and the Finance Inspector's way of presenting the case. The first day at the Appeals Court was curious, still according to *Göteborgs-Posten* (January 14, 2003): 'What a strange trial! On the one side, a supposed grand villain who leaves during the pause to pump milk from her breasts. On the other side, a pale prosecutor who has worked all night long and complains about shortage of time even though he has had four years to prepare'.

As it turned out, the prosecutor was 'sent home' a week earlier as his case had too many errors and even typing mistakes. But, said *GP* on the following day, this humiliation mobilized the whole Agency Against Economic Crime, whose honor was at stake. Indeed, the Appeals Court decided in March 2003 that 'convincing evidence' was presented showing that 'she was guilty as accused'. The Court was of the opinion that fines were not enough and ordered a psychiatric investigation to determine whether the woman could endure a prison sentence. If the result of the investigation was negative, she would be sentenced to psychiatric custody. The family considered appealing to the Supreme Court. The final comment from the prosecutor was reported thus: 'He perceives the case's tragic aspects and hopes that the woman, now on sick leave, will find a new place in society: this is an intelligent person with great qualities. But she will hardly find an appropriate job in this particular sector'.

Extraordinary intelligence and psychological instability are the two aspects that connect Lisa and Elin. Although Lisa's case is much closer to Nicholas Leeson's (basically the same type of misdemeanor, gambling tendencies), nobody analyzed Leeson's personality in such detail—the descriptions mostly concerned his behavior, with some comments on his not high intellectual powers (McDowell 1997: 172–3). To be fair, Leeson could not breast-feed in court, either. McDowell quotes also a journalist who, at the time of the Leeson affair, expressed a strong conviction that 'there could never be a female Nick Leeson' not merely because there are so few women dealers and traders, but also because of their characters' (1997: 174).

The working class background is no longer a factor with Lisa; it just seems that, in a popular rendition, the combination of high intelligence and instability is explosive. While in the case of men it is supposed to lead to criminality and sociopathic behavior, dangerous to society and its institutions, women are mostly themselves destroyed by it.

Again, as in the detective stories genre, the genre of journalistic accounts has its specificity. It prefers strong, dramatic plots (perhaps Lisa could become a journalist?), with an intense psychological element. Let me then move to yet another genre, that of social science.

## Games Women Play

The anthropologist Melissa Fisher studied US women in finances, and analyzed their autobiographical accounts. She used an analytical strategy close to that of Abolafia—letting in the drama as a phenomenon to be analyzed—although she exploits the metaphor of the game in place of the drama. She individuated two kinds of narratives employed by women in finances, neatly divided between their occupations: analysts and salespersons on the one hand (the majority), and the rare traders/investment bankers/bosses on the other. Both groups, however, reach for the traditional US repertoire to emplot their 'herstories'. In the first case, the narrative fits in well; in the second, it clashes, with foreseeable results.

She summarizes the narratives of analysts and salespersons in the following way:

The rhetoric of women in research and brokerage tends to draw on natural attributes of American femininity, such as conservative risk-averse behavior. In this way, femininity can be inserted within traditionally masculine areas. In particular, women in these fields invoke and reframe the figure of the 'consumer' as feminine in order to lay claims to their own ability to forecast, sell and buy stocks. To play the game of risk, they seem to use gender assumptions about their roles as mothers making family purchases in order to sell themselves as professional subjects of economic expertise in the market. (Fisher 2003: 289)

This is exemplified by the story of Patricia, 'the good mother'. It recalls other stories of women's entrance into the 'masculine professions', masqueraded as an extension of home services into the offices (Calás and Smircich 1993). In contrast, Maydelle's story seems to be a version of an 'alley-cat'. It also uses the traditional US narrative repertoire, but the one reserved for men, and therefore ends up as a story of deviation from the first, 'proper' one.

Women positioned in investment banking, on the other hand, provide a different articulation of playing games of risk. Their narratives draw on supposedly masculine characteristics of cool calculated rationality, adventure, and risk-taking. Investment bankers are directly responsible for capital accumulation, in contrast to women in research and brokerage. Risk-taking is important here. Yet, because risk-taking women invert all that is traditionally proper about gender, Wall Street treats these women as 'anti-mothers' of the professional-managerial class. Female bankers become demonic mothers who do not care about their employees or, in some cases, their real-life children (Fisher 2003: 289).

In fact, Maydelle hastens to assert that she does not 'beat her kids'—she invites her employees home to prove it.

The 'mother motif' was not present in the Swedish accounts, not only because of a likely difference in cultural narrative repertoires, but also because most women in Swedish finances are still too young to be mothers, especially to their colleagues. Unlike cashiers and other traditional bank employees, mostly female, they got into their jobs quite recently.

Fisher ends her essay by mentioning the fate of Mary Meeker of Morgan Stanley, 'the queen of the net', a crossbreed between a trader and an analyst. Her queendom, however, died with the dotcoms. 'Once more', says Fisher (2003: 308), 'a risk-taking woman has been taken to task for daring to exceed the gendered norms of the Street'.

What is, actually, 'the women's problem' in finances, and what do those who survive it actually do? I believe that Linda McDowell (1997) hits the nail on the head when pointing out that behind all the dramatization of the feminine 'character' there is one solid fact: the woman's body. A woman can think like one of the boys, can talk and act like one of the boys, but she cannot look like one of the boys, or not close enough. McDowell's fieldwork in three merchant banks in the City of London reveals that women in banking are 'marked' by their bodies. 'Without a single exception, the women I interviewed raised the question of appearance'. 'Every style available to women is marked, whereas men's styles are unmarked' (McDowell: 145). How do they survive? McDowell does not analyze the actual narratives, only their fragments, but she also employs the drama metaphor, claiming that they survive by employing the means of the masquerade, in several variations: playing an honorary man, doing a parody of femininity, etc. While not all the masquerades are equally successful, the idea of conscious masquerading seems to be gaining popularity among men and women alike. This, says McDowell, is because:

The public/private, home/work division which has a long heritage in western thought... is reflected in a duality between what is regarded as a necessary masquerade at work and an essential 'real' self that may emerge occasionally on the workplace stage but is allowed complete dominance only in off-stage activities—perhaps in leisure, but particularly in home life which has always been portrayed as more real or more authentic than the artificial and instrumental social relations of the workplace. As I shall show, the metaphors of performance, of reality versus masquerade, were also significant elements in the interviews I undertook. (1997: 161)

For all the incisiveness of McDowell's insights and the acuteness of her observations, here is a typical 'global language' speaker speaking for the whole of western culture. As an immigrant in Sweden with a work career in another country, I was struck by the absence of the public/private, reality/masquerade division in Swedish workplaces. This is Elin's problem: she has nowhere to hide, partly because the hiding places are few (the traditional family men have some; perhaps the division existed earlier on), partly because she exaggerates what is the general trend (she is 'swallowed' by banking). Her masquerade is of a criminal type; honest employees have nothing to conceal. But perhaps Teresa is into a successful masquerade: this is why the readers do not learn how she looks (she looks like any other woman, not playing a man, and not exaggerating her femininity), and are not invited to speculate about what she feels and thinks. She is not important enough to be material for a drama, but because of that she is left in peace (until the next redundancy campaign, of course).

## Strong Plots

As my readers have noticed, I have been using a variety of material here, starting with 'pure' fiction, continuing with a fiction based on an autobiography, a stylized autobiography, journalists' reports, ethnographic reports, and unstylized autobiographical accounts (interviews). Apart from the degree of fictionality, it is also the position of the narrator that varies: from self-accounts to accounts of others' actions. Finally, as there may exist national preferences for genres, plots, and characters, it must be pointed out that, although the context is that of global economy, the narrators are Swedish, British, and US American.

The motif of 'an unstable female genius' is present only in the two Swedish stories, those of Elin and Lisa. Rather than drawing from this a conclusion about Swedes' preference for high drama in female finances, it needs to be pointed out that, considering the timing, the actual 'Lisa' story was very likely an inspiration for 'Elin', that Elin is a highly dramatized version of Lisa. What is more, it is not improbable that the newspaper story of Lisa written in 2003 was inspired by the fictitious character of Elin, made known to the readers in 2001. The US 'anti-mother' and the UK 'alley-cat' are less dramatic versions of female deviance, in the genre 'she-turned-into-one-of-the-boys', not least because they are success stories, ironic as it may sound.

As the research literature seems to indicate, 'Teresa' is probably the most representative of the actual women in financial services. I am using the expression in its old-fashioned, statistical sense, but she is material for statistics in yet another sense. Her case will become anonymized, will vanish in the mass of numbers. She and Susan James are lucky to get a name in the stories told, unless it is a feminist story, like that of Fisher's, where Patricia Riley—the good mother—shares the spotlight with Maydelle Brooks, the anti-mother. It is, however, Elin and Lisa who are the popular dramatic material, the poor-girl-turned-dangerous-fanatic and the rich-girl-turned-gambler. Were an 'anti-mother' or an 'alley cat' to fail, they would probably be dramatized in a similar way (in local variations).

Why should highly stylized stories of exceptional women, presented by popular culture, be of interest for social studies of finance? There are at least two reasons. One is that popular culture—novels, films, mass media, and even how-to, and consultancy books captures the dominant view of the financial sector at any given time. The other reason is to be found in the old dictum 'art imitates life and life imitates art'. While I do believe, in a Tardean spirit, that people learn their jobs primarily by contact-imitation (Taussig 1993), a belief that Lewis' stories amply corroborate, the popular culture furbishes them with models and ideals. Somebody said that it is impossible to fall in love for someone who never read a romantic novel. It is obviously an old utterance, because at present a 'romantic novel' has been replaced by a 'Hollywood movie', but the idea still holds. It has been reported that neophyte mafia criminals in Sweden know by heart all the dialog in DePalma's *Scarface* (Czarniawska 2003). While the observation of everyday routines teaches everyday routines, popular culture, with its bigger-than-life heroes, provides material for dreams and rule-breaking behavior. As Linda McDowell puts it,

'Representations of fictional bankers influence the behaviour and attitudes of "real" bankers, and vice versa' (1997: 39–40).

Why can't young people learn their jobs through reading work ethnographies? Because contemporary ethnographies are modernist, as Manganaro (1990) rightly observed: complex plots, experimental structures, paradoxical resolutions. Popular culture, on the other hand, relies on strong narratives and traditional plots.

What are 'traditional plots'? Equally traditionally, one turns toward the Greek dramas and folktales. It is tempting to follow the example of Hayden White (1973) and look for the four genres of Greek drama (based on four major tropes) in management texts, as Sköldberg (2000) did. A closer look at the Greek drama, like, for instance, the insightful scrutiny of Mendelsohn (2003), reveals that even Euripides used much more complex plots, and embedded plots, not the least in his plays concerning women. Another possibility would be then to look for Propp's (1968) thirty-one functions of which, says McCloskey, economics uses but seven (1990). But then again, those thirty-one, or even seven, can be combined or trespassed against in an almost unlimited number of ways. A clever classifier can fit anything in a set of exclusive categories and if in trouble, there is always the 'and those belonging to the emperor' category. Northrop Frye (1957) achieved an impressive categorization of literary genres, but the main result was that his critics were busy for many years afterwards showing how the actual works poorly fit an abstract categorization. A defense of all such categorizations consisting in saying that actual works combine various categories amounts to saying that all literature is basically a combination of 25 (or 27) letters of an alphabet, which is correct, but not very instructive.

Besides, why should Greek drama survive so well? Contemporary journalists hardly need to follow classical theater to do their jobs. Shakespeare might fare better because of the school imprinting, but Shakespeare's plots are rather complex. Folk fairy tales are the best candidate for a strong place in collective memory, but even those were surely replaced by educational modern children literature. Those who believe in deep structures have an answer ready: traditional plots are archetypes, capturing the essence of human psyche and destiny. For those who, like myself, believe in surface connections, plots are strong because they have been institutionalized, repeated through centuries, well rehearsed. Their simplicity does not explain their success: it has to do with fashion (recall the times when Gothic novels were in fashion, or the extreme complications of D'Annunzio's prose, today undecipherable, yesterday read by all). One should therefore speak of conventional rather than traditional plots, and of dominant rather than strong plots: they are 'strong' in a given time and place. A complete list of such plots is neither possible nor necessary, but it might be instructive to delineate the presence (repetitiveness) of such dominant plots in accounts of and from the world of finances, and also point their connections to various types of traditional plots. Thus, Greek drama and folk tales, but as a loose inspiration, an invented tradition rather than as direct imitation or an expression of deep structure.

Whatever the essential or constructed traits of traditional plots may be, they are not known for carrying a feminist message. Extraordinarily intelligent and sensitive women who tried on masculine pursuits always ended badly in stories (Janion 1996). The stories of women in finances seem to be confirming the opinion of an egg trader quoted by Abolafia (1996: 93): women and children do not belong on the financial markets. If social science cannot, or will not, provide an alternative message, it can nevertheless show how the popular models are constructed, applied, and reproduced.

## Notes

1. The author uses the word *duktighet*, which in Swedish is used mostly in relation to children in school and women (in their study or work), rarely if ever in relation to men.
2. In Swedish they make an alliteration: *tro och tvivel*.
3. The connection between the chess master player and the world of finance starts with General Bank's marketing campaign, where the Russian master, of 'an overwhelming intelligence' makes a video for GB saying 'I want my money to be managed intelligently'.
4. Lewis (1999: 27) claims that the bankers use a degree in economics as a sort of standardized test of general intelligence (what he means is that such education has no other use); chess playing seems to be a global cultural indicator of extraordinary intelligence.
5. Played by Ewan McGregor.
6. I am grateful to David Renemark for collecting the material.

## References

Abolafia, M. Y. 1996. *Making Markets: Opportunism and Restraint on Wall Street*. Cambridge, MA: Harvard University Press.

Calás, M. and Smircich, L. 1993. 'Dangerous Liaisons: The Feminine-in-Management', *Business Horizons*, March–April: 73–83.

Czarniawska, B. 2003. 'Svenska företag 1943–2001 i deckarromaner', GRI Report.

—— 2004. 'Humiliation: A Standard Organizational Product?', Unpublished Manuscript.

Dostoyevsky, F. 1996 [1886]. *The Gambler*. New York, NY: Dover.

Fisher, M. 2003. 'Wall Street Women's "Herstories" in Late Financial Capitalism', in *Constructing Corporate America: History, Politics and Culture*, Lipartito, K. and Sicilia, D. (eds.). New York, NY: Oxford University Press.

Frye, N. 1990 [1957]. *The Anatomy of Criticism*. London: Penguin.

Janion, M. 1996. *Kobiety i duch innosci* [*Women and the Spirit of Otherhood*]. Warszawa: Wydawnictwo.

Lagercrantz, D. 2001. *Star Fall [Stjärnfall]*. Stockholm: Piratförlaget.

Lewis, M. 1999. *Liar's Poker*. London: Hodder & Stoughton.

Manganaro, M. 1990. 'Textual Play, Power, and Cultural Critique: An Orientation to Modernist Anthropology', in *Modernist Anthropology. From Fieldwork to Text*, Manganaro, M. (ed.). Princeton, NJ: Princeton University Press, 3–50.

McCloskey, D. N. 1990. 'Storytelling in Economics', in *Narrative in Culture. The Uses of Storytelling in Sciences, Philosophy and Literature*, Nash, C. (ed.). London: Routledge, 5–22.

McDowell, L. 1997. *Capital Culture: Gender at Work in the City*. Oxford: Blackwell.

Mendelsohn, D. 2003. *Gender and the City in Euripides'. Political Plays*. Oxford: Oxford University Press.

Norwood, R. 1989. *Women Who Loved too Much*. Flint, MI: Arrow.

O'Connell, C. 1994. *Mallory's Oracle*. New York, NY: A Jove Book.

Ohlsson, C. 2003. 'Bazaar or Business? The Language Practice in a New Swedish Pension System', Paper presented at APROS 2003 Conference, Oaxaca, Mexico, December 2003.

Propp, V. 1968. *Morphology of the Folktale*. Austin, TX: University of Texas Press.

Renemark, D. 2003. '(Wo)men Working in Financial Markets. A Study of Organizing of Work', Paper presented at Nordic Academy of Management, Reykjavik, August 14–16.

Sköldberg, K. 2000. *The Poetic Logic of Administration*. London: Routledge.

Taussig, M. 1993. *Mimesis and Alterity. A Particular History of the Senses*. London: Routledge.

White, H. 1973. *Metahistory. The Historical Imagination in Nineteenth Century Europe*. Baltimore, MR: The Johns Hopkins University Press.

# Section II
## The Age of the Investor

# 7

# The Investor as a Cultural Figure of Global Capitalism

## The Investor as a Figure of Global Capitalism

We see ourselves as small shareholders, as critical shareholders, as shareholders of ethical businesses, or of venture firms. We are against grand speculators, or dream of becoming one someday; we follow price movements every day, or only now and then, trade online, or go to a trusted broker, watch the news, look at price charts, discuss the market with friends, and so much more. Contemporary capitalism would not be the same without the investor. Against this background, it is surprising that we still lack a sociological analysis. How does this figure work and to what consequences? Its substantial presence and broad societal impact suggest that it is not a new phenomenon, but rather the outcome of a historical process. Since its public prominence is tied to the second globalization wave (the increased worldwide integration of capital markets since the 1980s), an adequate strategy of inquiry would be to investigate its shape in the first globalization wave (the period between 1850 and 1914, when capital markets witnessed a comparable level of integration). Concomitantly, the figure of the investor raises some crucial questions for the sociology of financial markets concerning the ways in which structural conditions are related to agency, economic action is shaped by cultural factors, and the categories of economic order translate into categories of individual experience.

I make here two arguments: the theoretical one is that the sociological concept of figure is a useful tool for analyzing how financial markets generate valid, socially legitimate types of social actors. The empirical argument is that in the first globalization wave (1850–1914)[1] the investor is reconfigured as having universal validity and as legitimating market globalization. I single out two interrelated aspects of this reconfiguration: (a) the transformation of the investor into a scientist bound to discover the universal laws of the markets and (b) the notion that investing is intrinsic to human nature and a basic social right. I begin my examination by developing the sociological concept of figure. I show then that the sociological tradition identifies four basic

This chapter has very much benefitted from the comments of Karin Knorr Cetina, Barbara Grimpe, Aaron Pitluck, and Peimaneh Riahi. My thanks to them all.

figures of capitalism: (1) the manufacturer, (2) the entrepreneur, (3) the accumulating capitalist, and (4) the religious capitalist. The missing figure here is that of the investor. In the next step I examine the reconfiguration of the investor along two lines: (a) the investor-scientist and (b) the right to invest. This reconfiguration occurs during the first globalization wave and marks a rupture with the eighteenth century figure of the investor. I show how (a) and (b) contribute to creating a cultural figure with universal validity, which legitimates global market expansion.

I rely in this examination on primary sources from the United States, United Kingdom, and France from 1850–1914. For comparison, I will also draw on primary sources from eighteenth century Britain and France (in the United States, institutionalized financial markets started around 1792). I refer here to investment books, magazines, newspaper articles, and reminiscences of investors; my arguments are grounded in the examination of over four hundred original documents directly related to and produced in investment activities. My method is that of an analytical reconstruction of the figure of the investor as constituted in the cultural field of investment activities (specified in the fourth section on 'The Figure of the Investor in the Eighteenth Century').

## The Sociological Concept of Figure

The investor as a figure of capitalism: is he or she then an abstraction, a fictionalized portrait of historical figures? We can easily imagine a fictionalized amalgamation of 'grand speculators', Jay Gould and Cornelius Vanderbilt mixed up with Carl Icahn and Warren Buffett. But is it not defining for these grand figures that they live through hyperbole, through countless stories about their exploits? And what about those investors who are absent from such stories? An amalgamation of historic characters would describe the grand figure rather than explain it. Shall we then understand the investor as a trope, a figure in the discourse of capitalism, a justification for engagement with financial markets, one which went beyond (uncertain) profit? This is intrinsic to the figure of the investor; yet, justification alone cannot bring unrelated actors to engage in similar paths of action, cannot completely explain how social responsibility is placed on them. There is more to the figure of the investor than justification.

If neither a fictional character, nor a trope, then what is the figure of the investor? Generally speaking, we encounter at least three meanings of the concept of the figure: (1) In rhetoric, the figure (of speech) or the trope designates a displacement of linguistic meaning, which takes place according to established rules of communication and is embedded in a pattern of persuasive argument. Thus, metaphors, litotes, or allegories as figures of speech are rule-governed elements of persuasive communication. (2) In literary studies, the figure designates a character in a novel or play, with the following properties: (a) placement in space and time; (b) development; (c) mimesis—that is, imitation of a person or class of persons from real life; (d) involvement in a pattern of action; (e) embeddedness in a web of relationships. (3) By opposition, the sociological concept of figure stresses neither exclusively linguistic aspects nor mimetic character. Note that the notion of figure does not entirely overlap with the sociological concept of role. While the latter is understood as a behavioral script which reflects social-structural constraints at the individual level, the figure implies the reciprocal adaptation between broad cultural categories, on the one hand, and categories of individual experience, on the other. The outcome of this process is a set of dispositions shaping individual paths of action. The concept of figure is grounded in a series of arguments which include, among others, Gabriel Tarde's examination of the economic act, Erving Goffman's analysis of the interaction order, and Norbert Elias' and Pierre Bourdieu's notions of figuration and figure, respectively.

There are two basic premises to this concept: the first is that the self cannot be constituted through solipsistic acts (i.e. pertaining exclusively to one's own character or private ego) but emerges in the interaction order. Thus, agency implies an interplay of forces, a system of different positions, roles, and performances on the part of social actors. An important argument in this sense is formulated by Gabriel Tarde: for him, the broader economic order requires a correlate at the individual level. The institutional categories of economic life need individual acts as a correlate, otherwise there would be no economy out there. These individual acts are grounded in beliefs; belief, however, is not a category of individual psychology, but of social interaction. The economic self is constituted at the level of the interaction order: none of her acts can be purely individual. Economic acts will always be coconstituted by interaction elements like commonly held values, moral projections, and collective representations (including fears, exuberance, and the like) (Tarde 1902: 290). Tarde's arguments resonate with Erving Goffman's. Goffman (in a larger context) sees the self as constituted by situated rules of interaction in the same way in which a theater figure is constituted on a stage in the interaction with coplayers (1959: 30–31). Since the interaction order is a sui-generis one (irreducible to individual psychological elements, or to biological determinants), it becomes necessary to analyze the process-like constitution of social selves and of the categories in which the social world is experienced. Norbert Elias formulates a related argument, in that he sees agency (a) as depending on the constitution of the self and (b) on the interaction between selves. Elias' case study is that of the European court societies at the dawn of the modern era. Court societies were intricate webs of social positions, roles, and forces, in which individual selves (i.e. of the king, the nobleman, the court lady) were shaped by the rule-determined interaction process. The self is then not an isolated creation, but a figure situated in a web of interactions in which other figures exert their forces. The concept of figure designates then the interplay between structure and individual agency in an interaction web. Figuration is the process through which individual selves and macrosocial processes are tied to each other: it ensures that social facts are created concomitantly on the collective and on the individual level (Elias 1983 [1969]: 21, 208–9).

This brings us to the second conceptual premise, namely that structural elements have to be matched by categories of experience on the part of individual actors. Without this match social actors cannot be explained but as robots. Paths of social action (and categories of experience with them), however, are not identical, but similar. Pierre Bourdieu explains (dis)similarities between these paths as being due to the position they occupy in the (literary) field (1996: 129, 132). During the Second Empire in France, for example, we do not encounter a single, homogenous figure of the literate, but several: the bohemian intellectual, the public intellectual, the popular writer, the social critic. These figures are situated in a field of cultural differences, according to the categories in which they experience the social world, to the social and cultural capital they dispose of, and to the resources they can mobilize. At the same time, external forces are exerted upon the literary field: for example, by the bourgeoisie who tolerates (or even sponsors) the bohemian, or by the political class. The consequences are that the notion of figure is neither a mechanical translation of structural constraints at the individual level nor reduced to a single set of determinants (economic or political). Figures shape the field (i.e. the structural conditions) in which they act.

## Figures of Capitalism

In the sociological tradition, we encounter a continuous preoccupation with the figures generated by the modern capitalist order: the expert, the public man, the consumer, the intellectual are only some major examples. Among the attempts to define capitalism by the figures it generates, at least the following categories figure prominently: (1) the manufacturer, (2) the entrepreneur, (3) the accumulating capitalist, and (4) the religious capitalist. Adam Smith's manufacturer and Joseph Schumpeter's entrepreneur belong to (1) and (2), respectively. Karl Marx's and Max Weber's respective figures of capitalists are examples of (3) and (4). Their authors saw these figures not as byproducts, but as key with respect to the capitalist order: they are the individual counterpart and the source of the entity called capital.

In the eighteenth century, 'capitalist' was understood by social philosophers, by economic thinkers, and by the educated public alike as a person who invests money in public debt or in stock, and expects an annuity or a dividend. A capitalist was someone who did not have to work for a living, nor lived off land revenue, nor had profits from manufacture or trade. His revenue was derived from the financial securities he owned and traded. At the dawn of the modern era, being a capitalist meant being an investor (DuPlessis 2002: 36). Only toward the end of the century did Adam Smith's (1991) *Wealth of Nations* give a new, abstract twist to the term 'capitalist'.

## The Manufacturer

A superficial observer may say that Adam Smith has not depicted a central figure of capitalism, being too busy with the grand tableau of the national economy. Yet, Smith's economic landscape is not an empty one, but populated by a whole array of figures, some of which are of central importance. Increasing the nation's wealth is, in Adam Smith's eyes, the ultimate aim of economic life. While agriculture, trade, and other economic activities may contribute to wealth increase, great nations excel in manufacturing (Smith 1991 [1776]: 12). All other economic activities—like banking and trade—are subordinated to increasing the manufacture industry of the country (p. 258). The manufacturer is skilled and innovative: he has a deep knowledge of production processes and of local conditions, is geared toward permanent productivity improvements, and is interested in long-term development. Of all social types, wrote Smith, the 'master manufacturer' plays the central role; the merchant, another important figure, is subordinated to the manufacturer in the social order of wealth. Manufacturers have the best knowledge of their own interest, a self-interest which is the very spirit of capitalism: 'during their whole lives (they) are engaged in plans and projects, they have frequently more acuteness of understanding than the country gentlemen . . . Their superiority over the country gentleman is not so much in their knowledge of the public interest, as in having a better knowledge of their own interest than he has of his' (p. 219).

## The Entrepreneur

Analogously, Schumpeter's entrepreneur (1934) is motivated by a constant, almost religious drive for (technical) innovation. In this respect, the entrepreneur combines Adam Smith's manufacturer with Max Weber's charisma. Capitalism is characterized by a 'habit of mind': that of striving toward technical innovation for economic profit. Innovation is the motor of economic growth and capitalist expansion. The entrepreneur is its major figure. He is not merely interested in science and technology for their own sake; he is interested in continuous innovation because he equates it with economic advantage. Innovations solve major economic uncertainties and set the stage for imitators. Technical and economic processes are closely related to each other; technology is endogenous to the capitalist economic system (Rosenberg 2000: 12). The entrepreneur is different both from the manager and the 'capitalist risk-taker' (i.e. the investor) (Schumpeter 1991: 407–8). He invents or innovates as a response to economic and social pressures and, in doing this, he promotes economic change. At the same time, Schumpeter's entrepreneur remains separate and independent from the investor; he may put his talents in the service of joint-stock companies, but financial speculation is not his defining feature (1991: 425 n4, n9).

## The Accumulating Capitalist

In the introduction to the first edition of the *Capital*, Karl Marx stated clearly that the figure of the capitalist was the 'personification of economic categories, bearer of class relationships and interests' (2002 [1872]: 37). Relevant here is the fact that in the *Capital*, this figure is determined by the process of accumulation.

For Marx, capitalism is reducible to two key aspects: the worker selling his labor force to the capitalist, and the capitalist being able to obtain surplus value by paying not for the labor, but for the reproduction of the labor force. Hence, the key relationship of capitalism is that between the capitalist and the worker: while the former accumulates, the latter sells his only possession. For the capitalist, the main type of social action is accumulation; for the worker, it is selling his labor force. Accumulation is a purely economic process, free of any ethical determinations. He who accumulates does not need to sell his labor force, and he who has to sell it all the time cannot accumulate. These two kinds of complementary actions are paradigmatic for capitalism and for the relationship between these two figures. Capitalism as a social order depends on the relationship between accumulation and the sale of labor force. Marx's entire analysis is geared toward deducing the laws of capitalism out of this relationship.

## The Religious Capitalist

While Marx's capitalist accumulation is free of ethical determinations, Max Weber saw the capitalist as a religiously motivated man: his drive toward redemption justifies getting rich as a self-contained aim. Since redemption is uncertain, all that is left is hope, which is supported by a constant strive toward accumulating riches. Accumulation, however, has to obey certain rules: the virtuous capitalist accumulates by his own ingenuity, frugality, sustained work, and constant preoccupation with economic processes. Religious asceticism forbids accumulation by speculation (Weber 1988 [1920]: 191). While witnessing waves of financial speculation in Germany, Weber did not really view financial markets as being at the core of the capitalist order. The most he could do about them was to write a popularizing brochure (Weber 2000 [1894]). Continuous work and profit through production (Weber 1988 [1920]: 175) are the legitimate means of religious salvation.

These figures are not mere traces in the history of political economy. Historically seen, they may coexist; from the conceptual point of view, however, each claims primacy in explanatory accounts of capitalism.

## The Figure of the Investor

Manufacturer, entrepreneur, accumulating capitalist, religious capitalist: some of them are easy to recognize in today's global capitalism. For instance, the figure of the dot.com entrepreneur was familiar and much cherished in the late 1990s. Other figures may be paler now than one hundred years ago. Nevertheless, striking in this enumeration is the fact that none of these figures is directly related to a fundamental institution of capitalism: financial markets. They are involved in production processes, in manufacture and technology; trade may play here a role too. Financial markets, however, are a notable absence. Of course, Adam Smith was aware of the merchant's role; but the merchant is subordinated to the manufacturer and is not involved in financial markets. In fact, Adam Smith did not consider these latter to contribute to national wealth; he saw financial markets as a noneconomic domain, a view clearly expressed in the last chapter of the *Wealth of Nations* (1991 [1776]: 534).

Yet economic opinion has radically changed: contemporary economic historians see financial markets—from the moment when they emerged—not as a mere byproduct of capitalism, but as its very motor (Sylla 1999a, b). This change of opinion goes hand in hand with the belief—rooted in eighteenth century illuminist thinking—that the market generates a fundamentally new human type (Hirschman 1992: 109): 'the archetype of capitalism is the shareholder who places his money in an enterprise and expects a profit' (Boltanski and Chiapello 1999: 39). Placing money, holding shares, expecting profit: all these actions, attitudes, and expectations are intrinsically related to financial markets as *the* capitalist institution. As early as 1901, Georg Simmel noticed that the stock exchange—characterized through permanent movement and continuous excitement—is an 'extreme increase in the rhythm of life' and the 'point of the greatest excitement of economic life' (Simmel 1989 [1901]: 708). If this is so, there must be a fifth, lost figure of capitalism: the investor. Understanding the 'spirit of capitalism' cannot ignore a figure tied to one of its core institutions, a figure which has positioned herself at the very center of this order, one on which so many hopes and responsibilities are placed and which has to take so many risks.

On the one hand, the figure of the investor is tied to the paths of action followed by so many unrelated actors: these actions cannot be seen as habit, as unreflected routine; they cannot be seen as coerced, or as automatically induced by education, income, social milieu, profession, and the like. They are similar or complementary, yet not identical: obviously, not everybody buys the same security at the same time. Thus, the figure of the investor should take these paths of action into account and show how they relate to the legitimacy of markets.

On the other hand, the figure of the investor is tied to the legitimacy of capitalist order: being an investor has to do with the social legitimacy of financial markets, with how enterprises are organized and property relations are structured. Among others, the investor is central for how relations of ownership are organized in capitalism, for how firms are conceived. This implies not only the right and the ability to own shares, but also to trade them, actively intervening on the market. The assumptions underlying this organization of ownership go well beyond the sphere of economic concepts: we own some part (however minuscule) of a corporation, we hold and trade securities not only because it is economically profitable (for this is uncertain), but also because it is socially and morally justified, because we accept this arrangement as legitimate. In short, the figure of the investor has to do with capitalism as a justified *and* just order (Boltanski and Thévenot 1991: 59).

This means taking into account the 'sets of beliefs associated with the capitalist order, which contribute to justify this order and to support, through legitimating, the modes of action and the dispositions coherent with capitalism' (Boltanski and Chiapello 1999: 46). Hence, we have to explain the bind between beliefs in the social and moral legitimacy of investments, and action categories which confirm and reinforce these beliefs. Belief in the social legitimacy of investments cannot be conflated with belief in their economic profitability. They are apparently flexible and multilayered enough to legitimate the grand speculator and the small investor, the billionaire and the employee, the day trader and the occasional buyer of treasury bills. As the recent account of a sociologist and amateur investor puts it, the grand speculator and the small investor, the full-time professional and the amateur alike belong to an 'imagined community' of market actors (Pollner 2002: 231).

In the same way, categories of social action cannot be limited to the financial marketplace, to trading securities. One reason is that financial transactions are tied to and dependent on larger categories of action: gathering information, evaluation procedures, knowing transactions partners, and the like. Another reason is that the notion of financial transaction, of investing in financial securities already presupposes that of the investor: it will be then a logical fallacy to reduce action categories to those of the marketplace.

A further aspect is given by the material arrangements and devices related to the categories of meaningful financial action. Gathering information, for example, depends on communication devices, on the material support of information. At the same time, devices and technologies can in themselves constitute paths of action: an economic study may require from investors different actions than economic gossip. Material devices play an important role in legitimating paths of action as well as the larger social order in which they are embedded (Mukerji 1997). They can make this legitimacy visible for several people at once, symbolize the legitimate order, and corroborate discursive formulations of this order. Consequently, we should not see the figure of the investor as exclusively constituted by (discursive) beliefs and action categories. In investigating this figure, we need to examine the configurations of mutually supporting beliefs, action categories, and material arrangements (devices, technical artifacts).

These configurations are not straightjackets. They do not impose courses of action; they make them possible, and make these possibilities inevitable. I argue here that the figure of the investor is constituted in a configuration (or field) of discourses about and of investing, material arrangements, and cognitive instruments. The discourses about investing establish how investment activities are conceptualized and represented; discourses of investing, related to activities, establish the communication modes between financial actors. Material arrangements, in their turn, determine the settings of investment activities, the quality of financial information, and shape the interaction modes of investors. Cognitive instruments determine how financial information is processed and by whom, affecting the discourses of investing. The field of investing is not isolated from the political, the technological, or the literary field; agency coming from these fields can produce significant changes in the material arrangements of investing activities or in their legitimacy.

## The Figure of the Investor in the Eighteenth Century

There is general agreement that investors are not a sudden, recent occurrence. There have been investors since the emergence of financial markets in Amsterdam, London, and Paris in the late seventeenth and early eighteenth century. While we still lack a systematic, comprehensive quantitative examination of investors in the eighteenth century, we possess descriptions of the financial marketplaces of this time (e.g. Schama 1997 [1987]: 343–71) and partial statistical analyses of company shareholders and of bondholders (e.g. Neal 1990; Carruthers 1996; Sylla 1998; Garber 2000; Wright 2001). The eighteenth century is the century of periodic enthusiasm with investing and speculation, of great periodic bubbles followed by periods of silence. The South Sea, the Mississippi, the Compagnie des Eaux, the Banque Saint Charles, and the Wall Street speculative manias have introduced a permanent notion into the vocabulary of finance: the bubble. If historical descriptions are to be believed, people from all social strata have participated in these speculative frenzies. At the same time, the eighteenth century is the century of heavy moral, economic, and political doubts about investing, of great anti-speculative tides. These doubts concern the relationship between investing and gambling, the effects of financial investing upon the character of the individual, upon the productive forces of society, upon social classes and the state. At the dusk of the century, the French revolution turned the tide against investing by asking for the death penalty on any kind of financial speculation. Edward Chancellor has recently argued that the culture of financial investments in the eighteenth century was carnival-like, characterized by popular participation coupled with 'a Utopian yearning for freedom and economic equality' (1999: 29). The notion of carnival culture, however, does not fit well with the overall deep skepticism about the social legitimacy of investments.

In the eighteenth century, the dominant discourses about investment activities were those of the moral pamphlet, comedy, satire, and visual allegory. The knowledge on which investments were based was marked by folly, 'the passion of avarice, the disease of fools and earth-worms' (*Truth* 1733: 13–14). Speculation is a 'deadly science, a most obscure and deluding game' (Mirabeau 1785: 77). Financial speculation is a 'scandalous mechanick' which has no reality in itself; it is bewitching, deadly, a perverted art which 'computes people out of their senses' (Some Seasonable Considerations 1720: 9). It is a mystery, a 'machine of trade with unheard-of engines'; it is an 'impenetrable artifice, poison acting at distance' (*The Villainy* 1701: 22). This small sample of metaphors, echoed in numerous publications, puts financial knowledge (and investments) in stark contrast with natural science and social philosophy, bound to discover the laws of the universe and of social order, respectively. A knowledge which is folly and 'devilish mechanick' can be integrated neither in the order of nature nor in that of the larger society.

While there are many descriptions of financial markets, we encounter throughout the century merely a single work claiming to be a manual on 'the Mystery and Iniquity of Stock-Jobbing': Thomas Mortimer's *Every Man His Own Broker*, published in 1761 in London and going through several editions. It had the declared aim of persuading 'the proprietors of our public funds to transact their own business; to make them the managers of their own property: the only effectual method that can be taken to reduce the great number of Stock-brokers; to diminish the extensive operations of stock-jobbing; and, in the end, to extirpate this infamous practice, which ruins many capital merchants and tradesmen every year' (Mortimer 1782 [1761]: xvi).

In the eighteenth century, investing was largely identified with gambling and clearly perceived as a noneconomic activity, which in no way can contribute to the wealth of the nation. Personal enrichment may occur, but it is socially illegitimate. Correspondingly, the discourses of investing were keyed as burlesque, treachery, blackmailing, and fraud. A widely used means of popular moral education were posters and illustrated brochures about wrecked lives. The prostitute, the pregnant unmarried woman, the thief, the robber, the liar, the dishonest merchant were among the usual figures. Crimes were told in lurid detail. Immoral lives always ended tragically, as a deterrent to the reader. Yet, these figures were not the only ones: the financial speculator, the gambler in stocks, was a constant presence in this panoply and his fate was not better than that of robbers (e.g. *The Life of Jonathan Wild* 1725; *A Complete Narrative* 1790).

Those who speculate are guilty of the sin of covetousness, which leads to fraud; they are disorderly, immoderate (*The Fatal Consequences* 1720: 8–10), degenerate, working against the public interest, dishonest, in a state of drunkenness and exaltation (Mirabeau 1787: 10, 19, 53). Stock trading is traffic by deception and cunning and a pernicious commerce. Financial markets destroy social order by attracting people from other professions into investments (*Sur la proposition* 1789: 8, 12). The public interest is 'screwed down' by 'the fraud, knavery, deceit and illusion' of financial speculation (*The Anatomy* 1719: 3–4).

Speculation is a poison which slowly destroys the state and leads to nonpayment of debts, which leads to disorder (Laporte 1789: 50). Financial speculation is a menace for the individual as well as for the social order.

The stage on which investors are encountered is the close universe of pubs, back alleys, and gardens, where the general rules of interaction are suspended. The communicative order of investing is predominantly oral: at the interaction level, the financial marketplace is constituted as a two-tiered conversational system requiring permanent agitation and presence. This conversational system, well adapted to multiple markets (the rule at the time) ascribes well-defined roles to investors, roles which require special ways of speaking and body techniques. Investors dispose of multiple price lists, more often than not forged. Forging whole issues of newspapers and staging political events for investment purposes was not very rare. A good example here is the staging of Napoleon's death for speculation purposes in 1814, a case that I have analyzed elsewhere (see for details Preda 2001). In this field, the typical investor figures are the bull, the bear, the sharper, the pigeon, the projector, the monkey, and the lame duck (see Figure 7.1). While some of these metaphors have become a staple of today's financial vocabulary, they do not

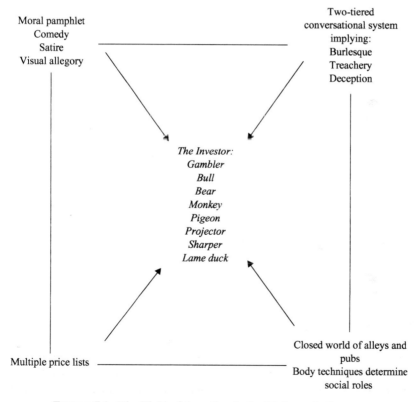

FIGURE 7.1. The Field of Investing in the Eighteenth Century

anymore identify investor figures in the way they did in the eighteenth century. One may still be bullish or bearish, but without being subjected to the behavioral scripts implied by these terms two centuries ago.

### The Reconfiguration of the Investor in the First Globalization Wave: The Investor-Scientist

In the mid-nineteenth century, under the impact of various social forces, the figure of the investor was reconfigured. Among the forces playing an important role here are railway engineers. Around 1845, construction and railway engineers became involved in railway economics and elaborated mathematical models of the demand and supply functions for railway transportation. While thus revolutionizing microeconomics (Ekelund and Hébert 1999: 54–5), engineers were responsible both for technical and economic aspects of railway companies, being involved in the evaluation of railway securities and their marketing to the public. We encounter examples of railway engineering treatises from the 1850s which discuss methods to evaluate railway securities and to speculate in them (Lardner 1850: 310). Engineers transfer the vocabulary of physics to the valuation of railway securities. They require observation and analysis in this process. Sheer luck or emotions are seen as irrelevant. The vocabulary of natural science replaces that of the moral pamphlet as *the* medium for representing financial investments.

This replacement is accompanied by the notion that financial markets are not governed by whims, emotions, or intrigues, but by objective laws. Discovering them is at the core of the efforts made by some stockbrokers in the same period. A prominent example in this respect is Émile Regnault's *Chance Calculus and the Philosophy of the Stock Exchange* (1863), which formulates for the first time the random walk hypothesis, crucial for the future development of mathematical finance (Jovanovic and Le Gall 2001; Preda 2004). Regnault argues that speculation should follow the example of physics and discover the objective laws which govern the market. True speculation must examine and know the constant laws of stock price variations; these laws are as universal as the gravitation laws (Regnault 1863: 143–4). No market actor can influence price variations in the long run since these obey to 'superior and providential laws' (p. 185). His contribution was two 'laws of differences', according to which (1) the differences between real and probable prices are a function of the square root of time and (2) prices tend toward the median value of this difference (p. 187). Regnault's work was followed by Henri Lefevre's (1870), another stockbroker who catered to individual, non-professional investors. Lefevre developed a graphic method for pricing derivatives; he started a mutual fund (the Union Financière) and devised a plan for national financial education; he invented a mechanical device for pricing derivatives (the auto-compteur), to be used on the floor of the stock exchange (see Preda 2004 for details). His graphic method was modified by Louis Bachelier (1964 [1900]) in his mathematical treatment of derivatives prices, which grounded the random walk hypothesis.

We should not underestimate the importance of the notion that financial markets are governed by objective, probabilistic laws, and not by a group of speculators. This notion relies on the assumption that large numbers of actors are present in the market, so that nobody can control it in the long run. It also purports to develop instruments for intervention in the market (e.g. for pricing financial derivatives). This implies not only describing, but changing the ways in which markets operate—a phenomenon analyzed by Donald MacKenzie and Yuval Millo (2003) as performativity. It should be stressed here again that these were investment manuals which did not address academic economists but investors. Developments crucial for derivatives markets and for financial economics were thus initiated in the mid-nineteenth century in the attempt to transform investors into scientists bound to discover the hidden, objective laws of financial investments.

The science of investing contributed to disentangling investments from gambling. The transformation of gambling into a medical condition (Brenner and Brenner 1990: 72–6), as well as the formal, probabilistic treatment of gambling problems (Bernstein 1996)—which occurred independently of medicalization—also played a part in this process. This new representation mode, disseminated by numerous investment manuals, stressed careful observation and analysis. It presented financial behavior as dispassionate, calm, grounded in permanent observation of market events and in problem solving (e.g. Castelli 1877; *Notions générales* 1877: 62–4).

Developments in price-recording technologies reinforced these demands. Until the late 1860s, prices were recorded on paper slips and circulated by courier boys (Downey 2000: 132–3). Multiple markets with multiple prices coexisted in the same building (Vidal 1910: 37–8; Walker 2001: 192–3). In 1867, telegraph engineers developed and introduced the stock ticker to Wall Street; in less than two decades, the ticker became a permanent fixture of Wall Street and of brokerage houses, as well as of the London Stock Exchange. One of the effects of the ticker was that it transformed parallel, sequential price information (as recorded on paper slips) into a continuous flow (Preda 2002). This flow demanded uninterrupted personal attention and observation on the part of investors. Since they had to react quicker to financial information, investors had to adopt artificial languages, exclusively expressing financial information. Telegraph companies edited and disseminated extensive code books for communicating this information. I will give here only two such examples: the first comes from *Hartfield's Wall Street Code* (1905) which contained over 450,000 cypher words. An investor would then telegraph his broker 'gabbiola baissabaci' instead of 'are you able to buy hundred shares?' Those using the manual of the Haight & Freese (a Philadelphia-based brokerage firm) would telegraph 'army event bandit calmly' instead of 'Cannot buy Canada Southern at your limit. Please reduce limit to 23' (*Guide to Investors* 1899: 385, 396). In this artificial language, one can build sentences using the word bandit, but one cannot build any sentence about bandits.

The new price-recording and communication technologies required body training: investors had to be able to observe the ticker tape uninterruptedly for hours (Wyckoff 1934: 37). Since the stock ticker recorded and visualized minute price differences, price charts became a new quality. A new analytical language was required in order to make sense of price movements, a language provided by chart analysis. In its turn, this reinforced the investor-scientist, bent on analyzing and understanding the hidden laws of financial markets. Here is how one of the pioneers of chart analysis defined the analyst emerging around 1900:

More and more I became impressed with the possibilities of making money through the study of the action of the market itself rather than the study of statistics. I wanted more knowledge on the subject; my subscribers continued to request more light. In many offices, active traders, more or less expert, scanned every transaction that appeared on the tape, evidently trying to scent out coming moves. They ignored statistics or earnings or such information, but they had great respect for previous swings, high and low prices, and other technical indications... Many of these traders sitting on high stools by the tickers had no other vocation; they devoted their entire time to this business of trading in stocks. As they became more expert, they seemed to operate a good deal on intuition. They were especially quick to detect the starting point of new moves, up or down, in stocks which had previously been inactive. (Wyckoff 1930: 171–2).

The general principles promoted by investment manuals (attention, observation, analysis) dovetailed with the categories of experience required by price-recording technologies (permanent attention to the price flow, concentration) and with the price charts which required a new analytical language. As Werner De Bondt shows in Chapter 8, constant study, information, and individual effort still rate high in the value hierarchy of contemporary investors. This does not mean, of course, that all deal-making, market manipulation, or emotions disappeared. Quite the contrary, but the investor-scientist distinguished between the tumultuous surface of the market and the hidden patterns of price movements which could be worked out through observation and analysis. In its turn, this reinforced the idea that the market cannot be consistently beaten in the long run and that its movements have an objective character, irreducible to individual intentions or manipulation. According to Jean Pierre Hassoun (Chapter 5 this volume), emotions do not disappear but become manageable. They are seen not as determining decisions, but as instruments in building up a personal relationship with the market.

The separation of the science of investing from ethics allowed grand speculators to represent themselves as strategists and planners, akin to military men, who (aided by technology) conceive, plan, and lead battles against their opponents. In his thinly disguised biography of the investor Jesse Livermore,

Edwin Lefevre described the grand speculator as follows:

Back to the ticker, one elbow leaning on the corner of the ticker-stand, tense, immobile, watching the cascading tape intently, his soul and mind and body merged into a pair of unblinking eyes to which every printed character was full of meaning, surcharged with significance, eloquent in his directness. The first volley had been fired by Dunlap; now Higgins; Willie was obeying orders; Cross and his artillery had arrived . . . The market began to go his way. Blood was being shed, and it was golden blood, and he was unscathed. There might be a day of reckoning later, perhaps tomorrow; to-day there should be one—for the bulls. He was a leader, and the unattached soldiers of fortune—the 'traders'—gathered under his flag and, without knowing it, fought for him, fought madly for dollars—more dollars—even as Rock fought for railroads, more railroads . . . the little ticker . . . sings its marvelous song of triumph and defeat in one. (Lefevre 1907: 53)

This heroic mode of representing grand investors is very much alive today; a fitting example is the styling of George Soros as the man who in the early 1990s single-handedly fought and won the battle against the Bank of England.

## The Right to Invest

In the early 1850s, parallel to the transformation of investment into a science, the question of the relationship between investing and human nature is reformulated. Crucial with respect to this was the distinction between 'true' and 'false' speculation made by some political thinkers and stock-brokers. False speculation or gambling is led by excess, emotions, and lack of study. True speculation is grounded in observation and study, conducted according to rules, useful and honest. It is nothing else than capital put to work and 'it cannot be lauded and encouraged enough by all governments because it is the veritable source of public credit' (Regnault 1863: 103). 'The speculator is the pioneer of progress, he foresees, combines in advance, forecasts' (Crampon 1863: 158). Pierre-Joseph Proudhon, one of the socialist leaders of the nineteenth century saw speculation as a creative social force (along with industry and trade), as an intrinsic feature of human nature and as an expression of human freedom; all human beings are endowed with this force and must therefore exercise it (1854: 23–5, 31). Consequently, everyone must have the freedom and the right to speculate. The working class must get the right to speculate too; for Proudhon, this meant abolishing the unequal access to the stock exchange and the monopoly of stockbrokers. Other authors concurred: 'Let the operations of the Bourse be free, give anybody the right to auction himself, at the auctioning hours, the commodities called stocks, bonds, public bonds, etc.' (Paoli 1864: 12). It also meant legalizing derivatives markets, which in France were illegal until 1885, yet a firm presence in Paris. New York and London made no difference in this respect.

Smaller investors could engage with lesser sums in derivatives trading, compared with the minimum order limits set by official stockbrokers. Consequently, the debates about broader social access to financial markets were enmeshed with arguments about the legality of derivatives markets.

Proudhon and his followers (some of whom, like Henri Lefevre, were stockbrokers) saw financial investments as a means of achieving social equality, of progress and self-enhancement for the working classes. Some prominent British Owenite socialists supported this argument (Thompson 1988: 158). The honest bourgeoisie should help the working classes by participating together in joint stock companies and hence speculating together:

Is it possible to admit that this societal movement [toward joint stock companies], resulting not from utopian theories but from economic necessities, and which invades all branches of production, shall stay eternally closed to the worker? That (financial) action is accessible only to the moneyed classes and that work will never accede to it? Shall we believe that the commercial society, by generalizing itself with an irresistible force, aims at reinstating a caste society, at deepening the cleavage between the bourgeoisie and the working class, and not at leading to the necessary and definitive fusion between these two classes, that is, to their emancipation and triumph? In fifty years, all national capital will be mobilized, all production values will be engaged to a social aim; the field of individual ownership will be reduced to the objects of consumption, or, as the [Civil] Code says, to fungible objects. Will the salary man, this old slave, excluded since the origins of the world from ownership, be still excluded from society, until the end of the world? In fifty years from now, work will have the weight of capital, and the former will write off the latter, and this will come true. (Proudhon 1854: 337)

The argument that the stock exchange can solve tensions between social classes was taken over by authors who saw investing as grounded in objective, scientific rules (e.g. Lefevre 1870: v–vii). The Stock Exchange was the heart of the social organism, recycling money in the same way the heart recycles blood (p. 243). 'The stock exchange is the expression of public credit. The public credit is the expression of society's state of progress. In our era, so material and so progressive, everything must converge toward the stock exchange. It's like the heart which, in a great body receives life and diffuses it throughout all the limbs' (Regnault 1863: 210).

Thus, the right to invest, grounded in human nature, was presented as an argument in struggles for widening social access to financial investments. In the late nineteenth century United States, the fights between bucket shops and official stockbrokers included the argument (coming from the bucket shops) that small investors have a right to accede financial investments and that bucket shops were fulfilling an important social function (Hochfelder 2003).

The figure of the investor as endowed with rights has come to play a significant role in the regulatory debates triggered by the Enron scandal (see Richard Swedberg, Chapter 9 in this volume). The regulations concerning fair access to financial information (like the Sarbanes–Oxley Act of 2002) rely on the assumption that smaller investors have a right to true information if financial markets are to allocate resources efficiently. The (information) rights of investors have to be protected as a necessary prerequisite of efficient markets (Spencer 2000: 104–5). With that, financial economics has transformed the issue of rights from a moral and legal topic into a scientific one: rights are embedded into the normative model of market efficiency.

Increasingly, the political economy of the nineteenth century acknowledged financial investments as an economic activity. Whereas for Adam Smith and other late eighteenth century thinkers, they were situated outside the economic sphere, political economists a century later began acknowledging financial markets as a key social institution. The most prominent figure here is perhaps Walter Bagehot (1874), though by far not the only one (e.g. Proudhon 1854: 31). This recognition meant that the investor was now conceived as an economic actor fulfilling important functions: his behavior is accounted for in terms of rules, not of emotions or whims (see Figure 7.2). The investor keeps the market moving, attracts capital which otherwise will

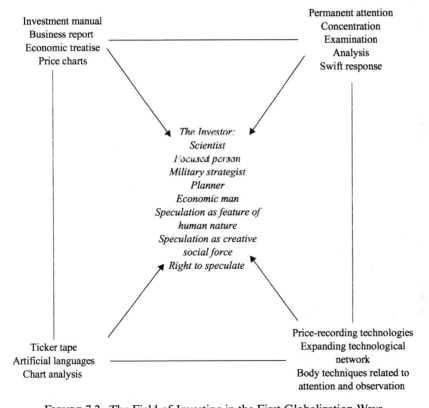

FIGURE 7.2. The Field of Investing in the First Globalization Wave

be idle, and does not let emotions prevail:

Above all, it is stagnation that we dread in the financial market, since with stagnation business is paralyzed and values vanish. The speculation, by contrary, by its sudden movements, its vain alarms, its failed illusions, its unexpected chances, its alternatives of high and low, keeps financial activity going and attracts on the stock exchange capitals which otherwise would be idle. Not only that speculation prevents markets from being invaded by apathy, but it also helps avoid the dangers of too high differences which menace from time to time public fortune; because, in the time of foolish trust, speculation coldly calculates tomorrow's deceptions and multiplies its sales; in moments of blind panic, speculation foresees the return to trust and doubles its acquisitions. (Guillard 1875: 539–40).

The acknowledgment of the investor from the left of the political spectrum does not mean that all tensions and criticisms against investing vanish or that all political doctrines suddenly embraced the investor. Nineteenth century US progressivism, for instance, was a vocal critic of speculation in commodities derivatives and of grand speculators (less so of stock markets). The field of investing was not void of tensions; representational modes like pamphlets and satire do not disappear. They continue to exist, but on the fringes of the field; the investor as a fool, an insider, or a manipulator are still with us. But they are counterbalanced by the strategist, the scientist, the planner: he who is not a scientist and a planner is a foolish investor nowadays. In other words, this field generates normative categories of action with respect to which other action paths are constructed as deviant.


## Conclusion

I have argued that the cultural legacy of the first globalization wave consists, among others, in the figure of the investor endowed with universal legitimacy and validity. It relies on the interrelated, universal principles that investment is a science and investing is grounded in rights. These principles may obscure the fact that deceit, manipulation, and inequality in the market are still very much with us. But they also open possibilities for action which otherwise would not be there: witness contemporary struggles around investor rights, access to financial information, and correct (true) information. If we would still believe that investing is knavery, fraud, and deceit—that these are perfectly legitimate means in financial transactions—we would accept loss of lifetime savings in financial scandals like Enron as normal. But we do not accept it as normal; we believe in the right to access true financial information, to study it, to make informed decision, and to defend our rights in the marketplace. We believe in the right to pursue in justice deviants from this norm. The cultural legacy of the first globalization wave (universally valid knowledge and rights) is still with us.

## Notes

1. The main characteristics of the first globalization wave are price convergence and market integration (O'Rourke and Williamson 1999: 2, 4; Rousseau and Sylla 2001: 7). While price convergence means a historically narrowing gap in real wages and cost of capital between the two sides of the Atlantic, integration designates the increasing interdependence (and reciprocal influence) of capital, production factors, and labor markets. This means, among others, that events in one market influence prices in other markets, and that this process gains in speed, so that the time gap between price changes in different markets narrows too. The first globalization wave is also characterized by social and economic transformations which led to the territorial diffusion of investment activities, their broader social outreach, and a considerable increase in the number of investors. These transformations, which cannot be detailed here, include the consolidation of the nation-state (Neal 1990), economic policy favoring joint-stock companies (Dobbin 1994; Alborn 1998), international migration (Wilkins 1999) and urbanization, and the rise of the news industry (Blondheim 1994; Leyshon and Thrift 1997). Economic historians however, have been quick to notice that factors like urbanization, international migration, the electric telegraph, or economic policy, while important, are not enough. As Jonathan Baskin and Paul Miranti (1997: 134) put it, market integration and the attraction of capital from wide geographic areas presuppose 'procedures enabling investors to evaluate the underlying worth of traded securities' in the same or similar ways. These procedures imply a knowledge framework mutually recognized and accepted over such an area: in other words, one with global features and a potential for expansion. In this framework, financial investments are acknowledged as socially legitimate and even desirable; moral doubts are, for all practical purposes, suspended; social actors can make sense of investing with respect to their personal and social lives.

## References

*A Complete Narrative of the Life, Adventures, Frauds, and Forgeries, of Thomas Tyler, the Celebrated Swindler, Who Was Executed November 24, 1790*. 1790. London.

Alborn, T. 1998. *Conceiving Companies: Joint-Stock Politics in Victorian England*. London: Routledge.

Bachelier, L. 1964 [1900]. 'Theory of Speculation', in *The Random Character of Stock Market Prices*, Cooter, P. H. (ed.). Cambridge, MA: MIT Press, 17–78.

Bagehot, W. 1874. *Lombard Street: A Description of Money Market*. London: King.

Baskin, J. and Miranti, P. 1997. *A History of Corporate Finance*. Cambridge: Cambridge University Press.

Bernstein, P. 1996. *Against the Gods: The Remarkable Story of Risk*. New York, NY: Wiley.

Blondheim, M. 1994. *News Over the Wires. The Telegraph and the Flow of Public Information in America, 1844–1897*. Cambrige, MA: Harvard University Press.

Boltanski, L. and Chiapello, E. 1999. *Le nouvel esprit du capitalisme*. Paris: Gallimard.

Boltanski, L. and Thévenot, L. 1991. *De la justification. Les économies de la grandeur.* Paris: Gallimard.

Bourdieu, P. 1996. *The Rules of Art. Genesis and Structure of the Literary Field.* Cambridge: Polity Press.

Brenner, R. and Brenner, G. A. 1990. *Gambling and Speculation: A Theory, a History, and a Future of Some Human Decisions.* Cambridge: Cambridge University Press.

Carruthers, B. 1996. *City of Capital. Politics and Markets in the English Financial Revolution.* Princeton, NJ: Princeton University Press.

Castelli, C. 1877. *The Theory of 'Options' in Stocks and Shares.* London: Mathieson.

Chancellor, E. 1999. *Devil Take the Hindmost. A History of Financial Speculation.* New York, NY: Farrar, Straus and Giroux.

Crampon, A. 1863. *La Bourse. Guide pratique a l'usage des gens du monde.* Paris: H. Durandin.

Dobbin, F. 1994. *Forging Industrial Policy. The United States, Britain, and France in the Railway Age.* Cambridge: Cambridge University Press.

Downey, G. 2000. 'Running Somewhere between Men and Women. Gender in the Construction of the Telegraph Messenger Boy', *Knowledge and Society* 12: 129–52.

DuPlessis, R. 2002. 'Capital Formations', in *The Culture of Capital. Property, Cities, and Knowledge in Early Modern England*, Turner, H. S. (ed.). New York, NY: Routledge, 27–50.

Ekelund, R. B. Jr. and Hébert, R. 1999. *Secret Origins of Modern Microeconomics. Dupuit and the Engineers.* Chicago: The University of Chicago Press.

Elias, N. 1983 [1969]. *The Court Society.* Oxford: Blackwell.

Garber, P. 2000. *Famous First Bubbles. The Fundamentals of Early Manias.* Cambridge, MA: The MIT Press.

Goffman, E. 1959. *The Presentation of Self in Everyday Life.* New York, NY: Doubleday.

*Guide to Investors. Haight & Freese's Information to Investors and Opérators in Stocks, Grain and Cotton.* 1899. Philadelphia, PA: Haight & Freese.

Guillard, E. 1875. *The Operations of the Stock Exchange [Les operations de Bourse].* Paris: Guillaumin et Cie.

*Hartfield's Wall Street Code.* 1905. New York, NY: Hartfield Telegraphic Code Publishing Company.

Hirschman, A. O. 1992. *Rival Views of Market Society and Other Recent Essays.* Cambridge, MA: Harvard University Press.

Hochfelder, D. 2003. *'The Stock Ticker, Bucket Shops, and the Small Investor as an Economic and Moral Problem, 1870–1929'*, Unpublished Manuscript.

Jovanovic, F. and Le Gall, P. 2001. 'Does God Practice a Random Walk? The "Financial Physics" of a Nineteenth-Century Forerunner, Jules Regnault', *European Journal of the History of Economic Thought* 8(3): 332–62.

Laporte. 1789. *Essai sur la legislation et les finances de la France.* Bergerac: J. B. Puynesge.

Lardner, D. 1850. *The Steam Engine Familiarly Explained and Illustrated.* Philadelphia, PA: A. Hart.

Lefevre, E. 1907. *Sampson Rock of Wall Street.* New York, NY: Harper & Brothers.

Lefevre, H. 1870. *Traité des valeurs mobilières et des opérations de Bourse.* Paris: É. Lachaud.

Leyshon, A. and Thrift, N. 1997. *Money/Space. Geographies of Monetary Transformation*. London: Routledge.

MacKenzie, D. and Millo, Y. 2003. 'Constructing a Market, Performing Theory: The Historical Sociology of a Financial Derivatives Exchange', in *American Journal of Sociology* 109(1): 107–46.

Marx, Karl. 2002 [1872]. *Das Kapital*. Köln: Parkland.

Mirabeau, H. G. 1785. *Lettre à M. Le Coulteux de la Noraye, sur la Banque de Saint Charles & sur la Caisse d'Escompte*. Brussels.

—— 1787. *Denonciation de l'Agiotage au Roi et a l'assemblée des notables*. Paris.

Mortimer, T. 1782 [1761]. *Every Man His Own Broker*. London: G. Robinson.

Mukerji, C. 1997. *Territorial Ambitions and the Gardens of Versailles*. New York, NY: Cambridge University Press.

Neal, L. 1990. *The Rise of Financial Capitalism. International Capital Markets in the Age of Reason*. Cambridge: Cambridge University Press.

*Notions générales de Bourse, de banque & de change*. 1877. Paris: le Moniteur des Fonds Publics.

O'Rourke, K. and Williamson, J. 1999. *Globalization and History. The Evolution of a Nineteenth-Century Atlantic Economy*. Cambridge, MA: MIT Press.

Paoli. 1864. *La Bourse et ses tripots*. Paris: Arnauld de Vresse.

Pollner, M. 2002. 'Inside the Bubble: Communion, Cognition, and Deep Play at the Intersection of Wall Street and Cyberspace', in *Virtual Society? Technology, Cyberbole, Reality*, Woolgar, S. (ed.). Oxford: Oxford University Press, 230–46.

Preda, A. 2001. 'In the Enchanted Grove: Financial Conversations and the Marketplace in England and France in the 18th Century', *Journal of Historical Sociology* 14(3): 276–307.

—— 2002. 'On Ticks and Tapes: Financial Knowledge, Communicative Practices, and Information Technologies on 19th Century Financial Markets'. www.coi.columbia. edu/ssf/papers.html#Preda.

—— 2004. 'Informative Prices, Rational Investors: The Emergence of the Random Walk Hypothesis and the Nineteenth-Century "Science of Financial Investments"', *History of Political Economy* 36(2): 351–86.

[Proudhon, P.-J.] 1854. *Manuel du spéculateur à la Bourse*. Paris: Garnier-frères.

Regnault, E. 1863. *Calcul des chances et philosophie de la Bourse*. Paris: Mallet-Bachelier.

Rosenberg, N. 2000. *Schumpeter and the Endogeneity of Technology. Some American Perspectives*. London: Routledge.

Rousseau, P. and Sylla, R. 2001. 'Financial Systems, Economic Growth, and Globalization', NBER Working Paper No. 8323, Cambridge, MA.

Schama, S. 1997 [1987]. *The Embarassment of Riches. An Interpretation of the Dutch Culture in the Golden Age*. New York, NY: Vintage.

Schumpeter, J. 1934. *The Theory of Economic Development*. Cambridge, MA: Harvard University Press.

—— 1991. *The Economics and Sociology of Capitalism*, Swedberg, R. (ed.). Princeton, NJ: Princeton, University Press.

Simmel, G. 1989 [1901]. *Philosophie des Geldes*. Frankfurt: Suhrkamp.

Smith, A. 1991 [1776]. *The Wealth of Nations*. Amherst, NY: Prometheus Books.

*Some Seasonable Considerations For Those Who Are Desirous, By Subscription, or Purchase, to Become Proprietors of South-Sea Stock*. 1720. London: J. Morphew.

Spencer, P. D. 2000. *The Structure and Regulation of Financial Markets.* Oxford: Oxford University Press.

*Sur la proposition du premier ministre des finances, relative à la Caisse d'escompte.* 1789. Paris: Baudouin.

Sylla, R. A. 1998. 'US Securities Markets and the Banking System, 1790–1840', *Federal Reserve Bank of Saint Louis Review* 80(3): 83–98.

——1999a. 'Emerging Markets in History: The United States, Japan, and Argentina', in *Global Competition and Integration*, Sato, R. (ed.). Boston: Kluwer, 427–46.

——1999b. *The State, the Financial System and Economic Modernization.* Cambridge: Cambridge University Press.

Tarde, G. 1902. *Psychologie èconomique*, Vol. I–II. Paris: Alcan.

*The Anatomy of Exchange-Alley.* 1719. London: E. Smith.

*The Fatal Consequences of Gaming and Stock-Jobbing.* 1720. London: T. Jauncy.

*The Life of Jonathan Wild, from his Birth to his Death. Containing His Rise and Progress in Roguery.* 1725. London: T. Warner.

*The Villainy of Stock-Jobbers Detected.* 1701. London.

Thompson, Noel. 1988. *The Market and Its Critics. Socialist Political Economy in 19th Century Britain.* London: Routledge.

*Truth. A Letter to the Gentlemen of Exchange Alley.* 1733. London: T. Cooper.

Vidal, E. 1910. *The History and Methods of the Paris Bourse.* Washington, DC: Government Printing Office.

Walker, D. 2001. 'A Factual Account of the Functioning of the 19th Century Paris Bourse', *European Journal for the History of Economic Thought* 8(2): 186–207.

Weber, M. 1988 [1920]. *Gesammelte Aufsätze zur Religionssoziologie.* Tübingen: Mohr Siebeck.

——2000 [1894]. 'Die Börse', *Theory and Society* 29: 305–38.

Wilkins, M. 1999. 'Cosmopolitan Finance in the 1920s: New York's Emergence as an International Financial Centre', in *The State, the Financial System and Economic Modernization*, Sylla, R., Tilly, R., and Tortella, G. (eds.). Cambridge: Cambridge University Press, 271–91.

Wright, R. E. 2001. *Origins of Commercial Banking in America, 1750–1800.* Lanham, MD: Rowman & Littlefield.

Wyckoff, R. D. 1930. *Wall Street Ventures and Adventures.* New York, NY: Harper & Brothers.

——1934. 'It's not the *Kind* of a Chart But Your Ability to Interpret That Counts', *Stock Market Technique* 3(2): 37–9.

# 8

# The Values and Beliefs of European Investors

WERNER DE BONDT

## Introduction

How are the values and beliefs of investors linked to the perceived attractiveness of asset classes and investment strategies? How do self-confidence, financial sophistication, and trust in expert financial advisors influence investment strategy? Little is known about these important questions.

Yet, that it is beneficial 'to know your customers' no financial practitioner will deny. In order to grow and to protect the wealth of their clients, banks, mutual funds, pension funds, money management companies, and other financial institutions do well to understand the behavior of investors. Globalization has greatly added to the complexity of money management since capital moves easily across borders. Today, large financial institutions have clients that live all over the world.

Saving and investment behavior varies between people because of differing economic circumstances (e.g. investment objectives and available resources) and differing institutional, legal, and tax arrangements. However, culture is also a fundamental contributing factor—a factor that, I regret, has often been overlooked by financial economists.

What is culture? Geert Hofstede (1980) defines culture as 'the collective mental programming that distinguishes one group of people from another'. Certain opinions, values, and beliefs tend to go together in what I call cognitive schemas or *mental frames*.[1]

I thank Arianna Arzeni, Nicholas Barberis, Vera Cooremans, Marilys Drevet, Maria Kousathana, Melissa Mallinson, Philippe Neve, Peter O' Farrell, Elias Khalil, Elke Persoons, Alex Preda, Eleanor de Rosmorduc, Dirk Schiereck, Steven Sharpe, Sandy West, and Patrick Zurstrassen for assistance, comments, and encouragement. Earlier summaries of this research were presented at the Board of Governors of the Federal Reserve System, the conference on 'Behavioral Economics and Neoclassical Economics: Continuity or Discontinuity' organized by the American Institute for Economic Research, the 'Bears' conference at the University of Illinois at Chicago, the Global Finance Conference, and the Boston Security Analysts Society. I thank Credit Agricole Indosuez Luxembourg and the University of Wisconsin-Madison for generous financial support. This article builds on earlier work that I co-authored with Patrick Zurstrassen and Arianna Arzeni and that was published in the Revue d'Économie Financière.

In *The Nature of Human Nature* (1937) Ellsworth Faris, an influential sociologist at the University of Chicago and a disciple of George Herbert Mead, said that with respect to the members of a group the cultural habits (i.e. the uniformities of thought, speech, and conduct) are preexisting 'so that the most important aspects of a given person are to be traced back to influences existing in the culture into which he comes'. Faris's conception of social psychology resembled what Peter Berger and Thomas Luckmann (1966) and others later called the social construction of reality. Faris considered the search for the irreducible elements of consciousness (e.g. instinct theory or the tabula rasa of behaviorism) to be futile because 'human nature is formed in social interaction'. Mind cannot be separated from culture. The interior life is a miniature of social life.[2]

How does culture influence behavior? Over the decades, this grand topic has been studied by nearly all the social sciences. The tradition goes back to the classic work of Max Weber in sociology, *The Protestant Ethic and the Spirit of Capitalism* (2002 [1904]). The topic has also been investigated in anthropology (Benedict 1959 [1934]), psychology (McClelland 1961; Smith and Harris Bond 1993), political science (Inglehart 1997; Harrison and Huntington 2000), economics (Landes 1998), and business (Hofstede 1980; Hampden-Turner and Trompenaars 1993).[3]

Cognitive schemas are connected to motivational strivings (D'Andrade and Strauss 1992). Jerome Bruner discusses how meaningful human action is situated in cultural settings and how it relies on folk psychology. '(P)eople are assumed to have world knowledge that takes the form of beliefs, and are assumed to use (it) in carrying out any program of desire or action' (1990: 40). For instance, an individual who sees himself as self-disciplined, who worries about the future, and who believes that the government ought to reduce the national debt, may prefer a low-risk portfolio heavily loaded with cash. Investors who tilt their portfolios towards equity may worry less about tomorrow, they may be more likely to see themselves as leaders, and they may believe more firmly that entrepreneurial values benefit society. Configurations of values and beliefs characterize groups of people.

The configurations are not random. Yet, it is impossible to derive them from axiomatic principles as suggested by rational choice theory. Mental frames are frugal. Most of the time they help decisionmakers. On occasion, though, they mislead. Mental frames can be very unsophisticated and yet resist change. Consider, for example, all the pseudoscience and superstition that envelop us on the benefits of herbal medicines. Hence, it is easy to see that financial literacy is at the core of investment decision making. What do people really know? When a financial problem presents itself, there may be no unitary model of truth even though there are degrees of knowledge. Many people use tacit models that are demonstrably false (Salter 1983). This should not surprise us. The logic of the mind is not Aristotelian or Cartesian. It is truly psychological and sociological.

The purpose of this study is to identify and to interpret relevant clusters of values and beliefs among semi-affluent and affluent European investors. Mental frames matter because they are correlated with decisions, for example, portfolio choice and asset allocation.

I rely on survey methods to investigate how people perceive themselves and their surroundings. Of course, much of what people know, they accept on faith. (What happened at Waterloo? Are milk and cheese rich in calcium? Is Ecuador a country in South America? Are stocks the best investment for the long run?) Every child that is born cannot possibly recreate from scratch all of our collective knowledge about the universe. Mental frames are socially shared. To a significant degree, they are fabricated by educators, opinion leaders, and men in advertising ('At Ford, quality is job one'). They are passed on from the old to the young. The study, therefore, examines the mind of the crowd, particularly as it relates to saving and investment.[4]

Evidently, my approach is very different from the standard economic perspective of modern finance. There, financial decision making is studied in deductive fashion. It is reduced to a mathematical optimization problem: What is the appropriate investment strategy for rational investors? Modern finance is based on the classical notion of *homo economicus*, that is, the normative axioms that underlie expected utility theory, risk aversion, rational expectations, and Bayesian updating. It assumes that individuals have considerable knowledge about the fundamental structure of the economy. Financial economics does not treat cognition as a scarce resource. Herbert Simon (1983) calls this approach the Olympic model. Within modern finance, there is little room for the study of cultural differences.[5]

The new field of behavioral finance takes a mostly inductive approach. It focuses on what people really do. Of course, what investors do may be very different from what, in principle, they should do. Richard Thaler and I (1994) present a survey of behavioral finance. In experiments, people often willingly violate the rational axioms that form the foundation of modern finance (Slovic 1972; Tversky and Kahneman 1986). Over the years, much empirical work has documented a wide gap between reality and the predictions of portfolio and asset pricing theory. In many instances, behavioral hypotheses led to the discovery of these anomalous facts. In past work (De Bondt 1998), I have listed four classes of anomalies in the behavior of individual investors. These anomalies relate to irregular perceptions of the dynamics of equity prices, perceptions of value, risk management, and trading practices. What is surprising is the failure of many people to infer basic investment principles from years of experience, for example, the benefits of diversification.

At this point in time, there is only limited prior research that takes a specific cultural/lifestyle/demographic point of view. Some early research was done by US financial planners and advisors, for example, Marilyn Barnewall (1987), Ronald Kaiser (1987), William Danko, and Thomas Stanley (Stanley and Danko 1996; Stanley 2000). With few exceptions (e.g. Warren et al. 1990; MacGregor et al. 1999), this work tends toward non-quantitative reports based on the writers' experiences with clients. A related line of work develops risk-assessment tools that help advisors determine what investment products are most suitable in view of their clients' risk tolerance (e.g. see Opdyke 2000).

Hereafter, I put forward a non-technical overview of the study. Limitations of space preclude a full statistical analysis.

## The Survey

As stated before, I use standard questionnaire methods. The survey—the largest ever conducted on this topic in Europe—was carried out in March/ April 2001 in cooperation with the surveying network TNS (Dimarso in Belgium, Sofrès in France, Emnid in Germany, Abacus in Italy, Demoscopia in Spain, and Taylor-Nelson in the United Kingdom). It was administered to households that were known to invest funds into stocks, bonds, or mutual funds. I received 3,125 valid responses, approximately 500 in each of the following countries: Belgium, Britain, France, Germany, Italy, and Spain.

The survey was written in English and translated into Dutch, French, German, Spanish, and Italian. My coworkers and I spent great effort making sure that the translations exactly matched the original English text. A limited number of questions were previously studied in the United States. In a pretest of the survey in March 2001, a focus group of Belgian investors responded to the questionnaire. They discussed every question at length.

Each survey contained 237 questions relating to (1) demographics and lifestyle, (2) income and wealth, (3) financial expertise, (4) personal values and beliefs, (5) values and beliefs about the world, (6) values and beliefs that guide investment strategy, and (7) the relative merit of different asset classes. Investors' values and beliefs are difficult to capture. For this reason, I asked multiple questions probing for the same underlying behavioral dimension, for example, whether people view themselves as being happy, as leaders, etc. The analysis is based on a total of more than 900,000 responses.

## The European Investor

I start with a brief statistical portrait of the respondents. Tables 8.1–8.4 show a selection of data organized by country. The text below often describes the average European respondent.

Judging from the demographic, economic and lifestyle data, it is unmistakable that I sampled semi-affluent, upper middle-class European investors. For a majority of respondents (56%), the investible wealth is between 100,000 and 1 million Euro (2% invest more than 1 million Euro), 40% are employed full-time while 34% are retired. These people are strong savers: 53% of the sample save more than 5% of their annual income; 59% receive interest income; 45% receive dividends; 17% receive real estate investment income. A large majority of respondents own a home (84%) and about 20% own a second home; 71% have no mortgage debt.

Most respondents (87%) are married; 56% are male; 44% have children who are financially dependent; less than 10% have parents who are financial dependent; 67% plan to leave a bequest.

Of the respondents, 74% are generally in good health, 57% are under the age of 55. They are educated (e.g. 43% are multilingual) and culturally sophisticated. For instance, a majority go to the theater and read books—54% read five or more books a year, assuming that the purchase of a book implies that it is read; 70% regularly use credit cards, 44% subscribe to a daily newspaper, and 43% use a personal computer regularly. The sample respondents' travel data: 54% have left the European continent; 21% have visited the United States.[6]

Because we want to learn about the links between culture and investment decision making, it is interesting to examine how the respondents perceive their own identity, for example, nationality and religious affiliation, 15% think of themselves as 'citizens of the world' (the highest percentage is observed for residents of Spain), 20% as 'citizens of Europe' (the highest score is for Italy), and 52% as citizens of the country where they reside (the highest score, 75%, is for Britain). Finally, 12% see themselves as citizens of a particular region within a country (the highest score is for Belgium). Four countries in the sample are overwhelmingly Catholic (Belgium, France, Italy, and Spain). The majority of British respondents are Anglican or Protestant. In Germany, 45% of the respondents are Protestant; 38% catholic. On average, 29% regularly

TABLE 8.1. Demographic Descriptors

|  | Belgium | Britain | France | Germany | Italy | Spain |
|---|---|---|---|---|---|---|
| Number of respondents | 515 | 492 | 502 | 550 | 560 | 506 |
| % Male | 49 | 41 | 53 | 61 | 80 | 45 |
| % Married | 88 | 85 | 84 | 87 | 93 | 94 |
| % No dependent children | 57 | 67 | 70 | 60 | 41 | 35 |
| % No dependent parents | 97 | 94 | 96 | 93 | 94 | 86 |
| Age < 35 | 16 | 6 | 13 | 17 | 7 | 18 |
| Age < 55 | 66 | 43 | 47 | 54 | 63 | 70 |

*Note*: Listed in the table are the number of survey respondents with their main residence in Belgium, Britain, France, Germany, Italy, and Spain; and the fraction of respondents who are male, married, without dependent children, without dependent parents, and aged below 35 or below 55.

TABLE 8.2. Employment, Income, Wealth, and Saving

|  | Belgium | Britain | France | Germany | Italy | Spain |
|---|---|---|---|---|---|---|
| Employed full-time | 48 | 36 | 42 | 42 | 63 | 52 |
| Self-employed | 5 | 5 | 3 | 6 | 12 | 6 |
| Homemaker | 9 | 7 | 3 | 7 | 4 | 22 |
| Retired | 28 | 43 | 45 | 35 | 30 | 17 |
| Income > 50,000 Euro | 13 | 14 | 11 | 16 | 10 | 30 |
| Income > 100,000 Euro | 1 | 3 | 1 | 2 | 1 | 5 |
| No dividend income | 61 | 22 | 62 | 45 | 61 | 51 |
| No interest income | 35 | 16 | 59 | 23 | 43 | 47 |
| No real estate income | 82 | 95 | 76 | 80 | 63 | 83 |
| Wealth > 300,000 Euro | 11 | 21 | 12 | 21 | 15 | 8 |
| Owns second home | 9 | 4 | 20 | 15 | 27 | 34 |
| Saving < 5% of income | 40 | 41 | 39 | 38 | 46 | 40 |
| C-debt < 5,000 Euro | 88 | 87 | 87 | 91 | 90 | 90 |
| M-debt < 20,000 Euro | 64 | 74 | 80 | 40 | 89 | 81 |

*Note*: Listed in the table are the percentage of respondents in each country who are employed, self-employed, retired, or who are homemakers. Also listed are statistics relating to income, savings, wealth, and home ownership, for example, the percentage of respondents with annual income above 50,000 Euro, with annual income above 100,000 Euro, and the percentage of respondents without dividend, interest, or real estate income, C-debt denotes consumer debt, M-debt, mortgage debt.

TABLE 8.3. Lifestyle

|  | Belgium | Britain | France | Germany | Italy | Spain |
|---|---|---|---|---|---|---|
| Citizen of country of birth/residence | 48 | 75 | 64 | 52 | 34 | 42 |
| EU/world citizen | 39 | 15 | 25 | 34 | 54 | 40 |
| Roman Catholic | 92 | 10 | 87 | 38 | 98 | 94 |
| Protestant/Anglican | 1 | 73 | 2 | 45 | 0 | 0 |
| Practicing | 23 | 24 | 18 | 21 | 49 | 39 |
| Travel outside Europe | 56 | 70 | 63 | 60 | 42 | 33 |
| Travel to US | 23 | 44 | 23 | 29 | 17 | 8 |
| Speak > 1 language | 67 | 23 | 31 | 64 | 36 | 44 |
| Higher education | 70 | 46 | 47 | 61 | 72 | 43 |
| Buys > 5 books/year | 44 | 57 | 55 | 65 | 49 | 55 |
| Computer literate | 71 | 72 | 63 | 75 | 63 | 69 |

*Note*: Listed in the table are the percentage of respondents in each country who describe themselves as 'citizens of their country of birth or residence', and as 'citizens of Europe' or 'citizens of the world'. Lifestyle variables related to religion, travel, and education are also listed.

attend church services. This percentage is significantly higher in Italy (49%) and Spain (39%), and it is significantly lower in France (18%). How do European investors manage their portfolios? Most go about the job themselves (77%), some do it with the help of family and friends (18%), press stories

(37%), and money newsletters (11%); 22% rely on professional advisors, and 44% count on guidance from bank employees. Surprisingly, 62% say that they spend more than 30 minutes a day 'reading financial magazines and watching financial news'.

Compared to investors in the United States, the average European investor looks conservative. The investments that are most favored are bank savings accounts and various fixed-income instruments. Relatively few investors trade stock options (6%), trade securities on-line (5%), or invest in assets outside Western Europe (12%). However, 38% of Europeans say that they invest in shares of large companies; 39% say that they invest in mutual funds. Five years ago, the corresponding figures were 29% and 28%, respectively. The respondents estimate that, for their own parents, the figures are, respectively, 13% and 12%. As seen in Table 8.4, these statistics differ quite strongly by country.

Of the survey participants, 63% believe that the average annual returns on their portfolios during the last five years were between 3% and 12%. Of the sample, 74% expect to earn a similar annual rate of return in the future, and 5% expect to earn more than 12% per year. The subjective estimates of GDP growth, unemployment, and inflation rates, also listed in Table 8.4, are remarkably sensible and more accurate than may have been expected based on opinion polls and other research in the United States.

TABLE 8.4. Financial Sophistication

|  | Belgium | Britain | France | Germany | Italy | Spain |
|---|---|---|---|---|---|---|
| Blue chips, now | 26 | 65 | 33 | 36 | 30 | 41 |
| Five years ago | 18 | 58 | 27 | 26 | 14 | 36 |
| Parents | 13 | 24 | 16 | 2 | 8 | 17 |
| Equity > 20% wealth | 12 | 12 | 6 | 10 | 15 | 6 |
| Fixed > 20% wealth | 30 | 26 | 14 | 15 | 25 | 12 |
| Traded options | 9 | 5 | 3 | 11 | 1 | 7 |
| Invested outside Europe | 13 | 14 | 4 | 13 | 17 | 6 |
| Expected rate of return | 5.7 | 5.2 | 5.1 | 6.6 | 5.2 | 4.9 |
| Past rate of return | 4.3 | 5.3 | 4.9 | 3.8 | 3.8 | 3.9 |
| GNP growth rate | 2.3 | 1.5 | 2.6 | 1.9 | 1.9 | 2.3 |
| Unemployment rate | 10.3 | 9.3 | 11.1 | 11.8 | 10.4 | 12.1 |
| Inflation rate | 3.6 | 4.0 | 3.2 | 4.3 | 4.9 | 4.1 |

*Note*: Listed in the table are the percentage of sample respondents who invest in blue chip companies, now, five years ago, and whose parents did; the percentage of respondents with more than 20% of their reported financial wealth in equity or fixed income; the percentage of respondents who have traded options, at least once in their lifetimes; and the percentage of respondents who invest outside Western Europe. I also report the average respondent estimates of (i) the future expected annual rate of return on the investment portfolio; (ii) the average annual rate of return over the last five years; (iii) the expected annual GNP growth rate; (iv) the current 'true' unemployment rate; and (v) the current 'true' annual inflation rate.

## Values and Beliefs

In order to capture the values and beliefs of investors, I was forced to make many judicious a priori choices about which opinions may be most pertinent in an investment context. I relied on the prior literature in financial psychology (e.g. De Bondt and Thaler 1995; De Bondt 1998; Warneryd 2001), the feedback from the focus group, as well as my own conjectures.

The respondents were asked to agree or disagree with thirty-nine statements listed in Table 8.5. I tried to capture (1) the sample respondents' personal values and beliefs (seventeen statements); (2) their values and beliefs about the world (nine statements); and (3) their values and beliefs that guide investment strategy (thirteen statements). However, the participants were not confronted with these exact statements. Instead, every statement was assessed with 2–5 questions. The questions about values and beliefs were presented in random order.[7]

Multiple questions allow me to cross-check the answers and to obtain reliable measures. Strong disagreement is coded as −1.0; weak disagreement as −0.5; a neutral position as 0.0; weak agreement as 0.5; strong agreement as 1.0. For every statement and for every respondent, I find the mean score.

For example, the statement 'I enjoy luxury' (A4) is scored based on the following three questions:

I save in order to buy luxury items.
I like a simple natural lifestyle. (-)
I like to dress with a touch of class. In a social setting, it is important how you look.

Since the enjoyment of a simple natural lifestyle is at odds with delight in luxury, I change the sign of the scores for question 2 (marked with (-)). As is seen in Table 8.5, the average European firmly denies that he or she enjoys luxury. The average score is −0.40 and the standard deviation across all survey participants is 0.49. The lowest average score is found in France.

A second example is the statement 'Globalization benefits society' (B2). In this case, I use four questions:

1. Globalization and free trade hurt the interests of workers. (-)
2. American culture is changing Europe for the better.
3. Cross-border corporate mergers and acquisitions are a big plus for consumers.
4. Our cities have become unsafe because of immigration. (-)

Here again, the scores for questions 1 and 4 are reversed. On average, Europeans oppose the statement but, compared to the other nations in the sample, Spaniards do so the least.

TABLE 8.5. Values and Beliefs

| | Average | Standard deviation | High | Low |
|---|---|---|---|---|
| Personal values and beliefs | | | | |
| A1. I am happy | 0.78 | 0.52 | B | E |
| A2. I like to work | 0.65 | 0.48 | E | F |
| A3. I like my family | 0.88 | 0.32 | I | B |
| A4. I enjoy luxury | −0.40 | 0.49 | UK | F |
| A5. I seek balance in life | 0.39 | 0.56 | D | F |
| A6. I am responsible for my own success or failure | 0.50 | 0.49 | D | I |
| A7. I am a leader | 0.36 | 0.50 | D | E |
| A8. I like to fit in socially | −0.47 | 0.44 | UK | I |
| A9. I am a thinking, serious-minded person | 0.30 | 0.47 | I | UK |
| A10. I take a long-term view | 0.60 | 0.42 | I | E |
| A11. I worry about the future | −0.29 | 0.53 | I | B |
| A12. I hate failure | −0.17 | 0.53 | UK | F |
| A13. I like self-discipline | 0.42 | 0.37 | I | D |
| A14. I make decisions quickly | −0.03 | 0.63 | D | UK |
| A15. I trust people and social institutions | −0.05 | 0.41 | E | F |
| A16. I respect tradition | 0.61 | 0.41 | I | D |
| A17. I feel compassion for the needy | 0.33 | 0.51 | E | D |
| Values and beliefs about the world | | | | |
| B1. Our society needs change | 0.49 | 0.48 | I | D |
| B2. Globalization benefits society | −0.17 | 0.42 | E | B |
| B3. The European Union benefits society | 0.02 | 0.62 | I | UK |
| B4. Regulation benefits society | 0.15 | 0.41 | B | I |
| B5. Entrepreneurial values and freedom benefit society | 0.58 | 0.38 | D | B |
| B6. Competence breeds success | 0.10 | 0.51 | F | E |
| B7. Many people are selfish and can't be trusted | 0.71 | 0.33 | F | D |
| B8. Government services often fail | 0.16 | 0.47 | F | UK |
| B9. Politicians often fail | 0.17 | 0.49 | F | E |
| Values and beliefs that guide investment strategy | | | | |
| C1. I like to invest | 0.02 | 0.75 | D | F |
| C2. I save | 0.71 | 0.54 | I | UK |
| C3. I need to save | 0.30 | 0.82 | UK | I |
| C4. It is difficult to save | 0.16 | 0.89 | E | UK |
| C5. I am competent to make financial decisions | −0.07 | * | * | * |
| C6. I love risk | −0.17 | * | * | * |
| C7. I take calculated risks | 0.29 | 0.41 | D | F |
| C8. I worry about inflation | 0.63 | 0.44 | I | B |
| C9. I worry about the volatility of the stock market | 0.14 | 0.50 | UK | D |

TABLE 8.5. (*Continued*)

|  | Average | Standard deviation | High | Low |
|---|---|---|---|---|
| C10. Successful investing requires effort | 0.52 | 0.32 | D | I |
| C11. Successful investing requires patience | 0.71 | 0.43 | UK | B |
| C12. Investing has an ethical dimension | 0.34 | 0.52 | F | D |
| C13. Bankers deserve our trust | 0.43 | 0.42 | D | F |

*Note*: Each value and belief statement is judged with two to five questions. Strong disagreement is coded as $-1.0$; disagreement as $-0.5$; neutral as 0.0; agreement as 0.5, strong agreement as 1.0. The various columns represent: (i) the values and beliefs that the sample respondents are asked to judge, (ii) the arithmetic average score (and standard deviation) across questions and respondents, and (iii) the countries with the highest or the lowest average scores. The country symbols are B for Belgium, UK for Britain, F for France, D for Germany, I for Italy, and E for Spain. * refers to missing data.

A final example is the statement 'I take calculated risks' (C7). Now, the average European agrees. The questions are:

> I am less concerned about losing money if there is a real chance that the risks that I take are worthwhile.
> You will never achieve much unless you act boldly.
> Investors have to take calculated risks. There is no other way.
> People should only invest in risky ventures if they are wealthy.

On average, the Germans obtain the highest score; the French obtain the lowest score.

In general, this study analyzes three types of information: (i) demographic information; (ii) financial information (e.g. income, investable financial wealth, home ownership, etc.); and (iii) psychographic information about values and beliefs. In addition, the nationality of the respondents is known. Tables 8.5 through 8.9 report average scores for selected groups of respondents. Table 8.5 lists the mean score for each statement, averaged across questions and across all respondents. Subsequent tables list average scores by gender, age, health, education, religion, as well as a range of financial variables.

Ideally, any investigation of how values and beliefs (say, related to the perception of self) differ for separate groups of investors will control for demographic factors. Similarly, any study of how values and beliefs (say, about investment strategy) differ for distinct demographic groups will control for financial variables. Below, I start from the values and beliefs of the respondents and present simple comparisons of means—usually for two groups of respondents. The purpose is less to estimate the precise differences between groups (which requires a set of control variables) than to illustrate large gaps between groups that often survive a multivariate analysis. In addition, to keep Tables 8.6–8.9 easily readable, I only list group averages for which the hypothesis of equality is statistically rejected ($p < .01$).[8]

### Personal Values and Beliefs

I find that the representative European in the sample very much loves his or her family (average score is 0.88), feels happy (0.78), likes to work (0.65), respects tradition (0.61), takes a long-term view of life (0.60), and feels responsible for his/her own success or failure (0.50). The average European does not aim to fit in socially (−0.47), does not worry about the future (−0.29) and, as already mentioned, does not admit to enjoying luxury (−0.40).

Of course, there are important differences in the responses of male vs. female participants, young vs. old, high-income vs. low-income, and so on. Table 8.5 illustrates some of the differences between nationalities. National identity may be a valuable proxy variable for persistent clusters of values and beliefs that people associate with national character. This assumption is usefully discussed by, among others, David Potter (1954) and Ake Daun (1996 [1989]).[9]

For example, more than any other nation in the sample, Frenchmen agree that 'money buys happiness'. Yet, the French (−0.67) and Italians (−0.50) score lower than other countries on questions relating to their enjoyment of luxury products. For Britain, the score is statistically indistinguishable from zero. Germans perceive themselves as natural leaders, 'taking responsibility in difficult circumstances'. On average, Europeans deny that they hate failure. The French, in particular, disagree (−0.42) that a hypothetical 10% drop in their total wealth would make them feel miserable.

Table 8.6 shows some interesting differences in values and beliefs by gender, age, health status, and religious affiliation. More than women, men like to work. They believe that they are responsible for their own success and they like self-discipline. More than the young, the old (>age 55) respect tradition and distrust people. Perhaps not surprisingly, the means by age group often resemble the means by health status. More than Catholics, Protestants see themselves as leaders. Religion is an astoundingly powerful predictor of values and beliefs. In contrast, education is a weak predictor (I only find statistically significant differences for three of seventeen statements). These results are repeated in later tables and in analyses not reported here.

Tables 8.7 and 8.9 allow the reader to characterize the thinking of wealthy investors, low and high savers, and so on. There is little doubt that savings and investment behavior are correlated with people's values and beliefs. In some instances, the opinion gaps are very large. Consider, for example, the answers to statements A14 ('I make decisions quickly'), B4 ('Regulation benefits society'), or C5 ('I am competent to make financial decisions').

### Values and Beliefs about the World

Europeans mostly agree that many people cannot be trusted (0.71), that entre-preneurial values benefit society (0.58), and that society needs change (0.49).

TABLE 8.6. Personal Values and Beliefs by Gender, Age, Health Status, Education, and Religion

| | Gender | | Age | | Health | | Education | | Religion | |
|---|---|---|---|---|---|---|---|---|---|---|
| | Male | Female | <55 | >55 | Healthy | Sick | High-school | >High-school | Catholic | Protestant |
| A1. I am happy | | | | | 0.83 | 0.63 | | | | |
| A2. I like to work | 0.68 | 0.60 | 0.67 | 0.61 | 0.68 | 0.58 | | | 0.66 | 0.60 |
| A3. I like my family | | | | | 0.90 | 0.84 | | | | |
| A4. I enjoy luxury | −0.45 | −0.35 | −0.39 | −0.44 | −0.38 | −0.51 | −0.38 | −0.42 | −0.49 | −0.21 |
| A5. I seek balance in life | | | | | | | | | | |
| A6. I am responsible for my own success | 0.56 | 0.42 | | | | | | | 0.46 | 0.62 |
| A7. I am a leader | 0.40 | 0.31 | 0.39 | 0.31 | 0.38 | 0.32 | | | 0.34 | 0.41 |
| A8. I like to fit in socially | −0.49 | −0.44 | | | −0.48 | −0.42 | | | | |
| A9. I am a thinking, serious-minded person | 0.38 | 0.21 | 0.29 | 0.34 | | | | | 0.32 | 0.27 |
| A10. I take a long-term view | 0.63 | 0.56 | 0.55 | 0.70 | | | 0.58 | 0.62 | | |
| A11. I worry about the future | | | −0.25 | −0.37 | −0.32 | −0.21 | | | | |
| A12. I hate failure | | | | | | −0.19 | −0.12 | −0.21 | −0.12 | |
| A13. I like self-discipline | 0.45 | 0.38 | | | | | | | 0.44 | 0.36 |
| A14. I make decisions quickly | −0.01 | −0.07 | 0.00 | −0.09 | −0.01 | −0.09 | | | −0.02 | −0.08 |
| A15. I trust people and social institutions | −0.08 | −0.03 | −0.01 | −0.13 | −0.03 | −0.12 | | | −0.04 | −0.09 |
| A16. I respect tradition | 0.65 | 0.55 | 0.55 | 0.70 | 0.59 | 0.65 | | | 0.63 | 0.55 |
| A17. I feel compassion for the needy | 0.29 | 0.38 | 0.30 | 0.37 | | | | | 0.39 | 0.18 |

*Note:* The table lists the values and beliefs that the respondents are asked to evaluate. The arithmetic average scores are presented across questions and respondents who (i) are male or female, (ii) of age below 55 or above 55, (iii) healthy or sick, (iv) with a high-school education or university education, and across (v) Catholic or Protestant. When there is no table entry, the difference in means is statistically insignificant. The scores shown in the table vary between −1 and +1. Positive scores indicate agreement; negative scores, disagreement.

TABLE 8.7. Personal Values and Beliefs by Wealth, Saving, and Asset Allocation

| | Wealth | | Saving | | Savings accounts | | Stocks/fixed income | | Real estate | |
|---|---|---|---|---|---|---|---|---|---|---|
| | <300K | >300K | Low | High | Low | High | FI>S | S>FI | Low | High |
| A1. I am happy | 0.77 | 0.83 | 0.80 | 0.74 | | | | | | |
| A2. I like to work | 0.64 | 0.70 | 0.67 | 0.58 | | | | | | |
| A3. I like my family | | | 0.89 | 0.85 | | | | | | |
| A4. I enjoy luxury | -0.43 | -0.34 | | | | | -0.42 | -0.35 | | |
| A5. I seek balance in life | | | 0.42 | 0.32 | 0.41 | 0.36 | | | | |
| A6. I am responsible for my own success | | | | | | | | | 0.52 | 0.48 |
| A7. I am a leader | 0.34 | 0.45 | 0.39 | 0.26 | 0.38 | 0.32 | 0.34 | 0.47 | | |
| A8. I like to fit in socially | | | | | | | | | | |
| A9. I am a thinking, serious-minded person | 0.30 | 0.36 | | | | | | | 0.33 | 0.28 |
| A10. I take a long-term view | 0.59 | 0.58 | 0.61 | 0.57 | | | | | | |
| A11. I worry about the future | -0.15 | -0.28 | -0.32 | -0.23 | -0.19 | -0.14 | -0.28 | -0.38 | -0.32 | -0.27 |
| A12. I hate failure | | | | | | | -0.16 | -0.26 | | |
| A13. I like self-discipline | | | 0.43 | 0.37 | | | | | | |
| A14. I make decisions quickly | -0.05 | 0.05 | | | 0.01 | -0.11 | -0.07 | 0.16 | | |
| A15. I trust people and social institutions | -0.05 | -0.10 | | | | | -0.07 | 0.00 | | |
| A16. I respect tradition | 0.35 | 0.23 | | | | | 0.62 | 0.55 | | |
| A17. I feel compassion for the needy | | | | | | | 0.34 | 0.26 | | |

*Note.* The table lists the values and beliefs that the respondents are asked to evaluate. The arithmetic average scores are presented across questions and across respondents who (i) have investable wealth above or below 300,000 Euro, (ii) are low savers or high savers (as a percentage of income), (iii) keep a small or a large percentage of their investable wealth in savings accounts, (iv) invest a larger percentage of their wealth in fixed income than in stocks, or the reverse, and (v) invest little or much in real estate. When there is no table entry, the difference in means is statistically insignificant. The scores shown in the table vary between -1 and +1. Positive scores indicate agreement; negative scores, disagreement.

TABLE 8.8. Values and Beliefs about the World and about Investment Strategy by Gender, Age, Health Status, Education, and Religion

| | Gender | | Age | | Health | | Education | | Religion | |
|---|---|---|---|---|---|---|---|---|---|---|
| | Male | Female | <55 | >55 | Healthy | Sick | High-school | >High-school | Catholic | Protestant |
| B1. Our society needs change | | | | | | | | | 0.51 | 0.42 |
| B2. Globalization benefits society | | | | | | | | | | |
| B3. The EU benefits society | 0.11 | -0.07 | -0.14 | -0.22 | -0.15 | -0.23 | -0.14 | -0.19 | 0.09 | -0.11 |
| B4. Regulation benefits society | | | | | 0.05 | -0.03 | | | 0.16 | 0.09 |
| B5. Entrepreneurship and freedom benefit society | 0.62 | 0.54 | 0.56 | 0.63 | | | | | 0.57 | 0.64 |
| B6. Competence breeds success | | | 0.08 | 0.16 | | | | | | |
| B7. Many people are selfish and cannot be trusted | 0.72 | 0.69 | 0.70 | 0.73 | 0.70 | 0.74 | | | 0.72 | 0.68 |
| B8. Government services often fail | | | 0.12 | 0.22 | 0.13 | 0.25 | | | 0.19 | 0.08 |
| B9. Politicians often fail | | | 0.12 | 0.25 | 0.15 | 0.25 | | | 0.16 | 0.21 |
| C1. I like to invest | | | 0.05 | -0.04 | 0.05 | -0.08 | | | -0.03 | 0.15 |
| C2. I save | | | 0.78 | 0.61 | 0.75 | 0.61 | 0.75 | 0.69 | 0.69 | 0.78 |
| C3. I need to save | | | 0.39 | 0.14 | 0.32 | 0.22 | | | 0.37 | 0.12 |
| C4. It is difficult to save | | | 0.12 | 0.21 | 0.11 | 0.30 | | | 0.22 | -0.01 |

| Question | (1) | (2) | (3) | (4) | (5) | (6) | (7) | (8) | (9) |
|---|---|---|---|---|---|---|---|---|---|
| C5. I am competent to make financial decisions | 0.35 | 0.08 | | | 0.26 | 0.16 | | 0.20 | 0.33 |
| C6. I love risk | −0.58 | −0.70 | | | | | | | |
| C7. I take calculated risks | 0.33 | 0.23 | | | | | | | |
| C8. I worry about inflation | | | 0.57 | 0.76 | 0.61 | 0.70 | | | |
| C9. I worry about stock market volatility | 0.10 | 0.18 | 0.09 | 0.20 | 0.10 | 0.22 | 0.16 | 0.16 | 0.07 |
| C10. Successful investing requires effort | 0.54 | 0.51 | | | | | | 0.51 | 0.57 |
| C11. Successful investing requires patience | | | 0.68 | 0.79 | 0.71 | 0.75 | | 0.70 | 0.75 |
| C12. Investing has an ethical dimension | 0.30 | 0.39 | 0.30 | 0.41 | 0.31 | 0.40 | 0.36 | 0.37 | 0.26 |
| C13. Bankers deserve our trust | | | 0.38 | 0.52 | 0.42 | 0.47 | | 0.41 | 0.48 |

*Note*: The table lists the values and beliefs that the respondents are asked to evaluate. The arithmetic average scores are presented across questions and respondents who (i) are below 55 or above 55, (ii) are male or female, (iii) healthy or sick, (iv) with a high-school education or university education, and across (v) Catholic or Protestant. When there is no table entry, the difference in means is statistically insignificant. The scores shown in the table vary between −1 and +1. Positive scores indicate agreement; negative scores, disagreement.

TABLE 8.9. Values and Beliefs about the World and about Investment Strategy by Wealth, Saving, and Asset Allocation

| | Wealth | | Saving | | Savings accounts | | Stocks/fixed income | | Real estate | |
|---|---|---|---|---|---|---|---|---|---|---|
| | <300K | >300K | Low | High | Low | High | FI>S | S>FI | Low | High |
| B1. Our society needs change | 0.50 | 0.40 | | | | | 0.50 | 0.43 | 0.47 | 0.51 |
| B2. Globalization benefits society | | | | | | | | | | |
| B3. The EU benefits society | 0.01 | 0.15 | | | 0.06 | −0.03 | | | 0.06 | 0.00 |
| B4. Regulation benefits society | 0.17 | 0.02 | 0.13 | 0.21 | 0.13 | 0.18 | 0.17 | 0.03 | | |
| B5. Entrepreneurship and freedom benefit society | 0.57 | 0.69 | 0.60 | 0.54 | 0.61 | 0.55 | 0.58 | 0.64 | 0.60 | 0.57 |
| B6. Competence breeds success | 0.09 | 0.20 | | | 0.70 | 0.74 | | | | |
| B7. Many people are selfish and cannot be trusted | | | | | | | | | | |
| B8. Government services often fail | | | 0.15 | 0.21 | 0.15 | 0.21 | | | | |
| B9. Politicians often fail | | | | | | | | | | |
| C1. I like to invest | −0.02 | 0.21 | | | 0.07 | −0.09 | −0.05 | 0.37 | 0.05 | −0.02 |
| C2. I save | 0.70 | 0.82 | | | 0.73 | 0.68 | 0.70 | 0.80 | | |
| C3. I need to save | 0.32 | 0.18 | 0.33 | 0.19 | | | | | | |
| C4. It is difficult to save | 0.23 | −0.20 | 0.09 | 0.35 | | | 0.18 | 0.01 | | |
| C5. I am competent to make financial decisions | 0.20 | 0.46 | 0.28 | 0.09 | 0.29 | 0.14 | 0.19 | 0.47 | | |
| C6. I love risk | | | −0.66 | −0.54 | | | −0.66 | −0.48 | | |

| | 1 | 2 | 3 | 4 | 5 | 6 | 7 | 8 | 9 | 10 |
|---|---|---|---|---|---|---|---|---|---|---|
| C7. I take calculated risks | 0.27 | 0.38 | | | 0.31 | 0.25 | 0.27 | 0.39 | | |
| C8. I worry about inflation | 0.65 | 0.59 | 0.68 | | | | 0.65 | 0.58 | | |
| C9. I worry about stock market volatility | 0.17 | −0.04 | 0.21 | 0.09 | | 0.21 | 0.18 | −0.15 | 0.09 | 0.18 |
| C10. Successful investing requires effort | 0.52 | 0.58 | 0.54 | 0.49 | 0.55 | 0.49 | 0.51 | 0.62 | 0.55 | 0.50 |
| C11. Successful investing requires patience | 0.73 | 0.68 | | | | | | | 0.74 | 0.70 |
| C12. Investing has an ethical dimension | 0.35 | 0.28 | 0.33 | 0.38 | 0.32 | 0.37 | 0.36 | 0.23 | | |
| C13. Bankers deserve our trust | 0.42 | | | 0.46 | 0.41 | 0.46 | 0.44 | 0.35 | 0.45 | 0.40 |

*Note:* The table lists the values and beliefs that the respondents are asked to evaluate. The arithmetic average scores are presented across questions and across respondents who (i) have investable wealth above or below 300,000 Euro, (ii) are low savers or high savers (as a percentage of income), (iii) keep a small or a large percentage of their investable wealth in savings accounts, (iv) invest a larger percentage of their wealth in fixed income than in stocks, or the reverse, and (v) invest little or much in real estate. When there is no table entry, the difference in means is statistically insignificant. The scores shown in the table vary between −1 and +1. Positive scores indicate agreement; negative scores, disagreement.

There is considerable skepticism with respect to globalization, the European Union, and the role of government, however. Only 8% of Europeans agree that 'American culture is changing Europe for the better'. The French, in particular, believe that globalization hurts workers. On balance, Europeans believe that regulation benefits society. However, many also say that the state bureaucracies and social services are failing—58% of Europeans think that private health care has become a necessity, 91% of the French agree. Interestingly, only 37% of the British do.

## Values and Beliefs about Investment Strategy

The respondents to our questionnaire are strong savers (0.71). In their minds, successful investing takes both patience (0.71) and effort (0.52). They take calculated risks (0.29) but they do not love risk per se (−0.17). The representative European worries more about consumer price inflation than about stock market volatility. Bankers are trusted advisors (0.43).

Fully 40% of the Spaniards in our sample admit that they lack self-confidence in financial matters. The equivalent number for Germany is merely 9%. Of the German investors, 60% further believe in their own good fortune, while only 33% of Spaniards do. Of the French, 64% state that, in investing money, one should consider the social and ethical consequences for other people in society; 42% of Germans disagree with this point of view and 15% agree (the remainder is neutral).

As before, there are notable cultural differences between countries, between age groups, and between religions. Table 8.8 confirms that education is a weak predictor of values and beliefs. What is more, the little that is found is unforeseen. If we accept the results at face value, university-educated Europeans are less enthusiastic about globalization than other Europeans (B2); they do not like as much to invest (C1) and they worry more about stock market volatility (C9). In contrast, age and religion are correlated with most statements listed in Table 8.8. Possibly because Anglicanism and Protestantism are strong in Britain and Germany, the results sometimes mirror the sorting of respondents by nationality. Since Britain and Germany have large Catholic minorities, the best way to study the effect of religious affiliation is to examine the data within these countries.

Many Europeans believe that, in the long run, stocks are the best invest-ment (0.20). On average, they favor value over momentum investing. When the stock price of a company has dropped, it is seen as a buying opportunity (0.40) (with 62% agreement, this opinion is most firmly held in France) and, when the price has risen a great deal, the participants in our survey deny that it is a good time to buy (−0.19).

## Asset Allocation

I asked the respondents in each country to judge and rank four asset classes, relative to each other, in terms of ten characteristics. The asset classes were (i) bank savings accounts and certificates of deposit (SA), (ii) stocks of publicly traded companies and stock mutual funds (EQ), (iii) government bonds and bond mutual funds (BO), (iv) and real estate (RE). The characteristics were (i) the potential for long-term performance, (ii) the required effort and attention, (iii) the overall risk, (iv) the level of protection against consumer price inflation, (v) the degree of easy access in case of financial emergency, (vi) the total costs of managing the investment, (vii) the level of worry, (viii) the favorable or unfavorable tax treatment, (ix) the overall tradeoff between risk and return, and (x) the overall comfort level with the investment.

The top panel of Table 8.10 presents selected results. I report the fraction of all European respondents who judge an asset class as either the best or the worst in terms of five of the characteristics mentioned above. Table 8.10 also shows statistics by country. (In this case, the rankings may be different from the European average.) It is widely believed that stocks have the best long-term performance potential, and that savings accounts have the worst. Equity investments are thought to be vulnerable to inflation, however. Savings accounts are preferred in terms of risk and tax treatment. Real estate is seen as the best hedge against inflation and is preferred based on its overall risk-return tradeoff. There are some striking differences between countries. In Britain, for instance, the risk-return tradeoff for savings accounts is judged somewhat better than the tradeoff for real estate.

Table 8.10 also lists the findings of a second thought experiment: 'If you had 1 million Euro to invest today, what percent would you invest, respectively, in bank savings accounts, stocks, bonds, and real estate?' I present the average 'perfect portfolio' in Europe and in individual countries, as well as the percent of respondents who invest zero in a particular asset class. Broadly speaking, the average perfect portfolio contains real estate for two-fifths, and stocks, bonds, and savings accounts for one-fifth each. In Belgium and Britain, the real estate portions are smaller. One of the practical uses of research in behavioural finance is that it documents statistical relationships between values, beliefs, investment strategy, and asset allocation. Hereafter, I present for illustrative purposes the profile of a semi-affluent European investor who puts a larger percentage of his portfolio in stocks than in fixed income (i.e. bank savings accounts, government bonds, and cash) and I also present the profile of a more typical European who puts more funds into fixed income than in stocks. The analysis is based on 2,258 responses: 356 investors that are primarily 'equity investors' and 1,902 'fixed-income investors'.[10]

Compared to other respondents, 'equity investors' believe more that they are leaders, and that they make decisions quickly. They admire entrepreneurship.

TABLE 8.10. Perceptions of Asset Classes and Preferred Asset Allocations

| | Europe | Belgium | Britain | France | Germany | Italy | Spain |
|---|---|---|---|---|---|---|---|
| *% of respondents who judge a particular asset class best and worst* | | | | | | | |
| Long-term performance | | | | | | | |
| EQ (best) | 41 | 43 | 33 | 53 | 50 | 43 | 24 |
| SA (worst) | 9 | 9 | 8 | 9 | 9 | 9 | 8 |
| Risk | | | | | | | |
| SA (best) | 62 | 69 | 70 | 69 | 67 | 47 | 55 |
| EQ (worst) | 3 | 1 | 4 | 2 | 4 | 5 | 1 |
| Hedge against inflation | | | | | | | |
| RE (best) | 50 | 51 | 38 | 42 | 64 | 59 | 48 |
| EQ (worst) | 13 | 17 | 14 | 14 | 10 | 13 | 8 |
| Tax treatment | | | | | | | |
| SA (best) | 52 | 57 | 55 | 75 | 51 | 47 | 24 |
| EQ (worst) | 10 | 20 | 6 | 5 | 10 | 11 | 12 |
| Overall risk-return tradeoff | | | | | | | |
| RE (best) | 36 | 26 | 29 | 35 | 29 | 45 | 46 |
| SA (worst) | 20 | 21 | 32 | 23 | 17 | 9 | 21 |
| *Preferred asset allocation* | | | | | | | |
| SA | 20 | 22 | 22 | 22 | 17 | 16 | 23 |
| EQ | 22 | 23 | 25 | 22 | 24 | 20 | 18 |
| BO | 22 | 25 | 23 | 17 | 22 | 25 | 19 |
| RE | 36 | 30 | 30 | 39 | 37 | 39 | 40 |
| *% of respondents who do not invest in a particular asset class* | | | | | | | |
| SA | 10 | 7 | 8 | 7 | 17 | 10 | 11 |
| EQ | 12 | 12 | 8 | 11 | 13 | 10 | 17 |
| BO | 11 | 8 | 11 | 15 | 14 | 4 | 16 |
| RE | 10 | 11 | 19 | 8 | 10 | 4 | 7 |

*Note*: Four asset classes namely, savings accounts (SA), investments in the stock market (EQ), in bonds (BO), and in real estate (RE) are represented. The table reports (i) the percentage of sample respondents in Europe who judge a particular asset class either best or worst in terms of performance, risk, inflation-protection, tax treatment, and overall risk-return tradeoff. It also shows statistics by country. (Note that, in this case, the rankings may be different from the European average.) Finally, (ii) the average preferred asset allocations in Europe and in individual countries, and (iii) the percentage of respondents who invest zero in a particular asset class are reported.

They feel that investment is fun. They 'love risk' and they claim to take calculated risks. They believe that successful investing requires effort. In their view, stocks are the best long run investments, small companies earn higher stock returns than large companies, and modern technology has made investing easier.

In contrast, 'fixed-income investors' worry more about the future than equity investors do and they fear failure. They agree more strongly that 'regulation benefits society', that 'working for government is a noble task', that 'social security will provide retirement income'. Fixed-income investors lack confidence to make money decisions, they say. Stock market volatility is something to worry about, and investing has an ethical dimension. More than other respondents, fixed-income investors believe that savings accounts and gold are attractive investment vehicles.

## Conclusion

I have sketched a psychological and sociological portrait of the semi-affluent investor in Western Europe. Little is known about how mental frames are linked to demographic variables and to investment strategy and portfolio choice. This study finds that identifiable clusters of values and beliefs, often correlated with national character, gender, age, and religion, predict portfolio choice. Culture matters. The results are preliminary but they have potentially valuable implications for financial marketing, product design, and other aspects of the money management industry.

One question that is often raised is the degree to which the statistical relations that are observed in survey data can be expected to be stable over time. Is it possible to make reliable out-of-sample predictions? Are the results vulnerable to dramatic worldwide events like the 9/11 terrorist attacks in New York or the bear market that started in the Spring of 2000? For instance, did 9/11 and the bursting of the stock market bubble cause many people to reassess their lives and, by implication, their investment strategies? The question is fundamental. For instance, Ronald Inglehart (1997) believes that there is a gradual postmodern shift in the value systems of advanced industrial societies and that people put less emphasis on economic achievement and more emphasis on the quality of life. On the other hand, in her survey studies of French values in 1981 and 1990, Hélène Riffault (1994) reports remarkable stability in the answers to at least half of the questions that were asked. Nevertheless, there are significant changes in specified domains, for example, the economy and employment.

Many more questions remain. I end, therefore, with the ritual cry for further research.

## Notes

1. Or to quote the anthropologist Clifford Geertz (1973: 49), 'there is no such thing as human nature independent of culture'.
2. It is an interesting intellectual question whether the idea of culture, a foundation stone of twentieth century social science, has lived up to its academic promise. Adam Kuper (1999) thinks that cultures are to be described and to be interpreted but that the idea of culture as a source of explanation has failed.
3. The wording 'mental frame' is open to debate. The term originates in cognitive psychology but psychologists restrict its meaning more than I intend. My definition here includes a broad range of mental representations, for example, how

184 *Werner De Bondt*

people experience and understand what happens to them in daily life (say, political beliefs; ideological and religious myths); how people see themselves; beliefs about instruments and practices (say, cooking recipes); and recollections in memory. I emphasize the social foundations of values and beliefs. All common sense knowledge is knowledge from a specific point of view (Shweder 1991). The problem is contained in Blaise Pascal's famous statement that 'there are thruths on this side of the Pyrénées which are falsehoods on the other'.

4. Some authors like Richard Dawkins (1982) or Dan Sperber (1996) are calling for a new epidemiology of mental representations. Ideas are contagious. Culture, Dawkins claims, is made up of 'memes' which in Darwinian fashion undergo replication and selection. (The notion of cultural contagion goes back to Gabriel Tarde and Gustave LeBon.) Whether Dawkins' approach will be fertile remains to be seen.

5. Rational choice theory does allow for differences in taste parameters but the differences are exogenous. They are not explained. In general, economists do not appreciate the role of cultural traditions and beliefs in human motivation. Many see cultural institutions either as (ultimately) neutral mutations that economic agents may have an incentive to circumvent, or as functionally optimal adjustments to human needs and desires. Because it suggests, contrary to the mainstream view, that cultural values and beliefs can promote or resist economic progress, the work of Landes (1999) and Harrison and Huntington (2000) that I referred to earlier is contentious.

6. Of the residents of Britain, 43% have visited the United States.

7. Remember, however, that the questionnaire was administered in six languages. The order of the questions was the same in every version.

8. Further steps are (i) to use factor analysis to identify the driving forces underlying the respondents' stated values and beliefs, and to relate the factors to demographic and financial variables; and (ii) to relate the factors to the seminal work of Hofstede (1980). I do not report this work for lack of space.

9. The discussion that follows regularly refers to specific survey questions, not to the thirty-nine statements listed in Table 8.5.

10. I built the profiles with the thirty-nine statements listed in Table 8.5 and with additional questions. All the $t$-statistics for tests of differences in means between 'equity' and 'fixed-income investors' exceed 3.0. Some of the evidence is found in Tables 8.7 and 8.9.

## References

Barnewall, M. M. 1987. 'Psychological Characteristics of the Individual Investor', in *Asset Allocation for the Individual Investor*, Droms, W. G. (ed.). Homewood, IL: Dow Jones-Irwin.

Benedict, R. 1959 [1934]. *Patterns of Culture*. Boston: Houghton Mifflin.

Berger, P. and Luckmann, T. 1967. *The Social Construction of Reality*. Garden City, NY: Doubleday.

Bruner, J. 1990. *Acts of Meaning*. Cambridge, MA: Harvard University Press.

D'Andrade, R. and Strauss, C. 1992. (eds.). *Human Motives and Cultural Models*. Cambridge: Cambridge University Press.

Daun, A. 1996 [1989]. *Swedish Mentality*. University Park, PA: Pennsylvania State University Press.

Dawkins, R. 1982. *The Extended Phenotype*. Oxford: Freeman.

De Bondt, W. 1998. 'A Portrait of the Individual Investor', *European Economic Review* 42(3–5): 831–44.

—— and Thaler, R. 1995. 'Financial Decision-Making in Markets and Firms: A Behavioral Perspective', National Bureau of Economic Research, Working Paper 4777, Cambridge, MA.

Faris, E. 1937. *The Nature of Human Nature*. New York, NY: McGraw-Hill.

Geertz, C. 1973. *The Interpretation of Cultures*. New York, NY: Basic Books.

Hampden-Turner, C. and Trompenaars, A. 1993. *The Seven Cultures of Capitalism*. London: Piatkus.

Harrison, L. and Huntington, S. 2000. *Culture Matters: How Values Shape Human Progress*. Boulder, CO: Perseus.

Hofstede, G. 1980. *Culture's Consequences: International Differences in Work-Related Values*. Beverly Hills, CA: Sage.

Inglehart, R. 1997. *Modernization and Postmodernization: Cultural, Economic, and Political Change in 43 Societies*. Princeton, NJ: Princeton University Press.

Kaiser, R. 1987. 'The Dynamics of the Investment Decision-Making Process for the Individual Investor', in *Asset Allocation for the Individual Investor*, Droms, W. G. (ed.). Homewood, IL: Dow Jones-Irwin.

Kuper, A. 1999. *Culture: The Anthropologists' Account*. Cambridge, MA: Harvard University Press.

Landes, D. 1999. *The Wealth and Poverty of Nations*. New York, NY: W. W. Norton and Company, Inc.

MacGregar, D., Slovic, P., Berry, M., and Evensley, H. 1999. 'Perceptions of Financial Risk: A Survey Study of Advisors and Planners', *Journal of Financial Planning* 12(8): 67–86.

McClelland, D. 1961. *The Achieving Society*. Princeton, NJ: Van Nostrand.

Opdyke, J. 2000. 'Bumpy Market Reminds Investors to Assess their Risk Tolerance', *Wall Street Journal* July 14.

Potter, D. 1954. *People of Plenty: Economic Abundance and the American Character*. Chicago: The University of Chicago Press.

Riffault, H. 1994. *Les Valeurs des Français*. Paris: Puf.

Salter, W. 1983. 'Tacit Theories of Economics', *Proceedings of the 5th Annual Conference of the Cognitive Science Society*, Rochester, New York.

Shweder, R. 1991. *Thinking Through Cultures: Expeditions in Cultural Psychology*. Cambridge, MA: Harvard University Press.

Simon, H. 1983. *Reason in Human Affairs*. Stanford, CA: Stanford University Press.

Slovic, P. 1972. 'Psychological Study of Human Judgment: Implications for Investment Decision Making', *Journal of Finance* 72(4): 779–99.

Smith, S. and Bond, M. H. 1993. *Social Psychology Across Cultures*. New York, NY: Harvester Wheatsheaf.

Sperber, D. 1996. *Explaining Culture: A Naturalistic Approach*. Oxford: Blackwell.

Stanley, T. 2000. *The Millionaire Mind*. Thorndike, ME: G. K. Hall.

—— and Danko, W. 1996. *The Millionaire Next Door: The Surprising Secrets of America's Wealthy*. Atlanta, GA: G. K. Hall.

Tversky, A. and Kahneman, D. 1986. 'Rational Choice and the Framing of Decisions', *Journal of Business* 59(4): 251–78.

Warneryd, K. E. 2001. *Stock Market Psychology: How People Value and Trade Stocks.* Cheltenham: Edward Elgar.

Warren, W., Stevens, R., and McConkey, C. W. 1990. 'Using Demographic and Lifestyle Analysis to Segment Individual Investors', *Financial Analysts Journal* 46(2): 74 ff.

Weber, M. 2002 [1904]. *The Protestant Ethic and the Spirit of Capitalism.* New York, NY: Penguin Books.

# 9

# Conflicts of Interests in the US Brokerage Industry

## RICHARD SWEDBERG

### Introduction

In this chapter, I will be focusing on the role that conflicts of interest have played in the brokerage industry during the recent corporate scandals in the United States. My reason for choosing this particular topic and this particular period has to do with the fact that a number of interesting cases involving conflicts of interest in the brokerage industry came to light during 2001–2. New important legislation on conflicts of interest was also introduced around this time, namely the Sarbanes–Oxley Act. Of particular interest, I argue, are two major cases of conflicts of interest, in which the Attorney General of New York State, Eliot Spitzer, was active: the fining of Merrill Lynch in 2002, and the 'global solution' with all the major brokerage houses on Wall Street that was finalized later the same year.

A few introductory words need to be said about the concept of conflict of interest. This concept has its origin in legal thought and is usually defined as a situation in which a private interest threatens to overtake a general interest. According to the most recent edition of *Black's Law Dictionary*, a conflict of interest is present when there is 'a real or seeming incompatibility between one's private and one's public or fiduciary duties' (Garner 1999: 295).[1] Conflict-of-interest legislation is basically prophylactic in nature and what matters, to cite a Supreme Court decision from 1961, is not so much what 'actually happened' as what 'might have happened' (*U.S. v. Mississippi Valley Generating Company*; see Stark 2000: 4). The notion of conflict of interest has gradually been expanded in US legislation, from the area of politics to the economy itself. In 1789, for example, an act was passed during the first Congress in the United States according to which the holder of the newly instituted office of Secretary of the Treasury could not invest in government securities (Association of the Bar of the City of New York 1960: 4, 27–8). During the twentieth century it became common that various forms of conflicts of interests were singled out and regulated in the professions, including the financial professions (e.g. Twentieth Century Fund 1980; Davis and Stark 2001).

We shall now return to the conflicts of interest that took place on Wall Street in 2001–2, especially in the brokerage industry. The usual explanation

*Richard Swedberg*

of these events in the media is that they had been caused by *greed*. The boom of the 1990s on the stock exchange, the argument goes, had whetted the appetite of many individuals, who now set aside the general interest that it was their duty to guard. Accountants, who were supposed to give honest accounts of the corporations that they audited, now began to rubber stamp dubious audits; and business analysts, who were supposed to give disinterested advice to investors about which shares to buy, now began to push for certain shares according to their employers' wishes. While the power of material interests as a source of motivation should not be underestimated, especially in a country with such a strong commercial culture as the United States, this explanation is nonetheless too simplistic and fails to address many of the key issues. What is seen as the general interest, for example, has varied quite a bit over time and is not to be seen as something given. As to the importance of greed as an explanatory factor, there is also the fact that money-making involves social interaction, and that the psychology of greed only goes so far in explaining actions that also involve social structures and institutions.

Sociologists, I argue in this chapter, can add to the conventional interpretation of why conflicts of interest take place during the corporate scandals of 2001–2, primarily by relying on the following two propositions: (1) *interests are always socially defined or constructed* and (2) *interests can only be realized through social relations* (e.g. Bourdieu 1990; Coleman 1990; Bourdieu and Wacquant 1992; Swedberg 2003). I will try to show this in two steps, after a brief introduction about the brokerage industry in the 1990s. First, I will give an account for what happened in the case of Merrill Lynch and how various attempts have been made to solve the conflicts of interest in the brokerage industry, including Spitzer's 'global settlement'. I will then suggest a sociological interpretation of the increase in conflicts of interest during the 1990s that draws on the two sociological propositions about interest, just cited.

### Conflicts of Interest in the Brokerage Industry in the 1990s

The main type of conflicts of interest that came to light during the corporate scandals of 2001–2 typically involved the relationship of business analysts to investment banking. Why this was the case had much to do with two important institutional changes on Wall Street: the deregulation of commissions in 1975 and the *de facto* repeal of the Glass–Steagall Act from the late 1980s onward (e.g. Demski 2003). The former made it much more profitable for Wall Street firms to do business with banks and institutional investors than with small investors; and the latter greatly increased the competition for big customers, since commercial banks were now allowed to buy and sell shares on behalf of their clients. Analysts, according to one experienced observer, now 'grafted themselves onto the investment banking team' (Levitt 2002*b*: 66). Small investors from now onward became much less interesting to brokerage firms, and were often treated with contempt. Buy and sell orders from this type of individual were, for example, referred to as 'dumb order flow' by NASDAQ market makers since they had so little information that it was always easy to make money out of them (Craig 2002: C3).

During the 1990s the relationship between business analysts and investment banks intensified. Business analysts now assumed the role of 'an adjunct of investment banking', and their pay was often directly dependent on how much business they could drum up (e.g. Levitt 2002*b*: 70). The financial firms publicly denied that any conflicts of interest existed and referred to 'the Chinese Wall' that has to exist between investment banking and research. Business analysts were nonetheless very useful in helping out with Initial Public Offerings (IPOs), which were a major source of profit for investment bankers during this period; they also assisted conventional brokerage. The analysts helped to attract business through overly optimistic analyses; and these overly optimistic analyses also helped to sell the IPOs. According to a study in the late 1990s, the long-run performance of IPO stocks which were recommended by analysts who worked for firms that lead the underwriting of these stocks, did significantly *worse* than stocks which were recommended by non-underwriting analysts. According to the authors of this study, 'it is not the difference in analysts' ability to value firms that drives our results, but a bias directly related to whether the recommender is the underwriter of the stock' (Michaely and Womack 1999: 683; similarly Hayward and Boeker 1998).

Many CEOs also leaked information about future earnings to analysts, in order to forewarn the market of what was to come. Uncooperative analysts got little information and were sometimes ostracized. According to a famous internal memo from Morgan Stanley and Co (which was quickly disowned when it became public), 'our objective is to adopt a policy, fully understood by the entire Firm, *including the Research Department*, that we do not make negative or controversial comments about our clients as a matter of sound business practice' (Hayward and Boeker 1998: 6; emphasis added).

Some business analysts now became superstars and could directly affect the market through their recommendations (e.g. StarMine, as cited in Der Hovanesian 2002). They appeared on television shows and wrote financial columns which reached a mass audience of small investors. The best analysts earned between $10 and 15 million a year, including bonuses, and the most famous of them all, Jack Grubman of Salomon Smith Barney, made $20 million. Grubman, who was an expert on the telecom industry, involved himself intimately with the corporations he analyzed, and helped them out with strategy, mergers, and sometimes even attended board meetings. In a much quoted interview from 2000 he said: 'What used to be a conflict [of interest] is now a synergy. Someone like me who is bank-intensive, would have been looked at disdainfully by the buy side 15 years ago. Now, they know that I'm in the flow of what's going on' (Rosenbush et al. 2002: 34).

This development toward a symbiotic relationship between business analysts and investment banking meant that the interest of the small investors was set aside. Business analysts sometimes said one thing in private, to the initiated few, and another in public. Grubman et al. issued practically no sell recommendations during the 1990s and often recommended investors to buy shares in corporations till these were close to bankruptcy. Grubman, for example, did not stop recommending WorldCom till April 2002, when its shares had lost 90% of their value.

By the end of the 1990s, it was apparent to many observers that business analysts were getting careless and irresponsible in their analyses (e.g. Sernovitz 2002). The big players fiercely opposed any intervention by the Securities Exchange Commission (SEC), including its efforts to stop CEOs from leaking information to analysts whom they were close to. Nonetheless, in late 2000, SEC succeeded in getting through a very important piece of legislation called 'Regulation Fair Disclosure' (RFD). The main point of RFD is that relevant economic information must be made available to *everyone*—not just a select few. This regulation has made immensely more information available to small investors. The attempt by SEC to get business analysts to behave more responsibly on public television, on the other hand, failed, largely because of the resistance of the television companies.

## The Case of Merrill Lynch

During 2002, a number of investigations were started that tried to establish that serious cases of conflicts of interest existed in a number of securities firms; and the US media has followed these with great interest. Many of these investigations were initiated at the state level since SEC, now under the Levitt's successor, Harvey Pitt, was reluctant to take action. The pioneer among these investigations, and also the most spectacular, was the one that involved Merrill Lynch in the state of New York (e.g. Scheiber 2002). On April 8, 2002 Attorney General Eliot Spitzer announced publicly that he had issued a court order requiring immediate reforms in Merrill Lynch, the largest brokerage firm in the United States. What was at issue, according to Spitzer, 'was a shocking betrayal of trust by one of Wall Street's most trusted names' (Office of New York State Attorney 2002: i).

Spitzer's charges against Merrill Lynch were based on a piece of state legislation known as The Martin Act of 1921. This law has two important advantages over SEC legislation and federal law. For one thing, it allows the attorney general to bring criminal charges; and in the case of Merrill Lynch a criminal conviction would have meant its death sentence. And second, the Martin Act, as opposed to federal law, allows you to proceed without establishing intent, which is typically hard to do. At the time when the case against Merrill Lynch was presented, Spitzer also announced that several other firms were under Martin Act subpoena to produce evidence about possible conflicts of interest between investment banking and research activities.

The evidence presented by Spitzer to the media on April 8 was based on a ten-month long investigation of Merrill Lynch, which involved some 30,000 documents and thousands of e-mails. The basic charge against Merrill Lynch was that its research had been presented to the general public as objective, while in reality it was biased by the fact that it had been produced in close association with investment banking. While noting that 'tension between various departments in a single (brokerage) firm is nothing new', and that 'this tension is usually addressed by the establishment of a "Chinese Wall"', it was also emphasized that this arrangement had failed in this particular case' (office of the New York State Attorney 2002: p. 14). According to the affidavit, Merrill Lynch had on a regular basis misled investors in the following ways:

(1) the ratings in many cases did not reflect the analysts' true opinions of the companies; (2) as a matter of undisclosed, internal policy, no reduce or sell recommendations were issued, thereby converting a published five-point rating scale into a *de facto* three-point system; (3) Merrill Lynch failed to disclose to the public that Merrill Lynch's ratings were tarnished by an undisclosed conflict of interest: the research analysts were acting as quasi-investment bankers for the companies at issue, often initiating, continuing, and/or manipulating research coverage for the purpose of attracting and keeping investment banking clients, thereby producing misleading ratings that were neither objective nor independent, as they purported to be. (Office of the New York State Attorney 2002: p. 3)

The main focus of Spitzer's investigations was directed as Merrill Lynch's so-called Internet Research Group, led by well-known analyst Henry Blodget. E-mails that were made available to the media revealed, among other things, that stocks that were publicly said to represent a sound investment (a '2'), were in private emails described as a 'piece of shit' and a 'piece of crap' (see Table 9.1). Blodget wanted the analysts to devote 50% of their time to research and 50% to banking; and he described his own work as '85% banking, 15% research' (p. 15).

Blodget and his staff were well aware that their involvement with investment banking would lead to biased research. According to one e-mail from a person on his staff, 'we bend backwards to accommodate banking', and according to another, 'the whole idea that we are independent of banking is a big lie' (p. 17). At one point Blodget noted that going against the wishes of Merrill's banking clients in the analysis would lead to 'temper-tantrums, threats, and/or relationship damage' (p. 19). This, however, did not present him from publicly pretending that the research produced by the Internet Research Group was objective. It was also noted in the affidavit that during 1999–2000 Blodget had made more than 120 appearances on public television, such as CNN and CNBC.

On May 21, 2002, after several weeks of discussions, a settlement was reached between Merrill Lynch and Spitzer. What exactly went on during these negotiations was not reported in the media and is currently not known.

TABLE 9.1. The Disparity between Private and Public Ratings of
Analysts at Merrill Lynch, 1999–2001— Selected Cases

| Company | Date | Contemporaneous analyst comments in e-mails | Published ratings |
|---|---|---|---|
| Aether System (AETH) | 03/15/01 | Might have announced next week ... which could pop stick ... but fundamental horrible (ML82578) | 3–1 |
| Excite @home (ATHM) | 12/27/99 12/29/99 | We are neutral on the stock Six months outlook is flat, without any real catalysts for improvement seen (ML37899; ML37956) | 2–1 |
| Excite @home (ATHM) | 06/03/00 | Such a piece of crap (ML51453) | 2–1 |
| GoTo.Com (GOTO) | 01/11/01 | Nothing interesting about company except banking fees (ML03806) | 3–1 |
| InfoSpace (INSP) | 07/13/00 | This stock is a powder keg, given how aggressive we were on it earlier this year and given the bad smell comments that so many institutions are bringing up (ML06413) | 1–1 |
| InfoSpace (INSP) | 10/20/00 | Piece of junk (ML06578) | 1–1 |
| Internet Capital Group Inc. (ICGE) | 10/05/00 | Going to 5 (closed at $12.38) (ML63901) | 2–1 |
| Internet Capital Group Inc. (ICGE) | 10/06/00 | No hopeful news to relate ... we see nothing that will turn around near-term. The company needs to restructure its operations and raise additional cash, and until it does that, there is nothing positive to say (ML64077) | 2–1 |
| Lifeminders (LFMN) | 12/04/00 | Piece of shit (ML60903) | 2–1 |
| 24/7 Media (TFSM) | 10/10/00 | Piece of shit (ML64372) | 2–2 |

*Source*: Office of New York State Attorney General (2002: 13).

*Comment*: This table comes from the affidavit of Attorney General of New York State Eliot Spitzer on April 8, 2002, against Merrill Lynch; and it shows the disparity between what Merrill's Internet Research Group said in public about certain stocks and what it said in private. E-mails, according to a 1997 decision, have to be retained for three years in the security industry.

The published ratings (in the right-hand column) are based on Merrill's 5-point system, with 1 meaning 'Buy'; 2, 'Accumulate'; 3, 'Neutral'; 4, 'Reduce'; and 5, 'Sell'. Further differentiation was accomplished in the following way: 2–1 would, for example, mean 'Accumulate [in the short run]/Buy [in the long run]'; 2–2, 'Accumulate [in the short run]/Accumulate [in the long run]'; and so on. One of the charges of the Office of the Attorney General was that the analysts at Merrill Lynch never used a 4 or a 5; when stocks dropped too low, they were simply not rated at all.

Nonetheless, since some 30% of the revenue of Merrill Lynch comes from retail investors and the firm has become known as 'a symbol of middle-class investing', it is often suggested that the firm may have been very sensitive to accusations that it had mistreated small investors (e.g. Scheiber 2002: 18). According to the press, Spitzer also threatened to indict Merrill Lynch, which would have meant the end of the company (McGeehan 2002: B6). Spitzer later noted that, 'we could have indicted, convicted, and destroyed Merrill [but] that would have been insane' (Rosenbush et al. 2002: 43). Some observers also feel that the quick drop in the stock of Merrill Lynch, as a result of Spitzer's investigation, was a further reason why Merrill Lynch chose to settle.

Without denying or admitting guilt, Merrill Lynch agreed to pay $100 million in fines (Levitt 2002*b*: 82–83). Much more importantly than the fine, however, was that Merrill Lynch now also had to introduce a number of structural changes into its ways of doing business, as dictated by Spitzer, to prevent conflicts of interest in the future. It was, for example, decided that an independent committee should be established at the firm to monitor the communications between the investment bankers and the analysts. The investment bankers would also have no say in issues pertaining to the compensation of the analysts; and the analysts would exclusively get paid on the basis of how well the stocks that they picked performed.

## Attempts to Solve the Conflicts of Interest in the Brokerage Industry

A large number of proposals for how to solve the conflicts of interest involving business analysis have been made in response to the corporate scandals of 2001–2, along the lines of Merrill Lynch. The most important piece of legislation that has been used to deal with these issues is the Sarbanes–Oxley Act, which was signed into law in July 2002. Much attention has also been devoted in the media to Eliot Spitzer's 'global solution' that was initiated in the fall of 2002 and completed by the end of December. More generally, it can be said that the decision has been made to maintain 'Chinese Walls', as opposed to the strategy of demanding that different functions are placed in different firms. A compromise has also been struck between using law to accomplish this, as opposed to self-regulation (see Table 9.2).

Under the impact of new scandals that kept happening one after the other during the spring and the summer of 2002, the Bush administration decided to take measures. The signing into law of the Sarbanes–Oxley Act on July 30 was the major result of this resolve. According to Bush, this law represented 'the most far-reaching reforms of American business practices since the time of Franklin Delano Roosevelt' (Bush 2002*b*).

From the Sarbanes–Oxley Act and various speeches by Bush it is clear that the US government's perception of the crisis of 2001–2 was primarily in terms of individual responsibility (e.g. Bush 2002*b*). According to the new

TABLE 9.2. Different Ways of Handling Conflicts of
Interest in the Brokerage Industry

|                 | 'Chinese Wall' | Different functions in different firms |
| --------------- | -------------- | ------------------------------------- |
| Law             | 1              | 2                                     |
| Self-regulation | 3              | 4                                     |

*Comment*: Conflicts of interest in the brokerage can either be
handled through legislation or self-regulation; and the two
activities can either be allowed to coexist in the same firm
('Chinese Wall') or be assigned to different firms.

The Sarbanes–Oxley Act of 2002 contains legislation about
Chinese Walls and allows for many forms of consulting and
accounting (1). A few suggestions for radically separating the
two activities were made in Congress early in 2002, as well as
by people such as Eliot Spitzer and Arthur Levitt (2). Before
the Sarbanes–Oxley Act most conflicts of interest of brokerage firms on Wall Street were handled through self-regulation,
typically in the form of a Chinese Wall (3). Self-regulation in
combination with assigning different functions to different
firms was suggested by Paul Volcker in the spring of 2002 for
the accounting industry, using Andersen as his model (4).

law, CEOs must vouch for the annual financial statements of their firms. The
penalty for white-collar crimes, which have been committed by those in
charge of a corporation, was dramatically increased to a maximum of twenty
years. From around July, it also became increasingly common in the US
media to see prominent businessmen being led away in handcuffs—another
indication that the Bush administration wanted to let the public know that it
had gotten tough with those who were engaged in 'corporate corruption'
(Bush 2002b). This tendency continued through the fall of 2002, and throughout 2003 Bush often lashed out at 'corporate criminals' (e.g. Bush 2003).

But even if the Sarbanes–Oxley Act to a large extent has been shaped by the
need for what Bush and his administration termed 'a new ethic of personal
responsibility in the business community', it also contains several paragraphs
expressly devoted to more structural issues such as conflicts of interest in business analysis (Bush 2002a). Bush was well aware that many average Americans
owned shares and had been badly hurt by the meltdown of corporations such
as Enron and WorldCom in 2001–2. 'More than 80 million Americans own
stock, and many of them are new to the market', as the President noted in
a major speech in early July of 2002 (Bush 2002a).

According to the new law, business analysts cannot be forced to submit
their analyses for clearance, before publication. The power of brokers and
investment bankers to decide salaries for business analysts, and in general
supervise their work, has also been limited. The goal of the legislation,
when it comes to business conflicts of interest, is as follows: '(to) improve the
objectivity of research and provide investors with more useful and reliable

information' (US Congress 2002: 47). The authority in charge of this task, as well as of other rules for business analysts, will be the SEC.

While the passing of the Sarbanes–Oxley Act may have given the general public the impression that a stern law now existed, with which to fight corporate misbehavior and corruption, it was soon pointed out in the press that its paragraphs on conflicts of interest were very flexible and could be interpreted in many different ways—either leniently or harshly. It may also have been the failure of the Bush administration to handle the conflicts of interest in a more decisive manner that made Eliot Spitzer, the attorney general of New York State, to act on his own. In any case, during the fall of 2002 Spitzer decided to push through a general or 'global solution' to the various wrongdoings in the whole brokerage industry on Wall Street. Instead of going after the major brokerage firms one by one, Spitzer wanted to get them all together in one room and negotiate a general settlement. SEC soon supported Spitzer's plan.

According to the press, Spitzer initially tried to get SEC to agree to a clear separation between investment banking and business analysis. This, however, was not accepted by SEC, and it was instead agreed that the existing 'Chinese Walls' inside brokerage firms should be strengthened, beyond the provisions in the Sarbanes–Oxley Act. The firms were also to be fined for their wrongdoings. The most innovative part of the plan, however, had to do with the attempt to get the firms to finance independent business analysis. One early version of this effort was to have the brokerage firms finance a board that was to buy research from some twenty already existing independent analyst firms, such as Value Line. This plan, however, was rejected by the brokerage firms.

Spitzer tried very hard to push through an agreement before the national elections in early November 2002. This did not succeed, and the fact that also the Senate now passed into republican hands encouraged the security firms to lobby Congress for support against Spitzer's plan, especially his innovative idea of having a panel dispense money for independent research. On December 20, it was nonetheless announced that an agreement had been reached, probably due to Spitzer's threat that he would otherwise proceed with criminal charges (e.g. McGeehan 2002; Morgenson and McGeehan 2002). The thrust of the agreement was a strengthening of the 'Chinese Wall', in relation to the Sarbanes–Oxley Act. The major brokerage firms on Wall Street also agreed to pay $900 million in fines and an additional amount of $535 million over five years to finance independent stock research ($450 million) and educate investors ($85 million). For these years, the agreement states, each firm has to buy independent research from at least three sources that do not have any ties to an investment bank, and it must also make this research available to its customers. According to a statement by Spitzer, when the settlement was announced, 'the objective throughout this investigation has been to protect small investors by ensuring integrity in the marketplace' (Morgenson and McGeehan 2002: C5).

## A Sociological Approach to the Conflicts of Interest

The two sociological propositions about interests that were mentioned at the outset of this chapter—that these are (1) *socially defined or constructed* and (2) *can only be realized through social relations*—can be illustrated by looking at the changes that the notion of the public or general interest of investors was going through in the 1990s. This way we can also get a better understanding of why the traditional measure of having 'Chinese Walls' did not succeed in containing the conflicts of interest during the 1990s. A public interest is by definition what is of interest to a large group of people, as opposed to the interests of these as single individuals. What constitutes a general interest is, however, not something that is given by nature. There always exist different public interests in a group of people, and it is a useless exercise, as Schumpeter (among others) has made clear, to try to define the one and only general interest. Schumpeter writes in *Capitalism, Socialism and Democracy* that 'there is ... no such thing as a uniquely determined common good that people could agree on [since] to different individuals and groups the common good is bound to mean different things' (Schumpeter 1975 [1942]: 250 ff.). A general interest, in other words, always has to be *constructed*. As part of this process, a general interest typically also needs to be recognized as *legitimate*.

Similarly, and closely related, general interests need to be rooted in social relations in order to survive and triumph. General interests that are embedded in durable social relations—in institutions, in brief—are extra well protected and also tough to challenge. What adds to their general strength is also the fact that these typically also are legitimate. General interests that are less firmly anchored are easier to fight and to uproot, even if it usually is hard to totally eliminate an interest.

Schumpeter's point about the multiplicity of potential general or public interests can add to our understanding of what went on in the 1990s and led to the corporate scandals of 2001–2. That there exist objective business analyses is in the general interest of the investors—but the structure of the investor public changed quite a bit during the 1990s, and so did the equivalent general interest. The number of small investors grew strongly, and these had typically no inside information about Wall Street but were instead exclusively dependent on public information of the type that can be found in accounting reports and reports from business analysts.

The more legitimate a general interest is, the stronger it will naturally tend to be. The problem for the increasing number of small investors, however, was that their general interest was not much acknowledged in the 1990s; it was not yet seen as the general interest of investors, and it was not protected in legislation. There was also an obvious collective action problem involved in this type of situation; until this had been solved, various people and institution felt that they had to step in and represent small investors. This is what Arthur Levitt tried to do during his chairmanship at SEC in the 1990s (1998; 2002*a*); and this is also what Eliot Spitzer was trying to do in 2002: 'I've got a job, and it's to protect small investors' (Traub 2002: 41).

When one switches from a general reasoning about the small investors and their general interest to an examination of empirical data about them, in order to better handle this interest, it quickly becomes clear that there is much less information about them than one would wish. This reflects the fact that there is a general lack of data in the United States on wealth, which in its turn appears to be related to the fact that American authorities collect very little information of this type because of the way that taxes are structured. According to one of the few sociologists who has studied this issue, the only time when the authorities need to find out exactly how much an individual is worth is when he or she dies, since in this case detailed estate tax returns have to be filled out (Keister 2000: 27; Spilerman 2000).

Whatever the reason may be for the lack of empirical data on wealth and the small investors in the United States, the most comprehensive and widely used type of information that does exist comes from the triennial surveys which are administered by the Federal Reserve Board, the so-called Surveys of Consumer Finance (SCF).[2] According to these, a little more than half of all American families (51.9%) owned stocks in 2001—that is individual stocks, mutual funds, retirements accounts, and what is known as 'other managed assets'. This figure can be compared to the one from 1989 which was 31.6% (Kennickell, Starr-McCluer, and Surette 2000: 15).[3] Together, these stocks accounted for nearly three-fourths (72.8%) of the financial assets of these families in 2001, up from one half (48.4%) in 1989. The median value of stocks for families in 2001 was $34,300, as opposed to $13,000 in 1992. It should also be noted that it was considerably more common to own stocks as part of one's retirement account than to own them as part of their savings. All in all, it is clear that stock ownership, measured in several complementary ways, increased sharply in the United States during the 1990s—but also that someone like Paul Volcker was wrong in his assertion that all Americans are shareholders ('a nation of shareholders'; see Volcker 2002).

But even if it is granted that about half of all American families do own stock, all of these families do not belong in the category of 'small investors'. A first step in addressing this issue may be to draw a line between what we may term the elite and the rest of the population, with the former being defined (in SCF categories) as families in the 90–100 percentile of income, and the latter as all other families (or in the less than 20, and in the 20–89.9 percentile). According to this way of reasoning, 'the small investor' would be defined as a residual (and abstract) category. Among 'elite families', the data show that 60.6% owned individual stocks in 2001, while the equivalent figure for the rest of the shareholding population of families ('small investors') ranged from 37% in the 80–89.9 percentile to 3.8% in the less than 20 percentile. The median value of the former's stock holdings was $50,000,

TABLE 9.3. Direct and Indirect Family Holding of Stock, by Selected
Characteristics of Families, According to the Consumer Finance Surveys
of 1992, 1995, 1998, and 2001 (%)

| Family characteristics | Families having stock, direct or indirect[a] | | | | Median value among families with stock holdings (thousands of 2001 dollars) | | | |
|---|---|---|---|---|---|---|---|---|
| | 1992 | 1995 | 1998 | 2001 | 1992 | 1995 | 1998 | 2001 |
| All families | 36.7 | 40.4 | 48.9 | 51.9 | 13.0 | 16.9 | 27.2 | 34.3 |
| *Percentile of income* | | | | | | | | |
| < 20 | 7.3 | 6.5 | 10.0 | 12.4 | 9.9 | 4.3 | 5.4 | 7.0 |
| 20–39.91 | 20.2 | 24.7 | 30.8 | 33.5 | 4.9 | 7.3 | 10.9 | 7.5 |
| 40–59.9 | 33.6 | 41.5 | 50.2 | 52.1 | 6.2 | 7.2 | 13.1 | 15.0 |
| 60–79.9 | 51.1 | 54.3 | 69.3 | 75.7 | 10.1 | 14.6 | 20.4 | 28.5 |
| 80–89.9 | 65.7 | 69.7 | 77.9 | 82.0 | 17.3 | 28.9 | 49.0 | 64.6 |
| 90–100 | 77.0 | 80.0 | 90.4 | 89.6 | 58.8 | 69.3 | 146.5 | 247.7 |

[a] Indirect holdings are those in mutual funds, retirement accounts, and other managed assets.

*Note*: In providing data on income and assets respondents were asked to base their answers on the calendar year preceding the interview.

*Source*: Aizcorbe, Kennickell, and Moore (2003: 16).

and that of the latter between $20,000 in the 80–89.9 percentile and $7,500 in the less than 30 percentile. If we include ownership of stocks to also include mutual funds and retirement accounts, the differences are in the same direction (see Table 9.3).

But even if our way of drawing a line between the elite and 'the small investor' is accepted, it is still an open question what the general interest of the latter would be. One factor that reminds us of this dilemma is the fact that there also exists a clear ethnic division in the investor community. According to the survey for 2001, it is, for example, twice as common for 'white non-Hispanic families' to own individual stocks (24.5%), than for 'non-white or Hispanic families' (11.0%). The median value of the former's holding was US$22,000 and that of the latter US$8,000. If we extend ownership of stock to also mean mutual funds and retirement accounts, the differences are roughly the same (see Table 9.4). In other words, what the general interest of 'the small investor' is, does not in some natural way emerge from social reality, as it might if small investors constituted a homogenous group. It very definitely has to be *constructed*.

Before leaving the issue of how many investors there are in the United States, there is one further issue that needs to be addressed. This has to do with the fact that the rapid growth in the number of shareholders in the 1990s took place during a period when overall wealth of Americans remained dramatically unequal (and when wealth inequality even slightly increased. In 1998 the top 20% of the population controlled 83.4% of all wealth, the next

TABLE 9.4. Family Holdings of Stocks, According to
the 2001 Survey of Consumer Finances

| Familiy characteristics | Stocks | Mutual funds[a] | Retirement accounts[b] | Other managed assets[c] |
|---|---|---|---|---|
| *Percentage of families holding assets* | | | | |
| All families | 21.3 | 17.7 | 52.2 | 6.6 |
| *Percentile of income* | | | | |
| <20 | 3.8 | 3.6 | 13.2 | 2.2 |
| 20–39.91 | 11.2 | 9.5 | 33.3 | 3.3 |
| 40–59.9 | 16.4 | 15.7 | 52.8 | 5.4 |
| 60–79.9 | 26.2 | 20.6 | 75.7 | 8.5 |
| 80–89.9 | 37.0 | 29.0 | 83.7 | 10.7 |
| 90–100 | 60.6 | 48.8 | 88.3 | 16.7 |
| *Race or ethnicity of respondents* | | | | |
| White nonHispanic | 24.5 | 20.9 | 56.9 | 8.2 |
| Nonwhite or Hispanic | 11.0 | 7.2 | 37.3 | 1.8 |
| *Median value of holdings for families holding assets (thousands of 2001 dollars)* | | | | |
| All families | 20.0 | 35.0 | 29.0 | 70.0 |
| *Percentile of income* | | | | |
| <20 | 7.5 | 21.0 | 4.5 | 24.2 |
| 20–39.91 | 10.0 | 24.0 | 8.0 | 36.0 |
| 40–59.9 | 7.0 | 24.0 | 13.6 | 70.0 |
| 60–79.9 | 17.0 | 30.0 | 30.0 | 60.0 |
| 80–89.9 | 20.0 | 28.0 | 55.0 | 70.0 |
| 90–100 | 50.0 | 87.5 | 130.0 | 112.0 |
| *Race or ethnicity of respondents* | | | | |
| White nonHispanic | 22.0 | 40.0 | 35.0 | 70.0 |
| Nonwhite or Hispanic | 8.0 | 17.5 | 10.0 | 45.0 |

[a] Excluding money market funds and funds held through retirement accounts; can be held in stocks or bonds.
[b] These may be invested in virtually any asset, including stocks, bonds, mutual funds, real estate, and other options.
[c] These include assets such as annuities and trusts with an equity interest and managed investment accounts.
*Source*: Aizcorbe, Kennickell, and Moore (2003: 13).

two-fifths 16.4%, and the remaining two-fifths 0.2% (Wolff 2000: 16). While the number of investors increased during the 1990s, there was no equivalent shift in ownership—only a change in what *type* of wealth people owned. If we use 'ideology' in its original Marxist sense of a set of ideas that conceal the nature of the economic 'base', then it is fair to say that the notion of 'the small investor', as it was understood in the 1990s, falls into this category.[4]

## Concluding Discussion

The attention given to conflicts of interests in the corporate scandals of 2001–2 represents a good opportunity for sociologists to turn to a topic that they have not paid much attention to (see, however, Shapiro 2001). Sociologists who follow in the footsteps of Bourdieu and Coleman, I argue, are nonetheless well equipped for an effort of this type since both of these assign an important role to interests in social life and also suggest various ways how these can be introduced into a sociological analysis. The latter, to recall, is basically to be done by following two propositions: (1) interests have to be socially constructed; and (2) interests are embedded in social relations.

These propositions have been applied to one of the major conflicts of interest that have received the most political and media attention in 2001–2, namely conflicts of interest in the brokerage industry. What happened in this case, according to the public discourse, is that self-interest got out of hand during the boom in the stock market in the 1990s. The general interest was set aside, and the scandals were a fact. In contrast to this type of analysis, which is fundamentally psychological in nature with its strong emphasis on the greed of the individual actor, I tried to show that social relations and institutions did indeed play a key role in channeling and directing various interests into conflict with one another. The way that the actors with their various interests were situated in the social structure is also of crucial import- ance in order to understand how they tried to realize their interests during the boom of the 1990s. I finally also argue that one of the reasons why the public or general interest of the investors was vulnerable during this period was that it was being redefined, as a result of the rapid growth in the number of small investors. These latter were especially vulnerable to various wrongdoings since they had little access to alternative information.

By looking at interests in this manner, the analysis in this chapter not only differs from the greed-centered analysis that can be found in the public dis- course, it also goes counter to quite a bit of contemporary economic sociology in that it explicitly assigns a central role to *interests*. My argument on this particular point is that interests have to be part of the sociological analysis, and this is something they tend *not* to be, since the focus is often exclusively on social relations. The main reason for taking this stance in favor of includ- ing interests in the sociological analysis is that interests drive human behavior, in the sense that they constitute the basic forces of motivation of the actor. Or to cite a line from Max Weber's famous passage about the so-called switchmen of history: '*action is pushed by the dynamic of interest*' (Weber 1946: 182; emphasis added). Simmel, Marx, and many other early sociologists, it can be added, basically agree with Weber on this point, and it is first in modern sociology that we find a tendency to leave interests out of the analysis.

## Notes

1. A second definition (of less interest here) is also given: 'A real or seeming incompatibility between the interests of two of a lawyer's clients, such that the lawyer is disqualified from representing both clients if the dual representation adversely affects either client or if the clients do not consent'.
2. For a general introduction to the Survey of Consumer Finance, see, for example, Fries, Starr-McCluer, and Sundén 1998 and Keister 2000: 24–7; for a discussion of similarities and differences between this and other surveys of wealth in the United States in the 1990s, see Wolff 2000: 11–3. It should also be noted that the longest historical time series on stock ownership in the United States has been published by the New York Stock Exchange (NYSE). Drawing on this latter type of data, as well as some other sources, James Burk (1988) has attempted to estimate the number of individual shareholders between 1927–80. In 1927, there were 4–6 million shareholders or 3.4–5.0% of the population (Burk 1988: 260–7), and in 1985 47.0 million or 20.2%.
3. The figures that are cited in this and other passages that come from SCF (apart from 1989) can be found in tables 3 and 4 in the appendix, 'Data from the Surveys of Consumer Finance about Stockholders in the 1990s'. On the assumption that each of the two adults in a family (or the only adult) does own shares, this means that something like 55% of the (adult) US population were shareholders in 2001 (cf. the calculation based on the 1998 figures in Poterba 2001: 1–2, 11).
4. Another issue that deserves to be mentioned in this context has to do with the fact that political power in the United States is built on voting—a fact that makes it important to know how many of the voters are also shareholders. I have not been able to find any reliable information on this point. One figure that circulates in the press, however, often together with the correct assessment that half of the American population owns shares, is that two-thirds of the voters own stock (e.g. Scheiber 2002: 16; Stevenson 2003: A1). People who are shareholders, in other words, have more say in the appointment of politicians than their mere number would indicate.

## References

Aizcorbe, A., Kennickell, A., and Moore, M. 2003. 'Recent Changes in U.S. Family Finances: Evidence from the 1998 and 2001 Survey of Consumer Finances', *Federal Reserve Bulletin* 89: 1–32.

Association of the Bar of the City of New York, Special Committee on the Federal Conflict of Interest Laws. 1960. *Conflict of Interest and Federal Service*. Cambridge, MA: Harvard University Press.

Bourdieu, P. 1990. 'The Interest of the Sociologist', *In Other Words: Essays Towards a Reflexive Sociology*. Stanford, CA: Stanford University Press, 87–93.

202                          *Richard Swedberg*

Bourdieu, P. and Wacquant, L. 1992. *An Invitation to Reflexive Sociology*. Chicago, IL: University of Chicago Press.

Burk, J. 1988. *Values in the Market Place: The American Stock Market under Federal Securities Law*. New York, NY: De Gruyter.

Bush, G. W. 2002*a*. 'President Announces Tough New Enforcement Initiatives for Reform'. *www.whitehouse.gov/news/releases/2002/07/20020709-4.html*. Downloaded October 24.

—— 2002*b*. 'President Signs Corporate Corruption Bill'. *www.whitehouse.gov/news/releases/2002/07/20020730.html*. Downloaded October 22.

—— 2003. 'President's State of the Union Message for Congress and the Nation', *New York Times*, January 29: A12.

Coleman, J. 1990. *Foundations of Social Theory*. Cambridge, MA: Harvard University Press.

Craig, S. 2002. 'Will Investors Benefit From Wall Street's Split?', *Wall Street Journal*, December 23: C1, C3.

Davis, M. and Stark, A. (eds.). 2001. *Conflict of Interest in the Professions*. New York, NY: Oxford University Press.

Demski, J. 2003. 'Corporate Conflicts of Interest', *Journal of Economic Perspectives* 17(2): 51–72.

Der Hovranesian, M. 2002. 'Don't Sell Analysts Short', *Business Week*, October 21: 122.

Fries, G., Starr-McCluer, M., and Sundén, A. 1998. 'The Measurement of Household Wealth using Survey Data: An Overview of the Survey of Consumer Finances', Paper presented at the 44th Annual Conference of the American Council on Consumer Interests, Washington, DC.

Garner, B. (ed.). 1999. *Black's Law Dictionary*, 7th edn. St Paul, MN: West Group.

Hayward, M. and Boeker, W. 1998. 'Power and Conflicts of Interest in Professional Firms: Evidence from Investment Banking', *Administrative Science Quarterly* 43: 1–22.

Keister, L. 2000. *Wealth in America: Trends in Wealth Inequality*. Cambridge: Cambridge University Press.

Kennickell, A., Starr-McClue, M., and Surette, B. 2000. 'Recent Changes in U.S. Family Finances: Result from the 1998 Survey of Consumer Finances', *Federal Reserve Bulletin*, January: 1–27.

Levitt, A. 1998. 'The Numbers Game'. Speech at NYU Center for Law and Business on September 28. *http://accounting.rutgers.edu/raw/aaa/newsarc/pr101898.html*. Downloaded October 18, 2002.

—— 2002*a*. PBS Frontline. *Interview: Arthur Levitt*. March 12. *www.pbs.org/wgbh/pages/frontline/shows/regulation/interviews*. Downloaded October 25, 2002.

—— 2002*b*. *Taking on the Street: What Wall Street and Corporate America Don't Want You to Know*. New York, NY: Pantheon Books.

McGeehan, P. 2002. 'Wall St. Deal Says Little On Individual', *New York Times*, December 21: C1,14.

Michaely, R. and Womack, K. 1999. 'Conflict of Interest and the Credibility of Underwriter Analyst Recommendations', *Review of Financial Studies* 12: 653–86.

Morgenson, G. and McGeehan, P. 2002. 'Wall Street Firms Are Ready to Pay $1 Billion in Fines', *New York Times*, December 20: A1, C5.

Office of New York State Attorney General. 2002. *Affidavit in Support of Application for an Order Pursuant to General Business Law Section 354*. April 8, 2002. *www.oag.state.ny.us/press/2002/apr08b_02.html*. Downloaded October 18, 2002.

Poterba, J. 2001. 'The Rise of the "Equity Culture": U.S. Stockownership Patterns, 1989–1998', Preliminary Paper, Cambridge, MA: MIT.

Rosenbush, S. et al. 2002. 'Inside the Telecom Game', *Business Week*, August 5: 34–40.

Scheiber, N. 2002. 'Eliot Spitzer's Message for the Democrats. Consumer Party', *The New Republic*, December 2, 9: 15–9.

Schumpeter, J. 1975 [1942]. *Capitalism, Socialism, and Democracy*. New York, NY: Harper & Row.

Sernovitz, G. 2002. 'Don't Shoot the Analyst', *New York Times*, November 15: A31.

Shapiro, S. 2001. *Tangled Loyalties: Conflict of Interest in Legal Practice*. Ann Arbor, MI: University of Michigan Press.

Spilerman, S. 2000. 'Wealth and Stratification Processes', *Annual Review of Sociology* 26: 497–524.

Stark, A. 2000. *Conflicts of Interest in American Public Life*. Cambridge, MA: Harvard University Press.

Stevenson, R. 2003. 'The Politics of Portfolios', *New York Times,* January 7: A1, A16.

Swedberg, R. 2003. *The Principles of Economic Sociology*. Princeton, NJ: Princeton University Press.

Traub, J. 2002. 'The Attorney General Goes to War', *New York Times Magazine,* June 16: 38–41.

Twentieth Century Fund. 1980. *Abuse on Wall Street: Conflicts of Interest in the Securities Market*. Westport, CN: Quorum Books.

US Congress. 2002. Sarbanes–Oxley Act of 2002. H.R. 3763. *www.findlaw.com*. Downloaded October 22.

Volcker, P. 2002. PBS Home. Online Newsletter. *Newsmaker*, Paul Volcker, March 12. *www.pbs.org/newshour/bb/business/jan-june02/volcker_3-12.html*. Downloaded October 18, 2002.

Weber, M. 1946. *From Max Weber*, in Gerth, H. and Wright Mills, C. (eds.). New York, NY: Oxford University Press.

Wolff, E. 2000. 'Recent Trends in Wealth Ownership, 1983–98', Working Paper 300, Jerome Levy Economics Institute.

# Section III
## Finance and Governance

# 10

# Interpretive Politics at the Federal Reserve

## MITCHEL Y. ABOLAFIA

### Introduction

One of the few things that can interrupt the flow of the US bond market during its trading day is an announcement from the Federal Reserve. Traders anticipate these announcements and trade on their implications. Every bond trading floor, whether in a bank or securities firm, employs economists, known as Fed watchers. They closely monitor the Fed's policy announcements and its reports on the economy, attempting to predict their contents. Fed watchers, journalists, and traders interact to create a collective set of expectations about how the Fed will act next to control the supply of money in the economy. But before anyone can interpret the Fed's reports and announcements, the Fed itself must make sense of the immense load of economic information flowing into it. The Federal Reserve, in this sense, is the chief sensemaker in a field of continuous sensemakers. The signals sent by its announcements and reports have the ability to elicit billions of dollars in trading and corporate investment. As such, even before the Fed's interpretation of the economic environment reaches the financial markets, the process of interpretation has begun.

At the October 6, 1982 meeting of the Federal Reserve's chief policymaking unit, the Federal Open Market Committee (FOMC), the members found themselves contemplating a major change: abandoning a monetary target (M1) as their chief policy tool. The policymakers were acutely sensitive to potential interpretations of their actions. Committee members spent most of the meeting framing the meaning of their action, assessing how others would interpret it, and crafting the policy directive so that it would be interpreted as they intended. The process of building consensus was contentious and members strongly contested each other's interpretations:

MR. ROOS: I believe that what we're about to do today will unquestionably be viewed by those who watch what we do as a major change. I don't think it will be possible to explain away the fact that, albeit temporarily, we are moving away from targeting a narrow aggregate that has predicted prices and output better than other variables.

I wish to thank Bien Baez, Steve Borgatti, Ralph Brower, Karen Knorr Cetina, Martin Kilduff. Mike Lounsbury, Alex Preda, Martha Starr, and Frank Thompson for their insightful comments.

It will be apparent, in spite of any disclaimers we may or may not make, that we are moving toward placing greater emphasis on controlling the Fed Funds rate. And I think it will be misconstrued by the markets. I think it will give comfort to those who, rightly or wrongly, have sat on the sidelines and implied that somewhere along the line we would cave in on our present policy posture. (FOMC 1982: 48)

This chapter suggests that students of financial markets need to pay more attention to the contest over interpretation that is part of every financial market. Information placed before traders is not neutral. It is interpreted or 'framed' by a diverse field of sensemakers competing for control of the understanding of market conditions. Preeminent among this field of sense-makers is the policymaking unit of the central bank of the United States, the FOMC. This chapter offers an approach for understanding the interpretive politics at the FOMC. These interpretive politics comprise the efforts of members of this Committee to influence the thinking of other group members and the wider community of market stakeholders. Interpretation, then, is not seen as a product, but a process made up of the 'framing moves' of various actors. The result of these moves is not a single idea, but rather a fabric of ideas and interests woven together by the participant's interaction.

## Framing Moves

From the perspective of interpretive politics, FOMC meetings are largely about 'meaning work', that is, the struggle over ideas and meaning construction. The object of this contention is control and definition of the dominant policy frame. Following Goffman (1974), frames are 'schemata of interpretation'. In the policymaking setting, they are 'narratives that guide both analysis and action in practical situations' (Rein and Schon 1996: 89). Rein and Schon explain that frames are the 'generic story lines' that one finds underlying policy controversies. In the area of welfare policy, we are familiar with the old frame of 'needs-based assistance' vs. the more radical frame of 'strengthening families' through abolishing welfare. In the monetary policy of the 1970s and 1980s, the competing narratives involved 'targeting monetary aggregates' vs. 'targeting interest rates'. Each tells a story about methods of regulating the supply of money in the national economy. In both cases, the frame is designed to guide both analysis and action in policymaking.

Framing is a fundamentally political act. On boards of directors as well as government agencies, this kind of linguistic contest is part of the ongoing politics (Hirsch 1986). Alternative frames may have significantly different policy consequences. As a result, framing is not haphazard. The statistics, reported events, and predictions that are at the narrative core of frames do not arrive in 'raw form' at policy meetings (Gamson 1992: 67). They have been previously organized and interpreted. Frames are therefore vulnerable to tampering (Goffman quoted in Gamson 1992: 67). They are reinterpreted to fit changing situations. Users of a frame will carefully calculate its timing and presentation. The narrative will usually be employed to legitimize one solution over another (Campbell 1998). Framing is itself an occasion for micropolitics or as Gamson puts it 'a locus of potential struggle'.

*Framing moves* are strategic actions meant to contest or maintain existing frames. Most of these moves are drawn from a repertoire of culturally available action to which every policymaker has access, although during occasions of crisis or change actors may devise innovative framing moves. Most typically, framing moves attack or defend claims of interpretation (frames). In this chapter, framing moves are used to contest dominant frames and project new ones at the Federal Reserve. They are used to promote or deflate efforts to make sense of economic events, statistical indicators, and previous policy actions of the policymaking group. They include such actions as casting doubt, preempting the old frame, or 'spinning' the new one. Any substantial change in monetary policy calls for the skilled use of framing moves to invoke a questioning of the taken-for-granted and a revision of the habitual.

Among the most important contextual factors shaping the employment of framing moves is time. The adoption of one framing move rather than another is structured by whether the actors are looking backward or forward. Emirbayer and Mische explain this temporality as a more general characteristic of human agency. 'As actors respond to changing environments, they must continually reconstruct their view of the past in an attempt to understand the causal conditioning of the emergent present, while using this understanding to control and shape their responses to the arising future' (1998: 968). Policymakers are challenged by an emerging present to reconstruct a coherent past and future. Policymaking, even under conditions of stability, includes three habitual, semiautomatic processes that reflect a continuous intertwining of past, future, and present. Policymakers *anchor* their analysis and action in the retrospective statistics and other indicators drawn from the immediate past. They *negotiate* to build a consensus for the continuing reproduction and application of the frame in the present. Finally, even as anchoring and negotiating proceed, they are carefully crafting *signals*; plausible accounts of their action constructed to influence future action by external stakeholders (Abolafia 2004).

Under conditions of stability, an exchange of instutionalized framing moves among policymakers will generally reproduce the existing policies from meeting to meeting. At the Federal Reserve, the regular reproduction of monetary policy involves a relatively diverse but recurring set of framing moves. When conditions are unstable, whether from exogenous or endogenous forces, political conflicts of interest create opportunities for policy entrepreneurs. Under such conditions, we may observe a different set of framing moves designed to break the old frame and construct the new one. These moves exhibit a similar temporal structure to the one described in the paragraph above, but a different interpretive politics in which actors exploit symbolic resources and employ social skills to accomplish policy change. Retrospective anchoring is replaced by questioning of past anchors and consensual negotiation is replaced by transformative framing. Under conditions of instability, the politics of framing is itself transformed.

This chapter applies a temporal perspective on framing to study the interpretive politics of policy change at the Federal Reserve. It uses verbatim, transcripts from closed-door policy meetings of the FOMC, the body responsible for setting monetary policy, to explore the framing moves involved in rejecting old frames and constructing and instituting new ones. The transcripts were obtained through a Freedom of Information Act request. A detailed coding of the verbal interaction of members of the FOMC is used to identify framing moves and the contexts in which they are used.

Framing moves will be presented throughout this chapter in italics. The moves identified do not represent an exhaustive population of all framing moves in the data. Rather, they are the framing moves that stood out in the data as important for accomplishing change. Specifically, they are the moves that elicited strong reaction among the participants, changed the direction of the discourse, or redefined fundamental issues. My aim here is to explore interpretive dynamics in the midst of a major policy change.

## Abandoning Monetarism

The FOMC meets every fifth or sixth week to decide whether the Fed should tighten or loosen the money supply, thereby influencing the availability and cost of money in the US economy. The voting participants at an FOMC meeting are the seven members of the Fed board of governors in Washington, the president of the Federal Reserve Bank of New York, and, on a rotating basis, four of the eleven presidents of the other regional reserve banks. Joining these twelve are a handful of staff economists as well as the nonvoting presidents of the regional reserve banks. Together, this group spends one and sometimes two days analyzing current economic conditions and setting monetary policy. At the end of each meeting, the Committee issues a directive to the Federal Reserve Bank of New York that may charge them to buy or sell relatively large amounts of government securities, thereby affecting the supply of money and credit in the economy. This in turn, influences individual and corporate investment and expansion or contraction of the economy.

In practice, there is no objective function or optimal rule for setting monetary policy (Blinder 1998). Rather, policymakers rely on the current mix of available frames. In the early 1980s, that mix included overlapping axes of choice: expansionary vs. contractionary, Keynesian vs. monetarist, discretionary vs. rule-based policy frames. They used these frames to interpret the current economic situation and to construct a course of action. For such a frame to be useful to the FOMC it must cut through the ambiguity of economic data and offer a mechanism for controlling inflation and maintaining growth.

During the period under study, Keynesianism and monetarism served as meta-frames, or policy paradigms. These were less tools than they were assumptions that constrained the solutions available to policymakers (Campbell 1998). From the late 1930s to the late 1970s, Keynesianism was the dominant narrative underlying macroeconomic policy. By 1979, the Keynesian consensus had unraveled due to a sustained period of high inflation and slow growth (stagflation). In October of 1979, the newly appointed chairman of the Fed, Paul Volcker, announced that in an effort to gain control over the expansion of money and dampen inflation, the FOMC would place greater emphasis on bank reserves and less on fluctuations in interest rates. According to the new frame, the Fed could gain greater control over the growth of the money supply by targeting the money supply itself and letting the interest rate float. This refocusing on the money supply is generally viewed as a strategic use of elements of a 'monetarist' meta-frame to justify the severe contraction in money growth that brought inflation down (Greider 1987; Heilbroner and Milberg 1995). The Fed could simply point to the contracting money supply without the political risk of having to raise or lower interest rates.

Whether the Fed truly went monetarist in 1979 or not, the enactment of the monetarist frame was successful. Targeting of monetary aggregates became the centerpiece of policymaking at the Fed. By 1982, inflation had been dampened and the growth in the money supply controlled. In July 1982, the Committee voted to begin easing up on the money supply, but was unwilling to accept Chairman Volcker's proposal to lower the acceptable range on interest rates. Volcker's response was 'Well, I don't like it much, but if that's what you want to do, let's do it. Let's have a vote'. The proposal to stick with monetary targets carried ten to one. In the six weeks between the August 24 and October 5 meetings, economic conditions grew substantially worse, especially outside the United States. Chairman Volcker knew that there was more support for the changes he wished to make, but there was still strong resistance, especially from the monetarist Reserve Bank presidents. In October 1982, with the US and world economy in a deep recession, Paul Volcker attempted to reframe monetary policy by abandoning monetarism.

### Breaking the Frame: Retrospective Interpretive Politics

The framing moves that constitute the interpretive politics of policy change are generally preceded by an external shock or internal contradiction that focuses attention on the situation. If the shock is sufficiently disruptive, the actors find themselves confused. As Weick (1995: 91) explains, they are confused by either too many interpretations (ambiguity) or the lack of any viable interpretation (uncertainty). As a result of this confusion, actors engage in a 'collective questioning' of the existing frame (Barley and Tolbert 1997: 102).

This questioning is largely retrospective, focusing on that which has already occurred, that is, the shock or contradiction, and trying to bring order and clarity to it.

This period of collective questioning represents a strategic opportunity for reframing. Contradictions and shocks can be made sensible. Such disruptions are labeled as systemic problems or, on occasion, crises. Actors who reject the status quo declare a crisis. The declaration of crisis is itself a statement that existing frames are inadequate to restore stability. Frame breakers attempt to convince others that their interests lie in rejecting the dominant narrative explanation of the policy problem and its logic.

These actors, whom we call reframers, are those with the resources and skill to develop and communicate a new frame, a new diagnostic and prescriptive story that will serve as a guide to change. Reframers work within institutionalized systems to significantly change not only the existing narrative, but some significant aspect of practice. They are skilled at sizing up the situation and molding a new collective identity for their group. Fligstein defines the skill of such 'institutional entrepreneurs' as 'the ability to motivate cooperation in other actors by providing those actors with common meanings and identities in which actions can be undertaken and justified' (1997: 398). Reframers may have been awaiting the opportunity offered by the shock or they may recognize new opportunities to pursue their interests because of the shock. They respond by mobilizing their resources and focusing their skills to reject the old frame and support a new framing of normative organizational practice.

Under conditions of stability, the retrospective element in policymaking is brief and consensual, largely an opportunity for grounding the projective and practical discussions in the legitimacy of past action. Under stable conditions, the data are interpreted as providing relatively useful signals and concern with ambiguity is at its minimum. Rather, attention is focused on what risks may lie beyond the horizon. Under conditions of severe disruption, reframers with the resources to do so may attempt to break the existing frame so that it can be replaced with a more plausible one. In this case, the retrospective element is neither brief nor consensual. It is extensive and conflictual. Strategic interpretations are proffered and contested. Ambiguity is identified as a locus for political action. Reframers attempt to establish that existing practices are no longer viable while defenders of the status quo use data to argue that frame change is unnecessary. In breaking the existing frame, issues of individual identity and organizational reputation are at stake.

*Calibrating the shock.* Among the first framing moves in a crisis setting is an effort to define the degree of disruption. Reframers advocating changed practices must be able to convince their constituency that the shock requires strong action. Early in the October 5, 1982 meeting of the FOMC Chairman Volcker departed from the ritualized discussion of staff reports to provide what he called 'a wider setting that has to be brought to bear' for reaching a policy decision. He gave a long bleak recitation of the state of the global economy including the following:

> We are in a worldwide recession. I don't think there's any doubt about that ... I don't know of any country of any consequence in the world that has an expansion going on. And I can think of lots of them that have a real downturn going on. This is not a time for business as usual, certainly, in the international area. I don't think it's time for business as usual in the domestic area either. *Extraordinary things may have to be done.* We haven't had a parallel to this situation historically except to the extent 1929 was a parallel. (FOMC 1982: 15)

Central bankers do not invoke 1929 lightly. Not only did 1929 mark the beginning of the Great Depression, but it is believed by many to mark the Federal Reserve Board's greatest failure. Volcker, known for his coolness, is anything but cool here. His long recitation was not a dry analysis of standardized indicators, it was a skillful effort to make sense of disturbing conditions. He uses rhetorical emphasis ('extraordinary things', no 'parallel', 'business as usual') to weave a narrative that is both an explanation and a frame for action. He has calibrated the shock as equal to the worst the Fed has experienced. He uses *dramatic comparison*, that is, 1929, as a framing move to signify the intensity and scope of the crisis and to suggest the potential consequences of unwillingness to act.

Another part of calibrating the shock involves establishing that the shock was big enough to create confusion, that is, ambiguity or uncertainty, about the future consequences of the disruptive conditions. The reframer claims not only that he or she is confused, but that the confusion is widespread. Volcker makes this claim for uncertainty after a review of nations in Europe, Asia, and Latin America on the brink of financial disaster:

> I'd say all of this leads to a considerable feeling in financial markets and elsewhere of developing disarray, a certain floundering. And that in itself contributes to uncertainty, which feeds upon itself ... But I do think we are in an extremely tricky period of transition that is complicated enormously by the factors not just of a period of potential transition for us, but for the world economy as a whole. There is not a single source of real strength or certainty out there. (FOMC 1982: 18)

The framing moves here are of two kinds. The first, *attributing confusion*, refers to his assessment of the retrospective data and is signaled by the statement 'There is not a single source of strength or certainty out there'. Volcker is making the claim that things are in such disarray, and weakening further, in the domestic and international economies that we cannot make reliable analytic or predictive statements. This claim will come up again throughout the meeting. The second is *attributing incapacity*. The reframer argues that no one knows how to respond to the situation in the present. In Volker's phrase, the 'uncertainty which feeds upon itself' is that consumers, businesses and financial markets are floundering and no one really knows what to do. This sort of uncertainty serves as the reframer's rallying point for his or her constituency.

Volcker tells his colleagues that 'unusual exertions' will have to come from the Fed because '... there is no other (institution) in a comparable position. It's the only possibility in terms of having the leadership and resources necessary to deal with some of these problems' (FOMC 1982: 20). The shock is so strong that no one else in the global economy is capable of responding.

*Rejecting the old frame.* Although establishing a sense of crisis and its magnitude is important, the reframer must also show that the existing frames themselves are inadequate to deal with the crisis. He or she does this by challenging the legitimacy of the old policy. The reframer attempts to persuade those responsible for maintaining the legitimacy of existing practice that it is no longer in their interest and the interests of the organization to support the old frame. This kind of *casting doubt* includes attacks on the efficacy and practicality of past practices and the frames that interpret them. The reframer attempts to convince others that continued commitment to the outdated frames is irresponsible. There is an implication in these questioning moves that those who do not see this are holding back the progress of the organization.

Early in the meeting on October 5, during the discussion of the staff economists' reports, Volcker begins to become quite pointed in his attack on M1, a measure of the amount of money in the economy and the leading indicator for monetary targeting for the preceding three years. During those three years, the Fed has attempted to control inflation by controlling the rate of growth of M1. At the October 5 meeting the FOMC members are anticipating the issuance of a new financial instrument, Super Now Accounts. They are debating whether this new form of money should be counted in M1 or M2. Volcker's rather testy response is 'I'm not sure it matters where we put it ... It makes a difference in the number, obviously. But in either case we don't know what the heck the number means' (FOMC 1982: 10). Volcker takes the strong position that the Committee cannot make sense of M1, therefore the frame is no longer reliable or useful. If a policy tool is no longer open to consistent interpretation, it has lost its practicality.

Not surprisingly, members of the policy group begin defending the frame. In this case, a monetarist member of the FOMC argues for the retention of M1 as the primary target. The reframer, Volcker, is compelled to strengthen his rejection adding emphasis and rhetorical flourish to his original doubt:

MR. ROOS. Mr. Chairman, I would agree with Frank (Morris), strange as it may seem, that before we bury my old friend M1 at this meeting there ought to be some work done by the various economic staffs to try to project the effect. There are a lot of people who don't like my old friend M1 and whenever anything changes they say this is a good time to bury M1.

CHAIRMAN VOLCKER. Well, yes and no is the answer, I think. Obviously, we can study the matter. I see no prospect that any amount of study is going to tell us what the behavior of M1 is going to be in the short run. It is unknowable, in my opinion, to all the best brains in the world. It's going to be an empirical question; we will discover what happens when it happens. And we have to look at it over a period of time. But I don't see that any amount of rumination—is that the right word?—is going to produce an answer to a knowable question but an unknowable answer. The wish for a study is fine; but the sense that it's going to give us an answer in a month before we get the new instrument I think is totally unwarranted just by the nature of the problem that we face. (FOMC 1982: 12)

Volcker, in unusually emphatic terms, has argued that the basis of monetarism, the targets used to monitor the growth of the money supply, are 'unknowable'. In doing so he has attempted to *close the door* on further study and debate. His rhetorical vehemence may be seen as an effort to create passivity in others. Once again he invokes the argument that uncertainty is too high to maintain the reliance on M1 as a dominant frame. Volcker has made clear his fundamental dissatisfaction with the status quo. He wants a significant departure from the old policy, a major policy change. His strong rebuttal of Roos suggests to all that he is not inclined to compromise or concede this time.

*Aligning moves.* Breaking the old frame is a social as well as cognitive activity. As we saw in the exchange above, the rejection of old and valued frames is not likely to go unchallenged. Participants in the policy process are committed to its frames. They have employed these frames for years and are invested in their importance and validity. As a result, the rejection of the old frame elicits *countermoves.* Mr. Roos' effort at defending the frame in the exchange above is typical. At one level, rejection of the old frame would be expected to generate resistance, even cognitive dissonance, in members who had voted more than twenty times to support its efficacy as a policy tool. For a subgroup of members, the commitment to the frame runs even deeper, based on competing policy paradigms. In this case, targeting M1 and M2 is the operationalization of monetarist theory. Monetarists fought long and hard to have their beliefs recognized and they are not likely to relinquish their position easily (Heilbroner and Milberg 1995).

The alignment process is a negotiation among those who feel most strongly about the old frame. Rejecting moves, like those made above by Volcker, are supported or contested by those with a strong interest in the attempted revision. If a policy change is to succeed, other members must back up the reframer's declaration of crisis and rejection of the frame. This kind of supportive move involves *a piggybacking* on the reframers' position. At the October 5 meeting other members of the FOMC affirmed Volcker's interpretation of crisis:

VICE CHAIRMAN SOLOMON. I just came back from Europe. I am struck by the degree of malaise and of nervousness there—fears of all kind—and the willingness of players to move enormous sums of money to Switzerland and the United States on gut instinct that things are just going wrong in Europe and that the future just doesn't look good for Europe. And, of course, this was happening even in Japan where the statistics look better. There is a lot of money going out of Japan. And the exchange rate now is ridiculous; it's 270 yen for the dollar.

MR. MORRIS. Well. I find the same kind of attitude among U.S. businessmen . . .
I am seeing an attitude that I have never seen before, not even in the depths of the
1974–75 recession. There is a feeling of apprehension, a vague apprehension that
maybe things are going to get out of hand. And it's leading businessmen to take a very
defensive posture . . .

CHAIRMAN VOLCKER. There's no question that that thinking is widespread. . . .
(FOMC 1982: 25–6)

This use of anecdote and impression is informal but pointed and mutually
supportive. It lays the groundwork for the needed consensus. But not all the
comments are supportive. The contentious statements tend to be less anec-
dotal, more analytic, based on aggregated data and projected trends. Even in
the early stages of the meeting, group members urge that an alternative interpretation be considered. In the following example, Robert Black, President of
the Reserve Bank of Richmond, is supporting the more optimistic views
of his monetarist colleague Lawrence Roos, President of the Reserve Bank of
St Louis:

MR. BLACK. Mr. Chairman, Larry rescued us from the straits of desperation and
said some of the things I had in mind. There are two things that might be helpful to
remember here. One is that it always looks very, very bleak right at the bottom and we
all get very pessimistic, and I'm much more pessimistic than any of my associates in
Richmond. The second point is that there's a very low pickup in velocity projected
over the next four quarters. And traditionally most forecasters at this stage of the
business cycle—maybe I should say at this apparent stage—have underestimated
the pickup in velocity. We ought to bear those things in mind as we move through the
meeting. (FOMC 1982: 28)

While claiming to share in the pessimistic consensus, Mr Black is laying the
groundwork for the argument against a major policy change at this time. At
its core, the argument is that things are not as bleak as claimed. Prediction is
still possible. Black's move is *claiming exaggeration*, that the reframers have
overestimated the problem. We are reminded again that reframing is a social
act that involves dispute and negotiation. Major institutional change is not
going to occur without resistance and conflict. Volcker is fully aware that his
efforts will not go uncontested. His long and belabored recitation of bleak
conditions suggests that he expects the new frame to be resisted. The
reframers' opponents will continue to contest the abandonment of the policy
throughout the meeting.

### Constructing the New Frame: Projective Interpretive Politics

Revision of a major policy cannot be accomplished in the retrospective
dimension alone. Reframers must move interested actors' attention beyond
the past and into the future to construct an image of the new policy frame
and its superior efficacy. Reframers do not stop at breaking the old frame,

they aspire to create an alternative. There is a temporal shift from retrospective to projective interpretive politics; a move from collective questioning of
the past to collective questioning of the future: what will happen in our future
if we change this fundamental practice? Emirbayer and Mische (1998: 971)
define projectivity as 'the imaginative generation by actors of possible future
trajectories of action, in which received structures of thought and action may
be creatively reconfigured in relation to actors' hopes, fears, and desires for
the future'.

Under conditions of environmental stability, the projective interpretive
politics of policymaking are relatively consensual and routine. The frames
are not in question. Rather, the object is to use existing frames as a tool
to interpret information. Negotiation is over the rate of expansion or contraction in the money supply, not the policy instruments themselves. In
conditions of crisis, projective action is taken not only to imagine the future
but to suggest the means of intervening in and changing it. The process of
constructing a new frame is accomplished by rearranging and transforming
the old one. This is not accomplished in a single imaginative act, but rather
by negotiation and argument in which participants challenge one another's
projections. The reframer offers a narrative account of the proposed new
practice. The reframer is challenged by those members defending the existing
arrangements. Ultimately, a resolution is offered that incorporates as many
concerns as possible and appeals to the largest constituency in the meeting.
The majority tries to minimize the number in the minority, mindful that the
policy will be revisited in five or six weeks.

*Projecting new frames.* At this point reframers engage in the riskiest
part of their entrepreneurial action. They shift from critic to advocate. They
are proposing to upset the routine, to change a fundamental practice. To do
this, they must get their colleagues to imagine along with them a future clouded
in uncertainty; one they can only loosely characterize. In the context of the
FOMC, the object of the meeting is to craft a policy that the members can vote
on before the end of the meeting. In periods of stability, this is generally done
in a collegial spirit (Kettl 1998). In the previous meeting in August, the majority
of members did not recognize a crisis. Despite Volcker's efforts, a consensus
emerged that monetary targeting would continue and a broad range for interest
rate fluctuation would be tolerated (Abolafia 2004). In the October 5, 1982
meeting, Volcker is not waiting for a consensus to emerge. As we have seen, he
is preempting the usual structure of the meeting. The challenge for a reframer
is to construct a frame that will reflect the largest possible consensus sharing
the recognition that a major policy change is necessary.

Once again Volcker *preempts the narrative arc* of the Committee's traditional meeting pattern. This framing move both signals the unusual circumstances and upsets the routine of shared decisionmaking to which members
are accustomed, thereby shifting power to the reframer. Volcker's preemption
not only involves disruption of the routine, but the introduction of a new text.

Instead of the usual circuit round the table to get each member's analysis of current conditions, Volcker departs from traditional procedure by distributing a draft directive in which boilerplate language has been rewritten to reflect the major policy change he intends. The draft is a technical document that describes the FOMC's outlook for the coming period and sets target ranges for the key indicators to which both the Fed and the army of Fed watchers attend. The indicators in Volcker's draft are sufficiently different from projections given at the last meeting and in the annual report to Congress that the intention is clear. Most telling is that the directive does not specify a target for M1. The distribution of this document to the group is a not so subtle means of projecting the new frame. Volcker gives a transparently disingenuous introduction:

CHAIRMAN VOLCKER: If we are ready, I think we ought to return to the policy discussion. The staff can distribute this draft text that I have for discussion purposes anyway. I have not read the directive probably literally for years; I don't know whether I've read it since I've been here. But for some reason I got this boilerplate part in front of me, which goes in front of the operative part of the directive, and it seems to me singularly inappropriate. It probably always is, but it is more so now. I think this could use a judicious sentence or two, making some allusion to the strains or pressures or whatever in the banking sector these days and to the problems of foreign lending in particular...
   MR. ROOS. This would mean that we would set no targets for M1?
[Secretary's note: The draft directive wording circulated at Chairman Volcker's request did not include a target for M1.]
   CHAIRMAN VOLCKER. You are ahead of us. I'm just referring to this general boilerplate now, which I will cease talking about with the understanding that you may see a new sentence or two in there, if that's acceptable. (FOMC 1982: 28–29)

   To this point in the meeting, Volcker had not stated this new frame explicitly, so Committee members have now seen just how far he thinks the Committee should go. Volcker's first attempt at proposing the new frame is an act of omission, that is, he simply leaves M1 out of the policy directive. President Roos, noting the glaring omission in the directive asks, 'This would mean that we would set no targets for M1?' But Volcker, looking to make his case and get support before engaging in debate, puts him off saying: 'You are ahead of us'. Volcker wants the directive to be more negative than the staff has written it. He is looking for support to add in a few sentences that would reflect his bleak outlook on international debt and the world economy. Before he can make his case any further though, the debate has begun. To this point Volcker has employed relatively subtle framing moves of preemption and omission to project his new frame. If this is not to be a repeat of the August meeting, the reframer must now effectively engage his opponents and enroll supporters.
   *Debating the new frame.* In a policymaking group reframers are dependent on others to adopt the new frame. Each member translates the projected

frame in accord with their own interests, their constituents' interests, and the agency's interests, as they perceive them. Supporters and opponents attempt to define and limit the interpretation of the new frame. Any negotiation of a new frame exists in the context of the old frame. The meaning of the new practice is culturally embedded in the old. The group looks back at the old to make sense of the new. Those members not ready to give up the old frame renew their defense by *questioning the benefits* of the change:

PRESIDENT ROOS. Mr. Chairman, why would this be preferable to continuing to specify the target for M1 but putting in a disclaimer or at least the warning that M1 might behave in an unusual manner and if that occurs, we would reserve the privilege of adjusting it accordingly? I'd prefer that for the sake of continuity. There is still a significant amount of debate between Frank and me and others; some of us think that M1 is not as unreliable as others do. (FOMC 1982: 31)

Volcker is now compelled to specify his argument for the new frame. After establishing that his new frame would target interest rates, rather than the money supply, Volcker clearly *reveals his agenda* both in terms of what it is meant to signal and what it is meant to accomplish. The omission of M1 is an effort to shift to framing high interest rates as the problem to be solved. He states, 'Let me clarify my comment. A 12 percent federal funds rate is totally unacceptable to me ... Eleven percent is also unacceptable to me' (FOMC 1982: 32). It is clear that Volcker wants to shut off the options chosen at the last meeting, to allow for a broad range of interest rate fluctuation. President Horn, who would favor the old approach, deferentially raises the possibility of using the August solution.

MS. HORN. Mr. Chairman, this indicates your dissatisfaction with the way we handled it last time—that is, to have a target that was sensitive to ...

CHAIRMAN VOLCKER. Yes, I am totally dissatisfied. What we did last time was unacceptable to me. I just want to make that plain. I think we made a mistake last time. I think we would not have so difficult a problem psychologically this time if we had not done what we did last time. (FOMC 1982: 32)

Having rejected the August solution as insufficient, he reiterates his commitment to bringing interest rates down, and ties it to his earlier analysis of the national and international situations. In this way the reframer 'problematizes' (Callon 1986) the new frame, specifying the issues that the new frame is meant to address and reinforcing the sense of urgency expressed in the retrospective frame breaking. This specification, of course, opens the new frame to more effective attack:

CHAIRMAN VOLCKER: What this is meant to convey is an operational approach that modestly moves the federal funds rate down. Whether it involves a discount rate change or not is something the Board is going to have to decide. But that is the tenor meant to be given here, rather straightforwardly, I might say ... All I'm saying is, looking ahead, that I don't want to end up a month from now with a 12 percent federal funds rate. I don't even want to end up with an 11 percent federal funds rate, based

220         *Mitchel Y. Abolafia*

upon everything I know about the market situation, the national situation, and the world situation.

MR. FORD. What you are saying quite plainly, if I hear you correctly, is that you think rates are too high now and you don't want even a tiny increase from the present rate of 10¼ percent on the fed funds rate. You don't want it averaging 11 percent.

CHAIRMAN VOLCKER. I surely do not.

MR. FORD. You want literally to cap interest rates where they are now, or better yet, to drive them down.

CHAIRMAN VOLCKER. Drive them down? I'd like to see them a little easier, yes, if we can get by with that. (FOMC 1982: 33)

Once the reframer has revealed his or her agenda, the opponents may try to *derogate the new frame* as inappropriate, counternormative, or even dangerous. These opponents will use disparaging language to characterize the proposal. In the segment given above, Mr Ford has characterized Volcker's new frame as an effort to 'drive down' interest rates or 'cap' them. These are derogatory characterizations of Keynesian policy that, at the time, had been discredited. Opponents may also suggest the negative consequences such action would have for the Fed's reputation as well as individual members' reputations and identity. After the clarification given above by Volcker, President Ford rejects the new frame even more strongly. At this point the lines of conflict have become transparent:

MR. FORD. I want to say, respectfully, that I'm flatly opposed to this... First of all, I'm not convinced that pegging interest rates at today's level or trying to push them down is best for the economy. Secondly, changing policy now in this context and saying overtly, as you said it, that we should hold interest rates where they are and trying to push them down is going to make us extremely vulnerable to charges—unfounded I feel, because I don't question the motives of the people here who would vote for this. I think the repercussions of this are going to be terrible.

CHAIRMAN VOLCKER: That's an enormous concession. (FOMC 1982: 33)

*Enrolling allies.* As Volcker's sarcastic remark suggests, his opponents are conceding only that his motives are sincere.[1] As positions begin to clarify, the reframer must build a coalition of supporters who buy into the new guiding narrative. The rejection of the prior consensus and the committee's mandate to issue a directive compel a process of alignment. Members enroll through active support for the policy change. As we have seen, Volcker has been laying the groundwork for such a coalition by offering a variety of alternative rationales for reframing. The reframer endeavors to enroll allies (Callon 1986; Latour 1987) by offering frames useful to a diverse group of participants. If the framing has been successful, allies will begin to express their support in terms of this variety of agendas. Sherman Maisel, a former member of the FOMC, explains how these multiple logics of action work in practice:

It would not be unusual to find two members voting to change policy because they fear a balance of payments effect; two others who are concerned over a possible slowdown in the economy; another who desires lower interest rates; and still another who feels that the policy would lead to higher interest rates but welcomes them. While in complete disagreement over the projection, goals, and policy result, they could concur on specific operating instructions. (Maisel 1973: 51)

Once the new frame has been projected, one or more synthetic solutions will be offered so that the new policy can be agreed on. Members of the group will either *echo the reframer* or *offer alternative agendas* that may be used to rationalize the policy change. A member, usually someone other than the reframer, will play the role of mediator in a ritualized effort to resolve the conflict. In this instance, three different agendas are offered. The first two are *echoes*, the third is an *alternative*. In the first, Charles Partee, one of the Governors, tries to offer the opponents, led by Bill Ford, an alternative interpretation of the new policy. He places the emphasis on the temporary uncertainty of the M1 statistic, rather than focusing on the new policy's rejection of the old monetarist frame. This interpretation is supported by Governor Wallich, who is not ready to reject the monetarist frame but shares the view that M1 has lost its usefulness:

MR. PARTEE. You know Bill, I would put the emphasis a little differently here. Maybe the wording needs to be changed some; I wouldn't put it in terms of moving interest rates down. I think the problem is that M1 could do almost anything in the period to come. In fact, it already has done almost anything.... (FOMC 1982: 33)

MR. WALLICH. I think we have to detach temporarily from M1 because it has become so uncertain both because of the All Savers Certificates bulge and the new instrument coming along. Even if that bulge were not to occur, we would have the new instrument and we simply don't know its likely effect, all we know is that it could be very major... and that gives us the opportunity to target on M2. That seems to me perfectly defensible substantively and still within the formal framework of our policy. (FOMC 1982: 34)

Wallich is making the case that one could vote for the policy change without rejecting the monetarist frame. Volcker gets Wallich's support here based only on the uncertainty around M1 as an indicator. Wallich's membership in the coalition is fragile and, in some sense, idiosyncratic. He is, in fact, opposed to Volcker's agenda of lowering interest rates. His own agenda is to shift to M2 without rejecting monetarism and he is trying to frame the policy change in this light. It seems likely that he is trying to shift members of the emerging coalition over to his interpretation. The tenuous nature of his membership was proven in future meetings when he joins Volcker's opponents who have an agenda closer to his own.

A second group of allies echoed Volcker's concern with the worldwide economy and his declaration of crisis stated early in the meeting. The first speaker, Mr Gramley, expands on the framing move in which Volcker dramatized the extent of dysfunction in the world economy. The second speaker uses Volcker's rhetoric about 'uncertainty that feeds upon itself', suggesting a downward cycle that must be broken by strong action. The third admits to having been swayed by Volcker's calibration of the crisis:

MR. GRAMLEY. My own judgment, however, is that the problem we face is much more fundamental than whether we target on M1 now because of All Savers Certificates and the new DIDC regulations that will come out as mandated by legislation. I think the world economy is literally starved for liquidity. And I'd liken this situation to the dietary analogy that suggests. I am worried that we have gone on long enough starving the world economy for liquidity and that we may be at a point of impending anorexia. (FOMC 1982: 38)

MR. RICE. Well, Mr. Chairman, I have very little to add to your tour d'horizon. I think it covers admirably the situation that we find ourselves in ... In your words, the developing disarray feeds upon itself, and until we see some evidence of a turnaround, I think we're in a very vulnerable situation. Therefore, I support this directive language. (FOMC 1982: 44)

MR. BOYKIN. Well. Mr. Chairman, when I came to the meeting this morning I was pretty much of the view that Bob Black and to some extent Bill Ford expressed. I must say that your review of the world situation prior to the coffee break woke me up. (FOMC 1982: 47)

A third group of allies expresses support for the policy change contingent on discretionary action by the chair. They do not simply echo Volcker's reframing, rather they raise practical issues about the presentation of the new frame and ask for an adjustment in return for their support. We will examine this practical adjustment and others in the next section. At this point, the new frame has been projected and clarified. A minority has raised strenuous objection. These objections, which have identified important practical consequences of the proposed change, must now be addressed to secure the largest possible coalition.

## Adjusting the Frame: Practical Interpretive Politics

To this point we have described the interpretive politics of policymaking in terms of deconstructing the past and projecting a changed future. Urgent situational contingencies impel policymaking groups to deal also in the present. The newly projected policy must be fine-tuned in keeping with the immediate context. Emirbayer and Mische, referring to this practical dimension of agency, explain that 'newly imagined projects must be brought down to earth within real-world circumstances' (1998: 994). This is accomplished through an open discussion about how others, especially consequential stakeholders, are likely to interpret and react to the new policy. It assumes that the new policy, in this case the directive, exists within a wider community of interpreters, and that the nature of this community's interpretation is not a foregone conclusion. Framing moves are used by the policy group to orchestrate this wider interpretive process. In this sense, the interpretive politics of policymaking extends to the worldwide network of financial, industrial, and political stakeholders.

Under conditions of relative stability, the practical interpretive politics of policy groups focus on carefully evaluating and constructing the signal that the new policy will send to stakeholders. The policymaking group endeavors to shape the sense that others will make of their work (Abolafia 2004). It tries to predict the expectations and probable actions of its audience. In the case of the FOMC, the members attempt to estimate how consumers, firms and markets will react to their actions, that is, how FOMC action will affect spending and investment. This requires 'psyching out' the markets, predicting response for the purpose of influencing it. Much of this is accomplished through the group crafting of the signal to be sent with an eye to its interpretation. Under conditions of instability, when policy groups are most likely to engage in major policy change, the practical interpretive politics focus on assessing a particular type of environmental response: reputational effects.

*Guarding reputation and identity.* Even, and perhaps especially, in the midst of dramatic policy change, policymakers are the guardians of institutional stability and survival. Survival of the organization demands protection of its reputation for effectiveness in the performance of its mission. At the same time, the individual policymaker's identity as skilled role incumbents is at stake. Reputation is the most prominent frame that members of the FOMC use to rationalize their policy positions. Its prominence in the transcript suggests its legitimacy as a guiding narrative for policymaking. Policy-makers are always aware that their actions will have consequences for their credibility. Reputation is important to FOMC members because the Fed is expected to hold the line on inflation as it sustains economic growth. If this expectation is undermined it may generate counterproductive activity on the part of corporations and investors. The salience of reputation for market psychology makes it a major locus of interpretive conflict in the politics of policy change.

Critical to any discussion of reputational effects is a sense of how stake-holders will calibrate the change. Members of the group engage in a framing contest for *defining the magnitude* of the perceived policy change:

MR. BOEHNE. Well, aside from whether this is a good idea or a bad idea, when this directive is made public I think it is going to be viewed as a substantial change in the way monetary policy is being directed.

MR. MARTIN. A substantial temporary change or a substantial change?

VICE CHAIRMAN SOLOMON. A change to reverse.

MR. BOEHNE. No, I wouldn't say it's a reverse, but it is a substantial change. (FOMC 1982: 31)

Members of the committee attribute this expected negative response to change to several factors, all of which relate to the group's credibility. For Mr Roos the central concern is that the policy change will be construed as an effort to pump up the economy before the midterm elections (FOMC 1982: 48). Vice Chairman Solomon expresses the concern of several others that it will be taken as a signal that the strong anti-inflationary bias of monetarism has been abandoned:

VICE CHAIRMAN SOLOMON. I think this is a rather momentous FOMC meeting. I had thought that we had until maybe 1986 before the pace of deregulation and innovation would bring us to this point... I recognize that there will be a good deal of questioning, not only in monetarist circles but more generally. I don't think there will be an avalanche of criticism given our credibility, but there will be major questioning as to what this means in terms of longer-run anti-inflationary policy. And it seems to me that there ought to be some words (to convey) our longer-run commitment and our expectations that inflation will continue to come down. (FOMC 1982: 49)

Reputation is important to organizations because of its influence on the flow of legitimacy and material resources from the environment. The legitimacy of the organization can, in part, be judged by the degree to which the wider community accepts existing frames. Policymakers are responsible for maintaining legitimate frames. The decision to change such a frame can have substantial consequences for maintaining or threatening an organization's legitimacy. As a result, efforts at *interpreting reputational consequences* can be quite conflictual. These consequences can be translated into more personal identity issues by the competing framers. In the following three excerpts, the discourse is couched in terms of integrity and credibility. Each speaker tries to put a positive or negative spin on stakeholder's potential interpretation of the new frame:

MR. FORD. I'm reacting to what the Chairman is telling us, which is I think commendably honest, in that he is saying he really doesn't want to see interest rates raised. That's what I'm reacting to regardless of what it says here. And I think that will be apparent in the marketplace well before this is published and our integrity will be brought into question if we proceed along that line.
    CHAIRMAN VOLCKER. Your vision of our integrity.
    MR. FORD. My vision, yes. (FOMC 1982: 34)

MR. MARTIN. I'd like to turn the integrity argument around and argue for the second thoughts of the commentators and the analysts of our policy... The second thoughts—which may be based on some analysis rather than on a knee-jerk reaction to what we do—would be that the integrity of the Federal Reserve is that they pursued policies with an eye to the growth of the economy, to the liquidity of the domestic and international system, and indeed, they did this despite the political consequences that occurred in the short run. They maintained their integrity as a central bank. (FOMC 1982: 35)

CHAIRMAN VOLCKER. Most people in the financial markets at least, to put it bluntly, think we've overstayed the course now. It gets into this great question of credibility that I suppose we're taking rather personally. At the risk of being misunderstood, following a mechanical operation because we think that's vital to credibility and driving the economy into the ground isn't exactly my version of how to maintain credibility over time. Credibility in some sense is there to be spent when we think it's necessary to spend it and we can carry through a change in approach. I don't think this is all as extreme as some have painted it. (FOMC 1982: 50)

The final major framing move is *spinning the announcement*. Even to the end of the meeting the alliance may be fragile. Some members are less comfortable with the new frame than others. Both supporters and opponents seek to make adjustments in order to buffer its potential reputational conse-quences. Toward the end of the October 1982 meeting, the proviso offered is that the chair will use his discretion to maintain the anti-inflationary bias of the Committee. This reflects the belief that monetarism provides a rule-based con-trol of monetary growth while interest rate targeting gives more discretion to the Committee and creates more inflationary expectations. Both speakers express their trust that Volcker, given his heroic reputation as an inflation buster, will not inflame such expectations. Nevertheless, such public expressions of trust may be seen as subtle constraints on the chair's discretion between meetings:

MR. BOEHNE. Well, I think how one comes out on this depends on whether one wants to take the risks on rules or on the side of discretion ... I must say, however, that whenever one bets on discretion versus rules, it depends a good bit on who is making the discretionary decisions. I believe this kind of directive puts much more than the usual amount of authority in the hands of the Chairman. And with this particular Chairman, I don't have any problems, given the circumstances. So, because of the situation and because of the person who is going to have to use a good bit of this discretion. I'm supportive of the general approach as proposed in the alternative directive language. (FOMC 1982: 43)

VICE CHAIRMAN SOLOMON. The presentation is critical. And judging from past history, the presentation is probably going to be more dependent on the Chairman's state-ments than it will be on the directive, particularly given the publication lag and the fact that we are expecting such a large bulge in the first week of October and something has to be said. Now, since the Chairman has a mind of his own, I would assume that if he gets a majority vote on the substance of this directive that it may not be worth spending a lot of time interpreting and arguing about the more marginal sentences. (FOMC 1982: 49)

Rather than deferring to the chair, this framing move seeks to constrain him. Both speakers acknowledge the discretion of the chair between meetings and state their expectation that his public statements will reflect their bias for noninflationary policy. Volcker gives a long balanced reply in which he acknowledges the anti-inflationary progress made under the old frame (monetarism), but strongly defends the new frame in terms of preventing an institutional legitimacy crisis:

CHAIRMAN VOLCKER. I don't think we're just dealing with the theory here. We are dealing with a real world and assessing where the risks are. It's quite clear in my mind where the risks are. I think I made it quite clear in terms of economic develop-ments around the world. But if one wants to put it in terms of risk to the institution: If we get this one wrong, we are going to have legislation next year without a doubt. We may get it anyway.

Despite the discussion of the chair's discretion and the Committee's expect-ations for its use, the members still try to craft the wording of the directive. They get down to arguing about single words and phrases. The issue is over what they convey by including or not including an interest rate target:

MR. WALLICH. If we drop it, that would convey less of an interest-rate-oriented directive. And I think it's desirable to avoid being very specific about our interest rate objective here.

MR. CORRIGAN. Who knows how the market will interpret it? I think the other argument is just as likely: That the absence of it would lead to the view that we really have zeroed in on a specific number. I don't know. (FOMC 1982: 67)

CHAIRMAN VOLCKER. Well, there are arguments on both sides. I don't feel strongly at all. Leave it out? (FOMC 1982: 68)

The final vote was nine to three in support of the frame change.

## Conclusion

This analysis of policy change suggests several observations about interpretive politics at the Fed. First, the participants in interpretive politics craft multivocal policy. Multivocality refers to the fact that a policy 'can be interpreted coherently from multiple perspectives simultaneously' and the fact that 'public and private motivations cannot be parsed' (Padgett and Ansell 1993: 1263). This is particularly true when the policy itself is constructed from multiple analyses and motivations. Even the dramatic reframing at the October 1982 meeting, so strongly influenced by Volcker, was interpreted by various members in different ways and voted for with differing justifications. This multivocality is enhanced by the shroud of secrecy behind which Fed policymaking lies. An army of interpreters (the Fed watchers) is paid to parse the meaning of every action. These interpreters can impart their own meanings to FOMC actions. The assignment of interests and motivations becomes a source of academic debate. Such multivocality, when accompanied by inscrutability, gives the producer the widest possible discretion in a turbulent environment (Padgett and Ansell 1993: 1310).

Second, our analysis suggests that interpretive politics at the FOMC has a temporal structure that is related to the group's epistemological assumptions. In the retrospective phase, group members place economic 'facts' before the group in order to influence the ongoing narrative of what is 'really' known about existing conditions. In the projective phase, group members are dealing with what is probable in an uncertain future. In predicting future consequences of policy alternatives, they engage in a heightened politics of positioning and derogating. In this phase their language reflects serious doubts about what is 'knowable'. In the practical phase, they attempt to shape what will be known about their policy decisions and about their interpretation of economic conditions. They engage in 'spinning' because they recognize that multiple interpretations are inevitable. All these phases overlap, but the framing moves are different in each because of the different assumptions about what is known, what is knowable, and what they want others to know.

Finally, the narrative arc of the meeting, from first ambiguity to final policy, is contested terrain. The reframer attempts to engage group members in a collective questioning that departs from the customary analysis. This questioning of dominant frames is resisted by those most attached to the frame. The reframer continues the disruption by introducing a new narrative; one that is further resisted. If a dominant coalition in support of the new frame can be created, the meeting may end in a dispute over the consequences for reputation and identity. Interpretive politics under conditions of market turbulence and interpretive ambiguity challenge the policy group to forego the comfort of its usual routine for the realm of unexpected moves and creative conflict.

By looking at interpretive politics as an interactional process with a repertoire of moves, this chapter has focused our attention on the social process of meaning construction. Reframers and their opponents engage in a contest of moves. The interpretive politics approach illustrates how these actors use their immediate contexts, shaping them and being shaped by them. Stage of meeting, existing customs, such as the directive, and prior decisions are all opportunities for influence as well as constraints. Members of the group compete to turn the constraints to opportunities. The ultimate goal of these moves is to interpret the environment, shape the framing process, and control the definition of market conditions. The study of interpretive politics reminds us that policymaking at the Fed is not only an exercise in discovering but also in shaping what is known in financial markets.

## Note

1. Volcker is responding to Ford's claim that the FOMC's action may be seen political, that is, designed to influence the upcoming midterm elections by pumping up the economy. See Ford's longer quote (FOMC 1982: 33).

## References

Abolafia, M. Y. 2004. 'Making Sense of Recession', in *The Economic Sociology of Capitalism*, Nee, V. and Swedberg, R. (eds.). Princeton, NJ: Princeton University Press, in print.

Barley, S. and Tolbert, P. 1997. 'Institutionalization and Structuration: Studying the Links between Action and Institution', *Organization Studies* 18: 93–117.

Blinder, A. S. 1998. *Central Banking In Theory and Practice*. Cambridge, MA: MIT Press.

Callon, M. 1986. 'Some Elements of a Sociology of Translations: the Domestication of the Scallops and Fishermen of St. Brieuc Bay.', in *Power, Action, and Belief*, Law, J. (ed.). London: Routledge, 196–223.

Campbell, J. 1998. 'Institutional Analysis and the Role of Ideas in Political Economy', *Theory and Society* 27: 377–409.

Emirbayer, M. and Mische, A. 1998. 'What is Agency?', *American Journal of Sociology* 103: 962–1023.

Fligstein, N. 1997. 'Social Skill and Institutional Theory', *American Behavioral Scientist* 40: 397–405.

FOMC. 1982. 'Transcript—Federal Open Market Committee Meeting October 6, 1982', Board of Governors of the Federal Reserve.

Gamson, W. 1992. 'The Social Psychology of Collective Action', in *Frontiers of Social Movement Theory*, Morris, A. and Mueller, C. (eds.). New Haven, CT: Yale University Press.

Goffman, E. 1974. *Frame Analysis*. Cambridge, MA: Harvard University Press.

Greider, W. 1987. *Secrets of the Temple*. New York, NY: Simon and Schuster.

Heilbroner, R. and Milberg, W. 1995. *The Crisis of Vision in Modern Economic Thought*. Cambridge: Cambridge University Press.

Hirsch, P. 1986. 'From Ambushes to Golden Parachutes: Corporate Takeovers as an Instance of Cultural Framing and Institutional Integration', *American Journal of Sociology* 91: 800–37.

Kettl, D. 1998. *Leadership at the Fed*. New Haven, CT: Yale University Press.

Latour, B. 1987. *Science in Action*. Cambridge, MA: Harvard University Press.

Maisel, Sherman J. 1973. *Managing the Dollar*. New York, NY: W.W. Norton.

Padgett, J. and Ansell, C. 1993. 'Robust Action and the Rise of the Medici, 1400–1434', *American Journal of Sociology* 98: 1259–1319.

Rein, Martin and Donald Schon. 1996. 'Frame Critical Policy Analysis and Frame Reflective Policy Practice', *Knowledge and Policy: The International Journal of Knowledge Transfer and Utilization* 9: 85–104.

Weick, Karl. 1995. *Sensemaking in Organizations*. Thousand Oaks, CA: Sage.

# 11

# The Return of Bureaucracy: Managing Dispersed Knowledge in Global Finance

GORDON L. CLARK AND NIGEL THRIFT

## Introduction

In the public mind, the paraphernalia of international finance are well known: the trading floor full of shouting, brightly colored bodies, the dealing room full of macho adrenaline addicts, periodic financial crises signaled by serious-looking commentators standing outside the headquarters of a troubled financial institution, and so on. It would be fair to say that these kinds of images are foremost in many academic minds as well, but translated into the underlying processes that they are assumed to represent: a frantic search for profit, the hyper-speed of communication driven by remorseless technological advance, and the crisis-prone nature of capitalism.

First amongst exemplars of these developments is usually counted the global foreign exchange (FX) market. A recurrent image is one of lone traders hunched over their desks secretly trading enormous amounts of other people's money around the world in the search for their own personal wealth. By many accounts, these traders are cowboys (at best) or renegades (at worst) putting in play not only the fortunes of their banks, but also the stability of national currencies and the entire financial world. Respectable versions of much the same idea are found in commentaries on the role and status of financiers like George Soros, and the hedge fund industry that has followed in his wake, and which is now deeply embedded in the global investment strategies of the largest institutional investors. At the limit, FX trading is the *deus ex machina* of 'hot money' undermining the stability of whole countries

This chapter was presented in seminars at the Philipps-University of Marburg and the University of Bonn. Our thanks go to Harald Bathelt (Marburg), Gernot Grabher (Bonn), and Alex Preda (Konstanz) for their invitations to present versions of the chapter. Comments on the chapter were provided by Dariusz Wojcik, Tessa Hebb, and Terry Babcock-Lumish. Support for revising and presenting this chapter was provided, in part, by the DAAD. Most importantly, the chapter was made possible by the insight and knowledge provided by Simon Ford and his colleagues at Credit Suisse First Boston (London). Data on foreign exchange trends and volatility were also provided by CSFB and, in particular, Christian Baraldo and Peter von Maydell. None of the above should be held responsible for any errors or omissions. Comments made about firms and the management process in this chapter are intended to represent larger processes rather than the particular events or circumstances faced by any one company.

and regions, thereby cementing the well-worn prejudices of critics concerning the tyranny of global finance and financialization in general.

In this chapter, we suggest that these kinds of accounts are both problematic in their own terms and historically outdated in a number of key aspects. We argue that the freest of free markets—which the FX markets are often presumed to represent—is more accurately represented as a *bureaucratic* process of risk management that is dependent upon assessing dispersed knowledge about market conditions and response within the firm and across the globe. As such, its purposes are really quite mundane and are characteristic of many firms and industries in which knowledge management and recursive learning are core components of competitive strategy (Nooteboom 2001). Perhaps more than in many other firms and industries, this kind of bureaucratic process is essential to corporate financial integrity and performance; indeed, these kinds of often mundane activities may also be essential to global financial stability given the range of what appear to be less-attractive alternatives (Stiglitz 2002).

The chapter is therefore structured in three main sections. The first section 'Leaving Behind the 1980s' sets out a series of four myths that continue to beset social commentaries on international financial markets, drawn from the experience of the 1980s, and the combination of forces that have now called them into question. We seek to dispel these myths through a close study of the global foreign exchange market. In the second section of the chapter on 'Foreign Exchange Markets', we introduce the FX market and consider its contemporary mechanics.[1] We show that FX trading is a continuous but time-sensitive process and is a global but also a spatially sensitive process. Understanding the time and space of FX markets is vital in understanding how the FX trading process and its attendant risks are institutionally managed. We then go on to document and explain how private financial institutions manage the trading process on a 24-h basis around the globe. In developing this account, we are conscious of the need to understand both the routine management of currency trading and the responsiveness of private institutions to events within the 24-h cycle of markets opening and closing one after the other.

At the core of the chapter is a basic proposition: global FX trading is a deliberate process of managing *dispersed* knowledge so as to account for and control total institutional risk exposure. While individual greed is always present, seeking-out the unrecognized blind spots in the management process, we contend that the real issue is institutional coordination and management and especially the maintenance of bureaucratic procedures that control trading exposures across time and space. The third section of the chapter on 'Global FX Market Structure' therefore considers the growth of bureaucratic procedures in large international financial services firms. This growth is associated with increased technological sophistication, new systems of risk management, and ever more demanding regulatory requirements regarding compliance. Thus, modern FX corporate trading floors are nearer to process-regulated accounting machines than entrepreneurial bear pits. Finally, we provide a brief summary of our argument and its implications.

The chapter utilizes three main sources of evidence. The first source is published quantitative research on global trading patterns and volatilities. The second source consists of insights gleaned from our own detailed interviews taken from a study of the FX operations of one global banking operation. We believe this operation to be representative of the large commercial organizations that now encircle the globe.[2] The third source is our knowledge of the internal structures of large multinational financial institutions drawn from our own interaction with the international financial sector over twenty years or more (see Clark, Thrift, and Tickell 2004). In any event, this chapter is deliberately exploratory although it is designed to report evidence and findings from close dialogue.[3]

## Leaving Behind the 1980s

Much of the critical literature on international financial markets is predicated on a set of myths for our time that retain a strong grip on the imagination. One myth finds its wellspring in a particular historical period being based on studies carried out in the 1980s, the high-noon of a particular set of entrepreneurial practices and representations. This was the time of Thatcher's 'big bang' in the City of London, as satirized in Caryl Churchill's (2002) *Serious Money*, and Reagan's Wall Street boom, brought compellingly to life in Tom Wolfe's (1990) *Bonfire of the Vanities* and Auletta's (2001) *Greed and Glory on Wall Street*. It was the time of 'greed is good', of red ties and braces, of champagne and oysters, of barrow-boy star traders and unfettered masculinity—what has been termed 'unscrupulous acquisitiveness' (Moran 1989: 59). It laid down a particular set of interpretations of international finance which continue to haunt us today (reinforced, of course, by the TMT—technology, media, and telecommunications—boom of the 1990s and the related activities of analysts in Wall Street-based financial institutions). These interpretations even have grip within international finance: some of its participants would have us believe that this is still the swashbuckling world to which they belong.

A second myth takes it that the world of international finance lurches from boom to bust, from unbridled optimism to scandal, and to irrational pessimism. This myth is usually framed as a moral lesson about the iniquities and necessary failures of neoliberal capitalism. Whether it is Orange County derivatives, the Long-Term-Capital Management (LTCM) crash, a rogue trader bringing down a bank, or some other manifestation, all are grist for the moral mill. The result is that exceptional events are written about to a much greater degree than the ordinary but vital day-to-day operations of international finance. The mechanics of everyday reproduction are ignored or lost in a rush to demonize the unruly nature of financial capitalism. The little things are lost.

The third myth centers around speed. According to many commentators, international finance has become a set of continuously moving markets, sustained by the seamless spread of information and the increasing speed of modern communications technology. Mythically, the world of international finance has become a uniform landscape over which money flows like mercury in response to the slightest variation in expectations. And the future holds out the promise of more of the same: it is supposed that each and every financial market which does not operate on this basis will gradually be forced to accommodate to the imperatives of global integration. If this is a myth, it is also a claim made about the functioning of financial markets now (O'Brien 1992) and in the future (Shiller 2003).

The fourth myth centers on the presumed ubiquity of information. And yet, commentators point to a paradox: on one side, the power of privileged forms of information exchange that still rely on unmediated communication whether these be the buzz of dealing floors or the power of gossip retailed in pubs and wine bars. On the other side, an environment characterized by more and more mediated electronic communication from the telephone to the screen, from instant messaging to electronic data display. At the limit, this myth would have it that it does not matter where in time and space we are located—we can all trade in the global marketplace on equal terms not withstanding the evidence to the contrary (see Clark and Wojcik 2004).

In this chapter, we seek to show through a detailed case study of global FX trading that each of these four myths is suspect. They persist because of a curious lack of attention to changing circumstances, a tendency to hyperbole instead of empirical analysis, and a large dollop of technological determinism. In particular, we wish to show how four forces have become intertwined and produced a global FX market rather different from the one commonly found in the critical social science literature if not in the expert studies of market performance.

The first and most obvious of these forces is the gathering global recession accentuating competitive pressures and scale. Since the burst of the TMT bubble at the end of 2000, the world's financial markets have been subject to a marked slowdown in the growth of transactions. Coupled with declining demand for advanced financial products and traded securities, the slowing rate of growth has put great pressures on the cost structures of international financial firms. In turn, this has been particularly problematic for smaller firms that do not have the operational reach or depth of liquidity to participate fully in markets where very large sequential trades across the globe are used to pick up the slightest of profits from the smallest differences of a few basis points.

The second force is technological efficiency. Since the 1980s, information technology has continued to grow in scale, effectiveness, and price. In turn, firms must now operate at much the same electronic speeds, have access to many of the same products (and, if they do not have them, be able to catch up more quickly than in the past), and have access to much the same information and expertise. Even though the set-up or sunk costs associated with market position have greatly increased in significance, competitive edge is much more difficult to have and to hold. Similarly, markets are less likely to be characterized by systematic inefficiencies than in the past. High levels of information flows and the application of advanced technology have ironed-out arbitrage opportunities, making for fewer of those opportunities while reducing the size of pay-offs when such opportunities arise.

The third force is increasing market concentration. The largest international financial firms dominate global market trading and dominate many developed domestic markets. Furthermore, market concentration measured in terms of the share of all transactions held by the largest firms is remorselessly increasing within and between capital markets and is especially apparent in the United States and Europe (Davis and Steil 2001). These firms are not the swashbuckling entities of folklore. As we shall see, they are very large and complex bureaucracies which depend on highly articulated hierarchies of control, management, and the flow of information. Their best interests are served by knowing what every one of their traders are doing on a near to continuous basis.

The fourth force is regulation. The intrusion of regulation on firms' operations is much greater than is often realized and is growing—the product of the crises of the 1990s and the concern of multilateral and national institutions charged with global financial stability. Not only do the requirements of regulatory compliance strengthen the bureaucratic impulse of corporate managers, not least by strengthening the hand of back-office oversight, it also produces its own bureaucratic layers with their own agendas outside of trading and making an immediate profit. In other words, regulation has become a corporate force in its own right, a point that, like the others, we come back to in the subsequent sections of the chapter.

## Foreign Exchange Markets

Foreign exchange trading is reckoned to be a vital cog in the global economy. It is essential for cross-border business transactions, trade and commodity exchange, and the flow of portfolio and direct foreign investment. It is also essential for governments of all political persuasions, and is especially important when offering sovereign debt. No national economy is immune from its effects.[4] At a most mundane level, and usually unnoticed by most people, FX trading greases the wheels of vacation travel and the like. In all, the unadjusted foreign currency cross-border assets of banks reporting to the Bank for International Settlements in September 2002 were just over $7 trillion (compared with $6.5 trillion in December 2001) (Bank for International

Settlements 2003, table 5A: 16). Average daily turnover on conventional FX markets is of an order of magnitude larger: on average, $1.2 trillion per day for April 2001 (Bank for International Settlements 2002). Large numbers indeed (roughly speaking, just one week of FX trading would be worth an entire year's value of international commodity exchange).

The FX trading comprises a series of markets which are usually bundled up together. But not only does it consist of standard trades between currencies (so-called vanilla) but it also takes in a series of more specialized sub-markets. For example, in the large financial institution we studied, there were dedicated teams involved in fixed income and various kinds of exotics ranging from vanilla FX options to far more complex options which involved several varieties of derivatives and spread betting. Each of these markets had their own range (e.g. exotics were rarely traded in more than seven or eight currencies), skills (e.g. exotics typically demand much higher levels of quantitative expertise to both develop and run), tempo, and spatial distribution.[5]

By contrast, much of the academic research devoted to FX is about long-term macroeconomic fundamentals such as relative money supply or relative velocity of circulation. However, of late, more and more research time has been devoted to analyzing and modeling the microstructure of FX markets, recognizing that the management of information and the behavioral responses to information are vital elements in all financial markets (Wilhelm and Downing 2001). This chapter focuses on short-term volatility in currency exchange rates, being conscious of the fact it is short-term volatility rather than long-term trends that preoccupies FX traders around the world. Further, and like Knorr Cetina and Bruegger (2002*a, b*), our contribution to understanding FX trading is focused on the management of the trading process, even if we conclude that bureaucracies and teams are more important than sole traders (perhaps the product of our particular focus).

Another contribution of the chapter is our argument that the management process is both systematic and is characterized by deliberate attempts at fostering intra-bank learning within and between related *teams* operating in markets over time, an issue dealt with by many analysts including Nooteboom (2002). Individuals are, of course, assessed in terms of their own performance. But, despite all the furor sparked by the large salaries and bonuses generated by some individual traders, the overall performance of FX trading within international financial institutions is much more a function of the formal and informal mechanisms of fostering teamwork and managing the shared knowledge and expertise that teams corporately generate and own (while recognizing that there are also substantial competitive pressures between individuals in teams and between teams; see Ackerman, Pipek, and Wulf 2002). Without the collaborative support of team members, all would be the poorer.

## Global FX Market Structure

Over the 1980s and 1990s, Western industrialized countries deregulated their currency exchange markets. Previous attempts at fixing exchange rates were shown to be problematic amongst the developed economies; witness the experience of Great Britain with the European exchange-rate mechanism (ERM) during the early 1990s. More recently, successive regional crises (in Asia, Russia, and Latin America) have also shown that nation-state attempts to manage global currency have proved extremely difficult to achieve in the face of enormous financial flows around the world, notwithstanding the fact that many countries outside the Organization for Economic Cooperation and Development (OECD) use administrative systems to dampen currency inflows and outflows.

At its core, the global FX currency market is a private market that uses the US dollar as the reference currency.[6] Evans (2002) characterized the structure of the FX market as follows. It is a decentralized, multidealer market with three types of FX trading: direct inter-dealer trading, brokered inter-dealer trading, and nonbank customer-dealer trading. The FX 'market' is actually a virtual set of sequentially related regional markets linked together by high-speed electronic systems (the Reuters system dominates all other systems). Being a system of exchange, it allows for simultaneous bids, offers, and trades wherein dealers 'call' one another for quotes on pairs of currencies with the expectation of acceptance or decline of those bids within seconds. In sum, the market is open 24 hours a day and 365 days a year, and is in theory accessible to traders from virtually any location in space and time. But, of course, most traders are the employees of large financial institutions just as the overwhelming volume of FX transactions come from those institutions rather than individuals trading on their own account.

The academic literature has focused upon currency exchange rates, being concerned about long-term macroeconomic trends in the value of individual countries' currencies in relation to the US dollar and the other core reference currencies, including the British pound, the Japanese yen, and the Euro. Over the long term, it is arguable that exchange rates should reflect nation-state comparative advantage in the trade of commodities and services (Sarno and Taylor 2002). Thus, long-term exchange rates should reflect nation-state economic growth potentials including expected rates of economic growth, labor productivity, and innovation. Indeed, much of the literature on national rates of economic growth and comparisons between national growth potentials assumes that there is no FX effect on those fundamentals. In other words, FX rates are assumed to be the medium through which national growth potentials are priced. For example, recent debate about the relative growth prospects of the US economy in relation to its European competitors suggests that the price of the US dollar in relation to the Euro fully reflects its potential.[7]

In fact, the available evidence suggests that much of the observed variance in exchange rates is short-term rather than long-term and is to be found *within* the day rather than between days, weeks, months, and years. Furthermore, it is widely conceded that theoretical models based on economic fundamentals are very poor predictors of short-term exchange rates and are virtually irrelevant to the question of exchange rate volatility.[8] It is not possible to work backward from long-term patterns in exchange rates to predicting intra-day exchange rate volatility. Whereas most theoretical models are focused upon exchange rates, the volatility of intra-day exchange rates is the issue that dominates the trading process. Not surprisingly, then, stochastic time series models clearly out-perform econometric models when intra-day data is taken into account. As a consequence, there is increasing interest in the microeconomic and behavioral processes that drive global day-to-day FX operations.

## Temporal and Spatial Trading Patterns

At the same time, it should be recognized that there *is* detailed information on both the temporal and geographical structure of FX trading patterns. In fact, recent statistical studies can provide us with a clear characterization of the various components that make up intra-day FX volatility (Andersen and Bollerslev 1998; Evans 2002). Most importantly, such characterizations depend a great deal upon knowledge of the opening and closing, as well as the moments of overlap, between the three core global FX markets: in order of GMT, Tokyo, London, and New York. To illustrate, Andersen and Bollerslev (1998: 221) characterized the then spot DM–US dollar market in the following terms: 'a 24-hour market composed of sequential and partially overlapping trading in regional centres worldwide, so it has no definite closures, except those generated endogenously by the market. This allows for the study of the volatility process over periods that would be non-trading intervals under centralised market structures'.

Evans (2002) showed that in each of these markets the 'home' currency is the most traded currency in relation to the US dollar, recognizing that London is both the center for trading in sterling and the Euro. In describing FX trade over the course of a day, he suggested that it can be characterized as 'triple-humped'. Beginning about 1 AM GMT in Tokyo, the first hump is relatively low volume. That is followed by the opening at about 7 AM GMT in London for trade in sterling and the Euro which records the highest volume of trade over the day, which is followed in turn at about 12:30 PM GMT by the opening of New York at a lower volume of trade than London. In terms of the management of the trading process within many FX companies, the close of trade in New York effectively closes the book for that day on FX operations.[9] This is customary practice for many such firms in the industry and around the world. We noted above that trade is anonymous in the market, and that the volume and volatility of trading is closely associated with the entry and exit of market traders by region. In fact, although trading can be continuous second by second, minute by minute, and hour by hour throughout the 24-hour cycle it is commonly observed that trade peaks at the opening and closing of each of the three markets.

Notice that London has an especially important place in the 24-hour cycle of FX trading. This is partly because of its historical role as a center of calculation collecting diverse market interests from around the world, and providing an unmatched depth of liquidity and range of risk preferences (Clark 2003). The role of London has also been important in recent financial history, being particularly associated with the 'big-bang' in the 1980s, the subsequent float of major European currencies, and the introduction of the Euro. Furthermore, London is very important as a switching point between Asia and Europe and Europe and North America, being a place where financial deals can be packaged and priced in terms of their currency exposure. As has been suggested many times in interview, if London did not exist it would have to be invented at much the same place in time and space between Tokyo and New York.[10] It could be in Paris or Frankfurt, but for all these reasons, reinforced by the concentration of related banks and trading talent, flexibility, and technological capacity, London remains the dominant international financial center.[11]

Considerable research has focused upon the role of information flow and sources in driving trading volume and volatility on an intra-day, daily, weekly, and calendar-basis. Anticipated public disclosures of relevant macroeconomic and monetary information have an impact upon FX trading by region. In some cases, especially those associated with news from New York, the impact of this kind of news can be distributed in time over the day. However, it has also been observed that anticipated public news has a limited temporal and spatial impact upon trading intensity even if public news may have an immediate and significant affect on the FX market concerned (Galati and Ho 2001). This type of information is thought to underpin long-term patterns embedded in observed short-run high-frequency volatility. Even so, since such announcements are regular, they are also, more often than not, anticipated in terms of their likely effects upon regional markets as well as the turnover between markets. Expectations are an essential ingredient in FX trading especially if there are marked differences between markets in the meaning attributed to anticipated announcements.

On the other hand, it appears that unanticipated private information has the biggest impact upon daily trading volume and intensity in FX markets. For Evans (2002), this is because of the apparent anonymity of FX markets and the fact that FX trades cannot be directly observed by third parties not involved in those trades. As a consequence, at any point in time there is a distribution of exchange rates and an intensive search by traders for an approximate reference point in making subsequent trades. In other words, just as there is a distribution of FX prices at any point in time and space, that distribution is itself partially dependent upon previous distributions of FX prices. More technically, it is observed that FX markets are characterized by informational asymmetries, by heterogeneous expectations, and by an ever-present need to trade when others trade so that current conditions are revealed to traders by sequential pairs of currency trades. By this logic, traders cannot afford to 'sit-out' the market awaiting new information that would propel local market traders to an expected equilibrium point in the relationship between currencies.[12]

The exact temporal and spatial decay function is therefore less important at this juncture than the realization that the significance of this component also varies by trading intensity. Although the electronic trading system is available for FX trading every second of every day, FX trading is not continuous but marked by identifiable trading peaks and troughs within each day by market. Evans' (2002) observations and arguments provide a compelling rationale for strong intra-day patterns. What is not often realized is that the significance of the 'sampling' component of FX volatility varies in terms of the volume of trading. Whereas it is the dominant component in normal market conditions, it declines in significance when trading intensity is very high suggesting that in these circumstances the distribution of FX prices narrows and converges toward a shared reference point only to diverge and once again spread as trading intensity declines. There appears to be no *necessary* intra-day temporal pattern of high activity *except* for the fact that all traders are aware of the peaks in trade associated with market opening and closing. Under conditions of risk and uncertainty, traders bunch together at those moments in time and space for more information and for the opportunity to off-set and share risk by discounting specific positions (characteristics of all securities markets; see Shin 2003).[13]

Added to this problem of managing the 24-hour market structure is the problem of managing speed. It cannot be gainsaid that, under pressure from improvements in information and communications technology, financial markets have tended to demand more and more rapid response, especially in markets like FX which depend on arbitrage to such a degree. But the problems presented by speed should not be overplayed for at least two reasons. First, the markets are only nominally 24 hour. There is still, in reality, a gap of an hour or so in the global 24-hour clock between New York and Tokyo. As well, there is the problem of settlement. We were constantly told that managing 24-hour books 'would be a nightmare'. Like the noonday sight at sea, there has to be a close of business in order to assess net positions. In any event, handing on a book from one market to another takes a considerable amount of time. The process is not instant: it occupies several hours each day, involving regional and global members of the FX team in constant conversation and what can often be a complex series of negotiations (see Table 11.1).

TABLE 11.1. A Typical FX Dealing Timetable for London

| | |
|---|---|
| 6.30 | Starting to pass the book from Tokyo |
| 7.00 | Update volatility curves |
| 7.00–7.30 | London and Tokyo make prices together |
| 7.30–8.00 | Take deltas (management of spot risk) |
| 8.00 | All prices made by London (RISK TRANSFERRED) |
| 12.00–15.30 | Same process gone through with New York |
| 15.00 | Option expiry time |
| 15.30 | London no longer actively involved in trading (RISK TRANSFERRED) |
| 15.30–17.30 | Administration |

## Corporate Management of FX Trading

Having outlined the nature of the FX markets, we can now consider the management problem that this poses for participants. We hope to identify the basic elements of the FX management problem by drawing upon the observations made above about the temporal and spatial patterns apparent in global FX trading. In doing so, we focus upon three kinds of 'agents and institutions': individual traders, their firms, and the markets in which they operate. Most importantly, we focus upon how global financial firms manage time and space on a 24-hour basis by being responsive to anticipated and expected events arising market by market, as well as the unexpected and surprising events that may drive high levels of intra-day market volatility. In the first instance, this requires conceptualizing the FX management problem. In the second instance, it allows us to emphasize the essentially *bureaucratic* nature of corporate decisionmaking in this arena which lies at the heart of this chapter.

Of course, bureaucracies have had notoriously bad press of late. In the face of 1990s, management paradigms focused around concepts like networks and communities of practice, hierarchical bureaucracies have often been depicted as shallow and energy-sapping forms of organization, sets of mundane routines that are inimical to the production of enterprising cultures and persons (Leavitt 2003): at odds, one might think, with what is often depicted as the free-wheeling nature of trading. In fact, as we have already argued, the FX markets rely on vast swathes of bureaucratic routine to function, from the day-to-day minutiae of settlement and compliance to the larger issues of regulation and general managerial oversight. Further, it is doubtful that bureaucracy is simply useful background for more entrepreneurial activities: most entrepreneurial activities like trading rely on bureaucratic routines for sustenance, whether these are embedded in software packages, organizational knowledge, or highly complex logistics. Indeed, du Gay (2000) goes as far as to argue that bureaucracy ought to be seen as a substantial ethical domain in its own right and not just an impoverished set of checks and balances on the real business of entrepreneurial effort.

Yet, in a series of descriptions of financial markets dating from the nineteenth century and from Weber (1978 [1919]), it has become commonplace to regard financial markets as the very opposite of bureaucracies. But, as we have tried to show, the scale of the management task of collecting and synthesizing dispersed financial knowledge is now so great that, for the main corporate players who constitute so much of the market, this no longer amounts to a realistic or even a desirable description. Large financial firms are highly structured, hierarchical operations that try to impose order and security as well as make a profit (the two by no means being inimical to one another). Though regional FX teams may work quasi-independently, they are all overseen by an inevitably authoritarian management hierarchy whose task is to manage risk on a global scale in organizations, which may have been put together through mergers and acquisitions and therefore may have a mix of quite different cultures and even quite serious rivalries. Thus the managerial imperative is consistently toward a classical nested organizational hierarchy with each team head reporting upward in a formal fashion to the global manager (see Thompson 2003). How might we characterize this situation and its consequences? This is the subject of the next section of the chapter.

## Managing Dispersed Knowledge

At the most general level, FX management is a problem of managing dispersed knowledge. This issue has been the subject of increasing amounts of research in the management literature, and is the focus of Becker's (2001) seminal paper, and related research by Girard and Stark (2002).[14] In essence, Becker contends that the issue of dispersed knowledge is representative of a most important aspect of modern economies, that being the utilization of knowledge where economic agents are themselves decentralized and coordinated through market exchange. Becker cites the relevant literature and goes on to reference Hayek's argument to the effect that in market economies characterized by the division of labor knowledge must be organized, codified, and deliberately managed if agents and their institutions are to be competitive with one another. Further, Becker suggests that this issue is now 'more salient than ever' (2001: 1039). Because many markets and systems of production and exchange are global rather than local, and because networks of communication allow access to markets by people from many more locations in space and time than ever before, dispersed knowledge is now one of the most important management issues preoccupying firms and their managers.

Assume that FX trading firms and their employees seek to maximize, respectively, reported profit (by division) and earned income (including yearly bonuses) while minimizing firm costs and potential catastrophic losses. Also assume that, given the robustness of firms' reporting practices and monitoring functions, it is difficult for any individual trader to build up over time positions that threaten the financial integrity of their firm. We must assume, however, that firms have an interest in allowing their traders sufficient discretion that firms may benefit from their employees' exploitation of market knowledge, experience, and intuition. In other words, the most important imperative driving the FX trading process is the interest of traders and their firms in making money day after day, week after week, and year after year. In this respect, traders and their institutions cannot afford to sit out market trading in the hope that collecting and organizing market knowledge will allow them an opportunity to make 'excess' profit out of a limited set of trades. For any firm seeking to maximize profit from FX trading, achieving this goal is a function of the strategic collection and dissemination of knowledge to and from their own traders located in different markets around the globe. This is an essential management function, and an issue of managerial control. It goes beyond the issue of setting correct incentives to the organization of the firm itself.[15]

This issue can be characterized in the following ways. With respect to intra-day FX trading, firms must manage the flow of knowledge (1) within each market and between their traders (within the firm), (2) between each market and between their market-based traders (within the firm), and (3) within and between markets with reference to external (nonfirm) traders. They must do so in ways that sustain mutual learning between team members and recursive response to changing conditions across the globe. This is a deliberately managed process because the costs of individual discretion and competition between team members are too high, even potentially catastrophic, for the firm and the global financial system.

Firms must therefore decide whether traders trade on their own account or trade as members of market-specific teams, and whether the geographical and temporal segmentation of FX markets should carry over into the accounting structure of the day-to-day performance of the firm itself. For the moment, let us assume that traders trade as members of market-specific teams and that those teams are held to account in terms of their contribution to the day-to-day performance of the firm in FX currency markets. We will explain how and why this is the case in the next section. All we need to suggest at the moment is that knowledge management and integration is more efficient if individual traders have a clear responsibility to their market-specific teams and if each team has a responsibility to the subsequent market team (in time and space). In essence, there is an operational hierarchy that culminates in just one FX team in the firm, a team that is local in its immediate functions but global in terms of its scope of responsibilities.

This type of managerial logic requires formal mechanisms of authority and accountability. It also imposes huge obligations on team managers to develop codes of practice that bridge time and space in a deliberate and predictable manner. In a world of settled expectations and the routine execution of transactions, there is little doubt that this type of managerial system would disappear into the fabric of the firm and its culture. But the recurrent and unpredictable currency crises emanating from emerging markets over the past few decades have meant that this managerial logic is an essential organizational device for handling episodes of great uncertainty and the consequent risks to the firm and its employees. When asked how they respond to such currency crises, managers suggested that they *rely* upon the firm-specific global management system for inter-market coordination and they *intensify* their use of intra-firm coordination mechanisms to respond to the temporal and spatial transmission of currency crises. This is not, however, a recipe for global market stability; it is a recipe for the survival of global financial firms in the hope that stability will be engineered by domestic and multilateral agencies (Kaminsky and Reinhart 1999).

## Bureaucracy and Regulation

This kind of managerial imperative has only been underlined by three further developments which strengthen the hold of hierarchy and general bureaucratic procedure. The first of these is the capacity for technological oversight of each trader's and team's performance. The growth of information and communications technology and, much more importantly, the increasing ability to stitch together often quite diverse systems into a functioning whole, has gradually allowed key managers to gain oversight of performance at all relevant points (in time and space) of the firm.[16] Thus, the global FX manager knows the position of every trader at the end of each day and should be able to pick up rogue traders within one day or a few days at most. Whereas some analysts of related phenomena emphasize the development of trust between related individuals as a crucial social regulatory determinant of information flow, it is clear that, in this particular context at least, this kind of device is fragile at best and is better handled by explicit oversight.

The second development is the growth of risk management which is meant to constantly monitor and assess risk exposure. All large international financial services firms have substantial risk measurement and management divisions which usually monitor trading according to limits set by a Senior Management Committee or equivalent. These divisions are hungry for data with which they assess the state of play of the firm at selected points in time and space. They use various software packages to help them achieve this goal, some of which are written in-house and some of which are proprietary. The goal is to speed up the system of monitoring so as to get as close to the close of business as possible. Even so, this has not proved easy. There have been significant problems in handling the flow of data.

The third development is the growth of regulation. The enormous growth in regulatory demands has in large part arisen from periodic financial scandals which have underlined the need for more control, as well as adding new semi-independent layers of bureaucracy. In our case study, trading teams may have acted to an entrepreneurial stereotype but this stereotype was encased in bureaucratic systems of oversight and regulation, much of which the teams themselves seemed to be only partially aware of. What seems clear, however, is that there has been a shift in the balance of power between the front and back office. The back office has become more important, partly because of all the requirements of oversight and regulation, partly because front and back offices have become closer through electronic booking, partly because more senior managers have had to take on certain back office functions, and partly because the entrepreneurial ethic, though still valued, has been in part subsumed under the imperative of safety.

Perhaps the best means of symbolizing this change is through what has happened to trading floors. Ten or even five years ago, trading floors were often noisy places. Traders existed in a noisy hubbub as information, rumor, and mood were passed back and forth as means of finding opportunities for arbitrage. That has now changed. Most trading floors are quiet. Most FX trading takes place through the medium of the screen and electronic booking systems. Most information also comes through the screen—through proprietary services (and especially Bloomberg) or through email and bulletin boards to which all the traders on the floor can contribute[17]—and through telephone conversations on open lines with company dealers in other locations.[18] Rumors no longer have the same place they once had in this world of 'response presence' in which much interaction is at a distance but, through the medium of teams and screens, can be gathered at one 'place' of management and control (see also Knorr Cetina and Bruegger 2002a). They are much less likely to move the market because so many of them can be verified as true or false—through a combination of the modern media and internal assessment—within 5 minutes of their launch.[19]

The focus now is therefore much more likely to be on 'sampling' market prices by reference to expected market-specific moments of collectivity and overlap, thereby providing those companies with the most resources (money and management) with the opportunity to arbitrage around unexpected events.[20] Of course, speed is still vital on the trading floor. Indeed, given the paucity of opportunities in recession and the accelerating impact of technological change, the discipline of speed on FX trading may have even become greater. But, speed is mediated to a much greater degree than ever before by technological and team backup so that its effects may be rather less than are often envisaged.

This does not mean there is no role for social glue, of course. But most of that glue is no longer the residue of local boozy nights out; FX traders may just as easily be a part of teams that stretch around the world. A good part of these dispersed teams will not therefore be physically present in the London trading room. Sociality is therefore deliberately engineered. Globally dispersed teams meet-up on a yearly basis and meet one-to-one much more frequently than that in order to talk strategy, swap new expertise, and hone existing communication skills.[21] Thus, at any one time, the trading floor consists of intra- and inter-floor linkages which cannot be separated out. The floor is partly a virtual society but one run on the assumption that teams interact face-to-face on occasion and learn the social assumptions and cues typical of other team members. Team membership is spun out of these assumptions and provides the cues for 'local' decisionmaking based upon certain well-defined parameters of shared experience (in ways consistent with Nooteboom's 2002 emphasis on managing the costs and consequences of 'cognitive distance').

Thus a crucial point that we want to end this section with is that it is dangerous to concentrate on just the traders and the trading floor, as has become common in a number of recent ethnographies which track the market as it is made. As we have tried to show, the management of these floors is more and more dictated from without by bureaucratic procedure which may or may not be crystallized in technological interfaces like the screen. Knorr Cetina and Bruegger (2002a, b) make this point but perhaps do not develop it far enough. In stressing the role of individual traders who are partially set apart from the rest of the corporate organization, they may have produced an account which is now historically misleading (Mitchell 2002). While it is clearly the case that traders constitute the market, they also increasingly represent corporate goals and organization, either in the form of codified rules of procedure, forms of oversight, and membership of a team which may stretch well beyond local traders' code (Thrift and French 2002). There are more and more 'traffic cops' within firms with the result that the boundary between explicit and tacit knowledge of the markets is shifting in the former's direction (Wilhelm and Downing 2001). In particular, as new metrics are invented and implemented (e.g. measures of overall corporate exposure), so they have become constitutive of organizations' work. Similarly, new opportunities for control have arisen (all the way from new kinds of higher management meeting called to consider the information arising from new metrics to a raft of new additions to the corporate rule book for traders).

## Conclusion

In this chapter, we have tried to puncture four myths about global financial markets by appealing to a mix of our own observations and existing empirical work. We used the FX market on the grounds that, if it were possible to find counter-narratives in even this fast-moving and in many ways stereotypical financial market, then existing accounts of the pathologies of individual decisionmaking and market volatility might require considerable adjustment.

What we found was a market which is increasingly coordinated by large bureaucracies that attempt to make money by threading a large number of administrative procedures through individual entrepreneurial behavior. Some of these bureaucratic procedures are activated through the medium of teams which are dispersed around the globe. Others involve overarching corporate organizational structures which are similarly global. In other words, maximizing profit and minimizing risk involves organizing time and space on a global scale which in turn has prompted these organizations to manage how proprietary knowledge of FX markets is dispersed through the organization and then put to best use; dispersed knowledge is both a problem *and* a solution.[22] In the process of dealing systematically and on a global scale with dispersed knowledge and expertise, the balance of power in large international institutions has subtly but inexorably shifted toward bureaucratic procedures of synthesis, oversight, and regulation—and away from the kind of untrammeled entrepreneurialism often associated with FX dealers.

Of course, all this can be overdone. Large international financial institutions are still driven by competition, regional divides and at times untrammeled entrepreneurialism is still allowed to let rip. But our argument is that large international financial institutions are learning how to do *global* finance and, as this process continues, so many international financial markets, often depicted as the domain of the get-rich-quick, are becoming the haunt of large bureaucracies. As more and more of the activity of these markets is taking place within these organizations, this argument becomes more and more relevant. Though markets are still fast-moving and, at least to a degree opaque, it would not do to overemphasize these features. International financial markets are not being domesticated but many of them are now moving into a new phase of coordination in which the broad contours of activity are understood and subject to the power of bureaucratic routine.

## Notes

1. Here, we are particularly interested in institutional investors, recognizing their importance in the FX trading process (Davis and Steil 2001; Chinn 2003). We do not investigate their clients in any detail.
2. At the end of 2001, this institution had approximately US$13.9 billion in revenues, US$10 billion in equity, and US$406 billion in assets. It operated in seventy-seven locations across more than thirty-six countries and was involved in a variety of activities including securities underwriting, sales and trading services, investment banking, private equity, financial advisory services, investment research, venture capital, correspondent brokerage services, and asset management.
3. This kind of inductive process of empirical analysis and theoretical interrogation is increasingly important in the social sciences (Beunza and Stark 2003), and is

characteristic of recent developments in economic geography and finance (see Thrift 1996; Clark 1998; Wrigley, Currah, and Wood 2003). It is also a vital research tool in finance and economics in building a better understanding of the behavioral structures underpinning global financial markets (see Shiller 2000, 2003).

4. To illustrate, consider the November issue of the OECD's (2002) *Financial Market Trends*. Therein, after a page devoted to broad trends and prospects, the report looks in detail at FX markets before considering recent developments in interest rates, equity and bond markets, and the management of global market volatility. Financial stability, domestic and international, is driven in part by FX markets.

5. The latest confirmed data on FX derivatives trading indicated that daily average turnover was in the order of US$1.4 trillion for April 2001 (Bank for International Settlements 2002).

6. This is a complex issue, beyond the scope of the present chapter. Suffice it to say that while there is a global market for transactions in the currencies of advanced western economies *relative to the dollar*, there is hardly any market for transactions in the currencies of emerging markets and developing economies. Given the risks associated with those currencies, any related FX transactions must be done directly in US dollars. And given the instability of many emerging market economies and domestic institutions, this has significant implications for the long-term stability of global financial markets.

7. This is the lifeblood of global investment banks. There is a premium for informed commentaries on the relative value of the US dollar compared to the Euro, GBP, and Japanese Yen which mix together current issues like the prospects and consequences of war with the productivity effects of the new economy and labor and capital market flexibility in the United States. See the recent reports by Quinlan and McCaughrin (2002), and McCaughrin, Kimbrough, and Roach (2002) from Morgan Stanley Dean Witter (New York) on these issues and more.

8. See Sarno and Taylor (2000: 136), who conclude their review of the value of theoretical models of long-term exchange rates with the observation that 'empirical work on exchange rates has not produced models that are sufficiently statistically satisfactory to be considered reliable and robust'.

9. In fact, in our global financial institution, close of play was taken to be 1615 EST with all subsequent trades going on to the next day. The situation is even more complicated because common books are not really passed on in the way depicted in many accounts. In our global financial institution, each region still had its own books even if positions were passed on between markets.

10. It has also been suggested that London is important because the Pacific Ocean is too wide (in time). If it were narrower, presumably New York would be able to bridge the gap, thereby being able to compete directly with London. Geography in this sense is a marvelously simple idea.

11. We would suggest, moreover, that the traditional virtues associated with London as being a place of gossip and face-to-face contact is less relevant than often assumed, given the significance of electronic linkages and networks on a second-by-second basis. In any event, like Cheung, Chinn, and Marsh (2000), we have not found any discernible firm-specific or market-specific collective view about the significance or otherwise of the determinants of long-term trends.

12. When asked, FX traders and managers had little to say about the underlying driving forces behind currency exchange rates. Their world is not theoretical; the significance of intra-day volatility is such that any long-term position on a set of

currency exchange rates informed by theory or related expectations would be practically irrelevant or worse. By implication, their actions are consistent with models of financial markets that emphasize herd behavior and informational asymmetries. That is, expectations may become self-fulfilling prophecies (Morris and Shin 1998). Even nation-specific cyclical patterns that drive the relative attractiveness of one country's currency as opposed to others may be treated by FX traders as long-term and therefore irrelevant to their daily positions. Only if cyclical patterns appear as unexpected time-dependent shocks would they be factored into the trading process (cf. Allen and Gale 2000).

13. In fact, the search for information by sampling others' expectations and positions is reputedly one explanation for the enormous volume of FX trading day in and day out (Harris 2002). Another possibility is the fact that any FX trade precipitates a sequence of trades designed by the institutions concerned to reduce their exposure to the risks associated with many of their clients' positions.

14. We use the term 'dispersed knowledge' because it captures succinctly the geography we wish to analyze. But other related conceptual reference points would work as well including 'cognitive distance' and the 'cycle of discovery' (see Gilsing and Nooteboom 2002).

15. By contrast, much of the literature in finance when dealing with similar issues emphasizes the cognitive and behavioral biases apparent in many individuals when dealing with risk and return, the valuation of reward and loss, and the response to time-dependent events. In this respect, the finance literature ignores the institutional management of knowledge and behavior. It is preoccupied with 'star-traders' rather than institutional structure (see Clark 2000 on related issues relevant to pension fund and investment decisionmaking).

16. This has proved an enormous problem in most international financial services firms. For example, in the firm we studied computer systems had been quite different in different world regions and there were still substantial problems with legacy systems. It is no surprise, then, that very large amounts of effort still go into developing software. Even a small team may have ten people on its IT side. Mainline FX teams may have upward of 120.

17. One major rite of passage now is inserting information on the very public bulletin board: if it is proved wrong the contributor's credibility obviously declines.

18. Open lines are crucial when, for example, London traders may be spending up to 2 h a day on the line to their counterparts in New York and half-an-hour to an hour on the line to their counterparts in Tokyo handing on the book and generally talking business.

19. The focus is therefore much more on set economic events (like interest rate changes) and analyzes and arbitrage opportunities around these events.

20. Similarly, it has become much easier to make educated guesses about the sources of activity in the market when relatively few key traders from relatively few financial services firms are making most of the running.

21. For example, the manager of one small team goes to Tokyo at least once a year to meet team members and to New York at least twice a year.

22. Consider, for example, the management 'solution' to this problem implemented at Barclays Global Investors (BGI): 'two global co-CEOs-located 5,371 miles apart' (London and San Francisco). When asked about how they divide their responsibilities, one of the CEOs indicated that the divide was functional along 'regional and product lines'. As for coordination, the other CEO responded as

follows. 'One of (the) things that has helped is that the two of us have worked together for a long period of time and we know each other extremely well'. As for the advantages of such an arrangement, 'the business benefits from having the leverage of two people who act as CEOs in different time zones. But it only works if we are joined at the hip in the way in which we are communicating'. (Reported in the industry newspaper *Pensions & Investments* April 14, 2003: 14).

# References

Ackerman, M., Pipek, V., and Wulf, V. (eds.). 2002. *Sharing Expertise. Beyond Knowledge Management*. Cambridge, MA: MIT Press.

Allen, F. and Gale, D. 2000. *Comparing Financial Systems*. Cambridge, MA: MIT Press.

Andersen, T. G. and Bollerslev, T. 1998. 'Deutschemark-Dollar volatility: Intra-Day Activity Patterns, Macro Economic Announcements, and Longer Run Dependencies', *Journal of Finance* 53: 219–85.

Auletta, K. 2001. *Greed and Glory on Wall Street: The Fall of the House of Lehman*. New York, NY: Overlook Press.

Bank for International Settlements. 2002. *Triennial Central Bank Survey of Foreign Exchange and Derivates Market Activity 2001—Final Results*. Basel.

—— 2003. *BIS Quarterly Review*. Basel, March 2003.

Becker, M. C. 2001. 'Managing Dispersed Knowledge: Organisational Problems, Managerial Strategies, and their Effectiveness', *Journal of Management Studies* 38: 1037–51.

Beunza, D. and Stark, D. 2003. 'The Organization of Responsiveness: Innovation and Recovery in the Trading Rooms of Lower Manhattan', *Socio-Economic Review* 7(1): 135–64.

Cheung, Y., Chinn, M., and Marsh, I. 2000. 'How do UK-Based Foreign Exchange Dealers Think Their Market Operates?', Working Paper 7524, Cambridge, MA: National Bureau of Economic Research.

Chinn, M. 2003. 'Explaining Exchange Rate Behaviour', *NBER Reporter* Spring: 5–9.

Churchill, C. 2002. *Serious Money*. London: Methuen.

Clark, G. L. 1998. 'Stylised Facts and Close Dialogue: Methodology in Economic Geography'. *Annals of the Association of American Geographers* 88: 73–87.

—— 2000. *Pension Fund Capitalism*. Oxford: Oxford University Press.

—— 2003. *European Pensions & Global Finance*. Oxford: Oxford University Press.

—— Thrift, N. J., and Tickell, A. 2004. 'Performing Finance: The Industry, the Media, and its Image', *Review of International Political Economy*, forthcoming.

—— and Wojcik, D. 2004. 'Financial Valuation of the German (Regional) Model: The Negative Relationship between Ownership Concentration and Stock Market Returns', *Economic Geography*, forthcoming.

Davis, E. P. and Steil, B. 2001. *Institutional Investors*. Cambridge, MA: MIT Press.

Du Gay, P. 2000. *In Praise of Bureaucracy. Weber, Organization, Ethics*. London: Sage.

Evans, M. D. 2002. 'FX Trading and Exchange Rate Dynamics', *Journal of Finance* 57: 2405–47.

Galati, G. and Ho, C. 2001. 'Macroeconomic News and the Euro/Dollar Exchange Rate', Working Paper 105, Bank for International Settlements, Basel.

Gilsing, V. and Nooteboom, B. 2002. 'Co-Evolution in Innovation Systems: the Case of Multi-Media', *Mimeo*. School of Management, Erasmus University, Rotterdam.

Girard, M. and Stark, D. 2002. Distributed Intelligence and the Organization of Diversity in New Media Projects. *Environment and Planning A* 34: 1927–49.

Kaminsky, G. L. and Reinhart, C. 1999. 'The Twin Crises: The Causes of Banking and Balance-of-Payments Problems', *American Economic Review* 89: 473–500.

Knorr Cetina, K. and Bruegger, U. 2002*a*. 'Global Microstructures: The Virtual Societies of Financial Markets', *American Journal of Sociology* 107: 905–50.

—— 2002*b*. 'Inhabiting Technology: The Global Life-Form of Financial Markets', *Current Sociology* 50: 389–405.

Leavitt, H. 2003. 'Why Hierarchies Thrive', *Harvard Business Review* 81(3): 96–102.

McCaughrin, R., Kimbrough, K., and Roach, S. 2002. 'Global Cross-Border Capital Flows', *Equity Research*. New York, NY: Morgan Stanley Dean Witter.

Mitchell, T. 2002. *Rule of Experts. Egypt, Techno-Politics, Modernity*. Berkeley, CA: University of California Press.

Moran, M. 1989. 'Investor Protection and the Culture of Capitalism', in *Capitalism, Culture and Economic Regulation*, Hancher, L. and Moran, M. (eds.). Oxford: Clarendon Press, 49–75.

Morris, S. and Shin, H. S. 1998. 'Unique Equilibrium in a Model of Self-Fulfilling Currency Attacks', *American Economic Review* 88: 587–97.

Nooteboom, B. 2001. 'Problems and Solutions in Knowledge Transfer', Mimeo. School of Management, Erasmus University, Rotterdam.

—— 2002. 'A Cognitive Theory of the Firm', Mimeo. School of Management, Erasmus University, Rotterdam.

O'Brien, R. 1992. *Global Financial Integration: The End of Geography*. London: Chatham House.

OECD. 2002. 'Finance and Investment', *Financial Market Trends*. Paris, n. 83.

Quinlan, J. P. and McCaughrin, R. 2002. 'Why the US Earns an "A" from Global Investors?', *Equity Research*. New York, NY: Morgan Stanley Dean Witter.

Sarno, L. and Taylor, M. P. 2002. *The Economics of Exchange Rates*. Cambridge: Cambridge University Press.

Shiller, R. J. 2000. *Irrational Exuberance*. Princeton, NJ: Princeton University Press.

—— 2003. *The New Financial Order. Risk in the 21ˢᵗ Century*. Princeton, NJ: Princeton University Press.

Shin, H. S. 2003. 'Positive Feedback Trading Under Stress: Evidence from the US Treasury Securities Market', Working Paper 122, Bank for International Settlements, Basel.

Stiglitz, J. 2002. *Globalization and its Discontents*. New York: Norton.

Thompson, G. 2003. *Markets and Hierarchies*. Oxford: Oxford University Press.

Thrift, N. J. 1996. *Spatial Formations*. London: Sage.

Thrift, N. J. and French, S. 2002. 'The Automatic Production of Space', *Transactions, Institute of British Geographers* NS27: 309–35.

Weber, M. 1978 [1919]. *Economy and Society*. Berkeley, CA: University of California Press.

Wilhelm, W. J and Downing, J. D. 2001. *Information Markets. What Businesses Can Learn From Financial Innovation*. Boston, MA: Harvard Business School Press.

Wolfe, T. 1990. *Bonfire of the Vanities*. New York, NY: Random House.

Wrigley, N., Curran, A., and Wood, S. 2003. 'Commentary. Investment Bank Analysts and Knowledge in Economic Geography', *Environment and Planning A* 35: 381–7.

# 12

# Enterprise Risk Management and the Organization of Uncertainty in Financial Institutions

MICHAEL POWER

## Introduction

Since the mid-1990s, enterprise risk management (ERM) has emerged as a set of ideas for rethinking the organization of risk management activities. There has been a conspicuous growth of normative and technical texts on the subject of ERM (e.g. Barton, Shenkir, and Walker 2001; Walker, Shenkir, and Barton 2002; Lam 2003), which is also characterized by related motifs of 'holistic', 'integrated' (AIRMIC 1999; Doherty 2000), and 'strategic' risk management. The discourse of ERM, although still aspirational, is gaining ground in leading financial organizations. ERM is the subject of multiple projects of codification and standardization, and is becoming constitutive of regulatory principles and practice.

Why has this happened? In this chapter, I argue that the rise of ERM can be traced to two convergent but different pressures for change in the concept of corporate control. First, ERM is a further mutation of the 'shareholder value' conception of the firm (Zorn et al., Chapter 13, this volume), one which involves an increasing technical and institutional focus on the risk measurement dimension of the risk-return relation underlying shareholder value. Value at risk (VAR) measurement technologies are at the very center of a project to know and calculate risk-based 'economic capital'. This strand of ERM posits a *risk-based conception of the firm*, which is most conspicuous for financial organizations and where a new intraorganizational politics is visible in the rise of the chief risk officer (CRO) (Oliver Wyman & Company 2002; Power forthcoming).

The second source of ERM thinking emerges from the corporate governance revolution of the early 1990s and from the increasing focus on, and formalization of, internal control as the bedrock of the 'good organization'. During the 1990s the idea of good internal control became explicitly

The author is grateful for the comments of Karin Knorr Cetina, Aaron Pitluck, and Alex Preda on earlier versions of this chapter. The financial support of the UK Economic and Social Research Council is also gratefully acknowledged.

informed and codified by concepts of risk, shaping a control-based concept of risk management focused more on organization design and process issues than on risk measurement. I argue that this source of ERM thinking is characterized by a *control-based model of risk management*. Both sources of ERM thinking are fundamental to the project of 'enforced self-regulation' (Ayres and Braithwaite 1992) inherent in the Basel 2 proposals for banking regulation and both serve to 'format' (Callon 1998) a new 'moral economy' of financial organizations.

Taken together, these two sources of ERM thinking express the win–win rhetoric of the 'new risk management' (Power 2000*b*), in which ideals of maximizing shareholder value can be reconciled to societal goals for good corporate governance and orderly capital markets. This ERM model promises a reconciliation of external demands for legitimate governance with functional demands for the efficient allocation of scarce capital. In this respect, ERM functions as a 'boundary object' spanning different interests and communities of practice.

There are a number of different definitions of ERM and the purpose of this chapter is not to police any specific understanding of the meaning and scope of the ERM concept. Rather, the intention is to examine the ERM model with a view to understanding its origins and logic. That said, a useful starting point is the following recent definition of ERM as: 'a process, effected by an entity's board of directors, management and other personnel, applied in strategy setting and across the enterprise, designed to identify potential events that may affect the entity, and manage risks to be within its risk appetite, to provide reasonable assurance regarding the achievement of entity objectives' (COSO 2003: 3).

From this strategic point of view, ERM demands the identification of all collective risks that affect company value as a whole and a key claimed benefit is the diversification benefits of a comprehensive view of risk, which have been traditionally managed separately. Functional claims for ERM in financial organizations relate to improved recognition of natural hedges and unanticipated correlations across risk categories (Rouyer 2002). In the non-financial sector, it is argued that ERM led initially to a rationalization of insurance strategies and the reduction of premium costs via multirisk policies (e.g. for the case of Honeywell, see Meulbroek 2002*b*: 58).[1]

For many years, lone pioneers and critics of risk-management practice bemoaned its balkanization, its insurance-based preoccupation with risk as a negative to be avoided and its bias toward the measurable (Kloman 1976, 1992). Now the aspiration has changed: risk management is to be regarded as a high-level practice of strategic significance of the firm embodying assessment and management techniques which address the whole range of risks facing the entity, particularly in recognition that some of the most important business risk effects, for example on reputation, have no ready markets for risk transfer or diversification and must be managed directly in the name of shareholder value.

This powerful functional 'storyline' (Hajer 1995) for the reorganization of uncertainty by ERM has different strands and elements, and the argument below is organized as follows: the next section deals with the finance-based conception of ERM and the search for a measurement basis for economic capital for organizational control purposes. The second section outlines the other main ERM thematic focused on organizational design and control systems. The third section explores the idea of ERM as a 'world model' and the fourth section reflects on the 'moral economy' of organizations, as projected by the idea of ERM as a regulatory system.

## ERM and the Risk-Based Concept of Corporate Control

Integrated Risk Management involves the identification and assessment of the collective risks that affect firm value and the implementation of a firm-wide strategy to manage those risks (Meulbroek 2002*a*: 56).

In 1998 Chase Manhattan Corporation became concerned that its assets were growing too fast and that its sales force was not making an appropriate trade off between risk and reward in developing new business.[2] In particular, traders were not relating their new business to the capital required to support it. Consequently, the bank decided to introduce the practice of 'Shareholder value-added' (SVA), a technique by which the profit of any business unit within the bank would be charged for capital, a variant of residual income methods for divisional control purposes. Thus, the 'free' cash flow that supports shareholder value was reconceptualized as 'free' only after charging units for the portion of risk capital they required the business as a whole to keep in reserve. The capital base on which such charges were computed was an allocated portion of the firm level risk, and this was calculated by two principal methods: VAR and stress testing.

The VAR has many different definitions and can be operationalized in a number of ways but the intention is to provide a measure of the potential financial loss from adverse market movements. According to Jorion (2001*a,b*), VAR is a simple integrating technology at the heart of the ERM model. It provides a common financial measurement framework for the whole firm, which simultaneously provides a calculation of 'economic capital', understood both as capital at risk *and* as a buffer for shocks. As a quantification of enterprise risk exposure over a period of time subject to a confidence level, the results of VAR modeling are relatively easily understood and visualizable for senior management.

First steps in the public standardization of whole firm VAR can be traced to J. P. Morgan's publication of *RiskMetrics* in 1993 and numerous applied textbooks have been published since then. However, the importance of the rise of VAR as a measurement technology for risk management lies as much in the idea as in the detailed practice. In reality, VAR techniques are heavily dependent on the availability of high-volume data sets and have developed most rapidly in the domain of 'market risk', that is, a category defined to capture the risk to the value of portfolios of assets arising from changes in market values. The techniques have been extended to the field of credit or default risk and are, at best, problematically and controversially applied in the more ambivalent category of operational risk.[3]

Notwithstanding this variation in specific applications, VAR is significant as an aspiration to measure capital at risk for the whole firm, across all categories of activity and to allocate that capital to individual business units. It is a vision in which capital for regulatory purposes is aligned with organizational control technologies like the SVA techniques at Chase Manhattan. But the idea of economic capital is itself far from unproblematic or uncontested. The accounting concept of share capital plus reserves is a traditional buffer concept, which is challenged by VAR. From this point of view it can be plausibly argued that VAR techniques 'perform' economic capital (MacKenzie forthcoming) in the sense that we do not have a clear concept of it, which is measurement independent. Furthermore, the fiction of VAR-based calculations of economic capital have real consequences as they are accepted by organizational agents. Two classes of agents matter in this respect: traders within the financial organization and regulators.

Getting traders in financial firms to accept VAR-based or other determinations of economic capital is the behavioral challenge of ERM. In practice, ERM only supports capital attribution to business units if these units actually accept its legitimacy: a fiction can only have real implications if it is accepted as real. It is clear from an extensive practitioner literature that these representations of capital at risk, even down to the level of individual transactions, can be highly adversarial within organizations. Consequently, normative commentaries continually emphasize the social support for measurement practices, namely the role of senior management buy-in, cultural commitment, and the need for champions of change (e.g. Cumming and Hirtle 2001; Sullivan 2001; Nash, Nakada, and Johnston 2002). VAR-based calculations of economic capital and related Risk Adjusted Return on Capital (RAROC) measures are institutional myths, in the sense that they are only effective if widely believed.

Getting regulators to accept ERM and VAR has also been an important dimension of its institutionalization. There has been increasing conceptual convergence between regulatory management of economic capital and internal business models. Banks have been permitted to use their own in-house models for determining a capital cushion for market risks since 1996, and this process is being extended to a new category of diverse and difficult to measure 'operational risks'. Although banking supervisors still constrain the use of in-house models, the changes in regulatory philosophy have been significant. The Basel Committee leading the reform of banking supervision (Basel Committee on Banking Supervision 2003a) is a key resource for conceptualizing ERM in financial markets and has published surveys of 'risk aggregation' practices, which realize the theoretical idea of ERM (see Basel Committee on Banking Supervision 2003*b*).

Despite specific technical difficulties of relating detailed risk-management investments to firm value, particularly in fuzzy areas like operational risk, the relation became newly thinkable in terms of VAR during the 1990s, and provided a new language for the business case for risk management. Accordingly, to Doherty (2000: 9–10), the fundamental theory of finance, in which returns on assets are always relative to risk, has made risk management a conceptually thinkable part of the corporate value creation process since the 1960s. However, though thinkable, that model had to wait until the early 1990s for diversification measurement technologies like VAR to become fully institutionalized as a calculation of risk capital.

The rise of this measurement strand of ERM is a further episode in institutionalization of the shareholder conception of the firm, driven in turn by the demands of financial markets that firms should manage their stock price. In the case of financial firms investing in other firms, the management of their own stock price is a function of how well they manage the impact of volatility in the stock prices of their investments, placing market risk management at the center of their own shareholder value strategies. ERM emerges from this double attentiveness to financial markets by financial institutions, first in terms of managing their own stock price and, second, doing this to a large extent by managing the effects of market movements on their portfolios of assets. This is slightly different from the two finance conceptions of control outlined by Zorn et al. (Chapter 13, this volume), focused more on the returns or earnings component of risk–return foundations of shareholder value. ERM represents a *risk-based concept of control* focused on the risk quality of earnings. As we shall see below, this concept of control is *regulatory as well as managerial*.

Zorn et al. (Chapter 13, this volume) argue that changes in the concept of control in organizations were a function of power struggles in organizations between management functions intent on claiming efficacy. In this respect, the most likely site of struggle in financial institutions is the challenge to the chief financial officer (CFO) by the rise of the CROs. The CRO is the organizational embodiment of ERM and the risk-based concept of control; the CRO reflects the repositioning of risk management in the management hierarchy (Lam 2000). Surveys (e.g. Conference Board of Canada 2001; Oliver Wyman & Company 2002) suggest a marked growth in the CRO role since the mid-1990s. In the case of Chase Manhattan discussed above, a risk policy committee of the main board is the organizational correlate of VAR and many organizations have similar committees headed by a new CRO role. In some cases, the CRO is subordinate to the CFO and in others they have equal and different status, one a facilitator of deals, the other a risk check on them. But while the general picture is presently unclear and demands further empirical research of the kind that Zorn and Dobbin have conducted for CFOs, the emergence of the CRO will further institutionalize the risk-based concept of control (Power forthcoming).

Where did the risk-based concept of control come from? To a large extent it had always been inherent or dormant in financial organizations, but there are several overlapping drivers in the 1990s. Its increasing significance is in part a rational response to volatility in financial markets and the need to manage asset growth more carefully in large financial institutions, such as we saw with Chase Manhattan. Second, it became institutionalized because of the organizational legitimacy and availability of a measurement technology, namely VAR, which promised a unifying, whole firm entity approach aligned with the whole firm philosophy of shareholder value. Third, it promised a new basis of divisional control of disparate units in financial organizations by determining risk-adjusted rates of return on capital for these units. Fourth, it provided financial organizations with a rational basis for contesting imposed regulatory capital requirements, resulting eventually in the regulatory recognition of in-house models for determining economic capital. Fifth, the technological domain of financial risk management was expanded by the increasing liquidity of markets for a broader set of financial instruments, extending the boundaries for risk transfer and management in fuzzy areas, such as 'weather bonds' (Meulbroek 2001).

To summarize: an important strand of ERM thinking has its origins in the project to improve control in large financial organizations. This project is epitomized by the idea and practice of VAR models which construct a concept of economic capital for two key audiences, internal traders and regulators. ERM provides a representation of economic capital supporting the interventions of senior management in the operations of divisionalized financial firms. But the idea of ERM is more than that of a measurement technology. It also projects a risk-based concept of corporate control, embodied in risk committees and in the work of CROs. In other words, ERM is not simply measurement focused; it is also about the management and control of risk-measurement practices and it is to this important strand of the ERM idea that we now turn.

## ERM and the Control-Based Concept of Risk Management

The second major strand of ERM is more generic in form and is visible in various attempts to codify the elements of a risk-management *system*. Building on the projects to codify quality management, a number of standards have been produced by standard setting organizations, beginning in 1995 with a joint document by the Australian and New Zealand Standards organizations (AS/NZS 1995), followed by counterparts in Canada (CSA 1997), United Kingdom (BSI 1999), and Japan (JIS 2001).[4] This generic risk-management thinking has been criticized, especially by those who do not see the utility of such general standards over and above specific risk-management practice, and this may explain why there is, at present, no ISO standard as such for the risk-management process, although a standard has been developed for a common risk-management terminology (ISO/IEC 2002).

Another related source of thinking for ERM has emerged explicitly from the codification of principles of internal control. Following a congressional investigation by the Treadway Commission in 1987 into fraudulent financial reporting, an internal control framework was developed (COSO 1991). This proposed a broad definition of an internal control *process* covering financial reporting, legal compliance and operations. Furthermore, the principles began to make explicit the connection between internal control and organizational risk management in its broadest sense: control processes must be designed on the basis of risk assessment and risk appetite, and their functioning must be reviewed. In the case of Chase Manhattan discussed above, the COSO framework was customized for use in the management of operational risk. Crucially, this rearticulation of internal control relates risks and controls explicitly to organizational objectives, and is part of a more general trend in the 'strategizing' of control functions.

The COSO in the United States, and the 'CoCo' framework developed by the Canadian Institute of Certified Accountants, have greatly influenced subsequent attempts to develop generic standards in the control/risk management area, not least for the Turnbull Report in the United Kingdom (ICAEW 1999) and the risk-management dimensions of the Control and Transparency Act (KonTrAG) in Germany, the latter passed in response to demands to strengthen the role of supervisory boards and requiring them to establish a monitoring system for risk identification.[5] In the case of COSO, a standing coalition of professional associations (The American Institute of Certified Public Accountants, the Institute of Internal Auditors, Financial Executives International, the Institute of Management Accountants, and the American Accounting Association) provides oversight for specific technical projects and the internal control framework has been republished as a draft framework for ERM (COSO 2003), which echoes and subsumes the earlier conceptual framework (COSO 2003: 18). This means that ERM is to be a standard for the design of internal control systems.

This strand of ERM represents a *control-based concept of risk management* and its key elements are clearly visible in the definition given earlier: risk management is related in ambition to entity objectives, to the production of value and thereby to organizational strategy; it is defined as a process requiring senior management direction and extending across the whole organization; it heralds a new organizational consciousness of 'risk appetite', and assurance. The document also represents a clear discourse of responsibilization: people must know their responsibilities and the limits of their authority. This linking of duties to entity objectives expresses a new 'moral order' to be discussed further below, as well as a strategizing aspiration for advisory markets. The auditing, control, and assurance conceptual heritage remains visible in the requirement to provide assurance that, inter alia, reporting and legal compliance objectives are achieved.

The COSO-based model of the ERM model is based on earlier PricewaterhouseCoopers architecture (e.g. PwC/IFAC 1998) and absorbs older internal control concepts. The internal environment of control is reconceptualized as a risk culture, a set of shared attitudes, values, and practices that characterizes how an entity considers risk in its day to day activities. COSO (2003) codifies the elements or stages of ERM understood in this context as a management process or system rather than a measurement practice. The ideal elements of this process are repeatedly visible in all the management process approaches to ERM and consist of:

*Event identification.* This reflects the intensified climate of concern during the 1990s for risk events which are not to be easily captured and understood by conventional information systems for example, rogue traders, reputational risks. Accordingly, the completeness of material risk identification, if not its precise measurement, has grown in significance as a management priority.

*Risk assessment.* This continues the quantitative tradition of risk analysis, including VAR, but is more pluralistic and includes qualitative techniques, such as focus groups, because of the importance of risk identification.

*Risk response.* This is the set of managerial action possibilities in terms of risk avoidance, reduction, sharing, and acceptance. Specific choices will reflect the *risk appetite* of organizations.

*Control activities.* These are designed in the light of risk responses and reposition longstanding control activities, such as segregation of duties, arithmetic and accuracy checks, and authority controls within the ERM process.

*Information and communication flows.* These are regarded as an essential feature of ERM, must be appropriate to the expectations of groups and individuals and must address the problem of cross-functional lateral communication.

*Monitoring.* As with COSO (1991) the ERM structure requires the ability to observe itself via periodic evaluation, by the internal and external audit functions and/or by the CRO.

This ideal ERM blueprint also acknowledges the limitations of control systems (collusion, ability to override) and emphasizes the roles and responsibilities of the various organizational agents who must realize ERM: the board, executive management who set the tone of an organization, the CFOs, CROs, and internal auditors. Possible conflicts and competition among these different agents are subordinated to the programmatic idea that ERM is the responsibility of all of them collectively.

From this generic point of view, ERM represents risk management as an *organizational process.* As in the case of financial institutions, there is a claim that risk-based control activities are value enhancing, but without the emphasis on a measurement technology such as VAR. Great emphasis is placed on senior management and the top-down ownership of the risk-control process. This emphasis grew out of the wave of corporate governance initiatives in the 1990s. Largely scandal driven, corporate governance thinking in different countries increasingly emphasizes internal organizational structures and processes. Boards of executive and nonexecutive directors, audit committees, internal and external auditors have all been subject to greater formalization of their roles, largely by voluntary codes of conduct but more recently in statutory form, with the Sarbanes–Oxley legislation in the United States. At the very center of these governance preoccupations is the nature of the internal control system and its management, which over time has been increasingly articulated in terms of risk (Power 2000a). For this strand of ERM internal control, risk management, and 'good' governance are almost coextensive.

There are of course differences and variations among the ERM standards mentioned above. Those emerging from national and international standard-setting organizations tend to have a strong project management flavor and there are important differences between the COSO and CoCo frameworks. But for the purposes of the present argument the similarities are more striking and significant.[6] First, risk is defined broadly in terms of both opportunity and harm, an essential strategy for reconceptualizing the value enhancing dimension of control activities and consistent with finance conceptions of risk as variance. Second, great emphasis is placed on risk communication rather than on specific measurement techniques, which may be diverse. In particular, communication with a wide range of stakeholders is countenanced, signaling greater sensitivity to the variations in risk perceptions of groups external to the enterprise. This is a critical extension of the risk-management field of vision and will be discussed further below. Third, ERM is part of a responsibility allocation process, which establishes risk accountability and authority; here the parallels with quality ownership are evident. Fourth, the system and process approach emphasizes documentation and auditability (Power 1999).

To summarize: COSO (2003) and other similar risk-management standards exemplify a generic control-based tradition of ERM thinking which is different in emphasis from that which has emerged from the financial risk-management practices of financial institutions. It is process- rather than measurement-based, and grows out of the varied discourses of corporate governance reform in the 1990s and their preoccupation with internal controls. This tradition is less concerned with internal management problems of divisional control and more with the integrity of senior management process. And although the control-based concept of risk management is also very much shareholder value focused, there is also another emphasis on stake-holder communication which places ERM in a potentially larger normative framework. With this in mind, we need to take a more critical look at ERM.

## ERM as World Culture?

ERM should not be presumed to be a self-evident and coherent set of ideas and blueprints for practice. It has been argued above that ERM ideas have emerged from two main conceptual frames for measuring economic capital and for organizational control processes, respectively. From this point of view, ERM is a reassembly of ideas, old knowledge perhaps (Deragon 2000), which has been subject to various attempts at codification. Although ideas about ERM clearly predate the development of standards and textbooks on the subject (e.g. Kloman 1976, 1992; Haines 1992), something distinctive takes place from about 1995 onward. Standardization projects for ERM are to be found at many levels, ranging from obvious standards issued by standard setting institutions to textbooks and commentaries. Even certain individuals can acquire the status of de facto codifier (e.g. Lam 2003).

Although the different elements of ERM thinking and conceptualization suggest a tension between a first-order emphasis on rational risk measurement and a second-order emphasis on the management of that risk measurement process, it can be suggested following Meyer et al. (1997) that ERM has all the apparent hallmarks of an emerging world cultural model. To unpack this argument, we can begin by considering practitioner surveys of ERM practice. Such surveys should not necessarily be taken at face value in terms of their analysis of degrees of implementation: they also constitute and perform the interorganizational world of ERM. Tillinghast Towers Perrin (2001, 2002) provides an example of an insurance industry survey, which not only describes practice, but also promotes the emergent discipline of ERM on the basis of its partial realization. Surveys like this typically conclude that industry is making progress (ninety-four companies, 49% of the sample, claim to have ERM and 38% are considering it, with the CRO role on the rise).

In terms of the operational reality of ERM, this survey suggests the continuing existence of barriers to a broad risk vision within insurance companies, with a strong cultural bias to existing ways of working. For example, 'overall the positive correlation between which risks are covered by ERM and satisfaction with the tools to manage those risks...suggests that risks may be included in an ERM program based on their ease of quantification more than their degree of importance' (Tillinghast Towers Perrin 2003: 6–7). With the exception of Canadian insurers, the general picture is one of a robust actuarial culture defining ERM to suit its own terms. This suggests that the concrete realization of the ideal elements of ERM is partial and subject to microcultural forms of resistance, such as intraorganizational turf wars and, in particular, the tension between the measurement and management facets of ERM identified above.

This decoupling between ERM claims and reality may be bemoaned at the level of practitioner surveys like this, but is not surprising. It should not blind us to the properties of ERM as an organizationally transcendent model with claims to universal applicability and with developed claims to functionality rooted in the shareholder value model. According to Meyer et al. (1997: 156), 'these models are organized as cultural principles and visions not strongly anchored in local circumstance'. The unreality of ERM principles, as embodied in the various codifications and texts described above, is also their strength as myths of control which serve to organize organizations.

To follow the thought experiment posited by Meyer et al. (1997), if we were to imagine the creation of a new banking organization, we know that it could not be founded without rapidly adopting the mission and principles of ERM, and would very quickly appoint a CRO and a whole host of other elements comprising the legitimated organizational actorhood of being a bank. In the 1980s and 1990s, the ideas of audit and of 'new public management' emerged as cultural models which could be made to look self-evidently functional and whose legitimacy was relatively immune to microcultural problems of implementation. From this point of view, ERM is the latest in a long line of world level (i.e. non-nation state level), organizational blueprints for the organization of uncertainty, and a new product in the market for advice which is increasingly legitimate via its codification in standards.

On this view, ERM is a product of 'world cultural forces', specifically organizations who can claim legitimacy as actors in the creation of collective goods and broad meaning systems (Meyer et al. 1997). We have already met these actors above: Chase Manhattan, J. P. Morgan, and other large banks; COSO and PricewaterhouseCoopers; national and international standards organizations; the Basel Committee on Banking Regulation; legitimized human actors, such as academics and practitioner commentators. It is important to note that not all so-called 'global' corporations are world actors in this sense; many do not actively participate in the creation of collective meaning systems, although as their operations are written up and disseminated as case studies by business academics and consultants, they may unintentionally come to play this role.

In picking our way through these actors, we can distinguish the two main sources of ERM thinking again. First, the risk-based concept of control derives from the position of financial economics as an increasingly powerful world cultural force, in general terms as a model of the firm (Whitley 1986) but also with a specific mandate to increase its scope via the financialization of all elements of risk management. Second, the control-based concept of risk management is built in part upon the older audit model, supplemented by a range of ideas to do with systems and communication. This suggests that ERM can be usefully imagined as a 'boundary object' at the world level which inhabits 'several communities of practice and satisf[ies] the informational requirements of each of them. Boundary objects are both plastic enough to adapt to local needs and constraints, yet robust enough to maintain a common identity across sites' (Bowker and Star 1999: 297).

To summarize: ERM can be understood as a world level boundary object which has emerged from a private market for risk-management norms and related discourses. A long-standing dissatisfaction with the insurance-based concept risk management (Kloman 1992; Dickinson 2001) was redeveloped in relation to a powerfully legitimate measurement technology on the one hand, namely VAR, and to a range of established ideas about management systems and processes on the other. ERM did not emerge from legislative or regulatory processes, although it has informed them as we shall see. However, whether ERM is a 'true' world model remains an open question. Some critics argue that continuing organizational barriers to the full implementation of ERM will diminish its legitimacy over time, reducing it to the status of mere fad (Banham 1999; Deragon 2000). These difficulties may feed back and be registered at the world level, namely the global conference circuit, the practice survey, consulting templates, handbooks of best practice, and world level standard setting bodies. Against this, we should expect at least some durability to the idea, irrespective of apparent specific failures. And part of that durability has little to do with the mechanics of risk management; it has more to do with ERM as a value system which appeals across different groups. As a boundary object, the ERM model importantly blurs the distinction between projects of risk measurement, organization, and regulation (Morgan and Engwall 1999), and posits a new normative order. It is to this that we now turn.

## ERM and the Moral Economy of Financial Organizations

The above discussion has focused on ERM as a model of organizational control. In this section, we consider its properties as a model of regulation or, more accurately, 'enforced self-regulation' (Ayres and Braithwaite 1992). First, ERM is a blueprint for regulatory regimes themselves and for financial regulators seeking to manage their own operating and political risk. Thus, elements of ERM are to be found in the policy thinking of the United Kingdom Financial Services Authority (2000) and elsewhere. Here, the legitimacy of ERM as a world model is evident as regulatory organizations are subject to isomorphic pressures to become, at least at the level of mission and purpose, more like the organizations they regulate. Notwithstanding the evident empirical operating variety of regulatory regimes (Hood, Rothstein, and Baldwin 2000), ERM is an increasingly legitimate template for such regimes, specifically what is now called the risk-based model of regulation. From this point of view states and state agencies are adopters of world cultural elements like ERM. ERM ideas have an important position in the KonTraG in Germany and in the recent Sarbanes–Oxley Act in the United States. And organizations like the World Bank have also begun to adopt ERM to structure their own working processes.

Second, the emergence of ERM makes a certain regulatory style possible, one that increasingly relies on the self-organizing resources of banking organizations and which monitors the quality of local risk-management systems. From this point of view, the 'auditability' and responsibility elements of ERM are critical in enabling regulatory oversight of essentially private processes, and the technology of VAR provides a common technical language of exchange between banks and regulators. Regulatory pressures have grown for ERM models to be introduced in financial institutions, such as the Office of the Superintendent of Financial Institutions (Canada), the Prudential Regulation Authority in Australia (where the HIH Insurance scandal has had a huge impact). More generally, the Basel 2 proposals also embody ERM ideas; pillar one corresponds to the risk-measurement ambition and pillar 2 corresponds to the control and communication emphasis (Basel Committee on Banking Supervision 2003*a*). From this point of view, world level norms are being relegalized at the level of regulatory policy. Indeed, Australia Standards acknowledges that failure to establish and maintain a proper risk-management program may be evidence that an organization is negligent.[7] In short, we can expect that national legal systems will reinforce the legitimacy of the ERM model.

In order for ERM models to fulfill this regulatory vision, they need to promote a new internal moral community in financial institutions. Ideals of integration and related internal responsibilities for risk envisage the construction of a normative operating climate in which risk is defined and, crucially, allocated to organizational agents. Historically, risk management in diverse areas, such as health and safety, internal control, insurance were decoupled from corporate policy and objectives (a matter for critical commentary by farsighted individuals) and managed on a fragmented basis. The ERM model recasts risk management explicitly in terms of organizational objectives, transforming risk management from a specialist control side-show to a (shareholder) value enhancing activity. This programmatic 'strategizing' of risk management, raising the profile of long-standing elements (e.g. control and risk assessment techniques), and repositioning them in the fabric of management knowledge, simultaneously represents a new 'moral economy' of the organization. This moral economy is governed by newly powerful actors, namely risk and audit committees and risk officers concerned with new objects, such as corporate reputation (Power 2003).

The sense of 'moral economy' should not be taken normatively to mean that organizations become 'moral' in some first-order sense. The intention of the concept is to highlight the normative structure of the ERM model, in particular the internal responsibility structures that banks like Chase Manhattan established in relation to risk management. However, there is also a larger sense in which ERM can be said to constitute a new moral economy, namely in the expanded role of risk management in processing social and environmental issues at the level of the organization. In short, historically visible anxieties and pressures for the democratization of risk analysis (e.g. Jasanoff 1999) are reworked and reframed by ERM as issues in the design of internal control and management systems, precisely the 'remanagerialization of risk' envisaged by Beck (1992).

The ERM world model translates potential public policy issues into matters of organizational process (rather than scientific expertise) at the enterprise level. Thus, the social and environmental externalities of financial and other organizations are reworked and *internalized* as matters of 'reputational risk management' (Power 2003). Reputation management as a component of ERM is arguably the organizational privatization of public policy. In particular, regulatory organizations begin to manage their own reputational and political risk in priority to their direct systemic obligations. For example, in the case of the World Bank, ERM functions to manage the risk to the Bank of not fulfilling its mission, rather than the risk to developing countries directly. The latter is reframed and internalized by ERM relative to the entity that is the World Bank organization. How this risk translation process might impact on the continuing legitimacy of the ERM model is an open question.

Another dimension of the moral economy of ERM is its role in providing the actors of corporate governance, namely boards, audit committees, internal and external auditors, a mediating semi-technical language through which to evaluate and monitor organizational process without becoming embroiled in technical risk analysis. Even VAR has the attraction of being relatively easily understood. This enfranchisement of nonexperts, with monitoring capacity within organizations is a critical feature of ERM as a template for good governance and appears to address the 'rogue' expert problem. Thus the ERM model restructures organizational handling of uncertainty with a greater accent on risk communication and dialog about a broader range of risk objects. Compared to older conceptions of financial risk analysis, ERM is much more democratic, at least at the organizational level.

To summarize: the ERM model repositions risk management within a new internal moral economy of the enterprise. This moral economy can be characterized in terms of heightened internal responsibilities for risk and its management, much in the manner of 'quality ownership', but it also has an external dimension in so far as ERM explicitly processes wider social, economic, and environmental problems at the enterprise level. This still leaves us with a puzzle about the moral economy of ERM which is both more open and responsive to these external issues than previous risk-management thinking, but which is also closed in so far as the operating premise is the rather old fashioned, pre-network idea of the discrete firm entity.

## Conclusions: ERM and the Organization of Uncertainty

Organizations have always been centrally, even definitionally, concerned with the management of uncertainty and the coordination of resources to create forms of order for identifying risk and making decisions (March and

Simon 1958). ERM can be regarded as yet another in a long line of programmatic technologies for rethinking the relationship between management, as the production of order, and uncertainty. Ideas about integrated, holistic, and enterprise-based risk management have existed for many years, in part as a discourse of dissatisfaction with narrow insurance based views of the subject. Since 1995, these ideas have found an institutional voice in the form of specific standards and guidelines on generic risk management, in supporting texts and commentaries, and in an increasing regulatory emphasis on organizational risk management. ERM in this sense has been transformed from the preoccupation of a small number of critical observers and pioneers, into something programmatic and operationally significant. As a potential world model, ERM has acquired the quality of a self-evident set of principles: the fundamental arguments are very well-rehearsed and, at the conceptual level, reasonably well accepted.

This chapter has argued that the ERM model has two convergent strands or currents, the *risk-based model of the firm* and the *control-based model of risk management*. Both these strands can be understood as the responses of discrete functional activities, risk-measurement and internal control, respectively, to the shareholder value imperative. To this end, ERM reorganizes and coordinates existing risk-management subdisciplines, a program for debalkanization (Kloman 1992), to create rational relations between risk management, control activities, organizational objectives, and strategy. These claims for functionality are fictional and unrealized to a large degree, but the ERM model as realized and legitimized in standards, texts, and now regulations makes it a thinkable imperative. If ERM is an illusion of control, it is also somehow one of a number of necessary illusions which constitute management practice. And as the rational reorganization of uncertainty, ERM is an 'organizational fix' in the same sense in which scholars of science and technology studies have used the concept of 'technological fix'.

This chapter has been concerned primarily with the emerging logic of ERM, its formalization in standards, and its status as a world level model of good governance. It has not been concerned with empirical questions of adoption and implementation, although a few things can be sensibly anticipated about what such studies will show, based on work in other areas. First, there can be no doubt that any implementation of ERM systems will be laden with organizational politics and negotiation, that objectives which should shape risk-management activity will become shaped by it, that traders will resist arbitrary capital charges and so on. So the official sequencing of ERM processes as represented in standards should not be assumed, and we can expect internal competition between various organizational actors, not least between the CFO and the CRO. Second, we should expect that ERM standards will become implicated in the legalization and proceduralization of organizations (Sitkin and Bies 1994), notwithstanding the enabling, innovatory language by which ERM is promoted. As regulatory systems depend increasingly on ERM at the organizational level, this tendency is likely to be observed as ERM and good organizational governance become increasingly codefined. Third, we should expect to see an active advisory market for ERM and its customized variants, a market in which consultants seek to articulate proprietorial versions of generic principles. From this point of view, standards and surveys exist in part to scare organizations into reform processes.

ERM has emerged, via standards and other texts, as an institutionalized basis for the self-observation of financial organizations based on the dual technologies of VAR and internal control. This second-order observation of operations is visible in the stated mission of the CRO role, an actor who is charged in part with providing a new basis for the self-description of management. However, languages of organizational self-description, such as ERM, may change precisely because there is no enduring rational way to deal with the management of enterprise (Simon 2003) and it remains an empirical question ultimately as to whether or not the ERM model leads organizations to change their substantive rules of internal communication.

## Notes

1. The case of BP in 1992 is also similar, informed by an academic study by Neil Doherty and Clifford Smith. See *Risk Management Reports*, December 1999, 4–5.
2. This case is based on Barton, Shenkir, and Walker (2001, ch. 3).
3. The categories of market, credit, and operational risk have emerged as legitimate classifications in the organizational field. Financial institutions structure their risk management activities in terms of these categories. However, they are far from being diagnostically useful; real risk events usually straddle these categories and their departmental embodiments.
4. It is interesting to note that in Germany the *Deutsches Institut für Normierung* (DIN) notably does not have such a generic document, part of a general German tendency to focus on product and service specific standards, rather than broad management templates.
5. This chapter does not deal with the regulation of risk reporting. It is important to note that the German Accounting Standards Board has issued an accounting standard on risk reporting.
6. Many standards are also supported by more specific guidance and amplification. See, for example, booklets 141, 142, and 143 published by Australia Standards.
7. See *Risk Management Reports*, January 2000: 5.

## References

AIRMIC. 1999. *A Guide to Integrated Risk Management*. London: Integrated Risk Management Special Interest Group, AIRMIC.
AS/NZS. 1995. *Risk Management*. Sydney and Wellington: Standards Australia and Standards New Zealand.

Ayres, I. and Braithwaite, J. 1992. *Responsive Regulation: Transcending the Deregulation Debate.* New York, NY: Oxford University Press.

Banham, R. 1999. 'Kit and Caboodle: Understanding the Skepticism about Enterprise Risk Management', *CFO Magazine*, April.

Barton, T., Shenkir, W., and Walker, P. 2001. *Making Enterprise Risk Management Pay off.* Morristown, NJ: Financial Executives Research Foundation Inc.

Basel Committee on Banking Supervision. 2003*a*. *The New Basel Capital Accord— Third Consultative Paper.* Basel: Bank for International Settlements.

—— 2003*b*. *Trends in Risk Integration and Aggregation.* Basel: Bank for International Settlements.

Beck, U. 1992. *Risk Society.* London: Sage.

Bowker, G. and Star, S. 1999. *Sorting Things Out: Classification and Its Consequences.* Cambridge, MA: The MIT Press.

BSI. 1999. BSI 6079–3. *Project Management—Part 3: Guide to the Management of Business Related Project Risk.* London: British Standards Institute.

Callon, M. 1998. 'Introduction: The Embeddedness of Economic Markets in Economics', in *The Laws of the Markets*, Callon, M. (ed.). Oxford: Blackwell, 1–57.

Conference Board of Canada. 2001. *A Composite Sketch of a Chief Risk Officer.* Ottawa: Conference Board of Canada.

COSO. 1991. *Internal Control: Integrated Framework.* Committee of the Sponsoring Organizations of the Treadway Commission.

—— 2003. *Enterprise Risk Management Framework: Exposure Draft.* Committee of the Sponsoring Organizations of the Treadway Commission.

CSA. 1997. CAN/CSA—Q850–97, *Risk Management Guideline for Decision Makers, A National Standard for Canada.* Mississauga, Ontario, Canadian Standards Association.

Cumming, C. and Hirtle, B. 2001. 'The Challenges of Risk Management in Diversified Financial Companies', *FRBNY Economic Policy Review* March: 1–15.

Deragon, J. 2000. 'Old Knowledge with a New Name', *Erisk.com*, November.

Dickinson, G. 2001. 'Enterprise Risk Management: Its Origins and Conceptual Foundation', *Geneva Papers on Risk and Insurance—Issues and Practice* 26: 360–6.

Doherty, N. 2000. *Integrated Risk Management: Techniques and Strategies for Reducing Risk.* New York, NY: McGraw Hill.

Financial Services Authority. 2000. *A New Regulator for the New Millennium.* London: Financial Services Authority.

Haines, Y. 1992. 'Toward a Holistic Approach to Total Risk Management', *Geneva Papers on Risk and Insurance—Issues and Practice* 17(64): 314–21.

Hajer, M. 1995. *The Politics of Environmental Discourse: Ecological Modernisation in the Policy Process.* Oxford: Clarendon Press.

Hood, C., Rothstein, H., and Baldwin, R. 2000. *The Government of Risk.* Oxford: Oxford University Press.

ICAEW. 1999. *Internal Control: Guidance for the Directors of Listed Companies Incorporated in the United Kingdom.* London: Institute of Chartered Accountants in England and Wales.

ISO/IEC. 2002. *Guide 73: Risk Management—Vocabulary.* Geneva: International Standards Organization.

Jasanoff, S. 1999. 'The Songlines of Risk', *Environmental Values* 8: 135–52.

JIS 2001. 'Guidelines for the Development and Implementation of Risk Management System', *JIS Q 2001*, Tokyo: Japanese Standards Association.

Jorion, P. 2001*a*. 'Value, Risk and Control: A Dynamic Process in Need of Integration', in *Mastering Risk*, Pickford, J. (ed.). London: Financial Times/ Prentice Hall, 119–24.

—— 2001*b*. *Value at Risk*. New York, NY: McGraw Hill.

Kloman, F. 1976. 'The Risk Management Revolution', *Fortune Magazine* July.

—— 1992. 'Rethinking Risk Management', *Geneva Papers on Risk and Insurance— Issues and Practice* 17(64): 299–313.

Lam, J. 2000. 'Enterprise-wide Risk Management and the Role of the Chief Risk Officer', *Erisk Magazine*, March 25.

—— 2003. *Enterprise Risk Management—From Incentives to Controls*. London: John Wiley.

MacKenzie, D. forthcoming. 'Models, Risk and Crises: The Global Financial System in 1998 and 2001', in *Organizational Encounters with Risk*, Hutter, B. and Power, M. (eds.). Cambridge: Cambridge University Press.

March, J. and Simon, H. 1958. *Organizations*. New York, NY: John Wiley.

Meulbroek, L. 2001. 'Total Strategies for Company-wide Risk Control', in *Mastering Risk*, Pickford, J. (ed.). London: Financial Times/Prentice Hall, 67–73.

—— 2002*a*. 'A Senior Manager's Guide to Integrated Risk Management', *Journal of Applied Corporate Finance* 14(4): 56–70.

—— 2002*b*. 'The Promise and Challenge of Integrated Risk Management', *Risk Management and Insurance Review* 5: 55–66.

Meyer, J., Boli, J., George, T., and Ramirez, F. 1997. 'World Society and the Nation State', *American Journal of Sociology* 103: 144–81.

Morgan, G. and Engwall, L. 1999. 'Regulation and Organization: An Introduction', in *Regulation and Organizations: International Perspectives*, Morgan, J. and Engwall, L. (eds.). London: Routledge, 1–14.

Nash, M., Nakada, P., and Johnston, B. 2002. 'Start Today for Enterprise Wide Risk Management in 2006', *RMA Journal* November 56–61.

Oliver Wyman & Company. 2002. *The Evolving Roles of the Chief Financial Officer and the Chief Risk Officer: A Global Survey of Financial Institutions*. New York, NY: Oliver Wyman & Company.

Power, M. 1999. *The Audit Society: Rituals of Verification*. Oxford: Oxford University Press.

—— 2000*a*. *The Audit Implosion: Regulating Risk from the Inside*. London: Institute of Chartered Accountants in England and Wales.

—— 2000*b*. 'The New Risk Management', *European Business Forum* 1: 20.

—— 2003. 'Risk Management and Corporate Responsibility', in *Risk and Morality*, Ericson, R. (ed.). Toronto: Toronto University Press, 145–64.

—— forthcoming. 'The Rise of the Chief Risk Officer', in *Organizational Encounters with Risk*, Hutter, B. and Power, M. (eds.). Cambridge: Cambridge University Press. forthcoming.

PwC/IFAC. 1998. *Enhancing Shareholder Wealth by Better Managing Business Risk*. New York, NY: International Federation of Accountants.

Rouyer, S. 2002.'Enterprise Risk Management for Financial Institutions', *Erisk.com* January.

Simon, F. 2003. 'The De-Construction and Re-Construction of Authority and the Role of Management Consulting', *Soziale Systeme* 8(2): 283–93.

Sitkin, S. and Bies, R. 1994. 'The Legalization of Organizations: A Multi-Theoretical Perspective', in *The Legalistic Organization*, Sitkin and Bies (eds.). Thousand Oaks, CA: Sage, 19–49.

Sullivan, L. 2001. 'Building a Risk Management Program from the Ground Up', *Risk Management*, December: 25–9.

Tillinghast Towers Perrin. 2001. *Creating Value Through Enterprise Risk Management— A Practical Approach for the Insurance Industry*. Tillinghast Towers Perrin, April.

—— 2002. *Enterprise Risk Management in the Insurance Industry: 2002 Benchmarking Survey Report*. Tillinghast Towers Perrin.

Walker, P., Shenkir, W., and Barton, T. 2002. *Enterprise Risk Management: Pulling it all together*. Altamonte Springs, FL: Institute of Internal Auditors Research Foundation.

Whitley, R. 1986. 'The Transformation of Business Finance into Financial Economics: The Roles of Academic Expansion and Changes in U.S. Capital Markets', *Accounting, Organizations, and Society* 11: 171–92.

# 13

# Managing Investors: How Financial Markets Reshaped the American Firm

DIRK ZORN, FRANK DOBBIN,
JULIAN DIERKES, AND MAN-SHAN KWOK

## Financial Markets and the Ideal Firm

What causes large numbers of firms to change strategy and structure in tandem? Organizational institutionalists find that managerial and professional groups that span organizations develop new models of organizational efficiency—models that are typically in the interest of the group pushing them (DiMaggio and Powell 1983; Baron, Jennings, and Dobbin 1988). These new models are often framed as responses to wider economic or political changes, and they serve to enhance the prestige and power of the groups behind them. The new models often diffuse before the jury is in on whether they are more efficient than the models they replace, suggesting that while changes are framed as efficiency-enhancing, they are not really based on rational learning.

We find that over the last three decades, experts promoted a new model of the firm. But in this case the experts were not part of a rising management specialty that hawked their new model from within the firm. They were outsiders. Institutional investors, financial analysts, and hostile takeover firms began to articulate a new ideal of the modern firm, an ideal that suited the professional interests of these three groups. Executives paid attention to this new ideal, in part, because firms were beginning to reward them differently. Executive pay had largely been tied to the size of the firm—the bigger the firm, the higher the chief executive officer (CEO) salary. Executives thus defined firm growth as job one. Agency theory (Jensen and Meckling 1976) led firms to compensate CEOs through stock options, tying CEO remuneration to stock price. Thus CEOs became more and more sensitive to how financial markets valued their firms, and paid more attention to institutional investors and securities analysts. We find that the new ideal of the firm that institutional investors, securities analysts, and takeover firms promoted led to a revolution in firm structure and strategy. The story offers important insights for organizational theorists. Early students of organizations traced practices to internal functional demands, such as size and technological complexity. Open-systems theorists (Scott 2002) traced practices to networks of specialists who spanned organizations, constructing management approaches. We show that emergent extra-organizational networks can successfully promote new management models. The power of those networks to discipline executives plays an important role. The availability of rhetorical devices, notably new theories of agency, core-competence, business process reengineering, and shareholder value, may matter as well.

We look at the effects of the new corporate ideal on the internal structure and strategy of over 400 large US firms for the period 1963–2000. Firms restructured their top management teams, installing chief financial officers (CFOs) to manage stock market valuation and eliminating the Chief Operating Officer (COO), a vestige of the diversification strategy. Firms also embraced the preference of institutional investors and securities analysts for focused firms, buying their competitors and suppliers rather than buying far-flung industries.

### Institutional Theory and the External Control of Organizations

Institutionalists were among the first organizational scholars to argue that corporations follow their peers—that groups of firms behave like herds of cattle (Meyer and Rowan 1977; DiMaggio and Powell 1983). Early studies covered practices that symbolized a commitment to equality (Edelman 1990; Dobbin and Sutton 1998). Recent studies (Fligstein 1990; Abrahamson 1991; Davis 1991; Dobbin and Dowd 2000; Davis and Robbins, Chapter 14, this volume) have examined core business strategies, finding that the social environment shapes ideas about efficiency just as it shapes ideas about equality.

Management fads often strike at the heart of corporate practices, and they often involve competing visions of how to best manage the firm. Fligstein (1990) has shown this with considerable subtlety in his study of the corporate revolution that put the conglomerate ideal of the firm into practice. For Fligstein (1990), diversification was promoted between the 1950s and the 1970s by managers with backgrounds in finance, as a replacement for the sales/marketing model of corporate strategy. Fligstein's argument was revolutionary, for it challenged the received wisdom of America's preeminent business historian, Alfred DuPont Chandler (1977), who had argued that conglomeration represented the functional evolution of American business, rather than the outcome of a power struggle between management cliques.

We build on the work of Fligstein and Markowitz (1993), Fligstein (2001), and Davis, Diekmann, and Tinsley (1994), who show that when finance managers faced a wave of hostile takeovers that disassembled undervalued conglomerates, they installed the 'core-competence' model of the firm. We show that both the top management team and the core business strategy were revolutionized. We underscore the role of extra-organizational groups in constructing and diffusing the new model of management. In the institutional tradition, we find that a new management ideal arises among a network of experts, who see an opening to push a strategy that serves their interests, but which they frame as in the interest of investors and managers. Yet we find that the key networks constructing and diffusing this new ideal were exogenous to the firm—they were major financial market networks (Zuckerman 1999, 2000).

Our core argument is that three key groups in financial markets retheorized their own interests, and the interests of investors at large, as synonymous. The successful promulgation of a new theory of interest turned out to be key to restructuring the firm. This is an important insight from institutional theory (Dobbin et al. 1993; Strang and Meyer 1994). Three groups that were newly powerful in financial markets theorized their own interests, and the interests of others. First, hostile takeover firms broke conglomerates up, demonstrating that the component parts could sometimes be sold for more than the previous market valuation—that the parts were greater than the sum of the whole. They argued forcefully that such break-ups were in the interest of investors, who reaped higher share prices, and ultimately benefited the economy as a whole. In the end, they convinced the world that what they did for a living, which was at first construed as illicit, was in fact efficient. Second, institutional investors, who controlled ever larger shares of corporate stock, had difficulty placing a value on the huge conglomerate and saw it as their job—not the job of the CEO—to diversify risk by building balanced portfolios. Thus they defined it as in their professional interest to invest in focused firms. By shunning conglomerates, they lowered their value. They defined focused firms as better serving the interests of investors, because focused firms now had higher share prices and because investors should, following financial economics, balance their portfolios themselves. Third, securities analysts typically specialized by industry, forcing diversified firms eager to attract analyst coverage to sell-off businesses unrelated to their core (Zuckerman 2000). Analysts preferred to evaluate single-industry firms, and they translated this preference into a theory that single-industry firms were superior and into an incentive for firms to focus their activities.

Management specialists and economists sketched new theories of the firm that would help to both explain and propel these changes. 'Core-competence theory' was given its name in 1990 by C.K. Pralahad and Gary Hamel in a *Harvard Business Review* article titled 'The Core Competencies of the Firm'. But General Electric's Jack Welch had argued since the early 1980s for hands-on management. 'Agency theory' in economics (Jensen and Meckling 1976) encouraged firms to tie executive compensation to stock performance, through stock options that paid executives to focus on increasing share price. The field of financial economists favored firms that were more focused, and favored allowing investors to diversify their portfolios on their own. The 'business process reengineering' (downsizing) movement (Hammer and Champy 1993) suggested that firms should eliminate unnecessary layers of management, including the conglomerate's extra layer of finance experts who handled acquisition strategy.

The new core-competence/shareholder-value ideal suggested that the firm's main job was to focus on the core business and to manage stock price. This carried implications for the structure of the top management team, and for acquisition strategy. Now the top manager—the CEO—was supposed to spend his time managing the core business. A COO signaled that the firm was still following the antiquated strategy of portfolio diversification. Managing stock price was now supposed to be the firm's primary task, and so the treasurer was promoted to the position of CFO, as part of the top management duo or troika. Because portfolio diversification was now defined as the job of investors, diversifying acquisitions gave way to horizontal and vertical acquisitions.

We chart changes over time in the importance of hostile takeover firms, institutional investors, and securities analysts. We also chart changes in the preferences in these groups—in their articulation of what the ideal firm should look like. We tie these changes to shifts in the top management team structures and acquisition strategies of 429 large American corporations, for the period 1963–2000.

## The Rising Importance of Financial Market Players

Over the past quarter century, firms have paid more and more attention to financial markets. We find that important actors in financial markets changed in character over time, as individual investors gave way to large institutional investors, stock analysts grew in number and in importance, and the activities of takeover firms, particularly in the 1980s, heated up the market for corporate control. While each group of actors articulated its own reasons for wanting firms that were less diversified and that catered more to investors, executives became increasingly attentive to share price. We present data from a sample of large public American corporations to document these trends.

### Constructing a Sample to Study What Changed

We collected data from a stratified random sample of 429 public corporations for the years 1963–2000. We stratified the sample by industry, collecting information on firms in twenty-two industry categories. We sampled from annual Fortune 500 lists and Fortune 100 lists, which cover the largest firms in each industry. To avoid survivorship bias, the sample was drawn from all Fortune lists published during the observation period rather than from a single Fortune list. Consequently, the sample includes firms founded later than 1963 and firms that cease to exist sometime before the year 2000.

We gathered information on management structure and business strategy from Standard and Poor's Register of Corporations, Directors and Executives, Thomson Financial's CDA Spectrum database, Institutional Brokers Estimate System (I/B/E/S), Thomson Financial's FirstCall database and SDC Platinum.

### New Financial Market Players: Takeover Firms, Institutional Investors, and Analysts

Important actors in financial markets changed in character over time, as individual investors gave way to large institutional investors, stock analysts grew in number and in importance, and the hostile takeover firms grew in number and in activity.

Davis, Diekmann, and Tinsley (1994) have linked the demise of the conglomerate to takeover specialists who bought firms only to break them up and sell off the parts. Their data from a Fortune 500 sample show that about 30% of large corporations received takeover bids between 1980 and 1990. Our sample is comparable. To track the rising importance of takeover firms, we examine not all takeover bids, but unsolicited (hostile) takeover bids. Figure 13.1 shows that between 1980 and 1990, slightly more than 11% of the firms received hostile takeover bids. This suggests that about one-third of

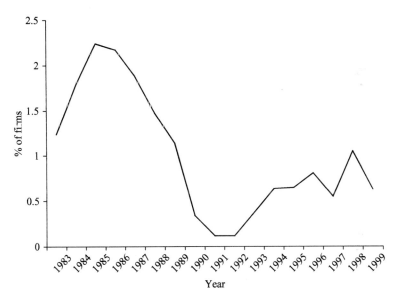

FIGURE 13.1. Firms Receiving Hostile Takeover Bid (Three-year Centered Moving Average)

*Source*: SDC Platinum.

the takeover bids that Davis et al. document were hostile. Every large American firm recognized the growing threat of hostile takeover. The phenomenon declined significantly toward the 1990s, as firms took precautions ranging from the poison pill (Davis 1991) to doing the job of takeover firms themselves, spinning off unrelated businesses.

Institutional investors and securities analysts were growing in importance at this time. Driven by both the explosion of pension plans that allowed individuals to direct their own investments and the democratization of stock market investment through mutual funds, institutional investors grew from minor players to major players. We document this in Figure 13.2, which displays the average percentage of shares controlled by institutional investors for the firms in our sample. From slightly more than 20% in 1980, the proportion grew almost threefold in twenty years time. Among large firms, in other words, institutional investors came to control the lion's share of stock. Institutional investors began to try to influence the internal workings of firms. Because they lost money when they sold stock in companies that were performing poorly, they found the strategy of voicing concerns rather than seeking exit more and more feasible. By sponsoring shareholder resolutions, they lobbied for changes in corporate governance and firm strategy. Davis and Robbins (Chapter 14, this volume) show how scrutiny by institutional investors and shareholder activism have led to changes in the board composition of large US corporations. We demonstrate the rise of this strategy in Figure 13.3, which presents data from the Shareholder Proposal Database

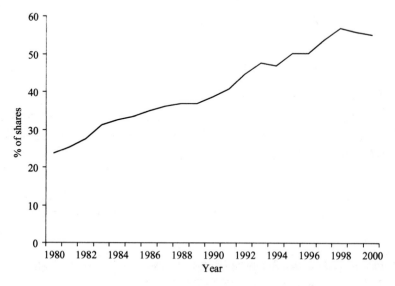

FIGURE 13.2. Shares Held by Institutional Investors

*Source*: CDA/Spectrum.

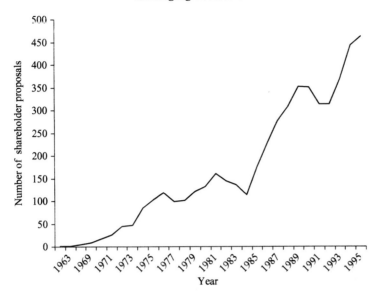

FIGURE 13.3. Number of Shareholder Proposals Sponsored by Institutional Investors (Three-Year Centered Moving Average)

*Source*: Shareholder Proposal Database (Proffitt 2001).

(Proffitt 2001) on institutionally sponsored proxy votes. Between the mid-1980s and the mid-1990s, the number of proposals supported by pension funds and other investment companies more than tripled.

The increasing role of stock analysts can be seen in Figure 13.4, which graphs the average number of stock analysts covering the firms in our sample over time. Between the late 1970s and the early 1990s, the average number of stock analysts following a firm rose from eight to eighteen. The importance of stock analysts to firms has been well documented in the studies of Ezra Zuckerman (1999, 2000). He shows that the conventional wisdom that firms were restructured in the 1980s as shareholders demanded the dismantling of diversified firms and their reconfiguration into more focused firms misses a key process. In the late 1980s and early 1990s, firms dediversified to please stock analysts, who had difficulty valuing diversified firms. He also shows that firms that were not covered by these industry specialists suffer, in terms of share price, relative to their peers. Their CEOs, now dependent on stock options for income, suffered as well.

### The New Corporate Metric: Stock Price

These newly influential groups in financial markets began to define a new way to judge the firm. In the 1960s, investors believed that stock price would

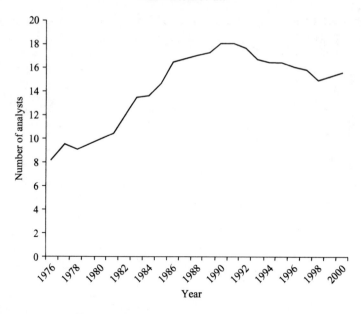

FIGURE 13.4. Securities Analyst Coverage

*Source*: I/B/E/S.

reflect profitability and dividends, and so firms that paid attention to the bottom line would succeed on all fronts. Even before the bull market of the 1990s, however, profits began to look like a poor measure of a firm's value. As during the heady days of railway expansion in the nineteenth century, prospects for future profitability seemed more important than current accounts. This was particularly the case for high technology firms. Institutional investors and securities analysts turned their attention from current accounts to stock price, particularly in growth industries.

This change was fueled by accounting technologies that improved the quality of quarterly reports, and by rise of services that provided data on analysts' profit projections. Journalist Joseph Nocera (1998: 59–60) notes that at Fidelity, a major institutional investor, the focus shifted from actual performance to beating the consensus estimates among analysts:

From time to time, young Fidelity hands would rush into Lynch's office to tell him some news about a company. They would say things like, 'Company X just reported a solid quarter-up 20%'. Eleven years later, as I review my old notes, I'm struck by the fact that no one said that Company X had 'exceeded expectations'. There was no mention of conference calls, pre-announcements or whisper numbers. Nor did I ever hear Lynch ask anyone—be it a company executive or a 'sell side' analyst on Wall Street—whether Company X was going to 'make the quarter'.

Whereas stock price used to rise and fall on the strength of the profits per se, now it rose and fell on the strength of profits vis-à-vis analysts' forecasts.

For many computer and Internet firms, after all, the bottom line was printed in red every quarter. Fortune magazine speculates that the emergence of firms making available consensus forecast data, based on the averages of these profit projections, has furthered managerial attention to analysts and to their forecasts:

Executives of public companies have always strived to live up to investors' expectations, and keeping earnings rising smoothly and predictably has long been seen as the surest way to do that. But it's only in the past decade, with the rise to prominence of the consensus earnings estimates compiled first in the early 1970s by I/B/E/S (it stands for Institutional Brokers Estimate System) and now also by competitors Zacks, First Call, and Nelson's, that those expectations have become so explicit. Possibly as a result, companies are doing a better job of hitting their targets: For an unprecedented sixteen consecutive quarters, more S&P 500 companies have beat the consensus earnings estimates than missed them. (Fox 1997: 76)

It was not only that analysts and institutional investors developed preferences for corporate strategy, but also that executives paid more attention to their preferences. Firms were, by their own accounts, relatively insulated from investor preferences in the 1960s and 1970s. Individual investors rarely had time to scrutinize firms, but with the proliferation of institutional investors and stock analysts, large firms now had many scrupulous overseers (cf. Davis and Robbins, Chapter 14, this volume).

With this increase in attention came more volatility in stock price. Stock price began to move more frequently in tandem with quarterly earnings reports and with analysts' buy and sell recommendations. At the same time, executive compensation had become more closely tied to stock price. Meeting the profit targets of stock analysts thus became a preoccupation among corporate executives, for their capacity to benefit from stock option grants depended on their capacity to drive up stock price. As Justin Fox wrote in Fortune in 1997:

This is what chief executives and chief financial officers dream of: quarter after quarter after blessed quarter of not disappointing Wall Street. Sure, they dream about other things too—megamergers, blockbuster new products, global domination. But the simplest, most visible, most merciless measure of corporate success in the 1990s has become this one: Did you make your earnings last quarter? (Fox 1997: 76)

Next, we turn to the implications the new corporate ideal carried for the structure and strategy of the large firm. We first explore the structure of the top management team and then take a look at acquisition strategy.

## A New Sidekick: From COO to CFO

When the conglomerate ruled the world, managers from finance backgrounds were defined as the optimal CEOs, because a key job of the top management team was to manage the acquisition strategy of the firm. Training in finance, at the MBA level, meant training in diversification strategy and in strategies for funding acquisitions. After that approach to management had been well institutionalized, the idea of naming a COO to take over day-to-day operations and freeing the CEO to focus on acquisitions became popular. Thus the ideal conglomerate had a CEO focused on the big picture, and a COO handling the mundane business of making the widgets.

Institutional investors and securities analysts helped to frame a new, investor-oriented theory in which the firm should focus on lines of business where executives held expertise, leaving the job of diversification to investors. The COO now became a liability—a signal to markets that the firm had not let go of the old conglomerate model. Now that the CEO was supposed to oversee the making of widgets, he needed a sidekick to handle financial markets. The head finance person *c.*1950 had been an accountant. The head finance person *c.*1970 had the added tasks of planning financing for diversifying acquisitions. The new finance chief, the CFO, was to manage stock price and market expectations.

### The Conglomerate Model and the Chief Operating Officer

When the conglomerate was king, the typical CEO was trained in finance and it mattered little whether he knew much about the main line of business (Fligstein 1987, 1990). For a sample of Fortune 500 firms in the early 1970s, Michel and Hambrick (1992) find that broad conglomerates are most likely to have top managers with finance backgrounds and without operational expertise in any of the business units. The early finance model of management suggested clear prescriptions for who should run the firm and for how it should be run. Beginning in the early 1970s, that prescription included a finance-trained CEO, to make long-term decisions about acquisitions, and a COO to manage daily operations. In the popular press, the COO was often described as the person who minds the store. Thus when David Rockefeller created the position at the Chase Manhattan Bank in 1975, *Business Week* (1975: 74) reported: 'a great deal more of the day-to-day job of checking the slide in Chase's return on assets, reducing its soaring loan losses, and fattening its capital base has fallen onto (the COOs) shoulders'. In a study of the rise of the COO (Dobbin, Dierkes, and Zorn 2003), we find that in the 1970s, firms that pursued conglomeration were most likely to install COOs. Profitable firms also created COO positions to allow their executives to focus on strategic decisions, evidently because they had the luxury of doing so. Hugh Hefner appointed a COO at Playboy Enterprises. From the end of the 1970s, however, COOs became associated with success because most high-growth firms had them. The single-industry firm now installed a COO as well, as an amulet to bring success.

**The Shareholder Value Model and the Chief Financial Officer**

From the early 1980s, the idea of having a COO became tarnished because it was associated with the broad conglomerate. The CEO–COO structure implied a top executive focused on diversification with a sidekick who was supposed to run the business. CEOs became more likely to name CFOs than to name COOs, for the CEO–CFO structure seemed to send the right signal to financial markets—that the CEO was minding the store.

Jack Welch at General Electric was among the first to eliminate the position of COO, in 1983, with the argument that he, as CEO, should be running the business. Welch went on to implement a new approach to managing the large conglomerate, by whittling down General Electric to a few broad domains. He spun off unrelated businesses and bought aggressively in the main lines of endeavor, pursuing both horizontal acquisitions of direct competitors and vertical acquisitions of suppliers. As General Electric's star rose, Welch became the poster boy for hands-on management.

We saw above that the number of securities analysts more than doubled in the first half of the 1980s, and that analysts successfully established their importance by making profit projections that investors took quite seriously. Firms paid closer attention to analysts and tried harder to meet their projections. To this end, firms implemented investor relations programs and promoted the corporate finance function to the level of chief. With the change in name came a profound change in the job of the top finance manager. For most of the twentieth century, the corporate finance function had been confined to bookkeeping, monitoring of debt and capital structures, and creating the budget—after strategic decisions had been made (Gerstner and Anderson 1976; Harlan 1986: xv–xvi; Whitley 1986: 181; Walther 1997: 3).

When the conglomerate came to prominence in the early 1960s, it paved the way for a more prominent role for financial tools that could relieve executives from the need for detailed operational knowledge in each of the firm's business segments. Now a small head office could monitor the financial performance of different units, and direct the flow of investment based on relative yields. Conglomerates were first to embrace the CFO title in the late 1960s. In 1970, Olin Corporation, with a product range that included books, chemicals, aluminum, and mobile homes, named James F. Towey vice president and CFO (*Wall Street Journal* 1970: 19). Sperry Rand Corporation, a large multiproduct firm, named Alfred J. Moccia CFO in September 1972 (Sperry Rand Corporation 1973), and Rockwell International Corp., a diversified aerospace and industrial manufacturer, recruited Robert M. Rice from CBS Inc. as its new CFO in 1974 (*Wall Street Journal* 1974: 19).

In those early firms, the CFO was to manage data flows for the top executives. But between 1980 and 1990, investor relations became a core function of the CFO (Useem 1993: 132). *The New York Times* reflected on the change in 2002:

Once upon a time, window-dressing was not in the job description. 'The CFO back 20, 30 years ago generally came out of the accounting profession', said Karl M. von der Heyden, former chief financial officer of both PepsiCo and RJR Nabisco. 'They were glorified controllers', he said, 'and strictly operated in the background'. Controllers generally report numbers and balance budgets, without arranging financing or offering strategic advice. Chief financial officers also served as treasurers, banking revenues, paying bills and investing reserves in new projects while ensuring that the company had enough cash to finance day-to-day operations. Yet in the 1980s, with the rise of junk bonds and more exotic ways to raise money cheaply, finance chiefs began to get involved in their companies' operations, deciding whether mergers were affordable and helping chief executives pick which parts of the business would deliver the best returns on investment. The role kept expanding in the next decade. 'In the 90's, the CFO more and more became the partner of the CEO in many good companies', Mr. von der Heyden said. 'At that point, the CFO became more visible in the public arena, because next to the CEO, he was the person that generally had the best grasp of the business as a whole'. As partners of chief executives, chief financial officers took on the task of growth, helping rapidly expanding companies capitalize on high stock prices with aggressive financing and by acquiring rivals. (Altman 2002: 10)

To track the effect of the corporate ideal on executive structures, we collect annual information on top management teams from Standard and Poor's Register of Corporations, Directors and Executives. Figure 13.5 shows the prevalence of each of the titles of CEO, COO, and CFO separately. Figure 13.6 shows changing combinations of these three titles. The rise and fall of the CEO–COO dyad and the steep rise of the CEO–CFO dyad are striking, while the CEO–COO–CFO triad is a model being phased out.

FIGURE 13.5. Firms with CEO, CFO, and COO Positions

*Source*: Standard and Poor's Register of Corporations, Directors and Executives.

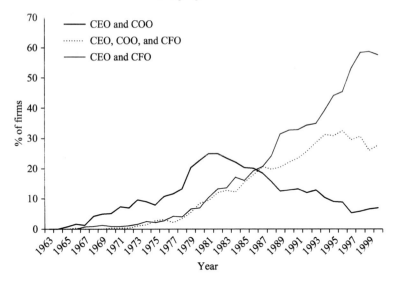

FIGURE 13.6. CEO, COO, CFO Combinations Over Time
*Source*: Standard and Poor's Register of Corporations, Directors and Executives.

Taken together, these two graphs show the rise of the COO toward the end of the conglomerate ideal of the firm, and then the stagnation of that position (in Figure 13.5) and its decline as one of the top two positions in the corporation (in Figure 13.6). Later in the period, few firms added new COOs, and firms were increasingly likely to eliminate the position when its incumbent moved on. We see clearly that the COO is no longer the preferred partner of the CEO. As we suggested, firms became reluctant to signal that the CEO was not minding the store. We also see that the CFO surpasses the COO quickly in prevalence (in Figure 13.5) and that the CEO–CFO duo becomes the dynamic duo of the 1990s.

### The Shareholder Value Model and Stock Market Management

With increased scrutiny from institutional investors and securities analysts, firms began to try to manage and manipulate analysts' projections. CFOs held conference calls to update sales and cost information. They introduced 'earnings preannouncements', in the hope of bringing analysts' predictions into line with their own projections. These changes can be seen in Figure 13.7, which charts the practice of earnings preannouncements in our sample. The first firms issued preannouncements in the early 1990s, and by 2000 some 50% of firms were doing so. Figure 13.7 also shows that firms became increasingly successful at meeting analysts' forecasts. The share of firms that meet expectations rose from about half in the 1980s to nearly two-thirds by the late 1990s.

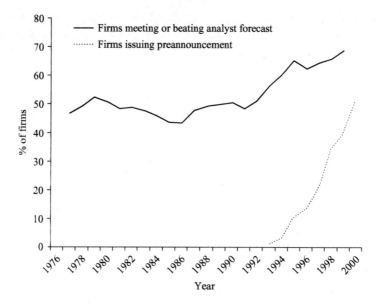

FIGURE 13.7. Firms Meeting or Beating Analysts' Consensus Forecast and Issuing
Earnings Preannouncements

*Source*: I/B/E/S and FirstCall.

This change was the result of two processes, for CFOs both learned to manage
analysts' projections and to manipulate earnings statements through accounting sleight-of-hand. The accounting specialist gave way to the spin doctor. As
Daniel Altman wrote in the *New York Times* in April of 2002:

In the 1990's, men like Mr. Fastow (CFO at Enron) and Mr. Swartz (CFO at Tyco)
were paragons of corporate ingenuity for meeting and beating ever-higher revenue
forecasts, but those values have backfired. That model made it hard for investors to
figure out how much companies are really worth. Now, even many scrupulous companies see earnings statements parsed for accounting gimmicks. In the last decade, as
Wall Street demanded more frequent reports of results and more guidance about
companies' prospects, chief financial officers became spokesmen and even salesmen,
conducting conference calls with analysts and often delegating to others the mundane
task of watching the numbers. Companies began recruiting lawyers, investment
bankers, and consultants as chief financial officers, more for their deal-making talents
than for technical expertise or fiduciary integrity. (Altman 2002: 10)

## The New Acquisition Strategy

By 1980, the conglomerate had come to dominate the Fortune 500. By one
common definition, the two-digit Standard Industrial Classification code,
only 25% operated in a single industry. Half operated in three or more

industries (Davis, Diekmann, and Tinsley 1994· 553) The level of diversification had increased dramatically since the Second World War, spurred in part by the Celler–Kefauver Act of 1950 which made vertical integration suspect under antitrust law and which thereby popularized diversifying acquisitions as an alternative growth strategy (Fligstein 1990).

Portfolio theory in economics reinforced the idea that the modern firm should be run as an internal capital market, investing in promising sectors and spreading risk across different sorts of industries. Oliver Williamson (1975) also reinforced this idea, arguing that conglomerates could acquire poorly performing firms and improve their profitability by managing them under financial accounting methods. Meanwhile, the major consulting firms—McKinsey, Arthur D. Little, The Boston Consulting Group— had developed technologies that simplified the management of diversified conglomerates. By the end of the 1970s, 45% of the Fortune 500 had adopted these portfolio planning techniques (Davis, Diekmann, and Tinsley 1994: 554).

This business model came crashing down in just a decade. It never made sense to financial and organizational economists, because it turned the firm into a diversified stockholder that could not easily sell off stocks that had turned into bad bets. Managers would have to turn around poorly performing units, which were often in industries they knew nothing about. Moreover, the Reagan administration helped to make a new model of the large firm possible. Reagan's antitrust officials relaxed restrictions against mergers among competitors and the courts relaxed controls of hostile takeovers, in the first place permitting firms to expand by moving toward monopoly and in the second allowing groups to acquire and break up conglomerates (Davis, Diekmann, and Tinsley 1994: 554).

As we saw in Figure 13.1, the hostile takeover became a popular solution to a new management problem, the relative undervaluation of conglomerates. Diversified conglomerates sometimes served the interest of their CEOs, who wanted to run huge firms, better than the interests of their investors, in whose interest stock price was paramount. Agency theorists cited this mismatch of interests as the reason for tying executive compensation to stock performance. The firm of Kohlberg, Kravis, and Roberts (KKR) showed how successful the strategy of buying up large conglomerates and selling off tangential businesses to raise the stock price could be. Beginning in 1976, they bought up over forty companies and restructured them, including such behemoths as Beatrice Companies and RJR Nabisco. They often played 'white knight', helping executives to fend off external suitors by taking firms private themselves, but the results were much the same: the diversified conglomerate was broken up and a streamlined firm emerged (Baker and Smith 1998).

The new theory of how the large firm should be managed was reinforced by four different theories of the firm, from different camps. The 'core-competence' movement among management consultants built on the classical theory of managerialism, which suggested that managers should stick to what they know best. Financial economics had long favored allowing investors to diversify their portfolios. 'Business process reengineering', a.k.a. downsizing, suggested that firms should eliminate the need that conglomerates produced for extra management layers. 'Shareholder value' theory defined the firm's first goal as pleasing shareholders by driving up stock price. 'Agency theory' in economics encouraged firms to tie executive compensation to stock price.

### The Changing Pattern of Acquisitions

Davis, Diekmann, and Tinsley (1994) show two effects of the decline of the conglomerate ideal. First, in the 1980s, firms that were diversified were significantly more likely to be acquired (and presumably broken up) than firms that were not diversified but were otherwise similar. Second, the lion's share of the acquisitions in the late 1980s were horizontal and vertical acquisitions. We look at two related indicators. We examine acquisitions over a long period of time, to show the decline of diversifying acquisitions and the rise of horizontal and vertical acquisitions. We use the mergers and acquisition database (provided by SDC Platinum) to retrieve information on domestic acquisitions patterns among firms in our sample. We follow extant research in the field of mergers and acquisitions and distinguish between horizontal, vertical, and deals that are unrelated to a focal firm's major business lines (e.g. Blair, Lane, and Schary 1991; Haunschild 1993). To assign a particular acquisition or divestiture to any of these three groups, we follow Davis, Diekmann, and Tinsley (1994: 560).

Figure 13.8 charts the change in acquisition pattern from 1983 to 1998 among 328 of the 429 large firms in our sample. This figure shows the relative numbers of unrelated (diversifying) acquisitions, horizontal acquisitions (those in an industry the firm currently operates in), and vertical acquisitions (those in an industry that supplies, or buys from, an industry the firm currently operates in) over time. The number of diversifying acquisitions rises until the mid-1980s, but then it declines and remains low. Meanwhile, the number of horizontal acquisitions—acquisitions of firms that are in one of the businesses that the corporation already covers—rises sixfold, and the number of vertical acquisitions—typically of supplier firms—rises fourfold. The investor-centered finance model is clearly reflected in these changes, for firms become less likely to try to diversify and more likely to buy other firms that are in the existing areas of strength.

Figure 13.9 represents changes in the level of diversification in a different way. Here we show the level of diversification in over time, plotting the number of four-digit industries firms operate by quartiles from 1963 to 2000. The firm at the seventy-fifth percentile rises in the number of four-digit industries it covers from five to nine, and then decreases to six over the period.

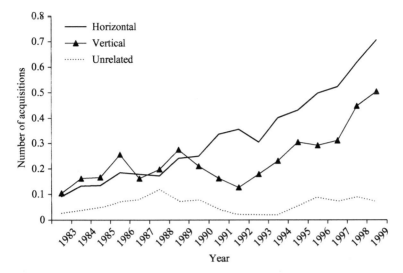

FIGURE 13.8. Horizontal, Vertical, and Unrelated Acquisitions
*Source*: SDC Platinum and Compustat.

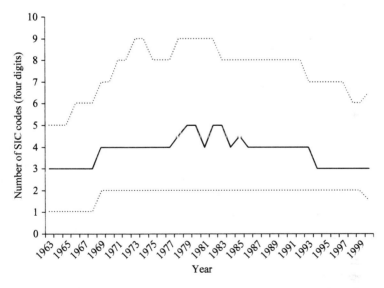

FIGURE 13.9. Distribution of Firm Diversification Levels
(Twenty-Fifth, Median, and Seventy-Fifth, Percentile)

Diversification in the median firm rises from three to five and then declines to three. Diversification in the firm at the twenty-fifth percentile rises from one to two, and declines to one. The overall pattern suggests that the average firm in 2000 is no more diversified than the average firm was in 1963—despite the fact that the average firm is much larger in terms of sales and workforce. The conglomerate model is clearly on the wane. The data on diversification, then, show a pattern consistent with that found by Davis et al. The rise of the new corporate ideals of shareholder value and core competence, as promoted by institutional investors, securities analysts, and takeover firms, led to changes in core corporate strategy. These huge corporations shed unrelated industries, and when they went shopping, they bought competitors and suppliers rather than branching out.

## Conclusion

In the last quarter of the twentieth century, key groups in financial markets came to play increasingly important roles in shaping structure and strategy among America's largest corporations. As investors evaluated firms in terms of how financial markets would value them in the future, firms became acutely aware of the norms for corporate governance that key players in financial markets were developing.

The diffusion of new models of how to manage the firm is anticipated by institutional theory in organizational sociology, but the mechanisms of diffusion we identified are not entirely anticipated. Institutionalists argue that new business models are developed and promoted in organizational fields, consisting of industry members and of people in important related industries. For the most part, the community of investors was exogenous in these models. The initial formulation, by Meyer and Rowan (1977), suggested that government agencies might promote new models of management, or that organizations and consultants might develop new models among themselves. In DiMaggio and Powell's (1983) version, executives could copy peer organizations, states could coerce firms to adopt new management techniques, or professional groups that spanned organizational boundaries could promote new management techniques. Many of the empirical studies (Edelman 1990; Dobbin and Sutton 1998) showed how these last two factors worked together—how professional groups actively interpreted public policy edicts and constructed compliance mechanisms that diffused among organizations.

The story of the rise of the shareholder value ideal of the firm does not quite conform to this theoretical model. Here the preferences of exogenous groups—emergent networks of hostile takeover firms, analysts, and institutional investors—became increasingly important to corporate executives. These groups expressed a new ideal of corporate structure and strategy, voting for this new ideal with their market power. They lowered the price of firms that did not abide by this new ideal (in the case of institutional investors), recommending against buying stock in them (in the case of stock analysts), or took them over and did the restructuring themselves (in the case of hostile takeover/white knight firms).

The result of these events was, to be sure, a new myth of the efficient firm. The myth of the ideal modern firm as an internal capital market, based in portfolio theory, gave way to the myth of the ideal firm as a focused single-industry oligopolist. Institutional theory describes the rise of successive myths of rationality in the modern firm, and to that extent we have provided evidence for the theory. But the agents of change in most institutional models are managers, not outsiders. And the mechanisms they use to change organizations are largely rhetorical. Our findings suggest that the agents of change can be professional groups in financial markets who have relatively little direct contact with the corporation, but who express their preferences for firm structure and strategy through their roles in markets. And the mechanism of change can be market power, which became salient to executives largely through agency theory's effect on compensation—from size-related-salaries to stock options. Our findings suggest that institutionalists should pay greater attention to the role of outside forces in constructing corporate strategies, and to the role of power in promoting new strategies.

# References

Abrahamson, E. 1991. 'Managerial Fads and Fashion: The Diffusion and Rejection of Innovations', *Academy of Management Review* 16: 586–612.

Altman, D. 2002. 'The Taming of the Finance Officers', *The New York Times* April 14 (Section 3): 1, 10–1.

Baker, G. P. and Smith, G. D. 1998. *The New Financial Capitalists : Kohlberg Kravis Roberts and the Creation of Corporate Value*. Cambridge: Cambridge University Press.

Baron, J. N., Jennings, P. D., and Dobbin, F. R. 1988. 'Mission Control? The Development of Personnel Systems in U.S. Industry', *American Sociological Review* 53: 497–514.

Blair, M., Lane, S., and Schary, M. 1991. 'Patterns of Corporate Restructuring, 1955–1987', *Brookings Discussion Paper 91*.

*Business Week*. 1975. 'The Change in Power at Chase Manhattan', February 17: 74.

Chandler, A. D. 1977. *The Visible Hand: The Managerial Revolution in American Business*. Cambridge, MA: Belknap Press.

Davis, G. F. 1991. 'Agents without Principles: The Spread of the Poison Pill Through the Intercorporate Network', *Administrative Science Quarterly* 36: 583–613.

Davis, G. F., Diekmann, K. A., and Tinsley, C. H. 1994. 'The Decline and Fall of the Conglomerate Firm in the 1980s: The Deinstitutionalization of an Organizational Form', *American Sociological Review* 59: 547–70.

DiMaggio, P. J. and Powell, W. W. 1983. 'The Iron Cage Revisited: Institutional Isomorphism and Collective Rationality in Organizational Fields', *American Sociological Review* 48: 147–60.

Dobbin, F. R. and Dowd, T. J. 2000. 'The Market That Antitrust Built: Public Policy, Private Coercion and Railroad Acquisitions, 1825–1922', *American Sociological Review* 65: 631–57.

Dobbin, F. F. and Sutton, J. R. 1998. 'The Strength of a Weak State: The Rights Revolution and the Rise of Human Resources Management Divisions', *American Journal of Sociology* 104: 441–76.

—— Sutton, J. R., Meyer, J. W., and Scott, W. R. 1993. 'Equal Opportunity Law and the Construction of Internal Labor Markets', *American Journal of Sociology* 99: 396–427.

—— Dierkes, J., and Zorn, D. 2003. 'The Rise of the COO: From Luxury Sidekick to a Significant Player in Corporate Management', Paper presented at the American Sociological Association Annual Meeting, Atlanta.

Edelman, L. B. 1990. 'Legal Environments and Organizational Governance: The Expansion of Due Process in the American Workplace', *American Journal of Sociology* 95: 1401–40.

Fligstein, N. 1987. 'The Intraorganizational Power Struggle: Rise of Finance Personnel to Top Leadership in Large Corporations', *American Sociological Review* 52: 44–58.

—— 1990. *The Transformation of Corporate Control*. Cambridge, MA: Harvard University Press.

—— 2001. *The Architecture of Markets: An Economic Sociology of Twenty-First-Century Capitalist Societies*. Princeton, NJ: Princeton University Press.

—— and Markowitz, L. 1993. 'Financial Reorganization of American Corporations in the 1980s', in *Sociology and the Public Agenda*, Wilson, W. J. (ed.). Newbury Park, CA: Sage, 185–206.

Fox, J. 1997. 'Learn to Play the Earnings Game (and Wall Street Will Love You)', *Fortune* 6: 76–80.

Gerstner, L. V. Jr. and Anderson, H. M. 1976. 'The Chief-Financial-Officer as Activist', *Harvard Business Review* 54: 100–6.

Hammer, M. and Champy, J. 1993. *Reengineering the Corporation: A Manifesto for Business*. New York, NY: Harper Business.

Harlan, N. E. 1986. 'Introduction', in *The CFO's Handbook*, Vancil, R. F. and Makela, B. R. (eds.). Homewood, IL.: Dow Jones-Irwin, xv–xx.

Haunschild, P. R. 1993. 'Interorganizational Imitation: The Impact of Interlocks on Corporate Acquisition Activity', *Administrative Science Quarterly* 38: 564–92.

Jensen, M. C. and Meckling, W. H. 1976. 'Theory of the Firm: Managerial Behavior, Agency Cost, and Ownership Structure', *Journal of Financial Economics* 3: 305–60.

Meyer, J. W. and Rowan, B. 1977. 'Institutionalized Organizations: Formal Structure as Myth and Ceremony', *American Journal of Sociology* 83: 340–63.

Michel, J. G. and Hambrick, D. C. 1992. 'Diversification Posture and Top Management Team Characteristics', *Academy of Management Journal* 35: 9–37.

Nocera, J. 1998. 'The Trouble with the Consensus Estimate', *Money* 6: 59–60.

Pralahad, C. K. and Hamel, G. 1990. 'The Core Competencies of the Corporation', *Harvard Business Review* 68: 79–91.

Proffitt, W. T. 2001. *The Evolution of Institutional Investor Identity: Social Movement Mobilization in the Shareholder Activism Field*. Evanston, IL. PhD Dissertation, Northwestern University.

Scott, W. R. 2002. *Organizations: Rational, Natural, and Open Systems*. Englewood Cliffs, NJ: Prentice-Hall.

Sperry Rand Corporation. 1973. *Annual Report 1973*. New York, NY.

Strang, D and Meyer, J W 1994 *Institutional Environments and Organization: Structural Complexity and Individualism.* Thousand Oaks, CA: Sage.

Useem, M. 1993. *Executive Defense: Shareholder Power and Corporate Reorganization.* Cambridge, MA: Harvard University Press.

*Wall Street Journal.* 1970. 'Commerce and Industry', February 6: 19.

—— 1974. 'Commerce and Industry', August 27, 15.

Walther, T. 1997. *Reinventing the CFO: Moving from Financial Management to Strategic Management.* New York, NY: McGraw-Hill.

Whitley, R. 1986. 'The Transformation of Business Finance into Financial Economics: The Roles of Academic Expansion and Changes in U.S. Capital Markets', *Accounting, Organizations and Society* 11: 171–92.

Williamson, O. E. 1975. *Markets and Hierarchies, Analysis and Antitrust Implications: A Study in the Economics of Internal Organization.* New York, NY: Free Press.

Zuckerman, E. W. 1999. 'The Categorical Imperative: Securities Analysts and the Illegitimacy Discount', *American Journal of Sociology* 104: 1398–438.

—— 2000. 'Focusing the Corporate Product: Securities Analysts and De-Diversification', *Administrative Science Quarterly* 45: 591–619.

# 14

# Nothing but Net? Networks and Status in Corporate Governance

GERALD DAVIS AND GREGORY ROBBINS

## Introduction

The argument that corporate action is embedded in social networks has moved from critique to conventional wisdom in organization theory in just over a decade (Granovetter 1985). Organizational scholars have come to pay explicit attention to the causes and consequences of the various ties linking corporations, such as the interlocks created when corporations share directors. Moreover, conceiving of corporations as nodes in networks allows researchers to build on the well-developed concepts and methods of network analysis to uncover unexpected regularities. Several studies find that a corporation's interlock network centrality (i.e. the number of other firms with which it shares board members) has a systematic influence on corporate decisions. Central firms are more likely than peripheral firms to adopt takeover defenses, to make acquisitions and divestitures, to be involved with political policy organizations and to be imitated when they adopt golden parachutes and switch stock markets. Centrality is not simply a proxy for other omitted variables: although correlated with size, it has little relation to corporate performance and at most a modest relation to alternative measures of 'prestige', and its effects persist when measures of size and performance are controlled for (see Davis, Yoo, and Baker 2003 for a review). And centrality proves quite stable over time, both during the 1960s and the 1980s and 1990s: among large US firms, centrality in 1982 was correlated 0.75 with centrality in 1994 (compared to a 0.85 correlation for sales during these years).

Centrality is thus both causally important and stable over time. Why should this be the case? The answer depends on what it is one thinks board members are for. A central board is composed of directors who sit on many other boards. The traditional managerialist view sees directors as 'ornaments on the corporate Christmas tree'—decorative objects chosen by the CEO to burnish the firm's image for the outside world (particularly the financial markets that evaluate them) while interfering as little as possible in the operations of the corporation. Directors who serve on many outside boards—particularly boards of prestigious firms—make better ornaments. In contrast, agency theorists see director centrality as a form of validation by the market for corporate directors, which rewards effective agents of shareholders with multiple board seats (Shivdasani 1993). A board's centrality is a proxy for its quality as a monitor; thus, the stock market responds differently to the same corporate actions according to who is on the board, indicating that the market 'trusts' some boards more than others (Brickley et al. 1995). But according to the first view, centrality should have little systematic influence on corporate action, while the second view implies that centrality should have a positive influence on corporate performance. Neither of these implications is true: centrality has a systematic influence on corporate decisionmaking but not on performance.

We argue that the construct of board status provides a means to integrate research on the causes and consequences of centrality. A producer's status in the market is the perceived quality of its products compared to those of its competitors (Podolny 1993: 830). What boards 'produce' is governance for the shareholders that elect them and for other constituencies of the corporation. Thus status—as an attribute of boards—is distinct from the reputation of the corporation as a whole. Status is particularly important in cases where more direct evidence of quality is missing. The quality of governance is largely unobservable, and the actual quality of any individual director is almost completely opaque from an outsider's perspective. In the absence of direct measures, shareholders and others have to rely on imperfect indicators of quality—such as what other boards directors serve on. Board centrality, as an indicator of status, can thereby insulate a corporation from shareholder oversight. Once in place, centrality will expose a firm both to a greater volume of information about governance at other firms and to more extensive normative pressures from other boards (Useem 1984), thereby influencing its practices.

This paper empirically unpacks interlock centrality by examining a panel of the several hundred largest US firms observed in four-year intervals from 1982 to 1994. We analyze the factors that contribute to centrality over time by examining the features of firms that prompt them to appoint central directors. Our results suggest that interlock network centrality is self-reproducing: independent of performance, size, and corporate reputation, central boards are better able to attract central directors and CEOs of major corporations, leading to a relatively enduring status order among corporations (White 1981). Moreover, while firms that out-perform their industry are somewhat better able to recruit CEOs and central directors, there is no evidence that boards composed of these individuals enhance subsequent performance. In other words, board composition appears to be an effect of performance, not a cause. We conclude with a discussion of the plausibility of proposed reforms in corporate governance in light of our findings.

## Corporate Boards and the Rhetoric of Governance

A recent review defined corporate governance as 'the ways in which suppliers of finance to corporations assure themselves of getting a return on their investment' (Shleifer and Vishny 1997: 737). Theory in the 'law and economics' tradition provides a set of tools for analyzing national systems of corporate governance in financial terms. In an economy where large corporations are typically owned by dispersed shareholders with only nominal control over the corporation's managers, as in the United States, the basic problem of corporate governance is to establish arm's length institutions that secure managerial devotion to increasing shareholder value. The American system is a matrix of such institutions that includes accounting rules, securities regulations, corporate law, the takeover market, and various formal and informal structures (such as compensation systems) adopted by corporations to promote accountability and align managerial and shareholder interests. At the center of this matrix is a shareholder-elected board of directors.

According to theory in law and economics, the institutions of governance mesh to create an environment that rewards managers who maximize share price and punishes those who do not. Both those who own and those who manage have an interest in maintaining these institutions: investors will not part with their money without reason to believe that they will get a return, and managers will not be able to raise capital if they cannot give credible accounts for how they will use it profitably (Easterbrook and Fischel 1991). Thus, those who run corporations spontaneously conform to best governance practices to demonstrate their fitness to the financial markets. 'The corporation and its securities are products in financial markets to as great an extent as the sewing machines or other things the firm makes. Just as the founders of a firm have incentives to make the kinds of sewing machines people want to buy, they have incentives to create the kind of firm, governance structure, and securities the customers in capital markets want' (Easterbrook and Fischel 1991: 4–5). By hypothesis, an invisible hand guides corporate practice to serve shareholder interests, from how to pay executives to who serves on the board.

A body of recent organizational research undermines this optimistic portrayal of a self-help corporate world. The rise of activist shareholders promulgating standards of corporate governance at odds with prevailing practice—and their vehement opposition by corporate executives—calls into question the imagery of an invisible hand. Experienced directors of large corporations are almost unanimous in their opposition to reforms pushed by some of the largest institutional owners, including separating the positions of CEO and Chairman of the Board, allowing shareholders to vote on executive compensation, and having shareholder representatives serve on the board (Neiva 1996). Because boards generally have the final word under the law, the proposed reforms have experienced little success. Either the large shareholders do not grasp their own interests, or boards are not interested in pursuing them.

A more fundamental challenge comes from research finding that conformity to best practices may be more symbolic than substantive, yet still achieve the ends of maximizing share price. In a series of papers examining the adoption of executive compensation plans, Westphal and Zajac (1998) elaborated a neoinstitutionalist perspective on governance that construes at least some structures as forms of impression management decoupled from actual practice. In part as a reaction to shareholder pressures, many large corporations adopted long-term incentive plans purported to align the interests of executives with those of shareholders. Yet a surprisingly large number of them announced the plans without ever actually implementing them—presumably as a form of shareholder impression management (Westphal and Zajac 1994). Moreover, firms experienced a significant spike in share price when they announced the plans, whether or not they ever followed through in implementing them (Westphal and Zajac 1998). Giving the appearance of conformity to the reigning 'shareholder value' model was sufficient to impress the stock market, even in the absence of genuine conformity. Share price increases were substantially larger when the announcement of the plan was accompanied by a rationale emphasizing shareholder value than when the identical plan was justified using a human resource explanation (Westphal and Zajac 1998). These findings suggest that 'cosmetic' governance reform and appropriate rhetorical spin can be used effectively to manage the demands of investors. Thus, while activists expect governance reforms to enhance corporate performance, it appears that governance reforms are themselves rhetorical performances, intended to persuade activists and other players in the financial markets of the corporation's fitness for investment. Creating 'the kind of firm, governance structure, and securities the customers in capital markets want' involves marketing through rhetoric, from the letter to the shareholders in the annual report, to how diversified the corporation portrays its operations on the income statement, to the choice of directors.

But choice of directors is distinguished from structural reforms in two ways. First, director choice entails what Aristotle called ethical appeals, which are rooted in the character of the individual, rather than appeals to reason, as in the case of structural reforms (McCloskey 1985: 121–2). Judgments about directors are judgments about character and ability, not about the validity of an argument (e.g. claiming a link between a form of compensation and shareholder interests). Boards are given great discretion under the law because it is assumed that well-chosen directors—being persons of good character—will do the right thing without being required to follow a set of detailed guidelines (which is infeasible in any event). Second, virtually every other structural reform is ultimately under the control of the board. Board composition is the master choice from which other reforms spring, and is therefore the most fundamental decision that shareholders make about governance. Unlike cosmetic structural changes, such as adopting a new incentive plan, boards cannot be decoupled from the process of governance.

The problem for those evaluating corporate boards is that the mysteries of corporate governance occur behind closed doors, and thus determining the quality of a given board or director from the outside is quite problematic. The legal requirements for board composition and structure are minimal, and boards composed of different individuals organize themselves differently to do what they do, for better or worse. As Pettigrew and McNulty (1998: 250) put it, 'the closer one gets to board process and dynamics, the more real becomes the generalization that all boards are different'. A profusion of academic research on boards in recent years provides little guidance on best practices: even the most basic proposed reforms, such as staffing the board with a majority of 'independent' outsiders, show little relation to subsequent performance. There is thus no template for outsiders seeking to evaluate a board's quality. Director candidates are virtually never made available to shareholders for the interviews that job candidates endure or the debates and press scrutiny expected of political candidates. Corporations are obliged to report certain information when directors are put up for election, but the requirements are scant. Shareholders and others are therefore left to assess director qualifications based on the thumbnail sketches included in proxy statements: the director's age, primary occupation, share ownership—and the other boards he or she serves on. These director characteristics can then serve as proxies (so to speak) for vigilance, dependability, integrity, and intelligence in folk theories about the qualities of good directors.

The concepts of signaling and status provide a useful way to parse the issues of board quality. A signal is an indicator of quality that is under some degree of control by a producer and whose cost goes down as the producer's quality goes up. An indicator that is effortlessly displayed by high-quality producers but extremely costly for low-quality producers to acquire (e.g. some types of health care certification) is a useful signal. Status is 'the perceived quality of (a) producer's products in relation to the perceived quality of that producer's competitors' products' (Podolny 1993: 830). Producers can be ranked into a relatively enduring status hierarchy. Status comes in part from connections to other producers: ties to higher status producers help elevate one's own status, while ties to low-status producers can compromise it (Podolny 1993). By the same token, we suggest that a board's status—the perceptions of quality held by the 'buyers' of the board's 'products'—is shaped by the number and perceived quality of the other boards that directors serve on. That is, the backgrounds of directors and the array of interlocks that they create act as signals in the 'market' for corporate governance.[1]

Given little other information to go on, outsiders appear to be swayed by director connections. For new firms, the addition of a prominent director can serve as a seal of approval to address the concerns of dubious investors.

Biotech firm ImClone gained credibility with investors through the appointment of renowned cancer specialist Dr John Mendelsohn to its board. ImClone's CEO later pleaded guilty to insider trading charges in 2002, having dumped much of his ownership stake ahead of the market after learning that the firm's only drug would not even be reviewed by the Food and Drug Administration (FDA).

Large firms can also benefit from prestige board appointments: Time Warner experienced a 5% stock price increase when it announced the appointments of the CEOs of Hilton Hotels and UAL to its board ('The rush to quality on corporate boards', *Business Week*, March 1997). Part of this effect is signaling: the ability to attract and retain prestigious directors indicates a high-quality board, while low-quality boards hold no appeal for such individuals. (Dissertation committees follow a similar dynamic: doctoral students may seek to signal their quality by inviting prestigious faculty to serve on their committees, but the faculty do not have to accept.)

Yet there is good reason to be skeptical that prestigious boards enhance corporate performance. The counter-examples are legion, as some of the best-known corporate meltdowns occurred on the watch of highly prestigious boards. Morrison Knudsen's board counted among its members the most successful mutual fund manager in history, a former National Security Advisor, a former Reagan administration official and judge, a former baseball commissioner, and other equally accomplished individuals, as it careened toward financial ruin in 1995. The boards of General Motors and American Express were accused of serious laxity during the periods before each fired their chief executives, despite being staffed with several major CEOs and other prominent directors. Money center commercial bank boards were packed with the CEOs of the largest corporations in America during the 1980s, even as the banks made disastrous loans that led some (such as Citicorp) to the brink of insolvency (Davis and Mizruchi 1999). Systematic research on the link between interlocks and overall corporate performance is agnostic at best (see Mizruchi 1996 for a review). From the shareholders' perspective, board status evidently does not merit much potency as a signal. Yet evidence for the effects of interlocks on corporate decisionmaking—if not performance—is compelling. Construing a corporation's portfolio of interlocks in terms of status connects our discussion of governance with the literature on the network created by interlocking boards of directors. We now turn to a brief examination of this network.

## The Meaning of Network Centrality

The insight that economic action is shaped by the social structures in which it is embedded helped usher in the widespread use of network methods in organizational research (Granovetter 1985). The core of this approach is the notion that organizations can be conceived as actors (nodes) connected to other actors through alliances, shared directors, and so on (ties), and that the resulting social structure could be analyzed as a network. Networks can be dense or sparse, centralized or Balkanized, with ties being strong or weak. Networks channel information flow, and thus the structure of a network is consequential: just as viruses spread faster in urban areas than rural ones, information flows more quickly in densely connected networks than sparse ones. Given that organizations are conceived as nodes in networks, an interorganizational network could be analyzed using well-developed theory in the literatures on anthropology, small groups, and diffusion of innovation, as well as sophisticated methodological tools. Notions of 'status', 'opinion leadership', 'contagion', and so on could then be applied fruitfully to firms.

If networks are construed as social systems, then centrality indicates an actor's position in this overall system. For a board, centrality comes from being tied to other boards through shared directors. Two measures of centrality have the most intuitive appeal for boards (see Knoke and Burt 1983, for a compendium). Degree is the simple count of ties—in short, how many other actors one is tied to. For a board, degree is the total number of other boards on which its directors serve. Prestige is the number of received ties (or in-degree)—how frequently the actor is the object of 'sent' relations. Boards 'send' ties when their executives sit on outside boards and 'receive' ties when executives of outside firms serve as directors. CEOs of outside firms thereby contribute to a board's prestige.

Centrality by these measures varies widely among firms. In 1994, Chemical Banking Corporation was the most central American firm, sharing directors with thirty-eight other large corporations.[2] Three of its officers collectively served on seven boards, and six executives of other firms served on its board. Sara Lee was the third most central with thirty-three ties, and Corning tied Union Pacific for tenth with twenty-eight ties. Conversely, of the seven directors of Microsoft, only one served on the board of another large corporation in 1994 (as an outside director), and Bill Gates (Microsoft's CEO) served on no other boards, making Microsoft one of the least central firms. Walt Disney Corporation was also peripheral, sharing outside directors with only two other large corporations. Like Gates, Disney CEO Michael Eisner served on no outside boards.

As the examples indicate, centrality is not simply a proxy for a firm's current size, performance, or a more nebulous 'importance'. Correlations between a firm's number of interlocks and its sales, assets, market capitalization, and number of employees in 1994 range between 0.39 and 0.45, and thus centrality is not merely an artifact or indicator of size. Correlations with measures of performance are modest or close to zero: centrality is correlated 0.12 with the market-to-book ratio and under 0.05 with return on assets (ROA) and return on equity. Interlock centrality is thus at best modestly related to other aspects of a corporation's importance.

One might then be tempted to dismiss centrality as random or irrelevant. Yet it is neither: a board's centrality is highly stable over time and is demonstrably important in shaping corporate governance. The stability of centrality is quite striking. Of the ten most central corporations outside the insurance industry in 1962, seven of them were still among the ten most central corporations twenty years later (cf. Mintz and Schwartz 1985: table 7.3 with Davis and Mizruchi 1999: table 1). And a corporation's centrality in 1982 was correlated at over 0.70 with its centrality in 1994, in spite of the fact that the median board had experienced 75% turnover in membership during that time. Well-connected boards tend to remain well connected independent of the particular individuals serving as directors. There is thus an enduring status order among corporate boards, indicating that, as in production markets, the interlock network is a self-reproducing social structure (White 1981: 518).

The stability of centrality would be curious but insignificant if being heavily interlocked had no important impact on corporate action. But centrality has documented effects on virtually every significant decision that boards make, and the effects are precisely what one would expect from theory about the impact of social structure on action. The diffusion of innovation literature, for instance, finds that central actors are quicker to adopt innovations that are consistent with the norms of a social system, and that when central actors adopt it triggers subsequent adoptions by others because their adoption helps legitimate the innovation (Rogers 1995). Both effects have been found repeatedly in the interlock literature (Davis, Yoo, and Baker 2003). It is as if the firms in the interlock network were individuals in a friendship network, with central firms acting as the opinion leaders. Centrality is thus an indication of status in the world of corporate governance.

The decisions made by boards are also frequently steeped in ambiguity. Whether it is appropriate to engage in takeovers or adopt a poison pill to ward them off; compensate the CEO at a particular level or using a specialized incentive contract; diversify into other industries or pare down to focus on a core competence—all are open to debate, and all have been found to be influenced by interlocks (see Mizruchi 1996 for a review). The microlevel mechanisms by which interlocks have their effects are fairly mundane: experienced directors with relevant information can say 'Here's what we did at my other company, and here's why we thought was a good idea'. Reasonable people can disagree about such matters, and thus precedent—what other boards facing the same questions did—helps resolve the ambiguity. Direct contact with other boards, via shared directors, provides detailed information about others' decision processes; the actions of central (high status) boards provide evidence for the legitimacy of a practice. Thus, one observes a surprising degree of conformity in the governance practices of the largest American corporations, as boards follow the precedents set by their immediate contacts and by high-status corporations (Davis and Greve 1997).

Conformity in practice is underlain by a common set of attitudes toward issues of immediate relevance held by directors who serve on multiple boards (Neiva 1996). These seasoned directors are particularly influential in boardroom discussions (Davis and Greve 1997); moreover, they are particularly likely to be called to account by other directors (Useem 1984). The late Harold Geneen of ITT wrote in reference to directors that he called 'asleep at the switch':

What can spur them to action? One thing: the fear of looking foolish. Most didn't join the board to make money or prove themselves; they joined for the prestige. To see that prestige threatened is their worst nightmare. The dread of humiliation is their one great motivating force. Thus, if a board member's golf partners start making wisecracks about the company that he is supposedly guiding, watch out. He'll get into fighting trim, fast. (Geneen 1997: 86)

Collectively, members of central boards have 'passive contact' with many more directors than do members of peripheral boards, and thus more frequently have to make sense of their actions to directors of the other boards they serve on. This makes them especially susceptible to following the 'group standard' of the corporate elite.

This interpretation helps make sense of the array of recent findings documenting the pervasive influence of centrality, and interlocks more generally, on corporate decisionmaking. Boards are embedded in social networks that follow the same regularities as other social networks. Central boards have access to greater information and are more susceptible to normative pressures than peripheral boards. They are therefore more likely than peripheral boards to conform to the norms of the social system in which they are embedded— for better or worse—and are quick to adopt practices and structures considered appropriate. Other boards in turn take their actions as signs of the legitimacy of a practice. Networks thereby channel individual decisions into collective outcomes: one board's decisions about where to place the boundaries of the corporation, how to respond to the threat posed by takeover, or to the opportunities created by a global economy, become inputs into similar decisions by other boards. Yet the 'morphology' of the corporate elite network is still dimly understood, in spite of its evident importance. The process configuring the status order of the interlock network—who becomes central, and why it is so stable—remains unclear.

## The Architecture of the Interlock Network

We take centrality to be an indicator of status and seek to understand the microprocess of status attainment: what makes some boards persistently central? A board's centrality results from decisions by the board itself (e.g. to follow a strategy of recruiting central or 'prestigious' directors) and by the directors it attracts and retains. We consider centrality from both perspectives. Our hypotheses are framed around two questions. First, what distinguishes boards that appoint directors who already serve on many boards (thus increasing the board's degree) from those that serve on few or no other boards? Second, what distinguishes boards that recruit CEOs of major corporations (increasing the board's prestige) from those that recruit non-CEOs?

With the exception of financial hegemony theorists (Mintz and Schwartz 1985), prior theory on boards of directors is largely silent with respect to centrality per se. Centrality could reflect the quality of governance being provided by the board—either positively or negatively. A corporation's managers may try to lure outside directors based on their likely appeal to shareholders and other constituencies, as implied by managerialists. Much like the elaborate false villages that Potemkin constructed to impress Catherine the Great, boards may be assembled as an attractive facade for corporate governance. Directors who serve on the boards of prominent firms, and particularly outside CEOs, may be perceived as providing an implicit endorsement of the organization from these other firms. Corporate managers' incentives to pursue a Potemkin Village approach increase to the extent that external displays of good faith are required (Meyer and Rowan 1977). Corporations that are owned proportionally more by institutional investors are perhaps more susceptible to scrutiny of their boards, and we would expect that such firms would be prone to appoint central directors. More direct forms of activism could also prompt the Potemkin Village approach; thus, firms that have been targets of shareholder activism may also seek to reassure their constituencies by appointing central directors.

Hypothesis 1a: Shareholder scrutiny will increase the likelihood of appointment of central directors to the board.

Hypothesis 1b: Shareholder scrutiny will increase the likelihood of appointment of outside CEOs to the board.

Agency theorists argue that directors become central by demonstrating their expertise at corporate governance. Multiple board seats are rewards for directors associated with superior performance (Shivdisani 1993), while executives become CEOs by compiling records of outstanding achievement at serving shareholder interests (Fama 1980). Thus, central directors and CEOs should be those most able to enhance the governance of a firm. Pressures on the board to recruit central directors and CEOs increase to the extent that prior performance has been poor. Firms with superior performance have little need to recruit 'prestige' directors, either as a signal to outside constituencies or in order to benefit from their expertise. Conversely, firms with poor performance stand to gain the most from improved governance, and thus have the greatest incentive to recruit central directors.

Hypothesis 2a: Poor prior performance will increase the likelihood of appointment of central directors to the board.

Hypothesis 2b:  Poor prior performance will increase the likelihood of appointment of outside CEOs to the board.

A third theoretical rationale for seeking to recruit central directors is that, regardless of their signaling value or their impact on governance per se, central directors provide access to a broad range of business intelligence. Board interlocks serve to enhance 'business scan', giving quick and reliable access to insider information across a range of industries (Useem 1984). The studies cited previously find that interlocks embed corporate boards in networks of information flow, supporting the business scan interpretation. Bank boards in particular are commonly composed of 'corporate diplomats' who are executives of major firms and tend to serve on numerous boards (Mintz and Schwartz 1985). Because the Clayton Act of 1914 prevents competing firms from sharing directors, individuals who serve on multiple boards by definition do so across different industries. Such individuals are an invaluable source of business intelligence and are thus attractive directors for banks and other firms. Financial institutions, particularly money center banks, historically used the intelligence brought by their board members to guide their broad investment policies (Mintz and Schwartz 1985). But any corporation that relies on information about diverse industrial sectors would benefit from the expertise of central directors. Thus, we expect to see firms seeking central directors when they are more highly diversified, and when they operate in 'network' industries such as communications, financial services, transportation, and business services.

Hypothesis 3a:  Diversified firms will be more likely to appoint central directors to the board.
Hypothesis 3b:  Diversified firms will be more likely to appoint outside CEOs to the board.
Hypothesis 4a:  Firms in 'network' industries will be more likely to appoint central directors to the board.
Hypothesis 4b:  Firms in 'network' industries will be more likely to appoint outside CEOs to the board.

Resource dependence theory argues that interlocks reflect power and dependence relations, and that firms invite executives of organizations on which they are dependent to serve on the board in order to coopt them (Pfeffer and Salancik 1978). Inviting a representative of a constituency that needs to be coopted has a venerable history, but pursuit of such ties can have potentially paradoxical effects for firms' centrality. On the one hand, firms that are in particularly dependent situations should routinely seek to appoint 'constraining' directors. On the other hand, the executives of powerful firms should routinely be sought in order to coopt their employers. If all board invitations were accepted, then both the weakest and most powerful boards would be central, as the executives of powerful firms joined the boards of many firms that were dependent on them, increasing centrality on both sides. There are two difficulties with this account. First, cooptive ties are quite rare: in the mid-1990s, fewer than 5% of large industrials had executives of firms in major buyer or supplier industries represented on their board. Second, it is unclear what would motivate executives of powerful corporations to serve on the boards of their dependents, whereas the pitfalls of potential cooptation are clear.

The intuition behind this approach, however—that ties to powerful actors are desirable—is surely correct. Powerful actors make useful allies, even if efforts to coopt them are problematic. We thus anticipate that the boards of powerful firms will be able to recruit central and prestigious directors. Other things being equal, whatever benefits board service achieves for oneself or one's employer are more likely to be available on the boards of large firms then small firms. Thus, large firms should be better able to recruit prestigious directors than small firms.

Hypothesis 5a: Large firms will be more likely to appoint central directors to the board.

Hypothesis 5b: Large firms will be more likely to appoint outside CEOs to the board.

Although size in this case is likely to matter, the network properties of the board are also an important consideration for potential directors. A board composed of corporate diplomats is likely to be appealing to potential directors independent of the underlying business: board meetings and the associated social events are an opportunity to hobnob with the elite, which has rewards of its own. A directorship on a central board is often a gateway to other board memberships, as the multiple directors with whom one serves can provide entree to the other boards on which they serve. It is likely that other business and social opportunities spring from the same source. The attractions to ambitious individuals of service on a central board are apparent (Mintz and Schwartz 1985: ch. 7). In addition, because their net is cast broadly, central boards have an advantage in locating and recruiting desirable directors through the first-hand experience of current directors. In short, central boards are more attractive to potential central directors and more likely to have contact with them. We therefore expect to see a network 'Matthew effect' (Merton 1968; Podolny 1993): those that are already central will be able to attract central directors, while those that are peripheral will not.

Hypothesis 6a: Central firms will be more likely to appoint central directors to the board.

Hypothesis 6b: Central firms will be more likely to appoint outside CEOs to the board.

## Data

Our interest is in unpacking the sources of interlock network centrality over time. We did this by studying the board compositions of the several hundred largest publicly-traded corporations in the United States in 1982, 1986, 1990, and 1994, examining their centrality at each point in time as well as the character of new board appointments between adjacent panels.

Our sampling frame consisted of public corporations appearing in the Fortune 500 largest industrials or the 50 largest commercial banks, 25 diversified financials, 25 retailers, or 25 transportation firms in 1980, 1986, 1990, or 1994. Firms appearing in earlier panels were included in subsequent panels even if their revenues no longer warranted inclusion among the largest, while the panels were expanded to include new entrants in later panels. Firms were removed from the sample when they were no longer separate public corporations (e.g. due to being absorbed by merger). A total of 647 firms were included in the 1982 panel, 591 in 1986, 591 in 1990, and 822 in 1994. Four hundred and ten firms appeared in all four panels, and their boards formed the core sample (which we refer to as the 'restricted sample'), although information about other sampled firms was included when appropriate for the analysis. Because centrality measures are sensitive to the size and boundaries of the network measured, use of the restricted sample ensures that these measures are maximally comparable over time.

We analyzed several outcomes of interest. Overall centrality was measured in several ways: using degree (i.e. the total number of other boards in a given panel with which a firm shared directors, and the total number within the restricted sample of 410), Bonacich centrality (calculated within the restricted sample to maintain a consistent scaling), and received ties (or in-degree), that is, the number of executives of other sampled firms that served on the board, as an indicator of prestige.

The Bonacich centrality measure is calculated by summing the Bonacich centrality score for each of the other actors to which the focal actor is connected. Since every actor's Bonacich centrality depends on the corresponding centrality scores for the other actors, this requires a simultaneous solution for the $N$ equations. That solution is calculated as the first eigenvector of the 'characteristic equation' of the matrix $Z$, where $Z$ is formed from the $(N,N)$ matrix of observed ties by normalizing it to be column stochastic (entries are nonnegative and sum to 1 within columns). We used UCINET IV to calculate this measure for each panel year, including only firms in the restricted sample in order to maintain maximum comparability over time.

We determined all new appointments of outside (nonexecutive) directors made by firms appearing in adjacent panels (i.e. between 1982–6, 1986–90, and 1990–4). Two outcomes were of interest: whether the new director was a CEO of one of the other sample firms (in the full or restricted sample), and the number of other sampled boards the new director served on at the beginning of the period. The analyses asked the following question: Given that a board is making a new appointment, what factors influence the likelihood that the new director is a 'prestige' or central director? The first outcome—appointing a CEO as an outside director—increases the board's prestige, while the second increases its centrality. The character of such appointments thus directly determines the board's centrality.

Our design allowed us to use lagged variables to model centrality and the character of new appointments. Centrality was measured as described previously. Data on board composition came from proxy statements as reported in Standard and Poor's Directory of Corporations, Executives, and Directors (for 1982) and Compact Disclosure (for subsequent panels). Extensive computerized and hand-checking routines ensured that directors and their positions as executives were uniquely and accurately identified across firms and over time.

Size was measured in three ways: using annual sales volume, number of employees, and total assets. There is a slight preference for using employment as an indicator of size, but we ran analyses using all three separately and note any differences in results below. Performance was measured using the market to book ratio (i.e. the market value of the company's common stock divided by its book or accounting value) and ROA (i.e. income before extraordinary items/total assets). Because market to book is a ratio measure, it is susceptible to extreme fluctuations when the denominator (book value of common) is close to zero or negative. We therefore truncated this measure at zero and ten, so that firms with nonmissing values below zero were recoded as zero and those above ten were recoded as ten. Book value of total assets is considerably more stable, of course, but because ROA and its variability differ substantially by industry, we adjusted this measure by taking the $z$-score of a firm's ROA relative to that of other sampled firms in its primary 2-digit SIC industry for that year. We then averaged this measure over three years to get an indication of sustained performance relative to one's industry competitors. All of these measures were taken from Compustat and Compact Disclosure for various years.

Shareholder scrutiny was measured in two ways. Ownership by institutional investors was the percentage of a firm's common shares held by 13F filers (i.e. entities holding $100 million in equity assets, primarily banks, insurance companies, mutual funds, and pension funds). This was measured using data reported in the Spectrum directory of ownership for 1980 and Compact Disclosure for 1986 and 1990. Ownership by executives and directors came from the same sources for 1980, 1986, and 1990. Being a target of activist investors was measured using the number of shareholder resolutions on governance issues appearing for shareholder vote at each firm's annual meeting. Resolutions can be included for a vote at the annual meeting by any shareholders meeting certain conditions. Shareholder resolutions are almost always opposed by management, and their rate of passage is quite low, but they have been used by activists to draw attention to firms that are considered to exhibit lax governance practices. Data on these proxy resolutions came from various publications of the Investor Responsibility Research Center, a not-for-profit organization that monitors issues of corporate governance. Data availability was incomplete for earlier years, and thus we included this variable only for the 1986–90 and 1990–4 panels. The measure was the sum of shareholder resolutions for the first two years of each observation period (i.e. 1986 + 1987 and 1990 + 1991).

Corporate diversification was measured using the entropy measure for 1980, 1985, and 1990. Sales data by segment came from Standard and Poor's, Moody's Industrial Manuals, and Compact Disclosure. Because this measure was only available for industrial firms and thus reduced the sample size, models including this variable were run separately. Industry was coded using a dummy variable for firms operating in telecommunications, transportation, financial services, securities, insurance, and business services. We also ran separate models coding each of these 'network' industries separately. Finally, we coded a measure of corporate reputation using Fortune Magazine's annual survey of 'America's most admired corporations', in which the more admired firms were assigned higher scores. This survey began in 1983, and so we used data for 1983, 1986, 1990, and 1994. Because only a subsample of firms were included in these surveys, its inclusion severely reduces our sample size, and we therefore report results on analyses with and without this variable separately.

## Method

First, we analyze new appointments of outside directors for non-banks. We compensate for unmeasured firm-level effects by specifying a random-effects model, with the data clustered by firm. We analyzed a firm's ability to attract a CEO director using a cross-sectional time-series probit regression in which the dependent variable was coded as one if the new outside director was a CEO of one of the other sampled corporations and zero otherwise. When the dependent variable was the number of sampled boards the director served on, the corresponding Poisson regression was used. In each case, we modeled either the appointment of a CEO director or the appointment of a 'central' director as a function of the independent variables described previously. We also controlled for director turnover using the number of new appointments during the observation period.

## Results

Table 14.1 reports the results for the analyses of new director appointments. We find that both measures of shareholder scrutiny (ownership by institutions

TABLE 14.1. New Appointments of Outside Directors (Non-banks): Results of Cross-sectional Time-series Models

| Variable | New CEO director | | | | | Degree of new director | | | | |
|---|---|---|---|---|---|---|---|---|---|---|
| Employees | 0.0005+ (1.68) | 0.0000 (0.12) | 0.0004 (1.37) | 0.0006 (1.52) | 0.0004 (1.23) | 0.0002 (0.79) | 0.0003 (1.19) | 0.0002 (0.63) | 0.0001 (0.22) | 0.0001 (0.29) |
| Return on assets | 0.1220* (2.99) | 0.1377* (2.92) | 0.1193* (2.76) | 0.1387* (3.05) | 0.1038 (1.32) | 0.0705+ (1.86) | 0.1254* (3.08) | 0.0658+ (1.67) | 0.0811 (1.92) | -0.0081 (-0.13) |
| Centrality | 0.0382* (6.56) | 0.0436* (6.43) | 0.0387* (6.07) | 0.0385* (6.07) | 0.0303* (4.16) | 0.0438* (10.00) | 0.0421* (7.73) | 0.0437* (9.62) | 0.0454 (10.11) | 0.0331* (6.74) |
| Institutional ownership | 0.0034+ (1.78) | 0.0051+ (1.94) | 0.0028 (1.44) | 0.0034+ (1.66) | 0.0025 (0.88) | 0.0044* (2.60) | 0.0047* (2.23) | 0.0030+ (1.77) | 0.0035 (1.92) | 0.0307 (0.28) |
| Shareholder resolutions | | 0.0120 (0.61) | | | | | 0.0294* (2.37) | | | |
| Reputation score | | | | | 0.0629 (1.03) | | | | | 0.0300 (0.67) |
| Insider ownership | | | -0.0012 (-0.38) | | | | | -0.0024 (-0.76) | | |
| Diversification | | | | 0.0110 (0.18) | | | | | 0.0352 (0.67) | |
| Industry | -0.0071 (-0.51) | -0.0130 (-0.85) | -0.0126 (-0.88) | -0.0136 (-0.77) | 0.0070 (0.33) | 0.0086 (0.56) | 0.0082 (0.51) | 0.0052 (0.34) | 0.0015 (0.08) | 0.0102 (0.53) |
| Constant | -1.5388* (-14.4) | -1.6758* (-11.2) | -1.4726* (-12.4) | -1.5327* (-12.1) | -1.8410* (-4.4) | -0.6100* (-5.9) | -0.6938* (-4.9) | -0.5111* (-4.6) | -0.5705 (-4.9) | -0.4214 (-1.4) |
| No. of directors | 2902 | 2032 | 2663 | 2471 | 1392 | 2902 | 2032 | 2663 | 2471 | 1392 |
| No. of firms | 370 | 367 | 367 | 332 | 213 | 370 | 367 | 367 | 332 | 213 |
| Chi squared | 143.29 | 569.78 | 609.4 | 186.85 | 46.43 | 419.69 | 205.86 | 168.87 | 549.98 | 141.35 |
| d.f. | 10 | 11 | 11 | 9 | 10 | 10 | 11 | 11 | 9 | 10 |

*p < .05. + p < .10. Reported significance levels are two-tailed.

and being subject to shareholder resolutions) increased the centrality of new
directors recruited, consistent with Hypothesis 1a. Neither measure had a
consistent positive influence on CEO appointments, however, in contrast to
Hypothesis 1b. The effects of prior performance were quite the opposite of
what we predicted in Hypothesis 2: both CEOs and central directors were
more likely to join the boards of superior performers, not weak performers.
We found little support for Hypotheses 3 and 4: neither diversification nor
operating in network industries (those industries requiring the greatest cross-
industry information) had a consistent positive influence on appointments of
CEOs or central directors. And while there was little support for Hypothesis
5—large firms were not significantly more likely to appoint CEOs or central
directors than small firms—there was quite consistent support for
Hypothesis 6: centrality strongly and consistently increased the probability
that a new director would be a CEO and the number of other board memberships held by the new director. Using alternative measures of centrality
(the Bonacich measure) and size (sales or assets rather than employment)
yielded substantively identical results.

*Effects of Centrality on Performance* We wanted to determine what effect
centrality has on subsequent performance. Unreported analyses regressing
a firm's subsequent performance (measured using the $z$-score of its ROA
relative to its primary industry for three years following the observation year)
on its centrality, size, and reputation found no significant effect for any measure of centrality. We did, however, find a positive effect of reputation (the
Fortune admiration score) on subsequent performance.

*Effects of Centrality on Reputation* We also treated a firm's admiration score
as the dependent variable. We find that centrality has a significant positive
effect on admiration. In other words, net of the more predictable effects of
size and performance, central boards enhance a firm's reputation, as one
would expect given our interpretation of centrality as status.

## Discussion

Our findings indicate that corporate boards seek to appoint well-connected
directors to the extent that their need for displays of status are great—when
they are owned by institutional investors rather than individuals, and when
they have been the subject of governance-related shareholder proposals. They
are able to recruit such directors when their firms have a history of superior
performance, but most importantly when they are already central. Central
boards are presumably attractive to potential directors for several reasons
and are able to locate these directors because of their broad scan. Whatever
the reason, the one constant across all models was the finding that prior

centrality increased firms' likelihood of appointing a status-enhancing director. This was invariant to model specification and is quite robust to the measure of centrality used.

Theorists have speculated on the process by which outside directors are appointed—whether these individuals are generally quiescent dupes of self-serving managers or vigilant agents of their shareholder principals—but the evidence to date does not support a simple interpretation in either direction (e.g. Zajac and Westphal 1996). What motivates boards to seek particular candidates is undoubtedly a mix of factors. But our results suggest two things that are new to the literature. First, central directors appear to be appointed in part to serve the 'Potemkin Village' function: they are most likely to be appointed by corporations owned proportionally more by institutional investors and those that have previously been subject to shareholder proposals on governance. It is precisely these firms that experience the greatest scrutiny of their governance practices, and whose boards therefore have the greatest pressures to make displays of good faith to the shareholders that elect them. The displays work to deflect scrutiny, if not to enhance governance: centrality evidently increases the corporation's esteem in the eyes of external constituencies while leaving operating performance unchanged. These results parallel those by Westphal and Zajac (1998): symbolic displays appear to be sufficient, even if detached from substantive reform.

Second, focusing on what the appointing firm gets out of recruiting a central director tells only part of the story: one must also consider what is in it for the director. Joining a corporation's board may be attractive as a means to learn from effective managers, because a firm is economically important, for career advancement, or to gain the opportunity to associate with other corporate diplomats and enhance one's business scan (Useem 1984). Central firms, and firms with a history of out-performing their industry, offer the best opportunities to serve these interests and therefore have the most success at attracting central directors, who presumably have their choice of which boards to join. Conversely, firms with a history of poor performance, which might benefit from the experiences of successful outside CEOs, have the least chance of recruiting them to their boards.

Some differences emerged between appointments of CEOs and central directors. Institutional ownership had its greatest effect on the appointment of directors holding multiple seats rather than on the appointment of CEOs, as did shareholder resolutions. To the extent that the appointment of new directors is intended to enhance status in the eyes of shareholders, it appears that central directors are more frequently the object of this strategy than CEOs. Conversely, CEOs may be more motivated by personal concerns—seeing first hand how a successful firm is run, and networking.

The effects of centrality on a firm's performance and reputation were intriguing. Neither central directors nor CEOs appeared to have a discernible impact on corporate performance, bringing into question whether they are valid signals of superior corporate governance from the perspective of shareholders. This null effect was consistent across our measures of performance. In short, while good prior performance may allow a firm to bag a CEO or central director, boards composed of such individuals have no discernible impact on subsequent operating performance. One might argue, following the logic of Demsetz and Lehn (1985), that centrality adjusts to meet the level required for acceptable performance; thus, in equilibrium centrality would have no relation to performance. But this would imply that central directors are recruited when performance is poor, bringing up subsequent performance to equilibrium levels. As we have seen, however, the opposite is true. Board composition appears to be a consequence, not a cause, of corporate performance.

Yet the appearance of central directors on the board enhanced the perception of the firm by analysts and other constituencies. They appear to serve as an effective symbol of commitment to shareholder value, even if in fact their relation to this construct is problematic. We must be cautious in interpreting this result, as the Fortune survey appears to change its methodology from year to year, but the result is tantalizing in light of our discussion of status.

The implication of all these results in combination is that interlock network centrality is self-reproducing: central boards appoint central directors, whereas peripheral boards do not (see White 1981). Sustained poor performance will eventually erode centrality by making it difficult to recruit central directors, but the effect is rather modest compared with the impact of centrality. Performing two standard deviations above one's industry average for three years had about the same estimated effect on CEO appointments as being one standard deviation above the mean in centrality. Moreover, turnover rates on large corporate boards were relatively low, particularly for central directors: the median board in this sample replaced roughly 21% of its members every four years, implying a relatively long lag period before a firm's centrality catches up with its performance. As a result, centrality is not a particularly reliable indication of current or future corporate performance, although it may be taken as such by outside constituencies. It is possible that centrality is a valid signal of the quality of governance (as distinct from a corporation's economic performance), but this must be taken on faith, not evidence.

## Conclusion

The overall results support construing centrality as status, a signal of governance quality when better information is not available. Outsiders have little direct evidence on whether a board is a good one, at least prior to a governance disaster. They are therefore compelled to rely on indirect indicators, such as what other boards directors serve on, whether they are executives of other major companies, and their age and tenure on the board—in other words, the things reported on proxy statements. Outsiders take these signals seriously, but there is little evidence that they should.

Boards may seek to appoint central directors because of the need to demonstrate good faith to shareholders and others, but whether intended or not, centrality has a number of consequences. The flow of information and normative influence works both ways: central boards have direct access to information and opinion about the governance practices at many other firms, but they also become susceptible to external demands as their directors are exposed to more occasions to explain the board's actions to outsiders. Central boards are thus quick to adopt governance practices considered appropriate and more prone to conform to the norms of the corporate elite, which need not map on to the expectations of shareholders and other constituencies (Davis and Greve 1997). Attempts to signal status by recruiting central directors may be directed at an audience of shareholders, but centrality also acts as a signal to other boards, which look to central firms for indications of the appropriateness of practices. Just as markets are constituted of mutually-regarding producers arrayed in a status hierarchy, the 'governance market' of interlocking boards is as well (White 1981; Podolny 1993).

Why does centrality appear to affect the most important aspects of corporate governance—including the ability to recruit high-profile directors—yet not operating performance? We would argue that the answer turns on the kind of information that can be transferred through ties such as interlocks. Outside directors can convey concrete information about what other boards do and opinions about the desirability of certain practices based on their experience, and they can locate new director candidates and vouch for their character. But they can't bottle an elixir that will help the firm out-perform its competitors. If this were the sort of knowledge that could be conveyed easily, such as through board meetings or hiring consultants, presumably the firm already would have implemented it. This situation parallels that described in public schools by Meyer and Rowan (1977): in the absence of cause-and-effect knowledge of how education occurs, schools seek to demonstrate their fitness by external displays of conformity to procedure. Central boards serve their legitimating function by being central, which signals their fitness to govern. Absent more reliable signals, their constituencies appear to buy it.

Activist investors have forwarded proposals for reforming corporate boards in order to enhance their performance. Two things are notable about most of these proposals: (1) they almost always prescribe standards for the small number of director attributes reported in the proxy statement (imposing a mandatory retirement age; preferring CEOs to others as outside directors; limiting the number of insiders; and so on) and not other attributes, and (2) they are rooted not in solid evidence about what works but 'common sense'. Our results suggest that boards can engage in displays of good faith (e.g. recruiting high-profile directors), but these displays may not have the intended consequence (improving performance) and may well have unintended ones. For better or worse, boards are social institutions first, positioning the firm in a larger network that influences what information it gets and what kinds of normative pressures it is susceptible to. The influence of network position on governance practices is indisputable, but its impact on quality per se is subtle at best.

## Notes

1. There are several disanalogies between the governance market and other markets, although scholars have discussed a market for corporate directors (Fama and Jensen 1983). To start, any competition among governance producers is muted at best. The boundaries of the market are largely unimportant, in contrast to the boundaries of industrial markets. What is produced is intrinsically intangible and evaluations of quality are particularly ambiguous. Finally, economic cost is largely irrelevant. Yet the notion of board status is intuitively plausible and helps explain several empirical regularities both in shareholder perceptions of board quality and in the dynamics of the interlock network.
2. The sample network for the descriptive statistics in this paragraph consists of 822 American corporations that were the publicly-traded members of the 500 largest manufacturers (by revenues), 100 largest commercial banks, 100 largest service firms, 50 largest retailers, 50 largest diversified financials, and 50 largest transportation companies in 1994, as well as 76 firms that had been among the largest during the 1980s but had dropped off the list.

## References

Brickley, J., Jeffrey, A., Coles, L., and Terry, R. 1995. 'Outside Directors and the Adoption of Poison Pills', *Journal of Financial Economics* 35: 371–90.

Davis, G. F. and Greve, H. R. 1997. 'Corporate Elite Networks and Governance Changes in the 1980s', *American Journal of Sociology* 103: 1–37.

—— and Mizruchi, M. S. 1999. 'The Money Center Cannot Hold: Commercial Banks in the U.S. System of Corporate Governance', *Administrative Science Quarterly* 44: 215–39.

——, Yoo, M., and Baker, W. E. 2003. 'The Small World of the American Corporate Elite, 1982–2001', *Strategic Organization* 1: 301–26.

Demsetz, H. and Lehn, K. 1985. 'The Structure of Corporate Ownership: Causes and Consequences', *Journal of Political Economy* 93: 1155–77.

Easterbrook, F. H. and Fischel, D. R. 1991. *The Economic Structure of Corporate Law*. Cambridge, MA: Harvard University Press.

Fama, E. 1980. 'Agency Problems and the Theory of the Firm', *Journal of Political Economy* 88: 288–307.

—— and Jensen, M. C. 1983. 'Separation of Ownership and Control', *Journal of Law and Economics* 26: 301–25.

Geneen, H. 1997. *The Synergy Myth: and Other Ailments of Business Today*. New York, NY: St. Martin's.

Granovetter, M. 1985. 'Economic Action and Social Structure: The Problem of Embeddedness', *American Journal of Sociology* 91: 481–510.

Knoke, D. and Burt, R. S. 1983. 'Prominence', in *Applied Network Analysis: A Methodological Introduction*, Burt, R. S. and Minor, M. J. (eds.). Beverly Hills: Sage, 195–222.

McCloskey, D. N. 1985. *The Rhetoric of Economics*. Madison: University of Wisconsin Press.

Merton, R. K. 1968. 'The Matthew Effect in Science', *Science* 159: 56–63.

Meyer, J. W. and Rowan, B. 1977. 'Institutionalized Organizations: Formal Structure as Myth and Ceremony', *American Journal of Sociology* 83: 340–63.

Mintz, B. and Schwartz, M. 1985. *The Power Structure of American Business*. Chicago: University of Chicago Press.

Mizruchi, M. S. 1996. 'What do Interlocks do? An Analysis, Critique, and Assessment of Research on Interlocking Directorates', *Annual Review of Sociology* 22: 271–98.

Neiva, E. M. 1996. *'The Current State of American Corporate Governance'*, Unpublished, Institutional Investor Project, Columbia University Law School.

Pettigrew, A. and McNulty, T. 1998. 'Control and Creativity in the Boardroom', in *Navigating Change: How CEOs, Top Teams, and Boards Lead Corporate Transformation*, Hambrick, D. C., Nadler, D. A., and Tushman, M. L. (eds.). Boston: Harvard Business School Press, 226–55.

Pfeffer, J. and Salancik, G. R. 1978. *The External Control of Organizations: A Resource Dependence Perspective*. New York, NY: Harper & Row.

Podolny, J. M. 1993. 'A Status-Based Model of Market Competition', *American Journal of Sociology* 98: 829–72.

Rogers, E. M. 1995. *Diffusion of Innovations*. New York, NY: The Free Press.

Shivdasani, A. 1993. 'Board Composition, Ownership Structure, and Hostile Takeovers', *Journal of Accounting & Economics* 16: 167 98.

Shleifer, A. and Vishny, R. M. 1997. 'A Survey of Corporate Governance', *Journal of Finance* 52: 737–83.

Useem, M. 1984. *The Inner Circle*. New York, NY: Oxford University Press.

Westphal, J. D. and Zajac, E. J. 1994. 'Substance and Symbolism in CEOs' Long-Term Incentive Plans', *Administrative Science Quarterly* 39: 367–90.

—— 1998. 'The Symbolic Management of Shareholders: Corporate Governance Reforms and Shareholder Reactions', *Administrative Science Quarterly* 43: 127–53.

White, H. C. 1981. 'Where Do Markets Come From?', *American Journal of Sociology* 87: 517–47.

Zajac, E. J. and Westphal, J. D. 1996. 'Director Reputation, CEO-Board Power, and the Dynamics of Board Interlocks', *Administrative Science Quarterly* 41: 507–29.

# INDEX

Greenspan, A., and the failure of LTCM 76; *see also* LTCM

GRS, performative and presentational capabilities of 53; and market unity 58; *see also* Global Reflex System

Hedge funds 21

Heterarchy, in the trading room 89; and organizational principles 90; *see also* desk; organizational model; trading room

Hostile takeover firms, and a new theory of interest 271

Hostile takeover, and management problems 283

Imitation, and the creation of a superportfolio 65; and extreme price movements 78; and models of behavior in financial services 134

Information, types of 27; and financial screens 42, 94; and financial news 43; and bulletin boards 44; information flows and the network society 53; and merger arbitrageurs 94; and emotions 105, ubiquity of 232; and volatility of currency exchange 237; *see also* financial markets; FX trading; global currency markets; Global Reflex System

Initial Public Offering, *see* IPO

Institutions, and uncertainty 90

Interests concept of 188, 196; conflicts of 187; of small investors 190, 196, 198; and socials relations 200; as an imperative in FX trading 241; *see also* investor; investing

Internal control process, and risk management in the financial industry 256

International Monetary Fund, and short-term loans 36 n16

Internet Research Group, at Merrill Lynch 191

Interpersonal liquidity 114

Interpretation, in financial markets 208; and policy-making 221; and multivocal policy 226

Investing, and human nature 155–6; as a science 158; *see also* investor, investment behavior

Investment behavior, and culture 163; *see also* investing; investor

Investor, as a figure of capitalism 141; and the legitimacy of the capitalist order 147; and action categories 148; as a scientist 154; small 188; changes in the structure of investors In the 1990s 196; and data on wealth in the US 197; ethnic divisions in the community of investors 198; and the reform of corporate bonds 309; equity investors 183; fixed-income investors 183; investors, institutional 21; institutional investors and risk diversification 271; institutional investors as major players in financial markets 274; institutional investors and attention to stock prices 276; *see also* equity culture; gambling; interests; stock investors; investing; investment behavior

IPO 189; see also Initial Public Offering

Keynesianism, as a policy paradigm 211; *see also* monetarism

Knowledge management, and competitive strategies 230; *see also* risk management

Leverage, and trading strategies 67

Lifeworld, and technical systems 41

London Stock Exchange 7; *see also* stock exchanges

London, as a financial center 237

Long Term Capital Management, *see* LTCM

LTCM 64, 231; structure of 66–7; and equity-index options 68; and the value-at-risk approach 69; and the aggregate risk model 70; and over-leverage 71; and imitation 72; and spreads 75; and the Federal Reserve Bank of New York 76; and mathematical models 77; *see also* arbitrage; Greenspan, A.; mutual susceptibility

Management, of the trading process 234; of the trading floor 244

Marché à Terme International de France, *see* Matif

Market act, and institutional arrangements 102; in its specific time frame 117

Market concentration, and international financial firms 233

Market emergence, patterns of 6, 7

Martin Act of 1921 190